The Girl on the Stairs

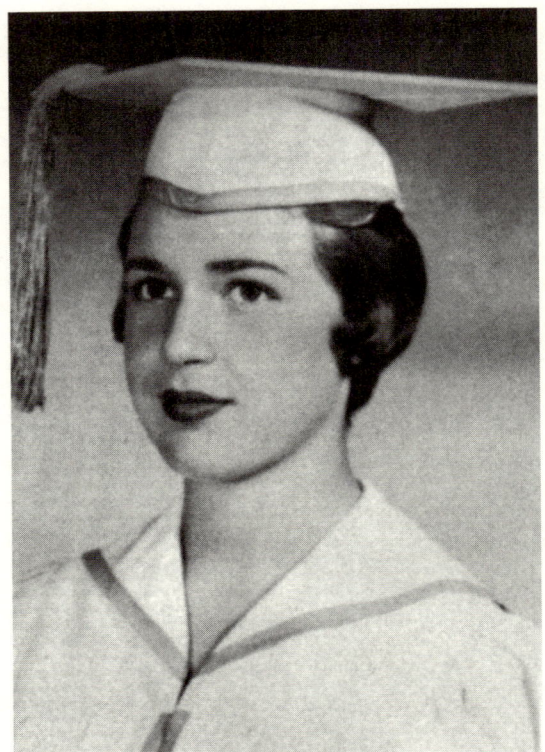

Victoria Adams was described as "jovial" and "blue eyed" while at St. Anne's Parish

The Search for a Missing Witness to the

JFK

Assassination

The

Girl

on the

Stairs

By Barry Ernest
Foreword by David S. Lifton

PELICAN PUBLISHING COMPANY
Gretna 2013

First Pelican edition, 2013

The word "Pelican" and the depiction of a pelican are
trademarks of Pelican Publishing Company, Inc., and are
registered in the U.S. Patent and Trademark Office.

Library of Congress Cataloging-in-Publication Data

Ernest, Barry.
  The girl on the stairs : the search for a missing witness to the JFK
assassination / Barry Ernest ; foreword by David S. Lifton.
    pages cm
  Includes bibliographical references and index.
  ISBN 978-1-4556-1783-8 (hardcover : alkaline paper) — ISBN 978-1-
4556-1793-7 (e-book) 1. Kennedy, John F. (John Fitzgerald), 1917-1963—
Assassination. 2. Adams, Victoria Elizabeth. 3. Witnesses—Texas—Dallas—
Biography. 4. Missing persons—Texas—Dallas—Biography. 5. Official
secrets—United States—Case studies. I. Title.
  E842.9.E76 2013
  973.922092—dc23
                        2012047607

Printed in the United States of America
Published by Pelican Publishing Company, Inc.
1000 Burmaster Street, Gretna, Louisiana 70053

*For my parents, who always encouraged me to seek the truth.
And for Patty, Jason, and Lisa, who put up with me as I tried.*

"The truth which makes men free is for the most part the truth which men prefer not to hear."

Herbert Sebastian Agar

"The great enemy of the truth is very often not the lie—deliberate, contrived, and dishonest, but the myth—persistent, persuasive, and unrealistic. Belief in myths allows the comfort of opinion without the discomfort of thought."

John F. Kennedy
Yale University Commencement Address
June 11, 1962

Contents

Foreword

Anyone who has ever become interested in the John F. Kennedy assassination probably starts with the idea that pursuing the truth is going to be relatively easy and then, in stages, learns that finding "the truth" and "answers" is more complicated than he or she ever really thought. Indeed, the Kennedy assassination is akin to a maze, and as with any maze, not all paths lead to the center—whatever "the center" really is. I am one who journeyed down that path, and Barry Ernest, whom I have known for decades, is another.

In my case, the "inciting incident"—to use screenwriter lingo—occurred when, as a close student of the Warren Commission Report, I was shown evidence that President Kennedy's head appeared to snap violently backward in response to the fatal shot, something unmentioned in the Report but obvious on the Zapruder film. Any U.S. citizen could telephone the U.S. National Archives, make an appointment, and then travel to Washington, D.C. for a private viewing of the motion picture, but of course, only a handful of people did that.[1] Especially because I lived in Los Angeles, pursuing my master's at UCLA, what I examined was the rather poor black-and-white reproductions of 158 frames of the Zapruder film that appeared as Warren Commission Exhibit 885 in volume 18 of the Warren Commission's 26 volumes.

Ray Marcus, one of the "first generation" JFK researchers, lived in West Los Angeles, and it was he who showed me those, in March 1965. Having recently graduated from Cornell's School of Engineering Physics (class of '62), and having had some six years of physics courses by that point, I was astounded. Until then, I believed the Warren Report, more or less. But after that demonstration, I wrote in *Best Evidence,* "For me, confronting the head-snap evidence was an almost revolutionary experience. For the first time, I looked at an official government pronouncement and said: 'No, I don't believe that.'"[2] In fact, my immediate response was, "That's impossible! Oswald was supposedly firing from behind. So he certainly couldn't have fired that shot—i.e., the fatal shot." Then came some elementary "political" questions. How could the attorneys on the Warren Commission—many of them young men who had gone to the best colleges and law schools and had access to this film—have watched it and believed that Lee Harvey Oswald was the assassin? Or, being more specific: how could they believe that he had fired the fatal shot? Indeed, how could anyone believe that Oswald was President Kennedy's assassin, if the film of the assassination showed he was struck fatally from the front? Moreover, if there was some explanation, why wasn't the matter investigated at the time of the Warren Commission inquiry? Why wasn't there a section in the Warren Report discussing the backward snap of President Kennedy's head? Was it possible the legal staff of the Warren Commission hadn't noticed?

In December 1965, still believing that I was privy to something that, for some reason, the Warren Commission had not "noticed," I had the opportunity to pose this question directly to one of the most important members of the Commission: former CIA director Allen Dulles.

During World War II, Dulles had joined the Office of Strategic Services and served as the OSS chief in Bern, Switzerland. He negotiated an early surrender of German forces in Italy. All of this made it into the American press and, says the official biography of Allen Dulles on the CIA Web site, "Dulles became famous in America as a spymaster and wartime cloak-and-dagger hero."

But Dulles was not that much of a hero to President Kennedy. He was one of those who "sold" Kennedy on the idea of the Bay of Pigs invasion as a way of overthrowing Castro. Kennedy fired Allen Dulles after the Bay of Pigs (mid-April 1961), and his next big venture into public service was when President Johnson appointed him to the Warren Commission (November 29, 1963). A year after the Warren Report was released (in September 1964), Dulles apparently was seeking to earn some extra money and went on the lecture circuit. That resulted in Dulles appearing at UCLA in December 1965 and being paid a princely sum for making a few speeches, and then meeting with students in an informal, coffee-klatch atmosphere.

So that's how I came to meet him. In fact, I had a rather heated confrontation with him, one that lasted some fifteen minutes (at least) and took place in front of about fifty UCLA students on December 7, 1965, at the Sierra Lounge, the main lounge of Hedrick Hall, one of the major UCLA dormitories. Allen Dulles was then seventy-two; I was twenty-six and dressed in my best suit, looking very "establishment." But what I had to say was not "establishment" at all. I had arranged with the student organizer to meet with Dulles in front of the assembled audience when he made this scheduled appearance at Hedrick Hall, and that's exactly what I did.

I was seated on a sofa with Dulles in the spacious lounge, and it began mildly enough. When I noted that the Warren Report had said there was no conspiracy, he corrected me. "Wasn't it," asked Dulles, punctuating the air with his finger as he spoke, "we have *found no evidence* of conspiracy?" I proceeded to bring up the eyewitness and earwitness evidence that one or more shots had been fired from the grassy knoll. Our debate then quickly escalated. When I brought up the fact that a number of witnesses reported smoke rising from behind some bushes on the grassy knoll, he chortled. "Do you think someone was smoking back there?"

Dulles became arrogant and sarcastic. After some general discussion, I opened a file folder and took out a sequence of Zapruder frames from volume 18. The photographs showed that, following Zapruder frame 313, which depicted the fatal shot, the president's head moved rapidly backward toward the rear seat of the car.

Dulles, now very irritated, took the photographs and looked at them closely. "I can't see a blasted thing here!" he exclaimed. Then he raised his voice and responded, "No, the head does not go back!"

Of course, despite Dulles's repeated protestations that it does not "go back," the president's head does indeed "go back"—violently, and rapidly, after the fatal shot—and the question is why.[3] Moreover, in looking at this confrontation decades later, I can only say that I find it shocking, and a bit depressing, that a former head of the CIA could sit there in front of some four dozen students and just lie.

I'm well aware that, with the advent of the Internet, and better imagery, it is possible to argue that the president's head moves forward for perhaps an inch or two, for a single film frame—an eighteenth of a second in time—but arguing about those subtleties came later, years later. The fact is that, to the naked eye, the head moves violently backward in response to the fatal shot. I have shown the film to many college audiences, and there is a shocked "Oh!" or "Wow!" when that film is projected. Audiences are truly stunned.

As noted by Thomas Stamm, one of the early JFK researchers who saw the film at the National Archives, the president looks as if he is being slammed backward by an invisible baseball bat. Yet none of this was discussed in the Warren Report. And now Allen Dulles, in front of some four dozen UCLA students, was denying the backward motion, denying that it existed at all!

Dulles had seen the film screened multiple times in the offices of the Warren Commission. If I had to trace the path by which I lost my innocence about the government in general—and the Warren Commission in particular—my encounter with Allen Dulles on that night in early December 1965 may have been the starting point.

Barry Ernest did not enter the Kennedy labyrinth at the exact time that I did, but we both entered the maze around the same period—the midsixties. For me, it was in late September 1964, the month the Warren Report was released; for Barry, it was 1967.

From rather early on, Barry became interested in a very simple question: *just where was Oswald when the shots were fired?* If you believed the Warren Report (which, in the beginning, Barry did indeed believe, just as I did), then Oswald was upstairs in a window of the Texas School Book Depository, firing the shots. After all, that's where the shells were found. And a rifle was also found, behind some boxes on that floor, in the opposite corner near the elevator.

The problem was (and still is) simply this: about ninety seconds later, Oswald was—indisputably—downstairs, in the second-floor lunchroom, drinking a cola (or at least had just opened a bottle of cola). That was known because that's when a Dallas Police motorcycle officer (one Marrion Baker) ran into the building and, with building superintendent Roy Truly leading the way and with his gun drawn, started to ascend the stairs. Between the second and third floors, Truly realized the officer was no longer following him, so he went back to the second-floor landing. There he found that Officer Baker had veered off into the lunchroom. Indeed, at that point, there was a very serious confrontation unfolding between Oswald and the police officer with his drawn gun. As noted in the Warren Report: "Truly thought that the officer's gun at that time appeared to be almost touching the middle portion of Oswald's body."[4] As I used to say in lectures, what was Officer Baker supposed to do? Say, "Drop that Coke or I'll shoot!"?

No, that didn't happen. What happened instead was that Oswald's supervisor, Roy Truly, who had run into the building with the officer and had entered the room just after Baker did, vouched for Oswald. (Truly said, "He works here," or some such thing.) The officer left the area and (with Truly) continued climbing the stairs, toward the roof.

Somewhere along the line, according to Truly's Warren Commission testimony, Baker said: "Be careful. This man will blow your head off."[5] (Baker never explained who "this man" was supposed to be or why he characterized his concern in just that fashion.)

Just as the Zapruder film documents the motion of Kennedy's head after the fatal shot, news films of the time show Officer Baker dismounting his cycle and then running, with apparent determination, toward the building. He stated in an affidavit he filed later that day: "I heard three shots. I realized these shots were rifle shots and I began to try to figure out where they came from. I decided the shots had come from the building on the northwest corner of Elm and Houston."

Exactly how Officer Baker "decided" that the shots "had come from the building" is not clear. What is known is that while films show dozens of people in a state of confusion, Officer Baker runs through the crowd, heading for the Texas School Book Depository, and then enters the building, gun drawn. FBI reports paint a picture of an officer who, for some reason, veered off the stairway at the second floor and then, gun drawn as if he was about to face a dangerous adversary, entered the lunchroom.[6]

Those who watch such shows as *Law and Order* or *CSI* might ask: what was Officer Baker's "probable cause"? A short while later, Baker came up with a more specific rationale for entering the building. He said he saw pigeons flying from its roof, and that's why he ran so swiftly inside. (He never did explain how his observation of pigeons flying from the roof led him to infer that Oswald was in the lunchroom. Oh well . . .)

But let's now return to Lee Oswald and his whereabouts at 12:30 P.M., the official version, and how Barry Ernest got drawn into all this.

"Upstairs" to "Downstairs"

Now the problem (as Barry learned rather early on) was that to get from "upstairs" (at the "assassin's window") to "downstairs" (at the soda machine), you either had to take an elevator (which Oswald apparently did not do, because the elevators were stuck on an upper floor) or run (if not race) down the stairs.

Another problem came in the form of a witness named Victoria

Elizabeth Adams, age twenty-two, who had trained to be a nun, then taught school in Atlanta and then Dallas. On November 22, 1963, Miss Adams was employed as an office service representative by Scott Foresman and Company, a publisher of schoolbooks located on the fourth floor of the Texas School Book Depository. Victoria—aka "Vicki" (often shown as "Vickie")—was watching the president's motorcade from a fourth-floor window—the "sixth window from the left," she said in a signed statement to the FBI on March 23, 1964.[7] With her were co-worker Sandra Styles, Dorothy Garner (their supervisor), and Elsie Dorman, who was sitting on the floor and attempting to take a motion picture through the raised window with her husband's camera. Adams said that when the motorcade passed, she heard "three loud reports which I first thought were firecrackers." But then "when I saw all of the confusion on the street below I knew they must have been shots." Adams stated—and then testified under oath—that "after the third shot I observed the car carrying President Kennedy speed away." At that point, she (along with co-worker Sandra Styles) immediately ran down the stairs, all the way to the first floor, and then went out a rear entrance and into the railroad yards. According to Adams, no one else was on the stairs. She didn't see (or hear) anyone ahead of her, and certainly no one came from behind and "passed her" on the way down.

So that became Barry's entry point into the maze. In his mind, he had the image of Vicki running down the stairs, and there was no Oswald on those stairs. Yet Oswald, it seemed, must have been on the stairs, if he had been at the sixth-floor "sniper's nest" and was then observed calmly having a cola on the second floor ninety seconds later.

Years later, Barry set out to find Vicki Adams and talk to her personally. Victoria Adams was "the girl on the stairs," someone who should have seen Oswald, if he was on those same stairs, at that time. Many years passed, and Barry's exploration of the Kennedy assassination went through many phases, as he wandered far down one after another of the Warren Commission rabbit holes in his pursuit of this particular question (among others) and in searching for Miss Adams. He indeed finally located (and interviewed) her. Along the way, he learned how the Warren Commission functioned, how it treated witnesses, how it ignored serious leads, how it mischaracterized their evidence—in short, how it failed to do its job properly.

During the same general period, I was having a similar set of experiences, and learning a similar lesson.

The Autopsy

Specifically, a major "point of no return" was reached, for me, on October 23, 1966. The previous summer, I had been hired by *Ramparts* magazine (in San Francisco) to write about the medical evidence of the assassination. The 30,000-word essay I co-wrote (with *Ramparts* staff writer Dave Welsh), titled "The Case for Three Assassins," was subsequently published as a cover story in the January 1967 issue.

I was proud of my article (it was the first to discuss the head-snap in detail)[8] but then decided to pack up my set of the twenty-six volumes and do no further work on the Kennedy assassination. Why? Because I did not see anything more that an ordinary citizen without police powers could do—there seemed no way to "break through" and get to the bottom of the crime. But then, shortly after returning to my studies, in the fall term of 1966, I made a rather astonishing discovery, which brings me back to the Kennedy head-snap, which Barry talks about in his book and which dominated my thinking when I wrote the *Ramparts* article.

I was convinced that the backward motion of President Kennedy's head indicated the fatal shot had been fired from the front. But the scientific examination of the president's body (and his wounds) conducted at Bethesda Naval Hospital on the night of November 22, 1963, reported that the president had been struck in the head from behind, and only from behind. Indeed, the Bethesda autopsy was quite clear on that point: there were no entry wounds on the front of the body, and no exit wounds on the rear.

Focusing on the fatal shot, the situation was simply this: if the autopsy could be relied upon, President Kennedy had been shot in the head from behind; but if the backward snap of Kennedy's head on the Zapruder filmed were considered to be the primary evidence, then he had been struck from the front. In the fall of 1966, I struggled with this "contradiction," persuaded not only that the president was struck from the front but, in addition, that the autopsy doctors must have lied.

There seemed no other way to resolve this apparent inconsistency in the evidence. Furthermore, I no longer gave the Warren Report much credibility, because not only had the Commission not addressed the backward motion of Kennedy's head, it was a fact that the chief autopsy surgeon, Cmdr. James Humes, had burned his original autopsy notes[9] and, in addition, testified that he had burned an earlier draft of the autopsy report. And the Warren Commission attorney who conducted his interrogation (the late Arlen Specter, who went on to become Senator Specter) did not even ask why!

During this period, I had made the acquaintance of UCLA law professor Wesley Liebeler, who had been one of the approximately fourteen assistant counsels on the Warren Commission. We had a number of meetings in his office at the UCLA Law School, and he asked me to attend a law seminar he was teaching on the Commission. We frequently debated this point: *had Commander Humes lied?* And wasn't *that* what the Zapruder film head-snap was really all about? Wasn't that the ultimate proof that the autopsy doctors had deliberately falsified their report and lied—under oath—about the wounds?

Professor Liebeler said no. He was adamant that, regardless of the deficiencies of the Bethesda autopsy, the two naval doctors—both pathologists—as well as the army colonel (Lt. Col. Pierre Finck, from the Armed Forces Institute of Pathology at nearby Walter Reed Army Hospital) would not (and could not) have lied about so basic a matter as the direction of the shot that struck President Kennedy's head. Liebeler believed this to be the case not only on the grounds of what he (apparently) viewed as common sense but also because the doctors could not be certain that the Warren Commission would not subpoena the autopsy photographs. And if the photographs showed that Kennedy had been shot from the front, the doctors could be indicted for perjury, obstruction of justice, and much else besides.

For a while, our debate centered on this issue and the integrity of the doctors. But then a paradigm shift occurred, and the debate turned to what I shall call, for want of a better term, "the integrity of the body"— that is, the president's body.

The President's Body as "Best Evidence"

In attempting to resolve this matter, I had an insight: that the doctors would not have to lie about the direction of the shots *if someone had altered the president's wounds prior to autopsy.* After all, the primary "evidence" was *not* the handwritten or even the typewritten autopsy report. *The primary evidence was the body of the president!* (It was the body, after all, that "contained" the wounds.)

So rather than postulate that the doctors had lied to the Warren Commission, suppose the president's wounds had been altered? Suppose the president's body, at the time of autopsy, was tantamount to a medical forgery? Suppose the body had lied to the doctors?

I had never thought of the problem in just those terms—that the primary evidence was "the body" and that the examining doctors were simply providing a written description of that evidence, i.e., what the president's body "looked like" (what wounds it contained) at the time of their examination. But that's all the autopsy report really was in this case: a description of President Kennedy's body some six and a half hours *after* his murder.[10]

So late on Saturday night, October 22, 1966, I began to think of the problem in just that way. Focused on this apparent contradiction between the backward snap of Kennedy's head and the Bethesda autopsy conclusion that the shot came from the rear, I started to question a basic assumption that I (and others) had been making: *that the president's body was in the same condition (at autopsy) as it was six hours earlier (in Dallas) at the time of the pronouncement of death.* I constructed a chronology of the movements of President Kennedy's body—from the moment of the fatal shooting in Dallas and the subsequent pronouncement of death at Parkland Hospital up till the time the body was brought to the Bethesda morgue, some six hours later and 1,500 miles away. At that time, Oswald was in the custody of the Dallas Police. He denied he had shot anyone, and, in one of the few "hallway appearances" he had made at the Dallas Police Department, he had exclaimed, "I'm a patsy," or—as often quoted—"I'm just a patsy."

Of course, that phrase has become legendary to any student of the assassination, but it is useful to go back to the dictionary definition. A "patsy" is *somebody who is easily victimized, cheated, or manipulated.*

That's what Oswald was saying, to explain why he had been arrested. In addition, he told his brother, in a brief jailhouse visit the next day: "Do not believe the so-called evidence."

Lee Oswald was probably thinking of such things as the bolt-action rifle (with scope) that he had ordered to his post-office box the previous March—under the name "Hidell"—and the fact that that rifle was found (at about 1:20 P.M. CST) on the sixth floor of the Texas School Book Depository.

Whether or not Oswald was on the sixth floor—or near the window—at the time of President Kennedy's assassination, one thing is certain. The critical link between the rifle found on the sixth floor and the assassination was the president's body. That is, the nexus between the body and Oswald, i.e., his gun, was to be found in the conclusions of the Bethesda Naval autopsy, because the body, at the time of autopsy, was tantamount to a diagram of the shooting. Moreover, any metal in the body would be retrieved at autopsy. So the autopsy report would not only contain legally authoritative statements describing bullet trajectories, but the autopsy examination would also be the time when bullets (or fragments) would be recovered and sent to the FBI Laboratory for ballistics tests.

Air Force One, carrying the new president—Lyndon B. Johnson—and the coffin that left Parkland Hospital with President Kennedy's body arrived at Andrews Air Force Base at about 6 P.M. EST. In terms of my own work, which—by October 23, 1966—was focused on "the body," a preliminary tally quickly revealed what seemed to be the "weak link" in the sequence of events that followed the offloading of the Dallas coffin, an event that was televised on national TV a few minutes after 6:04 P.M., EST, the official time that Air Force One rolled to a halt. The coffin was lowered to the ground and then placed in a naval ambulance. The ambulance (which also contained Jacqueline and Robert Kennedy) pulled away from the side of Air Force One at 6:10 P.M. and traveled directly to Bethesda Naval Hospital, where, according to Secret Service and press reports, it arrived at 6:55 P.M. EST. But then, over an hour passed before the autopsy started.

Exactly what happened during that hour was my initial focus, and within hours of viewing the problem in just this fashion, and carefully reviewing all the documents I then had pertaining to the autopsy, I made a remarkable discovery.

The Sibert-O'Neill FBI Report

Two FBI agents had accompanied the president's casket from Air Force One. The two agents—James Sibert and Francis O'Neill—would write a six-page single-spaced report dated November 26, 1963, which had just been located at the National Archives earlier that summer (1966) and made available to many of the early researchers by "first generation" researcher Paul Hoch. The report was also published as an appendix to two books that appeared in the fall of 1966: *Inquest,* by Edward Epstein, and *The Second Oswald,* by Prof. Richard Popkin.

My discovery, made late that night, was simply this. In the report appeared a passage that had been completely overlooked and ignored by the Warren Commission: that after President Kennedy's body was removed from the casket "in which it had been transported" and placed on the autopsy table, it was "apparent" that there had been "surgery of the head area, namely, in the top of the skull."

This was my *aha* moment, and the beginning of a completely new way of viewing the problem—not only the issue of "how many assassins?" (which immediately receded in importance), but the issue of fraud in the evidence. And what evidence was that? It was the most critical evidence linking the crime to Oswald—the body of the dead president. Because there it was, in plain English: if that FBI statement was true, then something indeed had happened to the president's body between the pronouncement of death and the start of the official autopsy.

Something else in the Sibert and O'Neill FBI report drew my attention. The agents reported that the doctors could find no bullets in the president's body and, quoting their language, actually stated that they were "at a loss to explain" why.

All at once, I had a major paradigm shift and realized that there was indeed a way to "break through" to the center of the Kennedy assassination mystery—not by identifying "the assassins" but by exposing the deception that had been employed to falsify the basic facts of President Kennedy's murder. I realized that the key to the Kennedy case was not who put the bullets *into* the president's body but who took them out. In short, I realized that the key to the Kennedy assassination was recognizing that the most important evidence of all was the president's body—and its covert alteration (i.e., the alteration of the wounds) was why the Zapruder film showed a backward snap, whereas the doctors stated that the head-wound pattern showed the shot came from behind. It then also became clear why the Dallas doctors, who saw the president at Parkland Hospital, had declared that he had been shot from the front, while the autopsy doctors concluded he had been shot from the rear.

It wasn't so much a matter of opinion (two groups of experts, with differing interpretations of the same data) but rather of basic facts— exactly what wounds were on the president's body at each point in time and what those wounds looked like. Both groups of doctors, I realized, could have told the truth about what they had seen. Their opinions (about the direction of the shots) differed because the wounds were different.[11]

Somehow, somewhere, the wounds had been altered. The diagram of the shooting had been changed. If my analysis was correct, then at the time of autopsy, the president's body was a medical forgery. Had the "Oswald case" gone to trial, I reasoned, Lee Oswald's statement, "Do not believe the so-called evidence," would have applied not just to the paraphernalia at the sniper's nest *but to the president's body itself.*

The timing of Victoria Adams' trip down the stairs at the Texas School Book Depository was one way of arguing that, just as Oswald claimed, he did not shoot President Kennedy, but the alteration of the body addressed the problem in an even more fundamental way. Victoria Adams, if she was correct, established that the Warren Report was wrong. If the president's body was covertly intercepted and altered, then the problem went even deeper: *there was fraud in the evidence.* In short, by altering wounds and removing bullets, someone had manufactured the legal foundation for a false story of the Kennedy assassination, one that would implicate Oswald as "the assassin."

The next day (Monday, October 24, 1966) I had a five-hour meeting with Professor Liebeler and showed him the passage in the FBI agents' report. I write about this at length in *Best Evidence,*[12] describing how Liebeler was astounded, not just that somebody might have altered the body (that was shocking enough), but even more so, that such explicit evidence—such a bald statement in an FBI report[13]—could exist in the Commission's own files, and yet, apparently, no one on the Commission legal staff even knew it was there! Here was a statement in an official FBI report that, if true, would mean that the president's body had been covertly intercepted and altered. Here was a statement that, if true, meant that the Commission's most critical evidence—the body of President Kennedy—had been altered *prior to the autopsy.* If true, the implications were huge. It would mean that the Warren Commission's "case against Oswald" was built on a foundation of sand—for it was based on autopsy conclusions that were, in turn, based on altered evidence.

If this was the case, then obviously, unknown (i.e., unreported) events had occurred prior to the autopsy. From the standpoint of the official record, those events did not exist. Certainly, no such thing had been formally reported to the Warren Commission.

Liebeler told me he wanted to call Arlen Specter but needed privacy. So he went into an adjoining room—we were in Joe Ball's Beverly Hills law offices at the time—and made the call. The two were on the phone for about ten minutes. When he emerged, I asked what he said. Liebeler replied (and I quoted this in *Best Evidence*): "Arlen hopes he gets through this with his balls intact." He also called Ball, who was responsible, along with David Belin, for the chapter titled "The Assassin" in the Warren Report, the one that identified Oswald as the assassin, largely based on the evidence at the sniper's nest. "Joe," he asked, "did you ever get the feeling we were being led down the garden path?"[14]

In a homicide, the body of the victim is the "best evidence," and that was no less true in the case of a president. The body—when properly examined—tells "the story" of the crime. Here, in the Warren Commission's very own files, was evidence the body had been altered, yet the Commission was so biased in its approach (and so oblivious to contrary data in the manner in which it had conducted its inquiry) that no one even knew such evidence existed!

In the days that followed, Liebeler mulled over the situation and decided what he would do: write a memorandum to Chief Justice Warren and every member of the Warren Commission, focusing just on the autopsy and prominently mentioning this passage. He also told me he was going to give me credit, in the text of his memo, for having made this discovery. Liebeler was amazed that a graduate student carefully studying publicly available records could find something of such significance that the entire Warren Commission staff had missed!

Copies of Liebeler's thirteen-page memo, dated November 8, 1966, went to every member of the Warren Commission, the entire staff, the Kennedy family, and the Justice Department. After detailing numerous problems with the autopsy, it zeroed in on that statement about "surgery of the head area, namely, in the top of the skull."[15]

Was the concept horrible, even ghoulish, that somehow, somewhere, unknown persons had messed with the body of President Kennedy, prior to autopsy? Sure it was. It was not just ghoulish but frightening. But it was also a fact that the FBI had reported the situation to the Commission—in some rather terse prose—and nothing had been done about it!

Would something be done about it now? The answer was no. On December 1, J. Lee Rankin, the former Commission general counsel, responded with copies to everyone on Liebeler's list. He told Liebeler that as far as he was concerned, the case was closed; furthermore (he said), the "best evidence" of what was seen and heard at the autopsy proceeding was the navy autopsy report, not what two FBI agents reported.

Considerably annoyed, Liebeler showed me the letter and said he was not going to pursue the matter any further. He had done all he could do, and that was the end of it. But that was not the end of it for me. To the contrary, that's when I set out to follow up on my discovery, which I did, and which—fifteen years later—resulted in my book *Best Evidence*, published in January 1981.

By that time, I not only had considerably more evidence that the wounds had been altered but also some rather dramatic evidence that the body had been covertly intercepted. Specifically, I found that:

1. the body left Dallas wrapped in sheets but arrived at Bethesda in a body bag;

2. the body left Dallas in a large ceremonial casket but arrived at Bethesda in a shipping casket.[16]

Furthermore, I found plenty of evidence that there had been organized cutting in the area of the head, prior to autopsy, which Commander Humes had disguised by reporting it as part of the gunshot wounding. (See chapter 18 of *Best Evidence*, which I titled "The Pre-Autopsy Autopsy.") For those interested in these details, I refer you to my book and to the many debates about it that have taken place on the Internet.

I bring all this up to let the reader know that, like Barry Ernest, I have done my share of following a particular lead, and then another, and then another. It's very hard work, and the process seems always to take much longer than was originally intended.

That's what Barry got involved in. Along the way, he also did a stint in the navy, got married, had a son, paid a mortgage, etc. But Barry kept coming back to the Kennedy case, and to Vicki Adams. Because, as many of us know, once you get hooked, it is very hard to just set it aside.

Barry wanted to find out exactly when Vicki Adams was on the stairs—to hear it from her own lips. I wanted to know what happened to the president's body. We each had our questions, and we both searched for answers.

Barry Ernest and Victoria Adams

The central witness in Barry's quest was Vicki Adams, and he finally made contact with her in February 2002. The two subsequently had very cordial communication. She was obviously pleased that someone was going to publish her story. In fact, Barry made an important discovery in the Warren Commission records: he found a June 1964 letter from Martha Joe Stroud (an assistant to Barefoot Sanders, U.S. attorney in Dallas) to the Commission that strengthens Vicki Adams' account as to the timing of her trip down the stairs. The letter, which was important evidence, was not followed up on, nor was it mentioned anywhere in the Warren Report.[17]

Barry and Vicki developed a friendship. She respected the fact that he had been working on the Kennedy case for so long, writing a book, and was going to be focusing on her story. Time passed, Barry was finishing his manuscript, and in September 2007 she called him with some sad news: she had been diagnosed with terminal brain cancer. As Barry recently explained to me, Vicki had delayed telling him because she didn't want it to affect the way he wrote about her. She just wanted her story to be published accurately; she was not seeking any pity. She died November 15, 2007. Just weeks before her death, she sent Barry a brief essay she wrote, titled "I Did It My Way."

Barry has pointed out that what she told him never had the quality of a "deathbed confession." Vicki's whole point was that she had *always* told the truth, and she was grateful and appreciative that, in writing his book, Barry would be bringing her truth to the American public and the world. To the end, she stuck to her story. Furthermore, Barry not only found the Martha Joe Stroud letter, he effectively tallies up the statements from Sandra Styles and Dorothy Garner that also corroborate Vicki's account. So Barry decided to write up the story of Vicki's experience, and of his own journey, and that's what his book is all about.

As far as I'm concerned—and I'm sure Barry feels the same way—the Kennedy assassination is an unsolved crime, and one question is this: are we really supposed to just leave it at that? I think that many of us who were "under thirty" at the time either liked President Kennedy (a lot) or identified with Oswald and his interesting life (he went to Russia upon leaving the U.S. Marines and arrived there on October 16, 1959, just two days before his twentieth birthday, then lived there through early June 1962). Many of us just simply believe Oswald when we see him in a film clip after his arrest, saying, "I didn't shoot anybody, no sir," or "I'm a patsy." Many of us can't believe the official version of the crime when so much seems to be so obviously wrong with that "official version," whether it's the Commission's "single bullet theory" or, in my case, the evidence that the wounds were altered.

So Barry has chronicled his journey, and it is not only the story of one man's investigation, but (also) of his loss of faith as, month after month and year after year, he learned more, his knowledge increased, and he was no longer the naïve trusting person he was back in the midsixties. He had now arrived at the conclusion that the Warren Report was fundamentally wrong and that Victoria Adams' account was, as far as he was concerned, one way of proving that Oswald could not have been Kennedy's assassin. The corroboration from the co-worker who ran down the stairs with Vicki (Sandra Styles) and the letter Barry found from the Dallas U.S. attorney's office both point, Barry believes, to Vicki's account being the truth. And if so, then Oswald could not possibly have been on the stairs, and—finally—if that is true, then he must have been downstairs all along and certainly could not have been upstairs, firing at the president.

I believe that each reader will have to be the judge of this for himself.

The true value of Barry's account is not the particular thesis that he presents but his chronicle of the search on which he embarked: what it did to him and how it changed him over the years. His account will acquaint the reader with what it means to "research the Kennedy assassination."

At each point along his journey, we learn of some new twist, some new puzzle, and even though we know how the story "ends," we still want to know "what happened next." That's a testament to Barry Ernest's writing and storytelling capability.

My literary agent—Peter Shepherd, in many ways the "godfather" of *Best Evidence*—said to me back in 1976, when he first saw my manuscript, "People aren't interested in 'facts' just out there in space. They want to know how those facts affected other people."

That's why I wrote *Best Evidence* as a personal narrative. That's why Barry's book is such an interesting read. He spells out how these facts affected him.

As a reasonably optimistic person, and as someone who believes that technology and the passage of time are eventually going to work their wonders in the Kennedy case, I do believe we're going to get an answer to the question: who did it? That answer is going to reverse the verdict of the currently accepted "official" version. I'm positive that's going to happen, and when it does, it's going to affect a lot of people. Barry Ernest is one of those who pushed very hard to bring that day closer. His book, *The Girl on the Stairs*, is one man's story of that journey.

David S. Lifton

Acknowledgments

One cannot write a book on a subject of this magnitude, spanning an era of this length, without the guidance and assistance of many people. I could, of course, list each one at the expense of space, the risk of forgetfulness, and the likely displeasure of my publisher. So let me just say instead that every name you see within these pages was of benefit to me in some way or another, and in many cases I suppose without them even realizing it.

The careful reader will be able to determine the extent of each one's contribution. There are a few others, though, who deserve a more special note of appreciation.

The frustrations of trying to dig out truths behind the JFK assassination in general, and a shunned witness to that event in particular, surfaced often along this lengthy journey. The careful reader again will have no problem spotting this unflattering characteristic. What that reader will not see are the efforts of one person in particular who, surrounded by frustrations of her own, persisted in providing much-needed support and encouragement. So I wish to express here my deep admiration for my wife, Patty, to whom this book is in part dedicated, for freeing up those many hours I needed by taking on various responsibilities that should have been mine alone.

Thanks go to:

My son, Jason, wise beyond his years, who answered all my legal questions (pro bono, I might add) while juggling his own busy career as a lawyer and his growing family.

And to his lovely wife, Lisa. I could not have had a better first-run promotions director.

Also to the memory of my parents, who, despite being disappointed in my initial attempt at college, nevertheless continued to push me onward throughout the years in my studies of this subject. I trust they somehow realize that their efforts were not in vain.

And to Janet Kleffman, who edited early drafts of this manuscript, which back then had the dubious title of *Just an Ordinary Guy*—a long story. Although the finished product is somewhat different than what she initially red-lined, her editorial advice has carried forward.

Also to Carol Anne McQuiggan, my computer guru, who helped untangle the electronic knots on a device that still keeps invading my attempts at sleep.

Finally, a collective note of appreciation goes out to other family members, friends, and acquaintances—even those many strangers—who have read and learned and listened to me talk about Victoria Adams, then taken the time and much-welcomed initiative to foster even more awareness of her story. You know who you are.

A long time ago Harold Weisberg, in his preface to *Whitewash*, wrote that self-publishing was the "least desirable of possible forms." This was back in 1966, when he had to resort to that method because the book firms he contacted were hesitant about printing the truth about this historic and significant topic. I too found that to be the case when this book was born and offered to a long list of publishers, many of whom told me they found the story fascinating and enlightening. Several actually went further and said they'd be more interested if I agreed to write a concluding chapter that provided a highly speculative and theory-based "solution" to the crime.

I felt that such a finish would be dishonest to my own efforts, which all along have been targeted toward the pursuit of truths. I also felt that it would be an insult to the girl of the book's title, whose very life centered on maintaining those truths. And so, I refused.

Yet getting people to understand what really happened to Victoria Adams, this little-known and neglected witness scorned simply for doing what we are all taught to do, was important to me. It was vital to her.

Then along came Pelican Publishing Company.

Without exaggeration, it is with the utmost of gratitude that I thank Pelican and its professional team for having confidence in this book, for the courage to print it without adding the literary garbage that often pervades this subject, and for the opportunity of getting the real story of Victoria Adams into the hands of more people than I ever thought possible.

Miss Adams once said that the only thing she ever wanted was for people to know she told the truth. The people now have that opportunity.

November 22, 1963

At first she thought it was firecrackers.

But when she saw the chaos and the terror on all the faces below, she knew it was something far worse.

She turned from the window and grabbed the arm of a co-worker.

"Come on," she whispered. "Let's find out what's going on down there."

In this split second, her innocence—and that of a nation's—came to an end.

The
Girl
on the
Stairs

CHAPTER 1

February 1967

I really don't know what it was that made me want to find her.

Perhaps I thought she was somehow important in this mess. Perhaps it was because the government tried so hard to convince me otherwise. Maybe I was just bored.

That afternoon began like any other at Kent State University. It was three years before innocent kids would be gunned down there; three short years before America would suffer still another debilitating blow to its sense of stability. I had just turned nineteen and found myself stuffed into an overcrowded Moulton Hall on an overpopulated campus.

On this cold day, a guy I recognized from one of my classes hurriedly approached. I was minding my own business, content in waiting for the cafeteria doors to open.

"Hi. I'm Terry. Why is it you believe the Warren Report?"

I blinked. "Huh?"

"In class one day when we were asked if anyone had read the Warren Report, you said you had and you felt it was true. I'm wondering what makes you think so."

I recalled a debate on the Kennedy assassination in a U.S. history seminar some weeks earlier. Terry was accurate with his recap. "I guess it's because all the evidence points to Oswald being the lone assassin. The rifle was his; he was the only one who ran from where the shots were fired; he killed a Dallas police officer—J. D. Tippit, I think his name was."

Terry nodded.

"And I've read enough testimony that supports those conclusions."

"Have you read *all* of the testimony?" he prodded. Before I could answer, he continued. "Have you ever heard of the grassy knoll? What about the violent backward motion of Kennedy's head in the Zapruder film? How about all the witnesses ignored and never called before the Warren Commission?"

"What are you talking about?" I asked.

"Ah! Never heard of those things, huh?" Terry was pleased at making his point, a point that, quite frankly, eluded me. "The government is not telling us the truth about the assassination."

"Why would the government lie about something like this?" I asked.

Terry persisted. "Our library has a set of the twenty-six volumes of testimony. Take a look at them. In the meantime, read this." He pushed a magazine into my arms. "I'll be in touch." Then he was gone.

His comments hit a nerve. I settled down with my tray of food. Like others, I had read the Warren Report, every word of its 888 pages—twice, as a matter of fact. The accompanying twenty-six volumes of supporting evidence weren't readily available, so I had done the next best thing and read highlights of that evidence in a paperback put out by the *New York Times*.

I had admired John F. Kennedy, his style, his goals. He was a breath of fresh air. His wife, I had to admit, was my first infatuation. Lee Harvey Oswald ended all that.

Oswald worked in the Texas School Book Depository. The shots came from there. Bullet fragments matched the rifle that had his fingerprints on it. People saw him do it. He was picked from a police lineup. He had no alibi and he tried to escape. He even shot a policeman.

Why all the fuss? But I still glanced at the magazine Terry had left behind: *Playboy*. It was already opened to what he apparently wanted me to read, that month's interview. Staring back at me was a bespectacled attorney-turned-author from New York named Mark Lane. Lane had written a book about his private investigation into the assassination. His remarks revealed a heavy bias against the Warren Report.

By the time I lifted my nose from the lengthy article, my food was cold and I was alone. Everyone else had finished lunch and had left for afternoon lectures. My "How to Think Straight" logic class was now nearly over.

I decided to salvage the day by visiting a local bookshop to pick up a copy of Lane's work, titled *Rush to Judgment*. Along the way I stopped at the university's library. As Terry said, the Warren Report and its twenty-six volumes were there, occupying forty inches of shelf space, impressive in their dark-blue covers and gold lettering.

That night I settled in to read, accompanied by a sack of heart-stoppers from McDonald's. It was good to be young.

Lane was brutal as he sliced his way through the Warren Report's conclusions. He quoted witnesses who saw smoke rising from the grassy knoll, a raised plot of ground to the right front of Kennedy's motorcade; witnesses who saw someone running from there; or saw *two* gunmen instead of only one in the sixth-floor window; or saw Oswald in places he wasn't, shouldn't have been, or couldn't have been. He discussed the backward snap to Kennedy's head when the final bullet struck home. He named names and brought up contradictions between what witnesses said they saw and what the government ultimately said happened.

I had never read anything like it. I was mesmerized. And he introduced me, inadvertently as it may have been, to Victoria Adams.

Miss Adams worked on the fourth floor of the Texas School Book Depository. She witnessed the assassination from there, the shots coming from only two floors above. Lane, quoting from her official Warren Commission testimony, wrote that following the last shot, "she and a co-worker 'ran out of the building via the stairs and went in the direction of the railroad where we had observed other people running.'"[1]

Since "the railroad" was located on the grassy knoll, Lane used her remarks as further evidence that shots originated from there. What caught my eye, though, was her comment that she "ran out of the building via the stairs." I remembered that Oswald had escaped the sixth floor by running down a back staircase. Could that staircase have been the same one Miss Adams was on?

"So, do you still believe the Warren Report?" Terry inquired when I returned his magazine a few days later.

"Yeah, I do," I said. "But Lane raises some interesting points in his book. Ever hear of Victoria Adams?"

"Ah, so you were interested enough to buy his book, huh? I knew you would. And yes. I've heard of her. Why?"

"Lane mentioned her. I was curious, that's all."

"Check what the Warren Report said," Terry advised, "then go read her testimony in the twenty-six volumes. You should compare a lot of the witnesses that way. You might be surprised."

My professors weren't doling out this much work.

"We should get together on a regular basis and compare notes," he added. "Might be good. For both of us." The guy had an ego. But I liked him anyway.

That night, after checking out the relevant books from the library, I focused on the story of Miss Adams. According to the Warren Report, Oswald fired three shots from a sixth-floor window. He then hurried across that floor, hid his gun under some boxes at the top of the back staircase, and descended those stairs. For some reason, he exited the stairs on the second floor and ducked into a nearby lunchroom. Seconds later he was confronted there by Dallas policeman Marrion Baker and building superintendent Roy Truly, who had run up the stairs from the first floor.

Baker, riding a motorcycle in the parade, wanted to get to the roof of the Depository. He thought shots might have come from there. Truly was showing him the way when the policeman spotted a man later identified as Oswald through the window of a door leading to the lunchroom.

The timing was crucial. Could Oswald have fled the sixth floor and arrived in the second-floor lunchroom within the ninety seconds allotted by the Report? Shouldn't Miss Adams, if she was descending the same stairs after the shots were fired, have been privy to this footrace?

The Warren Report had little to say about her:

> Victoria Adams, who worked on the fourth floor of the Depository Building, claimed that within about 1 minute following the shots she ran from a window on the south side of the fourth floor, down the rear stairs to the first floor, where she encountered two Depository employees— William Shelley and Billy Lovelady. If her estimate of time is correct, she reached the bottom of the stairs before Truly and Baker started up, and she must have run down the stairs ahead of Oswald and would probably have seen or heard him. Actually she noticed no one on the back stairs. If she descended from the fourth to the first floor as fast as she claimed in her testimony, she would have seen Baker or Truly on the first floor or on the stairs, unless they were already in the second-floor lunchroom talking to Oswald. When she reached the first floor, she actually saw Shelley and Lovelady slightly east of the east elevator. . . .
>
> Shelley and Lovelady, however, have testified that they were watching the parade from the top step of the building entrance when Gloria Calvery, who works in the Depository Building, ran up and said that the President had been shot. Lovelady and Shelley moved out into the street. About this time Shelley saw Truly and Patrolman Baker go into the building. Shelley and Lovelady, at a fast walk or trot, turned west into the railroad yards and then to the west side of the Depository Building. They reentered the building by the rear door several minutes after Baker and Truly rushed through the front entrance. On entering, Lovelady saw a girl on the first floor who he believes was Victoria Adams. If Miss Adams accurately recalled meeting Shelley and Lovelady when she reached the bottom of the stairs, then her estimate of the time when she descended from the

fourth floor is incorrect, and she actually came down the stairs several minutes after Oswald and after Truly and Baker as well.[2]

It seemed cut and dried. Miss Adams may have come down the stairs, just as she said. But the question was, when? If it was right after the shots, as she claimed, she should have heard or seen Oswald. Yet she didn't.

The most convincing detail proving that her timing was wrong was her statement that she saw Shelley and Lovelady on the first floor. Both men, according to the Warren Report, had remained outside the building after the shooting for several minutes before entering. Therefore, if Miss Adams saw them on the first floor when she arrived there, she must have come down the stairs later than she thought. No wonder she saw and heard no one on the staircase. Oswald had already descended it.

Something was gnawing at me, though. I was uncomfortable with all the ifs—*if* her estimate of time was correct; *if* she descended from the fourth to the first floor as fast as she claimed; *if* Miss Adams accurately recalled . . .

What *if* she was right? And how convincing was Billy Lovelady's statement that he saw a girl he only *believed* was Miss Adams?

I decided to examine her official testimony.

CHAPTER 2

March 1964

By now, four months after the assassination, Victoria Adams was getting nervous.

From day one since that horrific event, authorities had been nosing around her office. The FBI, Secret Service, Dallas Police, Sheriff's Department—they were all there. It seemed understandable, of course. After all, she had been a witness to the assassination of a United States president. How often does that happen?

But what about Sandra Styles and Elsie Dorman and Dorothy Ann Garner? They had all been there too, right beside her at the window, watching the same thing she had watched. Why weren't they being questioned as much or as often? Why were they focusing on her?

And it didn't stop at her workplace. They even came to her apartment, the same men from the same offices. Couldn't they just share their notes?

She had moved to another part of town and left no forwarding address, not even yet alerting her boss or the local post office as to her current whereabouts. Plus the new place was leased in her roommate's name. And still they had found her, coming up late at night, knocking loudly, dark shadowy figures on the doorstep scaring the bejeezus out of her.

Each time they appeared, they asked her about the same thing: her trip down the stairs and when exactly she had made it. It was almost as if she were a suspect.

When she left her office for lunch or at the end of the workday, she saw some of those same men watching her as she walked from the building. One time she even caught one of them—an FBI agent who had been in her office that morning—following her through town. The afternoon of the assassination, she had written and sent a lengthy letter to John O'Connor, editor of a newspaper in San Francisco where she had worked while in high school. In that letter she had described in detail what she had seen and done that day.

He never received it.

And there always seemed to be funny noises on her phone.

She was young, alone, and in a big city. The memories of her parents abandoning her when she was just a child still haunted her. There was no one she could turn to for help or guidance.

She had told them all, over and over again, that she heard three shots, no more, no less. They were not concerned with the number.

She had told them she saw the president's head explode after that final shot. They did not seem to care about that.

But when she told them that within moments after the final shot, she and Sandra had left the office to go outside and had heard absolutely no one on the stairs, then they were all ears. This, for some reason, seemed to bother them.

Sandra, Elsie, and Dorothy—they too were becoming concerned, but for a different reason. The trio wondered why all the attention seemed to be focused on Miss Adams, when they had seen the same thing from the window. Yes, they had been interviewed as well, but certainly nowhere near as much as Miss Adams. All the officers and agents went directly to her. She had become, well, the target.

She would be singled out again one day when a registered letter from Washington arrived. Now Miss Adams was being summoned to appear in front of a staff member of the Warren Commission who would soon arrive in Dallas. Sandra, Elsie, and Dorothy were left behind once more.

At 2:15 P.M. on April 7, 1964, Miss Adams arrived at the U.S. attorney's office in the Post Office Building at Bryan and Ervay streets. There, she was met by David Belin, an assistant counsel for the Commission. He did not rise from his chair when she entered his office, merely motioning for her to sit down. He chatted with her briefly. The emphasis was on how the proceeding would take place: what he expected from her; how she was to answer his queries; and how she was not, under any circumstances, to veer from his line of questioning by offering extraneous and unsought details.

Then he signaled for a stenographer to enter and begin transcribing the session.

CHAPTER 3

February 1967

Victoria Adams' testimony was taken on April 7, 1964, and the first thing that surprised me about her was the fact that she had wanted to become a nun.

The second thing was her age. At the time of her questioning by the Commission, she was twenty-three years old. For some reason, I had envisioned her as being much older. She was, in fact, only a few years beyond me.

Born in San Francisco, Miss Adams graduated from high school there before moving to Ohio, where she entered the Ursuline Order in St. Mary's. She taught at Catholic schools in Atlanta and Dallas, then suddenly switched gears to become an office-survey representative for the Scott Foresman Company in the soon-to-be-famous Texas School Book Depository.

What must she have felt in her dogmatic youth as she watched her president get murdered just outside her office window? What must she have felt to now end up sitting in front of a high-powered Washington attorney like David Belin, having to undergo scrutiny of her actions during one of the most significant historical events of all time? Did she relish it? Was she nervous or scared? Or did she look at it as some kind of an opportunity?

Those questions went unasked. Belin was not there for that kind of personal detail. Instead he focused his attention on the fourth-floor window behind which Miss Adams had stood.

Belin: Were you standing with anyone?
Miss Adams: Yes, sir.
Belin: With whom?
Miss Adams: I was standing with Sandra Styles, Elsie Dorman, and Dorothy Ann Garner.
Belin: Will you state what you saw, what you did, and what you heard?

Miss Adams: I watched the motorcade come down Main, as it turned from Main onto Houston, and watched it proceed around the corner on Elm, and apparently somebody in the crowd called to the late President, because he and his wife both turned abruptly and faced the building, so we had a very good view of both of them.

Belin: Where was their car as you got this good view, had it come directly opposite your window? Had it come to that point on Elm, or not, if you can remember?

Miss Adams: I believe it was prior, just a second or so prior to that.

Belin: All right.

Miss Adams: And from our vantage point we were able to see what the President's wife was wearing, the roses in the car, and things that would attract women's attention. Then we heard—then we were obstructed from the view.

Belin: By what?

Miss Adams: A tree. And we heard a shot, and it was a pause, and then a second shot, and then a third shot.

It sounded like a firecracker or a cannon at a football game, it seemed as if it came from the right below rather than from the left above. Possibly because of the report.

And after the third shot, following that, the third shot, I went to the back of the building down the back stairs, and encountered Bill Shelley and Bill Lovelady on the first floor on the way out to the Houston Street dock.[1]

Her reference to Shelley and Lovelady seemed odd. In a recitation of her general actions, the sudden mention of those two men seemed out of place. Maybe it was just me.

Belin next asked about her trip down the stairs.

Belin: Was anyone going along with you?

Miss Adams: Yes, sir; Sandra Styles. . . .

Belin: Are there any other stairs that lead down from the fourth floor other than those back stairs in the rear of the stockroom?

Miss Adams: No, sir.

Belin: Those stairs would be in the northwest corner of the building, is that correct?

Miss Adams: That's correct.

Belin: You took those stairs. Were you walking or running as you went down the stairs?

Miss Adams: I was running. We were running.

Belin: What kind of shoes did you have on?

Miss Adams: Three-inch heels.

Belin: You had heels. Now, as you were running down the stairs, did you encounter anyone?

Miss Adams: Not during the actual running down the stairs; no, sir.

Belin: After you left the Scott Foresman office and went into the stockroom, did you see anyone until you got to the stairs on the fourth floor other than the person you were with?

Miss Adams: Outside of our office employees; no.

Belin: Would these office employees that you might have seen, all be women?

Miss Adams: Yes, sir.

Belin: Then you got to the stairs and you started going down the stairs. You went from the fourth floor to the third floor?

Miss Adams: That's correct.

Belin: Anyone on the stairs then?

Miss Adams: No, sir. . . .

Belin: As you got off the stairs on the third floor, did you see anyone on the third floor?

Miss Adams: No, sir.

Belin: Then you immediately went to the stairs going down from the third to the second?

Miss Adams: That's correct.

Belin: As you ran down the stairs, did you see anyone on the stairs?

Miss Adams: No, sir.

Belin: All right. You got down to the second floor. Did you see anyone by the second floor?

Miss Adams: No, sir.

Belin: Did you immediately turn and run and keep on running down the stairs towards the first floor?

Miss Adams: Yes.

Belin: When you got to the bottom of the first floor, did you see anyone there as you entered the first floor from the stairway?

Miss Adams: Yes, sir.

Belin: Who did you see?

Miss Adams: Mr. Bill Shelley and Billy Lovelady.

Belin: Where did you see them on the first floor?

Miss Adams: Well, this is the stairs, and this is the Houston Street dock that I went out. They were approximately in this position here, so I don't know how you would describe that.

Belin: You are looking now at a first floor plan or diagram of the Texas School Book Depository, and you have pointed to a position where you encountered Bill Lovelady and Mr. Bill Shelley?

Miss Adams: That's correct.

Belin: It would be slightly east of the front of the east elevator, and probably as far south as the length of the elevator, is that correct?

Miss Adams: Yes, sir.

Belin: I have a document here called Commission's Exhibit No. 496, which includes a diagram of the first floor, and there is a No. 7 and a circle on it, and I have pointed to a place marked No. 7 on the diagram. Is that correct?

Miss Adams: That is approximate.

Belin: Between the time you got off the stairs and the time you got to this point when you say you encountered them, which was somewhat to the south and a little bit east of the front of the east elevator, did you see any other employees there?

Miss Adams: No, sir.

Belin: Any other people prior to the time you saw them?

Miss Adams: No, sir.

Belin: Now when you were running down the stairs on your trip down the stairs, did you hear anyone using the stairs?

Miss Adams: No, sir.

Belin: Did you hear anyone calling for an elevator?

Miss Adams: No, sir.

Belin: Did you see the foreman, Roy Truly? Did you see the superintendent of the warehouse, Roy S. Truly?

Miss Adams: No, sir; I did not.

Belin: What about any motorcycle police officers?

Miss Adams: No, sir.

Belin: Now what did you do after you encountered Mr. Shelley and Mr. Lovelady?

Miss Adams: I said I believed the President was shot.

Belin: Do you remember what they said?

Miss Adams: Nothing.[2]

After encountering those two, Miss Adams said she and Miss Styles ran out the rear of the building and attempted to go in the direction of the railroad yards, where numerous people were running. They were prevented from doing so by a police officer, who told them to return to the building. The women then walked to the front of the Depository.

Miss Adams: When I got there, I happened to look around and noticed several of the employees, and I noticed Joe Molina for one, was standing in front of the building, and also Avery Davis, who works with me, and I said, "What do you think has happened?"

And she said, "I don't know."

And I said, "I want to find out. I think the President is shot."

There was a motorcycle that was parked on the corner of Houston and Elm directly in front of the east end of the building, and I paused there to listen to the report on the police radio, and they said that shots had been fired which apparently came either from the second floor or the fourth floor window, and so I panicked, as I was at the only open window on the fourth floor.[3]

Of critical importance, of course, was when Miss Adams had descended the stairs. If it was immediately after the shots, then she might have been in a position to hear an assassin escaping down those same stairs from only two floors above. This naturally seemed to be the focal point in Belin's next line of questioning.

Belin: Now trying to reconstruct your actions insofar as the time sequence, which we haven't done, what is your best estimate of the time between the time the shots were fired and the time you got back to the building? How much time elapsed? If you have any estimate. Maybe you don't have one.

Miss Adams: I would estimate not more than 5 minutes elapsed.

Belin: Is there any particular reason why you make this estimation?

Miss Adams: Yes, sir; going down the stairs toward the back, I was running. I ran to the railroad tracks. I moved quickly to the front of the building, paused briefly to talk to someone, listened only to the report of the windows from which the shot supposedly was fired, and returned to the building.

Belin: How long do you think it was between the time the shots were fired and the time you left the window to start toward the stairway?

Miss Adams: Between 15 and 30 seconds, estimated, approximately.

Belin: How long do you think it was, or do you think it took you to get from the window to the top of the fourth floor stairs?

Miss Adams: I don't think I can answer that question accurately, because the time approximation, without a stopwatch, would be difficult.

Belin: How long do you think it took you to get from the window to the bottom of the stairs on the first floor?

Miss Adams: I would say no longer than a minute at the most.

Belin: So you think that from the time you left the window on the fourth floor until the time you got to the stairs at the bottom of the first floor, was approximately 1 minute?

Miss Adams: Yes, approximately.

Belin: As I understand your testimony previously, you saw neither Roy Truly nor any motorcycle police officer at any time?

Miss Adams: That's correct.

Belin: You heard no one else running down the stairs?

Miss Adams: Correct.

Belin: When you got to the first floor did you immediately proceed to this point where you say you encountered Mr. Shelley and Mr. Lovelady?

Well, you showed me on a diagram of the first floor that there was a place which was south and somewhat east of the front part of the east elevator that you encountered Truly [*sic*] and Lovelady?

Miss Adams: I saw them there.

Belin: I mean; you saw them?

Miss Adams: Yes.

Belin: Would that have been a matter of seconds after you got to the bottom of the first floor?

Miss Adams: Definitely.

Belin: Less than 30 seconds?

Miss Adams: Yes. . . .

Belin: During the trip down the stairs on the way down did you ever encounter Lee Harvey Oswald?

Miss Adams: No, sir.[4]

Belin then began to wrap up his inquiry. He asked a final question.

Belin: Is there any other information that you have that could be relevant?

Miss Adams: There was a man that was standing on the corner of Houston and Elm asking questions there. He was dressed in a suit and a hat, and when I encountered Avery Davis going down, we asked who he was, because he was questioning people as if he were a police officer, and we noticed him take a colored boy away on a motorcycle, and this man was asking questions very efficaciously, and we said, "I guess he is maybe a reporter," and later on on television, there was a man that looked very similar to him, and he was identified as Ruby.

And on questioning some police officer, they said they had witnesses to the fact that he was in the Dallas Morning News at the time. And I don't know whether that is relevant or what.[5]

Apparently that was not important to Belin, because seconds later he ended the session.

Comparing what Miss Adams said in her testimony with what had been written about her in the Warren Report, I found the government's version to be logical. Oswald fired the shots from the sixth floor and ran down the back stairs. Certainly the government had proven that. There was no other avenue of escape for him, no other way he could have arrived in the second-floor lunchroom in less than ninety seconds after the assassination for his encounter with police there.

If Miss Adams was accurate with what she remembered and she went down those stairs when she said she did, she would have seen Oswald or at least heard his mad dash on the steps. It couldn't have been avoided. And yet, she saw and heard no one.

Therefore, she must have come down later than she thought. She must have made a mistake about her timing. In the excitement of it all, she had made a human error. That would explain everything.

And let's not forget Shelley and Lovelady. They said they had been outside the building for several minutes after the shooting. If Miss Adams saw them on the first floor when she arrived there, that alone proved she was on the stairs later than she figured. It seemed so simple.

Maybe it was the aftereffects of what once occupied the now-empty hamburger wrappers and fries tubs I noticed lying on the floor. Maybe it was because the clock read 4 A.M. I couldn't put my finger on it yet, but something about this young girl still didn't seem quite right.

CHAPTER 4

February 1967

Victoria Adams' testimony had taken only thirty minutes. During it, Belin had handed her a diagram of the first floor of the Depository— Commission Exhibit (CE) 496. According to the transcript, she had indicated on that exhibit the spot where she saw Shelley and Lovelady. When I looked up CE 496 in the twenty-six volumes, however, I found that document to be a copy of the application Oswald filled out for his job at the Depository.[1] Curiously, I could not find the diagram Belin had introduced anywhere in the Commission's published exhibits.

The transcript mentioned Sandra Styles, the woman who accompanied Miss Adams. The Commission never questioned her. Nor did it bother with the two others who were with Miss Adams at the window, Elsie Dorman and Dorothy Garner. If the Warren Report wanted to establish when Miss Adams went down the stairs, why hadn't any of them been examined?

Miss Adams seemed adamant that she left her office immediately after the shooting. How then could she have encountered Shelley and Lovelady?

The questions just kept coming.

William Shelley was a manager at the Depository. He was also Oswald's immediate supervisor. Like Oswald, Billy Lovelady filled book orders. Photographs reveal he also bore a strong resemblance to Oswald: both were nearly the same height and weight, both had dark, thinning hair with a wide forehead, and they each wore the same style of clothing. From a distance, it was difficult to tell them apart, and employees often kidded each about the similarities.

Shelley and Lovelady provided testimony about one hour after Miss Adams' appearance. Commission counsel Joseph Ball, Belin's partner in this phase of the investigation, did the questioning. Both witnesses went through lengthy explanations of how they observed the shooting from the front steps of the Depository. Each said they next went toward the railroad yards to see what the commotion was about. Then they returned to the building, entering the first floor a couple of minutes later. Did they see Victoria Adams?

Ball: When you came into the shipping room did you see anybody?
Shelley: I saw Eddie Piper.[2]
Ball: What was he doing?
Shelley: He was coming back from where he was watching the motorcade in the southwest corner of the shipping room.
Ball: Of the first floor of the building?
Shelley: Yes.
Ball: Who else did you see?
Shelley: That's all we saw immediately.
Ball: Did you ever see Vickie Adams?
Shelley: I saw her that day but I don't remember where I saw her.
Ball: You don't remember whether you saw her when you came back?
Shelley: It was after we entered the building.
Ball: You think you did see her after you entered the building?
Shelley: Yes, sir; I thought it was on the fourth floor awhile after that.[3]

Like Belin, Ball must have been aware of the timing difficulties inherent in Miss Adams' testimony. Shelley had to be more precise with when and where he saw her.

Ball: Did you see Vickie Adams after you came into the building and did you see her on the first floor?
Shelley: I sure don't remember.
Ball: You don't.
Shelley: No.[4]

I flipped back to the Warren Report. It indeed said nothing about Shelley seeing Miss Adams on the first floor. The Report, however, did say Lovelady "saw a girl on the first floor who he believes was Victoria Adams."

But that wasn't exactly what Lovelady said in his testimony.

Ball: You came in through the first floor?
Lovelady: Right.
Ball: Who did you see in the first floor?
Lovelady: I saw a girl but I wouldn't swear to it it's Vickie.[5]

I nearly jumped from my chair. Did he just say her name? Where had that come from?

Lovelady's sudden reference to "Vickie" was certainly strange. Up to that utterance in Lovelady's testimony, Ball had not mentioned a single word about Victoria Adams or any derivation of her name. What brought forth this unsolicited and impromptu reference to Miss Adams? How did Lovelady know what Ball was leading up to?

Ball: Who is Vickie?
Lovelady: The girl that works for Scott, Foresman.
Ball: What is her full name?
Lovelady: I wouldn't know.
Ball: Vickie Adams?
Lovelady: I believe so.
Ball: Would you say it was Vickie you saw?
Lovelady: I couldn't swear.
Ball: Where was the girl?
Lovelady: I don't remember what place she was but I remember seeing a girl and she was talking to Bill or saw Bill or something, then I went over and asked one of the guys what time it was and to see if we should continue working or what.[6]

If "Bill" was William Shelley, as it most surely must have been, then why didn't Shelley remember talking with Miss Adams?

There were just too many questions.

I quickly learned that the twenty-six massive volumes of Commission evidence represent a researcher's nightmare. They are all un-indexed, and that fact alone forces the curious to leaf through hundreds and hundreds of pages, searching document by document until, with no small degree of luck, whatever is being sought is located.

During one of my forays late at night, I discovered CE 1381. It was a collection of statements made to the FBI by the seventy-three people at work in the Texas School Book Depository on November 22. Alphabetically, Miss Adams was first. Her statement was made March 23, 1964, two weeks prior to her Commission testimony.

"I am a Caucasian female, born February 8, 1941 at San Francisco, California and I presently reside at 4906 Wenonah, Dallas, Texas. I am employed as an Office Service Representative by Scott, Foresman and

Company, Room 401, Texas School Book Depository Building, 411 Elm Street, Dallas, Texas, and was so employed on November 22, 1963, the day President John F. Kennedy was assassinated.

"On November 22, 1963 at about 12:20 P.M. I was in my office and I went to the sixth window from the left to watch the Presidential Motorcade. Also viewing the parade with me were Elsie Dorman, Sandra Styles and Dorothy Garner, all employees of the Scott, Foresman and Company. I recall that at about 12:30 P.M., just after the car carrying President Kennedy had passed on the street below, I heard three loud reports which I first thought were firecrackers. But, when I saw all of the confusion on the street below I knew they must have been shots. After the third shot I observed the car carrying President Kennedy speed away. Sandra Styles and I then ran out of the building via the stairs and went in the direction of the railroad where we had observed other people running. We had not gone far when a Police officer stopped us and instructed us to return to the building, which we did.

"I never knew Lee Harvey Oswald, but I believe I did see him on one occasion in the Depository Building about two weeks before President Kennedy's assassination. I did not see him on the day President Kennedy was assassinated, nor did I observe any strangers in the Texas School Book Depository Building on the morning of November 22, 1963.

"I believe I left the Texas School Book Depository Building between 2:00 PM and 2:30 PM on November 22, 1963 and I went home."[7]

Except for maybe forgetting about her encounter with Shelley and Lovelady on the first floor, her statement was consistent with what she would later say before the Commission.

Co-worker Elsie Dorman made no mention of Miss Adams in her FBI statement, other than to say both women were together at the window. Interesting was her admission she was filming the event with her husband's camera.[8] I made a note about this.

Dorothy Ann Garner, who was beside the other women at the window, also said nothing about when Miss Adams left.[9]

The tagalong, Sandra Styles, was questioned March 19, 1964.

"I am a white female, born February 6, 1940, at Dallas, Texas and reside at 2102 W. Grauwyler, Irving, Texas. I am employed as Office Service Representative at Scott, Foresman and Company located at room 401 in the Texas School Book Depository Building, 411 Elm Street, Dallas, Texas.

"On November 22, 1963 I was in my office at a window facing Elm Street watching the Presidential motorcade at the time President Kennedy was shot. Also present at this window with me were Dorothy Garner, Elsie Dorman, and Victoria Adams all of whom are employed at Scott, Foresman and Company.

"I never knew Lee Harvey Oswald, not even by sight as an employee at the building, and did not see him at the time the President was shot. I do not recall seeing any strangers in the building on the morning of November 22, 1963.

"I recall that on the afternoon of November 22, 1963, while watching the motorcade at sometime between 12:15 PM and 12:30 PM, possibly about 12:20 I heard shots but thought at the time that they were fireworks. I was unaware of the place the shots came from. I saw people running and others lie down on the ground and realized something was happening but did not know exactly what was happening. Victoria Adams and I left the office at this time, went down the back stairs and left the building at the back door. We then went around to the side of the building where we saw a policeman talking to someone whom I did not recognize. I was told by a policeman to go around to the front of the building and out of that area. I then re-entered the building through the front door, took the elevator to the fourth floor and returned to my office. I did not see any strangers or Lee Harvey Oswald between the time I left my office and returned to it inside the building, however I saw many persons milling around outside the building and did not recognize any particular person.

"I believe I left the Texas School Book Depository Building at approximately 2:00 PM on November 22, 1963."[10]

"Victoria Adams and I left the office at this time. . . ." Did Sandra Styles just corroborate Miss Adams' statement? Did both leave the window right after the final shot after all? Wouldn't that have put them on the stairs when Oswald was there? Why wasn't Miss Styles called as a Commission witness?

In the same group of statements were those made by Shelley and Lovelady. On March 18, Shelley told the FBI, "Immediately following the shooting, Billy N. Lovelady and I accompanied some uniformed police officers to the railroad yards just west of the building and returned through the west side door of the building about ten minutes later."[11]

On March 19, Lovelady said, "I recall that following the shooting, I ran toward the spot where President Kennedy's car had stopped. William

Shelley and myself stayed in that area for approximately five minutes when we then re-entered the Depository building by the side door located on the west side of the building."[12]

If their estimates of time—Lovelady at five minutes, Shelley at ten—were anywhere near correct, then Miss Adams was very wrong. She would have had to descend the stairs considerably later than she said, if she saw both men on the first floor.

Deep in the twenty-six volumes one night, I discovered even more discrepancies. I found the original affidavits of both Shelley and Lovelady, sworn to on the day of the assassination. They had been taken by the Dallas County Sheriff's Department. In his, Shelley said:

> The President's car was about half-way from Houston Street to the Triple Underpass when I heard what sounded like three shots. I couldn't tell where they were coming from. I ran across the street to the corner of the park and ran into a girl crying and she said the President had been shot. This girl's name is Gloria Calvery who is an employee of this same building. I went back to the building and went inside and called my wife and told her what happened. I was on the first floor then and I stayed at the elevator and was told not to let anyone out of the elevator.[13]

Lovelady said:

> After he [Kennedy] had passed and was about 50 yards past us I heard three shots. There was a slight pause after the first shot then the next two was right close together. I could not tell where the shots come from but sounded like they were across the street from us. However, that could have been caused by the echo. After it was over we went back into the building and I took some police officers up to search the building.[14]

What happened to their journey through the railroad yards? How quickly did Shelley go "back to the building" and call his wife? What exactly did Lovelady mean when he said he reentered the Depository "after it was over"?

Could they have been on the first floor when Miss Adams arrived after all? If so, did that mean their trip to the railroad yards was a story concocted simply to prove her wrong?[15]

CHAPTER 5

March-June 1967

"I'm going to trace Oswald's movements from the day before the assassination up until the time he was arrested."

Terry looked at me but said nothing. We were at one of what had become regular meetings in my dorm room. I had brought him up to date with my progress on the story of Victoria Adams.

"I'm curious about what the Report says Oswald did versus what the witnesses who saw him said."

"Do you realize how much time that's going to take?" Terry finally responded. "What about your schoolwork?"

"No problem."

"By the way," Terry added, "still believe the Warren Report?"

I smiled. "Catch you later."

During the normal workweek, Lee Harvey Oswald stayed in a rooming house in Oak Cliff, a Dallas suburb only a few miles from the Depository. On Friday afternoons, he routinely caught a ride with fellow employee Buell Wesley Frazier to Irving, about fifteen miles from Dallas. Oswald's wife, Marina, and their child (later children) stayed there with an accommodating friend, Ruth Paine. Oswald visited with his family during the weekends, returning to Dallas on Monday mornings.

Frazier, a neighbor of Mrs. Paine, lived with his sister, Linnie Mae Randle.

On the eve of the assassination, a Thursday, Oswald asked Frazier for a ride to Irving. The Warren Report thought the day-early trip suspicious, although evidence showed it may not have been unique.[1]

Oswald told Frazier that he wanted to pick up curtain rods for his rooming house. He planned on returning to Dallas the next morning.[2]

The Report concluded that the trip was for a more sinister purpose: to allow Oswald to retrieve his rifle. The rifle was stored in an old blanket on the floor of Mrs. Paine's garage.[3]

On Friday morning, as Kennedy prepared for a breakfast speech at the Texas Hotel in Fort Worth, Oswald overslept.[4] He had to be nudged awake by his wife ten minutes after the alarm went off. Once aroused, Oswald hastily dressed, gulped a cup of coffee, and walked the half-block to Frazier's house. He carried a long, brown, handmade paper sack. Inside the sack, according to the Report, was his disassembled rifle.

In all probability, the paper and tape used to construct the bag was on Oswald when he rode home the previous evening. Kennedy's visit was first announced in newspapers two days earlier, on Tuesday, November 19. Therefore, Oswald would have had no reason to take those materials to Irving otherwise. But Frazier testified he never saw those items on Oswald during the Thursday ride home.

Ball: On Thursday afternoon when you went home, drove on home, did he [Oswald] carry any package with him?
Frazier: No, sir; he didn't.[5]

Based on the evidence, Oswald would have had to carry at least six feet of paper to construct the sack. The Report concluded that the paper and tape came from rolls used at the Depository to wrap and ship textbooks. Since Oswald had access to this material, the Report states he "took paper and tape from the wrapping bench of the Depository and fashioned a bag large enough to carry the disassembled rifle."[6]

There was no evidence presented to support that claim, however. Plus, the Report ignored Troy E. West, an employee so dedicated to his job at the wrapping bench that he even ate his lunches there. He said he never once saw Oswald near that area.[7]

The Report also failed to explain when Oswald would have had the time to fashion the bag at Mrs. Paine's residence. Both Marina Oswald[8] and Mrs. Paine[9] told the Commission they did not see any brown wrapping paper like that around the Paine residence Thursday evening. Nor could Mrs. Oswald[10] or Mrs. Paine[11] recall a period during that evening when Oswald had the undisturbed opportunity to make such a sack.

Nevertheless, Oswald *did* carry a long paper sack to Frazier's car the next morning. Frazier's sister, Linnie Randle, saw it from a kitchen window and thought the sack was "a little bit more" than two feet in length.[12] Frazier described the package as taking up "around two feet, give and take a few inches," of the backseat of his car, where Oswald placed it.[13] That size was later verified when the FBI measured the area of the backseat pointed out by Frazier.[14]

Since the shortest length of the disassembled rifle measured 34.8 inches, the two-foot estimates of both Frazier and Mrs. Randle posed problems.

"The Commission," the Warren Report eventually concluded, "has weighed the visual recollection of Frazier and Mrs. Randle against the evidence here presented that the bag Oswald carried contained the assassination weapon and has concluded that Frazier and Randle are mistaken as to the length of the bag."[15]

Apparently mistaken as well was Depository employee Jack E. Dougherty. He testified that he saw Oswald enter the back door of the building that morning. He said he saw nothing in Oswald's hands, despite the Commission's persistence along this line:

Ball: Do you recall him [Oswald] having anything in his hand?
Dougherty: Well, I didn't see anything, if he did.
Ball: Did you pay enough attention to him, you think, that you would remember whether he did or didn't?
Dougherty: Well, I believe I can—yes, sir—I'll put it this way; I didn't see anything in his hands at the time.
Ball: In other words, your memory is definite on that, is it?
Dougherty: Yes, sir.
Ball: In other words, you would say positively he had nothing in his hands?
Dougherty: I would say that—yes sir.
Ball: Or are you guessing?
Dougherty: I don't think so.[16]

Other than Howard Brennan, who was seated outside the Depository, the Commission could find no one within that building who saw Oswald on the sixth floor at 12:30 P.M., the time of the shooting. The Warren Report said Brennan, who became a "star" witness as a result, "made a positive identification of Oswald as being the person at the window."[17] On November 22, Brennan told sheriff's deputies that the man he saw was in his early thirties and weighed between 165 and 175 pounds.[18] In his Commission testimony four months later, he repeated that same description, adding that the man was about five feet ten inches tall and was wearing "light colored clothes, more of a khaki color."[19]

Oswald, however, was twenty-four, five feet nine inches tall, 132 pounds, and wearing a dark-brown shirt and dark trousers.

Brennan also was unable to pick Oswald out of a police lineup. His testimony states that he told Dallas police, "I could not make a positive identification."[20] Why then did the Report turn around and say that he had?

The closest the Commission could come to putting Oswald in the sniper's window was the testimony of Charles D. Givens, who said he observed Oswald on the sixth floor at 11:55 A.M.[21] Although the Report stated nobody saw Oswald after this time, it ignored two other witnesses, Eddie Piper and William H. Shelley, who both said they observed Oswald around noon, a half-hour before the assassination, on the first floor.

Ball: Was that the last time you saw him [Oswald]?
Piper: Just at 12 o'clock.
Ball: Where were you at 12 o'clock?
Piper: Down on the first floor.[22]

Shelley also noticed Oswald slightly earlier on the same floor.

Ball: Did you see him [Oswald] from time to time during the day?
Shelley: I am sure I did. I do remember seeing him when I came down to eat lunch about 10 to 12.[23]

The Commission also discounted the testimony of eighteen-year-old Arnold Rowland, who was standing in Dealey Plaza and claimed he saw *two* men on the sixth floor at 12:15.[24] The Report claimed he lacked credibility because he once fibbed about his high-school grades[25] and also because he supposedly never told his tale of seeing two men to anyone prior to his appearance before the Commission.

Yet he had told his tale, according to Deputy Sheriff Roger D. Craig. Craig testified he talked with Rowland ten minutes *after* the assassination, "and the boy said he saw two men on the—uh—sixth floor of the Book Depository Building over there."[26]

If little was known about Oswald's whereabouts in the half-hour prior to the assassination, there was plenty discovered about him starting moments after. The Report concluded that within ninety seconds of the final shot, Oswald made his way across the cluttered sixth floor[27] to the northwest corner, where he hid his rifle under several boxes. He then descended four flights of stairs to the second-floor lunchroom.[28]

A Dallas policeman confronted him there. Officer Marrion L. Baker told the Commission he was on his motorcycle facing the Depository when the shots were fired. He dismounted and ran into the building, he said, when "all these pigeons began to fly up" from the roof of the building.[29] Baker said his intention was "to go all the way to the top where I thought the shots had come from."[30]

He and building superintendent Roy S. Truly began running up the back stairs of the Depository. As Baker emerged onto the second floor, he glanced through a small window in a nearby door and "caught a glimpse of this man walking away."[31] Revolver in hand, Baker flung open the door. He called to the man, who then "turned and walked right straight back to me."[32] It was Lee Oswald.

Truly verified that Oswald was an employee. Baker and the building superintendent then continued up the stairs. Both Truly and Baker described Oswald as being calm and cool—not out of breath—even though the police officer's gun was "almost touching him."[33]

Oswald was next seen by clerical supervisor Mrs. Robert A. Reid, who said "he was moving at a very slow pace" through her second-floor office area while carrying a bottle of Coke.[34]

He apparently felt thirsty after his extraordinary morning's activities. Following his purchase and sighting by Mrs. Reid, he casually walked out of the Depository.

These oddities were suddenly becoming the norm. So did the huge amounts of time I was investing in this. McDonald's was getting rich from me, and I was burning the oil long past midnight at the sacrifice of sleep. I began to skip classes, reasoning that many of the missed lectures were those that strayed from the syllabus anyway. My assassination reading had become nonstop.

"You're obsessed!" a concerned Terry announced at our next meeting.

I was indeed. How had that happened?

Escape from the Depository

Oswald left the Depository about "3 minutes after the assassination" and walked seven blocks east on Elm to board a bus heading back, oddly enough, to where he had just come from.[35] Suddenly, he is a changed man. No longer is he calm, cool, and collected.

Mary Bledsoe, a former landlady of Oswald's, happened to be on that bus. She had rented a room to Oswald in September 1963, but after taking an immediate dislike to him, a week later she requested that he leave her premises. When she saw Oswald on the bus, he looked "like a maniac," Mrs. Bledsoe testified. "His sleeve was out . . . his shirt was undone . . . all the buttons torn off . . . he was dirty . . . I didn't look at him. That is—I was just—he looked so bad in his face, and his face was so distorted."[36]

The Report stated that bus driver Cecil J. McWatters "picked Oswald from the [police] lineup as the man who had boarded the bus."[37] Then it admitted that McWatters' selection had been made in error, since the witness actually had confused Oswald with another passenger.[38] Finally, it simply stated, "McWatters' recollection alone was too vague to be a basis for placing Oswald on the bus."[39]

It did give credence to the words of Mrs. Bledsoe, who didn't even attend a police lineup. Her identification instead came from an incriminating picture that police had confiscated, which showed Oswald posing while brandishing a gun.[40]

More convincing, though, was what police said they found in Oswald's pocket hours later. Stuffed there, according to authorities, was a bus transfer ticket that was traced back to McWatters from the mark used by that driver's individual punch.[41]

After leaving the bus when it became stalled in traffic, Oswald walked about two blocks to the Greyhound Bus Station. About to enter a taxi driven by William W. Whaley, he politely offered his ride to an elderly woman, who declined the gentlemanly gesture.[42]

Whaley told the Commission that Oswald wanted to be taken to 500 North Beckley in Oak Cliff. The address was about five blocks beyond Oswald's rooming house. A trip manifest submitted by Whaley verified the destination as "500 North Beckley."[43] Yet when the Commission questioned Whaley a second time a month later, he gave the address as 700 North Beckley, now only *three* blocks from Oswald's rooming house.[44] The change occurred after Whaley participated in a reconstruction of the cab ride conducted by an agent of the Secret Service.[45]

Whaley also testified he later picked Oswald from *six* men in a police lineup. The Report, however, disputed this:

> Whaley's memory of the lineup is inaccurate. There were four men altogether, not six men, in the lineup with Oswald. Whaley said that Oswald was the man under No. 2. Actually, Oswald was under No. 3.[46]

As Whaley drove away, Oswald walked back to his rooming house. He entered about 1 P.M. Moments later, said landlady Earlene Roberts, "there was a police car stopped and honked" right in front of the rooming house.[47] She thought the car's number was either 106 or 107.[48] The Commission found nothing to substantiate that claim.[49]

Shortly after the police car left, so did Oswald. He now wore a jacket and carried a revolver in his pocket. He had been in his room for about three or four minutes.[50]

Mrs. Roberts last saw him waiting at a bus stop in front of the rooming house.[51] The stop was for busses heading back into downtown Dallas.

He was next sighted nine-tenths of a mile away at Tenth Street and Patton Avenue, scene of police officer J. D. Tippit's slaying. With no witnesses to Oswald's movements from the bus stop outside his rooming house to this location, the Report could only guess how he arrived there, suggesting it was by way of a "brisk" walk.[52]

Near Tenth and Patton, Helen Markham watched as a police car pulled up beside a man on the sidewalk. Tippit conversed with him through a passenger-side window. As Tippit slowly, and without drawing his gun, got out and approached this man, the pedestrian shot the officer several times.

Tippit was killed at about 1:16 P.M.[53] Mrs. Markham, according to the Warren Report, "identified Lee Harvey Oswald as the man who shot the policeman."[54] It reinforced that statement by saying, "In testimony before the Commission, Mrs. Markham confirmed her positive identification of Lee Harvey Oswald as the man she saw kill Officer Tippit."[55]

But that is not quite the way it happened. During her questioning, she was asked repeatedly—a total of six times by Commission attorney Joseph Ball—whether she recognized anyone in a police lineup she attended shortly after the Tippit slaying. In each case, although Oswald stood in that lineup, she replied no. It was only after Ball offered hints about "a number two man"—a position in the lineup occupied by Oswald—that Mrs. Markham acquiesced and said that was the man she had picked out.[56]

According to the Warren Report, after throwing the spent shells into nearby bushes Oswald made his way to Jefferson Boulevard, one block away. Witness Warren Reynolds provided a positive identification of Oswald as the man he saw fleeing the scene, gun in hand, "no question about it," when he was deposed by the Commission in Dallas in July 1964.[57] This was in stark contrast to an FBI report made six months earlier, on January 21, 1964, when Reynolds said "he would hesitate to definitely identify Oswald as the individual" he had seen.[58] Perhaps his mind was changed when, two days after that January statement, an unknown assailant shot him in the head as he closed his business. Reynolds attributed that act to his being a witness to the events surrounding the Tippit murder.[59]

Taxi driver William Scoggins was eating lunch in his parked cab when he heard the shots,[60] and a man with a revolver "passed within 12 feet" of him.[61] "The next day," according to the Report, "Scoggins viewed a lineup of four persons and identified Oswald as the man whom he had seen the day before at 10th and Patton."[62] Scoggins, however, might have been influenced by a picture of Oswald that he thought he saw in the morning newspaper only hours prior to the lineup.[63]

The Report also failed to mention that Scoggins made his identification from the same lineup attended by William Whaley, the cabby who took Oswald to his rooming house. Whaley admitted that Oswald was very easy to pick out of the lineup "because he was bawling out the policeman, telling them it wasn't right to put him in line with these teen-agers and all of that."[64]

Domingo Benavides was perhaps the closest to Tippit when the shooting occurred. He was only fifteen feet away.[65] When police wanted him to attend a lineup, a nervous Benavides declined. He said he was unsure he could make an identification.[66] In a bit of levity from the witness stand, Benavides offered a physical description of the man he saw that fit so perfectly with that of Commission counsel David Belin, the lawyer questioning him, that it prompted Belin to deny on the record that he had been in Dallas that day.[67]

Benavides described the shooter as being average weight and about five feet ten inches tall, wearing a dark shirt with dark trousers and a light-beige jacket, and having dark, somewhat curly hair. This description matched Oswald, except for the curly hair and the fact that Benavides felt the assailant had "a little bit darker than average" and "a little bit ruddier" complexion.[68]

After the shooting, several witnesses started following the assailant, who at one point ducked into the parking area behind a gas station. Police later found a discarded jacket there. The Report claimed it was Oswald's.[69]

Under closer examination, authorities discovered that the recovered item had "laundry mark 30, and 030 in collar" and "laundry tag B-9738 on bottom of jacket."[70] The FBI questioned Marina Oswald and wrote, "She cannot recall that Oswald ever sent either of these jackets [the one in question plus another one Oswald owned] to any laundry or cleaners anywhere. She said she can recall washing them herself."[71]

If it wasn't Oswald's jacket, then whose was it?

Johnny Calvin Brewer, a shoe-store manager, noticed a man step into his lobby along Jefferson Boulevard as police cars, sirens sounding, sped past. "His hair was sort of messed up and looked like he had been running, and he looked scared, and he looked funny," Brewer said.[72] Not only did Brewer watch the "funny" man, he also followed him—right to the nearby Texas Theatre, where he said the man ducked into the place without buying a ticket.

Julia Postal, the ticket seller, stated she observed a "panicked" man come around the corner of the theatre entrance but did not see him actually go into the theatre.[73] Nor did Warren H. Burroughs see him, even though Burroughs was inside and in charge of taking tickets from patrons as they entered.[74] Nevertheless, Mrs. Postal summoned police, who arrived in force and frenzy seconds later.[75]

Even though Brewer, by now on the theatre's stage and with the house lights shining brightly, pointed directly at the man he had seen furtively enter the theatre, Patrolman M. N. McDonald decided to forgo an immediate capture. Instead, he conducted a slow search of some of the other "14 or 24" patrons who had entered from the time the theatre opened at 12:45 P.M.[76] McDonald displayed remarkable restraint in light of the opportunity of arresting a suspected presidential assassin and cop killer. It was done that way, he testified, "to make sure that I didn't pass anything or miss anybody."[77]

When he finally confronted the man Brewer had been fingering all along, a scuffle ensued and the suspect was handcuffed. He was led out to a police car, past rowdy onlookers who by now had gathered, resembling a lynch mob.[78] Lee Harvey Oswald had been nabbed.

There were nights in my dorm when I tossed and turned, thinking about this whole shrouded storyline.

On the morning of his evil deed, the soon-to-be presidential assassin restfully overslept.

The only two who saw him carrying a paper sack, both consistent and corroborated, are deemed mistaken. So too was the Depository employee who saw Oswald enter empty handed.

Arnold Rowland was unreliable because he once exaggerated about his grades in high school; Howard Brennan and Mrs. Markham, notoriously unreliable in their testimony, became star witnesses.

The Commission appeared to give little consideration to the Jekyll-and-Hyde routine Oswald pulled from the Depository (where he was calm under an officer's gun), to the bus (where he looked like a maniac), to the cab (where he had impeccable manners with an elderly woman), to the Tippit murder (where he was described as being both calm *and* wild looking by the very same witness).

The Commission stimulated a change in William Whaley's timetable yet failed to be stimulated by the startling words of Earlene Roberts, who said a police car sounded its horn outside the rooming house immediately before Oswald departed.

It neglected to investigate how Oswald got from the rooming house to the Tippit murder; it simply said that he did.

It said the jacket belonged to him yet ignored evidence showing otherwise.

And the Commission commented that it was "satisfied that the lineups were conducted fairly," despite evidence to the contrary.[79]

"Still believe the Warren Report?" Terry asked me, once again.

I could not answer that question. Although it was hard to think of the government purposely wanting to deceive the public, I told him I was finding it increasingly difficult to believe it was simply a matter of human error.

But that proved to be my downfall.

In my zeal of research, I had completely overlooked the fast-approaching final exams for the spring term. I muddled my way through them under the delusion they weren't difficult and that earlier good grades would carry me.

Before leaving the campus, Terry and I met for a last time, promising to write weekly until we could resume our endeavors in the fall.

Several weeks later, two letters appeared in my home mailbox. One diplomatically informed me that because of poor grades, my days at Kent State were over. I had flunked out.

The other was from my government. I was now classified 1-A. My college deferment was done, and I had become qualified for active military service.

CHAPTER 6

July 1966

Victoria Elizabeth Adams had simply had enough. The FBI, the Secret Service, the Dallas Police, the David Belins . . . it had finally dawned on her what all the fuss was really about and why she was asked over and over again about exactly when she made that seemingly innocent trip down the back staircase. Oswald had escaped from the sixth floor right after the shooting by running down the back stairs—the same stairs she had been on.

And she had seen and heard no one. Why was that?

When the Scott Foresman Company offered her a transfer to its home office in Chicago, Miss Adams jumped at the chance. She had no family in Dallas, and while she had friends at her job, when work was done, everyone seemed to go his or her separate way. There was no after-hours socializing. Plus, she was in a dead-end position there, and Dallas had too many bad memories. She needed a fresh start.

Yet the memories went with her, packed somewhat neatly in her mind.

Of course, she was aware of the growing number of books and theories about the assassination. She refused to read them. She had been there. She had seen it. She knew what had happened.

But it kept nagging at her, and in Chicago one lazy afternoon, she decided to read what the government had written about her—for the first time, belatedly. She picked up the library's copy of the Warren Report. She was shocked by its words.

The Report was calling her wrong, branding her a liar in her statements, or at the least portraying her as being naively mistaken about when she ran down the stairs, claiming it was much later than she had said. But she had been there. She knew when it had happened. It was not her who was wrong.

And what was all that business about her seeing Shelley and Lovelady on the first floor? Where had that come from? She had seen a black guy standing there, yes, that was true. She remembered asking him if the president had been shot. He was the one who never responded.

But Shelley and Lovelady? No, they were not there. She was sure of that. Why then did they write that she had seen them when she hadn't?

Suddenly, she saw her government in a different way. It was not the honest body of people devoted to the common good, as she had been taught to believe. Now, it was this faceless conglomeration of far-off individuals intent on twisting the truth to placate a public craving closure. She became even more frightened.

Things weren't right at her job in Chicago either. She was getting bored and she wanted more from it, desperately seeking to be a saleswoman instead of languishing as the executive secretary to the vice president of sales. She was told no. She asked if the company would provide her with funds to attend college at night to prepare her for advancement. She was told no.

Once again, she had reached a plateau. She was getting older, with not a whole lot to show for it. She needed a change. She thought of fleeing town . . . once again.

During her stay in Chicago, Miss Adams met and then married a man who lived in the suburbs. This became the opening for her to quit her job with Scott Foresman and move with her husband to San Diego, where she went into a completely new line of work. She found herself traveling farther and farther away from the memories of Dallas. And that was—good.

CHAPTER 7

March 1968

After getting kicked out of Kent State, I sorely missed the twenty-six volumes of Commission testimony and evidence. The library in my hometown of Altoona, Pennsylvania, didn't have a set. Bookstore managers gave me incredulous looks when I asked about ordering them.

"Why would anyone want something like that?" they asked me. I was at a loss.

And so I waded through the writings of the pioneers of JFK assassination literature: Mark Lane, Edward Epstein, Harold Weisberg, Josiah Thompson, Sylvia Meagher, Richard Popkin. By now, many writers were offering their own explanations, viewing Oswald as a fall guy, dupe, or scapegoat; Oswald as a KGB, FBI, or CIA agent run amok; or Oswald as the original *Manchurian Candidate*. Then came the oddity of Jim Garrison, a New Orleans district attorney who publically claimed he had "solved" this most famous of cases with the arrest of a prominent business owner in that city named Clay Shaw.

The media seemed full of theories. What I needed were more definitive answers. That is how I ended up standing on Elm Street in Dallas on a cold and rainy March morning. My eyes instinctively went to the infamous sixth-floor window, looming high above me, in the Texas School Book Depository.

Next door were the Dal-Tex and County Records buildings, then Elm Street made its lazy *S* curve down into the three tunnels of the Triple Underpass. The picket fence on the grassy knoll looked mysterious on this dreary morning. But it was real. I was actually here.

Cars must have been passing. People must have been walking by. The sounds and smells of Dallas surely must have been sweeping across this expanse. But I was oblivious to everything, entranced by this landmark. It was only Eugene Aldredge, tugging hard on my arm, who finally brought me back.

"Come on," he was saying. "I'll show you the bullet mark."[1]

Aldredge was not a witness to the assassination. He had learned through the local media of a mark on the sidewalk near the Depository that possibly had been caused by a missed shot. He alerted the FBI to all this, but he said the agency had done little.

I had read about Aldredge in one of my books. After writing him for more details, a lengthy correspondence ensued. Now he had become my self-appointed guide through Dealey Plaza, the parklike section of town where Kennedy was murdered.

We made our way down the gradually descending sidewalk on the north side of Elm, moving toward the Triple Underpass. I lagged behind, spellbound. Suddenly, he stopped and pointed to the ground.

There, in line with the center of the plaza and the westernmost portion of the Depository, nearly perpendicular to Elm Street and certainly not in a position it should have been if it was fired from the sixth floor, was a rather long gouge in the sidewalk. It still appeared fresh in comparison to the aged color and texture of the surrounding cement. The mark was smooth sided, sloping in then out of the concrete. It was about a quarter-inch in width for most of its length. It did indeed look like a bullet mark.

Moments later, when it began to rain harder, we were off to Midlothian, a suburb of Dallas and home of newspaperman and author Penn Jones, Jr. His forte was the strange and mysterious deaths of witnesses or those connected in some way with the assassination. His list of victims included Rose Cheramie, an employee of Jack Ruby, who said two days before the president's murder that Kennedy would be killed in Dallas (she died of an unsolved hit-and-run accident); Lee Bowers, who observed two men behind the stockade fence on the grassy knoll moments before the assassination (he died in a one-car accident); Robert Perrin, who saw Ruby at a meeting to discuss illegally running guns into Cuba (he died of an apparent suicide); James Worrell, who saw a man run from the rear of the Depository building moments after the assassination (he died of a motorcycle accident); William Whaley, the cabdriver who took Oswald to his rooming house after the assassination (he died of an auto accident). I was familiar with Jones' name and his unusual ideas from various magazine articles, but I had been unable to find his books anywhere.

Thirty minutes later, we arrived in Midlothian, the so-called Cement Capital of Texas. It didn't take long to find the offices of the weekly *Midlothian Mirror* on Avenue F. Jones owned the newspaper. He also wrote its editorials. As we entered, I spied him talking to a customer.

The building smelled of newsprint and ink. Linotype machines sat in the background. All the desks were cluttered with copies of the *Mirror*. On the wall hung several pictures of John Kennedy. Nearby were two posters, one of Batman and one of Robin. A plaque revealed that Jones had won the Elijah Parish Lovejoy Award for Courage in Journalism in 1963. He had written editorials back then that were highly critical of the John Birch Society. Not long after, someone firebombed his newspaper office during the night. No one was caught or claimed responsibility for the act.

Jones, at fifty-three, was a short man with glasses and close-cropped hair. He seemed scrappy, a man who, if involved in a fight, would be right in there and throwing punches long before his opponent would look down to find him. He was pure Texas, in his clothing, his accent, and his language. And he was generous with his time, inviting us to his home only a few blocks away, where he felt we would be more comfortable. I liked him immediately.

Jones was genuinely interested in my fascination with the subject and my motives for coming to Dallas. He labeled me a "young student" of the case. He thought my naiveté might prove beneficial with some witnesses. He also felt it might benefit him.

"Would you like to do a little work for me while you're in town?" he asked. "I'm too well known locally."[2]

I had only come to buy his books.

He told me of a strange notation Oswald had written in his notebook.[3] As was his meticulous custom, Oswald wrote a name or address next to each telephone number he jotted down. But with one—FR 55591—there were no details. It stood conspicuously alone.

And it appeared twice, once on the next to last page in his notebook and again on the last page. It may have been one of the final things Oswald wrote in his life.

Jones discovered that the number belonged to Kenneth Cody, a bus driver for Continental Trailways in Dallas.[4] "But Cody refuses to speak with me on the phone," he explained. "I thought of approaching him in the bus terminal, but I'm too well known in this area. He'd never talk to me. You may get to at least ask him a few questions."

"What do you think his involvement is?" I asked.

"I think he has a pilot's license and was supposed to fly one or more of the assassins out of Dallas that day."

And I was expected to talk with this guy?

When I agreed to do my best, Jones gave me copies of his two books, *Forgive My Grief I*[5] and *Forgive My Grief II*,[6] as compensation. I told him I was also looking for the twenty-six volumes. He said he had squirreled away two sets and would sell me one. I quickly wrote a check for seventy-six dollars, and he agreed to ship them to my home.

Alone and back in Dallas that evening, I was drawn once again to Dealey Plaza. Striking on this second visit was how compact everything was, the buildings and surrounding grounds being much closer to each other than pictures suggested.

I took my time with it now, absorbing the nuances. As the day drew to a close and traffic lessened, this tract of land was overpowering, solemn, almost haunting.

I stood on the Triple Underpass, where witness S. M. Holland had gazed on the presidential motorcade as it directly approached him. I looked to my left at the grassy knoll, then made my way there, retracing Holland's steps as he went behind the picket fence following the shooting. I felt uneasy, standing at the corner of the fence where many critics said a gunman had fired the fatal shot.

It was, indeed, a perfect hiding place. Low-growth trees planted in front of the five-foot-high fence would have obscured anyone standing there. Behind was nothing but a small parking area and an open expanse of railroad yards.

And it was close, surprisingly close. From there to where Kennedy received his fatal wound was a mere ninety-five feet.

I climbed the pedestal that Abraham Zapruder had stood on as he unwittingly filmed the murder. I sat where Howard Brennan had sat and stared at the Depository's sixth-floor window. I walked across Houston Street and turned to look at the sixth floor from where Arnold Rowland and his wife had stood.

I tried my best to imagine how it must have felt to see President Kennedy, one moment waving and the next mortally wounded, from the spots where witnesses Charles Brehm, Jean Hill, and Mary Moorman watched. And I looked back to the Depository, especially its front entrance, from the location where James Altgens took his photograph that many said showed Oswald standing in the crowd as Kennedy passed.

These were all people I had read about. And now I was here.

Only darkness forced me to leave.

Snooping on the Second Floor

The sun was just coming up the next morning as I entered the

Continental Trailways bus terminal. A dispatcher told me Kenneth Cody was off duty that day, but I could catch him the next before his 6 A.M. run to Shreveport. So I was off to the Depository to talk with whomever I could find there, hopefully Victoria Adams, the main reason for this trip.

In one of his letters, Eugene Aldredge told me he once tried but was refused admittance to the sixth floor of that building. He was a local, though. I was a "young student" from far-off Pennsylvania.

"It doesn't matter where you're from," Roy Truly emphasized to me. "Only employees are allowed on the sixth-floor."[7]

"Are you hiring?" I teased. Truly's stern face broke into a smile. The humor worked, for he invited me into his first-floor office.

Still the building's manager, Truly consented to a rare interview. He took me back five years.

He had been standing outside when the motorcade passed. Truly "distinctly heard three shots," he said, and then accompanied "a running" police officer, Marrion Baker, into the Depository. The officer was looking for a way to the roof, Truly said. The freight elevators weren't available, so both began climbing the wooden stairs in the northwest corner of the first floor.

Truly told me he was ahead of the policeman by "several feet" when, on his way up to the third floor, he noticed Baker was no longer behind him. Returning to the second-floor landing, Truly found Baker in the lunchroom. He had his gun drawn and pointed "at close range and directly at the stomach area" of Lee Oswald, who was standing in the lunchroom. When Truly identified Oswald as an employee, Baker holstered his gun and he and Truly continued their ascent to the roof.

"How quickly did Officer Baker enter the building?" I asked.

"*Very* quickly," Truly responded. "We were actually pushing people out of the way."[8]

"And once you two were inside the building, how quickly did you move from the front entrance to the elevators and up the stairs to the second floor?"

"We were hustling, that's for sure. I led the way 'cause I knew the layout, but we were moving fast. Much faster than the time tests we did for the Warren Commission."

I then asked Truly if anyone or any motion caught his attention as he emerged onto the second floor ahead of Baker. Specifically, was the door leading to the lunchroom closed?

This was an important point. The door was pneumatically operated.

Once opened, it took several seconds for it to close completely. I was curious about whether it may have been in the process of closing, an indication that a fleeing Oswald had just used it.

"I didn't notice anyone or anything," he said. "And as I recall it that day, the lunchroom door had to be closed, or I would have noticed it moving."

"Was Oswald holding a bottle of Coke or did he have anything in his hands?"

Truly gave me a sly smile. This too was a key point. For Oswald to be holding a soda, he would have had to arrive in the lunchroom earlier than the Warren Report concluded. Since he was on an extremely tight schedule already, the additional seconds required for the purchase of a Coke from a machine spelled trouble. Curiously, Officer Baker initially submitted a report that noted Oswald held a Coke in his hand, but the policeman later changed his mind to say Oswald was empty handed.[9]

"I know this is important," Truly said. "But I can't recall one way or the other. He may have been, or he may not have been. I just don't know."

"How did Oswald appear as the officer was pointing his gun at him?"

"That's the strangest part," Truly replied. "Here's a man who just shot the president of the United States, and he was as calm and collected as anyone I'd ever seen. I didn't see any fear in him."

Truly, who had hired Oswald in October 1963 as a temporary order filler, told me Oswald was a quiet person who kept to himself and had always displayed good manners and respect.

"Do you think he shot the president?" I asked.

Truly said nothing. He gave me only a furtive smile, raised eyebrows, and a slightly cocked head.

"Are you sure I can't get up to the sixth floor?" I pleaded once more.

"Not even CBS was allowed to film from up there," he answered.

But Truly did relent a bit and agreed to let me look around the first floor. I began by nonchalantly walking toward the back of the building along its east wall. I was heading for the Domino Room, an employees' lounge where Oswald said he had been eating lunch when the assassination occurred.

Turning left, I passed the back door where Oswald entered on the morning of the shooting. Then there were two large freight elevators with wooden gates. In the far northwest corner, I found the old wooden stairs that Truly and Baker had hurriedly climbed to the second floor.

Other than a man talking on a telephone that hung from the wall next to the stairway, no one else was around. When he finished his conversation and left, I ambled over to the stairs, peeked up the dark passageway, casually glanced around to ensure no one was watching me, and then started up them.

I expected to get caught at any moment, arrested for trespassing, and sent straight to jail. But I kept going anyway.

The stairs were old and narrow, the front edges of the treads worn by heavy use. They were very creaky. Every step I took created squeaks and cracks so loud I was sure the noise would summon Truly from the opposite corner of the building and get me roughly thrown out.

But no one reacted, and I ended up emerging onto the second floor.

As I stood there for a moment, I noticed that slightly ahead of me and to my left was the door leading to the lunchroom where Baker confronted Oswald.[10] Baker testified that when he reached the second-floor landing, he happened to gaze through a small window in that door at a vestibule and caught a "sudden glimpse" of a man, "and it looked to me like he was going away from me."[11] Suspicious, he ran over, flung open the door, and confronted Oswald, who by now had walked some twenty feet beyond into the adjacent lunchroom.[12]

The implication was that Baker saw Oswald just as Oswald hurried through this door. The Report made the same inference when it stated Baker "intended to continue around to his left toward the stairway going up but through the window in the door he caught a fleeting glimpse of a man walking in the vestibule toward the lunchroom."[13]

As I opened that door, I now noticed the small vestibule inside. I also found that once inside the door, I had to quickly bear left to actually enter the lunchroom. From Baker's perspective at the top of the stairs, a person on the other side of the door would be visible through the door's window for only a split second before that person moved left and was out of sight. The Report confirmed this, saying, "If the man had passed from the vestibule into the lunchroom, Baker could not have seen him."[14]

Therefore, Baker must have spotted Oswald precisely as Oswald opened the door and entered the vestibule but before he moved left toward the lunchroom and out of Baker's line of vision. This presented problems.

The door had an automatic closing mechanism that, once opened, caused it to move slowly back to a shut position. I tested it several times and found it took a full three seconds to become completely closed. If Baker saw Oswald just inside that door, then the door should still have been in the process of closing, unless Oswald stood there waiting for the door to shut before turning left into the lunchroom. Assuming he kept walking, three seconds was more than enough time for him to move out of Baker's sight.

When Baker testified, he told the Commission he wasn't sure if Oswald had even used that door. All he felt safe in saying was he caught "a glance at him" and "this door might have been, you know, closing and almost shut at that time."[15]

It was Truly, several seconds ahead of Baker in the race up the stairs, who told the Commission he saw no one when he reached the second floor.[16] And he told me the same thing, adding that he remembered the door to the vestibule being shut, completely.

If that door already was closed as Truly passed in advance of the policeman, why would Oswald stand stationary behind it until Baker appeared?

As I confirmed on site, Baker could also have spotted Oswald along the same line of sight if Oswald had been farther back in the vestibule, not just inside the door.

During his testimony, when it was suggested that Baker had seen Oswald in the *front* part of the vestibule, meaning near the automatic door, he clarified those words, saying, "Well, to me it was the back of it."[17] This was odd, though, for if Oswald had entered through this door and been at the back part of the vestibule, it would mean he already had walked *past* the lunchroom entrance and then inexplicably retraced his steps *back* to the lunchroom.

Perhaps Oswald had entered that vestibule from another direction. Snooping around more, I discovered a hallway that led out of the vestibule at the "back" portion, where Baker thought he could have spotted Oswald. When I followed that hallway, it led me to the front of the building, then down a flight of stairs to the first floor, ending up just inside the main entrance to the Depository. In other words, the hallway provided access to the second-floor lunchroom from the first floor. In fact, it was the same hallway Miss Adams had taken on her return to the fourth floor after her venture outside.

Could Oswald have used this hallway to get to the lunchroom? But that would have meant he wasn't on the sixth floor.

Officer Baker had initially introduced that very same idea when he was asked during his testimony if the back stairs provided the only access to the lunchroom. Baker casually mentioned the hallway leading to the first floor. But he discounted the idea of Oswald coming from that direction since, according to Baker, "he had no business in there."[18]

Why not?

Oswald told police that he was on the first floor eating lunch during the assassination and that he went up to the lunchroom for a drink. Could he have been telling the truth?

Could Baker have seen Oswald as he entered the "back" of the vestibule from the hallway? That too would explain why Truly did not see him and why he did not observe the door in motion. Yet if this scenario were correct, it would mean Oswald wasn't the assassin.

Back on the first floor, I walked into Truly's office to thank him for allowing me to roam around. I asked him if the second-floor lunchroom looked now as it had in November 1963, and specifically if the automatic door leading to the lunchroom was the same.

He gave me a quizzical look but didn't pursue it. "The lunchroom," he said, "is unchanged. So is the door."

I hadn't forgotten about Miss Adams, though. Before I left the Depository, I rode the elevator near the front entrance to the fourth-floor offices of the Scott Foresman Company. From what I had covertly found in the lunchroom and hallway, Victoria Adams' claim of hearing nothing and seeing no one on the stairs suddenly took on added meaning.

"Miss Adams no longer works for us," a receptionist curtly said. "She left no forwarding address."

With her, it was only the beginning.

On the Witness Trail

The bus dispatcher was right. When I arrived at the terminal at 5:15 the next morning, Cody was already there. He was standing near the open door to his bus, checking some paperwork on a clipboard.

I stood back a bit and watched as he moved about the vehicle, opening the baggage compartments and making everything ready. Why in the world did Penn Jones believe that a man like this, a bus driver of all things, had been recruited to fly a presidential assassin out of Dallas? Still, there had to be a reason why Oswald had jotted down his telephone number.

Cody began to sweep dirt from the steps leading into his bus. I took a deep breath, hitched up my pants, and slowly moved forward. As I walked up, I did a quick run-through of how I would start. I knew I had to be calm, courteous, inoffensive. I'd have to immediately put him at ease—make him willing to talk with me and confide the darkest secrets that apparently only he knew.

"Why was your telephone number in Oswald's notebook?" I blurted out.[19] It was a wonderful start.

He quickly looked up from his work. "What?" he asked. "Who the hell are you?"

"I'm sorry." I told him I was a bit nervous, then introduced myself. I explained I was from Pennsylvania—far away—and was here doing some research.

Cody did not respond.

"I noticed your telephone number in Lee Oswald's address book and I was just curious if you knew him?"

He had that if-looks-could-kill stare. "Never met him. Never talked with him. You know," he continued, "I've been asked that question a lot. If there was anything on me, don't you think the FBI would have picked it up a long time ago?"

"Then why do you feel Oswald wrote your number down?" I said.

"I have no idea. Maybe it's because I had some land for sale out in Oak Cliff." Like Oswald, Cody lived in that suburb.

"Did you ever receive a call about your property from someone named Oswald?"

"Not that I know of," Cody replied. By now, he had moved into the driver's seat of his bus. I followed him inside. He quickly pulled the lever that shut the doors behind me, the clamor loud in my ears and the doors missing me by only inches. He clearly was not pleased.

I asked if he knew Jack Ruby.

"Nope."

I asked if he had a pilot's license or knew how to fly a plane.

"Nope."

"Where were you at the time of the assassination?" In hindsight, I realized that query could easily have sent him over the edge. Fortunately, it didn't.

"At my home," he said.

"Can you tell me a little about the property you had for sale?" I inquired. "Was it a house or an apartment or . . . "

"Listen. I'm busy," he snapped. "I don't have time for this."

He flung open the doors. The fresh air and sudden freedom smelled wonderful. I took the hint and stepped outside, thanking him for his time and trouble, my acknowledgments clipped short as he quickly slammed the doors shut again.

It seemed likely that Cody was telling the truth, and Oswald had merely jotted down that telephone number with the innocent intention of someday inquiring about a property. He had, after all, expressed a desire as late as the eve of the assassination to find a place where he and his wife, Marina, could live together.

At the public library, I searched through 1963 issues of the daily newspapers for a real-estate listing of property being sold or offered for rent by Cody, or with Cody's telephone number included for inquiries. There was nothing. Maybe Oswald had simply copied the number from a handmade sign posted in Cody's yard.

I called Jones later that day to bring him up to date on my visit with the bus driver. He expected as little. Then I asked him about Victoria Adams. Jones said he knew nothing about her whereabouts, having given up searching for her a while back when "all the leads went dead." Interesting choice of words, I thought, from a man focused on expiring witnesses.

I also placed a call to S. M. Holland, a local railroad official, who had been standing on the Triple Underpass when the assassination occurred. He was the one who claimed he saw smoke on the grassy knoll when the fatal shot was fired, and I wanted to ask him about that. His secretary put my call through, and Holland came on the line.

Would he consent to an interview?

Instead of answering that question, he hit me with twenty of his own, about my full name, age, home address, phone number, high school, parents' occupations. . . . After this barrage, he said he'd call back later and quickly hung up. Perhaps he had misunderstood me and assumed I was applying for a job.

Then the idea hit me that maybe I should take a cab out to 4906 Wenonah. It was the address where Miss Adams testified she lived.

But it was where she *once* lived. She had moved, and no one knew where.

I had the same luck at the library and various state, county, and city offices. There were no tax records, residency records, employment records—any records on Victoria Adams. I called every *Adams* listed in the phonebook. Not a one was her, was any relation to her, or had any knowledge about her. It seemed as though Miss Adams had simply disappeared.

CHAPTER 8

March 1968

Penn Jones was quite the character. During my telephone chats and meetings with this crusty editor, he told me about his research. He had at this point compiled a list of forty-five people connected in some way to the assassination who he believed had died under mysterious circumstances.

Jones was a firm believer in conspiracy. He thought that five guns fired at Kennedy, in a textbook case of crossfire. Under his theory, Kennedy was hit four times, and Texas governor John Connally, seated in front of the president, was hit by "at least one different bullet and it appears Connally was probably hit by two bullets."[1]

That scenario was 180 degrees from the Warren Report, which concluded Connally's wounds were caused by only one bullet, which had first passed through Kennedy. Known as the single-bullet theory, it was the crux of the government's case for a lone assassin.

"We know there were at least two shots that missed," Jones said. "If your friend [Aldredge] is correct the other day, there's one. And certainly we know that the bullet that hit the curb by James Tague was a miss." Tague was standing near the Triple Underpass and was wounded on the cheek when something, perhaps a bullet or bullet fragment, struck a nearby curb.

"If Oswald's gun was fired at all that day, it was fired simply for evidence and I rather doubt that it was fired. I certainly don't think it was firing to kill anyone. That rifle is too unreliable; it's too dangerous; it's too inaccurate to be used for serious marksmanship. And certainly when you're shooting at the president, you're serious about it."

Jones felt that shots also came from the Dal-Tex Building and the roof of the Dallas County Jail Building. Other snipers were "behind the wooden fence, underneath the trees" on the grassy knoll and in a storm-sewer drain along the north side of Elm Street.

Still focused on Oswald's escape, I inquired about Roger Craig, a deputy sheriff who thought he saw Oswald run from the Depository some fifteen minutes after the shooting and hop into a passing car driven by another man.

"I certainly think that the man who got into the station wagon was Oswald," Jones declared. "If you go straight down Elm Street, if you go straight across the river from there, about the first street that you take across the river is Beckley [the street where Oswald lived]. So all he did, in my opinion, he drove across the river and turned to the left on Beckley and he's home in just a few minutes."

Jones did not believe that Oswald took a cab ride with William Whaley. "If you read his [Whaley's] testimony, the cabdriver signed his [blank] affidavit . . . and let the police fill it in for him." Jones chuckled. "I don't know how much more cooperative they'd want anyone to be and that might have been the reason he was killed later on."[2]

"Yes, I think that Earlene Roberts was telling the truth," Jones said when I asked about Oswald's landlady. "And I think her testimony was amazing and so damaging there's a reason they had to keep her hid [*sic*] until she died. I think [she] was a very important witness and I know of no newspaperman in the world who talked to Earlene Roberts after she gave her testimony. I searched for her for many, many weeks. I bet I spent a total of two months looking for [her]. And I never did find her.

"They hung her with a driving-while-intoxicated conviction and the police had an arm on her then after that. I doubt very much that she was drunk. She had a bad case of diabetes and, hell, you don't drink when you got a bad case of diabetes."[3]

Was it possible that Tippit was in the police car that honked its horn in front of Oswald's rooming house?

"I certainly say flatly that the police was [*sic*] completely involved in the assassination," Jones answered. "Tippit was in East Dallas at the time of the assassination; he was not in South Dallas as was stated by the Warren Commission. I know where he was and I know who he was talking to at the time the assassination took place. The policeman he was talking to headed straight for the Book Depository building while Tippit unexplainably headed towards Oak Cliff.

"I certainly think Tippit was involved. I certainly think he was as big a patsy as Oswald. Whether or not that was him that pulled up in front of the rooming house, I don't know.

"I think the police car's visit to the rooming house was important and was not handled adequately at all by the Warren Commission and they knew they were not handling it adequately. The police would come by checking with her [Mrs. Roberts] so frequently that it indicates to me that there was something going on between that house and the police. Certainly they were not coming by for the brief purpose of talking to Earlene Roberts. First place she was sixty, she was fat, she had bad eyesight, she was uneducated."

What about Tippit's murder?

"When Domingo Benavides was questioned," Jones explained, "David Belin asked Domingo what the killer looked like and Domingo said, 'He looked like you.' Now Belin didn't put into the record a description of himself. He did hurriedly put into the record where *he* was on the day of the assassination. I would much prefer that he had put in his own physical description."

After failing to identify Oswald, Benavides received threats on his life, and his lookalike brother was fatally shot in the head during a February 1964 barroom brawl.[4]

Two gunmen were involved in the Tippit slaying, Jones surmised. Oswald, he felt, was nowhere near the Tippit murder scene, having gone directly to the Texas Theatre from his rooming house.

Were They All Wrong?

S. M. Holland apparently had completed his background check. He called my hotel to say he would meet with me after all. His conditions were that it be unrecorded and in a public place. He suggested the lobby of my hotel.

At the appointed time, I was seated on a sofa near the bustle of the revolving doors. I had seen Holland's picture in several books but wasn't sure if I'd recognize him in person. Strangely, he somehow knew me, because he came up from behind, tapped me on the shoulder, and introduced himself.

Holland was a lean man, in his early sixties I guessed, and wore glasses and a brimmed hat. He was nattily attired in a business suit and overcoat. On each side of him stood two big, mean-looking men. They hovered over me like a pair of hawks but were not introduced. Bodyguards, I suspected—as if he needed them with me.

"I know more about you than you do," he immediately began.[5]

At my age, what was there to know? I smiled politely and glanced up. The hawks were expressionless.

Holland, a supervisor for the Union Terminal Railroad, said he arrived in Dealey Plaza about noon on November 22 and took up a position on top of the Triple Underpass, above the center of Elm Street. The president was expected to pass directly beneath him. Dallas Police officers were also on the underpass, Holland said, preventing all but railroad employees with credentials from gaining access. He assured me no shots had been fired from there.

As the motorcade approached in the middle lane of Elm, "I heard four shots; the first two sounded like they were behind the president with that shot from the knoll being different from the rest." When I asked what he meant by "different," he said it sounded, "I don't know, just different than the others, like it was a pistol or a different type of rifle or something."

"The third and fourth shots were very close together, almost at exactly the same second."

Holland said his eyes were focused directly on Kennedy when the "second, or possibly the third shot," caused the president's head to "suddenly lurch backward." At that moment, he said, his attention was immediately drawn to the left, straight to the far corner of the wooden fence on top of the knoll, from where he felt that shot, the "different" shot, had originated. "And I saw a puff of smoke come out from that corner and it didn't just hang there but it slowly drifted out under the trees and over the grassy area toward the street below."

The smoke, he added, traveled out about twenty feet from the fence and was located slightly behind a large tree on the knoll. Holland said he had been shown private and unpublished pictures that "confirm the presence of smoke coming from the knoll." He refused to discuss that tidbit further.

"How do you know it was smoke?" I questioned. I sensed the hawks drawing closer.

"I don't know what else it could have been. I've heard some people say that it was steam from a pipe that runs behind the fence. But there is no steam pipe back there. The only steam pipe is at the end of the underpass there, which is far from the corner of the wooden fence where I saw the smoke.

"Me and some others ran around behind the fence and I made my way up to that corner, and when I got there, I saw footprints and cigarette butts on the ground in the *exact* [his emphasis] spot where I had seen the smoke come from."

"Were the footprints and cigarettes fresh, do you think?"

"It had rained that morning," Holland said, "and those cigarette butts were all dry. I looked close at them. And there were quite a few of them there."

Holland said the footprints he saw were the only ones along the entire length of the fence. "It appeared as if whoever was behind there had been there for a while and was pacing back and forth like a caged animal. There was the same kind of mud on the bumper of the car parked there and it looked like someone had been standing on it to look over the fence."

"Let's say there *was* someone there," I said. "How could that person get away so quickly?"

"It would have been very easy to jump into the trunk of one of those parked cars and be driven away later," Holland speculated.[6]

At this point, I grabbed a piece of paper and drew an *L* shape to depict the fence. I asked Holland to put an *X* where he had seen the smoke. The mark he drew was, he said, about ten feet back from the corner on the long part of the *L*. He had me draw a line representing the bumper where he saw the muddy footprints. He said that vehicle was the third car in from the corner and was a "Pontiac station wagon, sandy or light brown in color, with a luggage rack." A white Chevrolet sat on one side of the station wagon, he said, and the muddy footprints on the ground seemed to come from the corner of the fence and pass between those two cars on their way into the parking lot beyond.

Holland admitted he rarely granted interviews, because he had been misquoted so often. "It started with the Warren Commission, which misused what I had told them in their Report. Then I wasn't too pleased with the way Mark Lane handled my interview. And that program for CBS ["CBS News Inquiry: 'The Warren Report,'" broadcast in June 1967] was very biased, especially concerning the statements I made. They only used certain parts of what I said and that didn't provide the whole story."

I assured him of my care. I showed him my notes, which he carefully read.

"Are you writing a book?" he asked.

"No. I took notes only for my own memory."

He laughed. "You're too young to worry about that."

As we walked out of the hotel, I asked Holland if he would mind retracing his steps for me from the underpass to the knoll. He paused, then said he was very busy, but if I ever got to Dallas another time, I should give him a call.

That evening I stood with my elbows on the cement wall on the

Triple Underpass, trying to visualize what Holland must have seen. The compactness of Dealey Plaza, and his position above and in front of the oncoming motorcade, certainly had given him a unique view. Kennedy was shot right in front of him, then the car sped underneath. The grassy knoll was within his peripheral vision, to the left.

I walked the short distance to the knoll. Peering over the fence ten feet from the corner, I was again struck by the closeness of Elm Street. It would have been an easy shot.

Someone could have stood right here and gone virtually unnoticed. It was the perfect location.

Something at this exact spot definitely drew the attention of many on November 22. Were they all wrong?

A Startled Man

One of the leads Penn Jones provided to me was Carroll Jarnagin, a Dallas attorney who claimed he had seen Oswald in Jack Ruby's Carousel Club not long before the assassination.[7] An Oswald/Ruby tie-in was a popular theory. Many claimed to have seen the two together. Some critics thought Oswald was on his way to Ruby's nearby apartment when Tippit stopped him.

My phone calls to Jarnagin went unanswered. So I decided to visit his office at 511 North Akard Street in the midtown section of Dallas. I expected to find a typically busy legal practice. But when I opened the door, I walked into an eight-foot by eight-foot room. A few feet ahead was a single chair for visitors. To my left, a startled man rose from a small metal desk so quickly that his chair slammed into the wall inches behind. Jarnagin was working out of a broom closet.

Jarnagin was a frail person and of average height. Probably in his early forties, he wore glasses and a business suit. He smiled as I entered. He then offered me his hand, no doubt expecting me to be another—maybe his only—client. As he sat back down, I told him the nature of my visit. Would he mind answering a few questions?

The smile left his face more quickly than it would have taken to traverse his meager office. He motioned for me to sit down as he reached for a cigarette.

I settled into his only other chair. Minutes of silence drifted by. "I don't want to talk about it," he finally said.[8]

I told him I only wanted to know what it was that made him so sure the man he saw was Oswald. He refused to answer. Instead, he nervously puffed on one cigarette, then another, and another. The guy was making *me* uneasy.

After ten minutes of this, I got up to leave. Jarnagin motioned for me to sit again. He apologized for his silence, saying he had already provided the FBI with a full statement. That agency had disbelieved him, he said, labeling it a case of "misidentification."

"And that is the way I'm going to accept it," he added. He stared at me intensely. Then he averted his eyes, as if it was *me* giving *him* the creeps.

Hoping to break the ice, I said it was Penn Jones who had mentioned his name. He immediately asked how many deaths had occurred to witnesses up to that point. I told him Jones had the number pegged at forty-five.

"I don't want to be number forty-six," he muttered.

That was when it hit me. Jarnagin wasn't toying with me. He wasn't playing games. He was scared.

"Well, if I make you uncomfortable . . . " I said.

He did nothing to stop me from leaving this time.

Jones told me there were people in Dallas who would be afraid to talk. I had just met one of them.

"But Boxes Don't Move"

Carolyn Walther told the FBI on December 4, 1963, that shortly before the presidential motorcade entered Dealey Plaza, she saw *two* men in either the fourth- or fifth-floor, southeast-corner window of the Texas School Book Depository.[9]

She was not interviewed by the Warren Commission.

"I fully expected to be questioned by them," Mrs. Walther told me in a phone conversation. "I guess they weren't interested in what I had to say."[10]

She and a co-worker were standing on the east side of Houston Street about five minutes before the assassination when she began looking around at the crowd and to her right, toward the Depository. When she moved her eyes upward, she noticed a man holding a rifle and gazing south down Houston. She told the FBI the man was "on either the fourth or fifth floor" and she was "positive this window was not as high as the sixth floor."

"But I now know it was the sixth floor," she told me that day.

Mrs. Walther explained to me she initially thought and thus told authorities that the man with the rifle was on the "fourth or fifth floor because I just wasn't sure which it was at the time." But she said she clearly remembers that this man was on the floor directly above where "two colored men were hanging out a window looking at the motorcade." Her reference most likely was to Harold Norman and Bonnie Ray Williams, who were in fact watching from the fifth-floor window of the Depository. This would have put the man with the rifle on the sixth floor, in the window from where the Warren Report said the shots originated.[11]

She described that man as having light hair and wearing a white shirt.

"Next to the man with a rifle and in the same window was another man. I could only see him from about his waist up to his shoulders and never got a good look at his face. But there was definitely another man there."

That second man was wearing "a brown suit coat." Could she have been looking at the brown cardboard boxes that were stacked in that window?

"That's what the FBI accused me of doing," she answered. "But boxes don't move on their own, do they?"

Her point was taken. "Did you report this to anyone, a nearby policeman, your friend?"

"No, I didn't say anything. I thought this man was a guard or something and that they had guards everywhere. And just after I saw these two, someone yelled, 'Here they come,' and the president turned the corner and I stopped looking at the two men."

Mrs. Walther said she "heard four shots, and right after the last shot I saw this police officer drop his motorcycle and immediately run into the Depository." This would have been Marrion Baker.

She described the sounds as having a definite pause between the first and second shots. Then the second and third shot sounded as if they were fired "at the same time." After that there was another slight pause, and then she heard a fourth shot.

She moved across Houston and looked down Elm in the direction of the motorcade. She saw two children lying on the grass on the knoll and, thinking they may be injured, walked that way.[12]

"There was mass confusion and chaos in Dealey Plaza. Everyone seemed to be running to get up behind the fence and into the railroad yards."

Along the way, she recognized a bystander.

"And I passed Abraham Zapruder, who I knew from working in the same building. He said, 'Kennedy is dead.' He [Zapruder] took his finger and pointed to his forehead, shook his own head, and said, 'They got him in the forehead, from the front.'"

"From the front? Those were his exact words to you?" I asked.

"He said, 'from the front.'" I could hear sobbing on the other end. Mrs. Walther had begun to cry.

"It's not you," she assured me. "It's just that it still affects me when I think back on it. I know what I saw and I know what I heard. And it's not what the government is telling us how it happened."

I apologized for the bother, thanked her for her time, and hung up.

Like Arnold Rowland, who was standing near her, Carolyn Walther had seen two men in the window. This type of independent corroboration shouldn't have been overlooked. It should have been fully investigated.

Why hadn't it?

Time Tests of My Own

I was standing where Oswald took his last conscious breath, the basement of the Dallas Police Department. Two days after the assassination—on a Sunday morning—Oswald was led through here, like a sheep to slaughter. He was flanked by Dallas police officers, ironically being moved to what was intended to be safer housing in the county jail.

Seeing the accused assassin and, so he would later say, wanting to spare the Kennedy family a return trip for Oswald's trial, Dallas nightclub owner Jack Ruby made his move. He burst forward through the crowd and fired the revolver he had been carrying for his own protection. The bullet entered Oswald's abdomen. He died at Parkland Hospital, without saying a word.

Like in Dealey Plaza, everything was much closer, much tighter here than pictures and film suggested. To my left was the vehicle ramp Ruby was said to have walked down. To my right, an identical ramp led up the opposite way, onto Commerce Street. In front of me in this rather dismal underground parking garage were numerous police cars, and in the far wall straight ahead was a door to a stairway leading up to the first-floor lobby.

The media had swarmed all over this constricted area that day. It wouldn't have taken many bodies to label it overcrowded. Why had Oswald been escorted into that madness?

An hour drifted by before I decided to walk back to Dealey Plaza.

At Kent State, I had spent many hours studying Oswald's timeline from the Depository to the Texas Theatre. Today, I did it in person. Stopwatch in hand, I began by walking east from the front entrance of the Depository to the corner of Elm and Murphy streets, where Oswald boarded a bus.

Still on Elm but now between Poydras and Lamar, where Oswald left the stalled vehicle, I followed his footsteps for two blocks south along Lamar to the Greyhound Bus Terminal, coincidentally where Kenneth Cody worked and where Oswald met taxi driver William Whaley. At the bus terminal, I hailed a cab and asked to be taken to the 700 block of Beckley Avenue. From Beckley and Neely, I walked back three blocks to Oswald's 1026 North Beckley rooming house. The single-level home, with its distinctive arched roof over the entryway, looked exactly as it did in 1963.

Curiously, a wooden sign stuck in a front yard that was barren of grass advertised a *Bedroom for Rent*. I knocked on the front door, figuring I'd get to examine the interior under the pretense of inquiring about the room. No one answered.

To the left of the door were three windows. Looking through them, I made out the communal living-room area of the house, where tenants could watch a television and where the landlady, Earlene Roberts, had been when Oswald came in that day. I also tried to peek into Oswald's former room, but someone had placed heavy curtains over the windows.

Back on the sidewalk, I found the bus stop where Mrs. Roberts said Oswald briefly waited after leaving his room. From that stop, I turned back to look at the rooming house. I had an unobstructed line of sight directly to the living-room windows. The landlady clearly could have seen her tenant standing there.

It was, according to the Report, about nine-tenths of a mile from this point to where Tippit was killed.[13] Bus schedules for the area of the rooming house did not conform to the time or direction of Oswald's movements, so the Commission assumed he walked from there. The government gave Oswald twelve minutes to get to the scene of the Tippit murder.[14] I clicked my stopwatch.[15]

The path as shown by the Report proceeded due south along Beckley Avenue for five blocks to Davis Street, where it turned east for a short block, then went diagonally on Crawford Avenue for three blocks. It then turned left onto Tenth Street. Another block in an easterly direction on Tenth brought me to the intersection of Patton Avenue. Just 100 feet ahead was where the shooting had taken place.[16]

I walked at a steady and "brisk pace," just as the Report presumed Oswald had done.[17] I was taller than Oswald, so my stride was probably a bit wider. Traffic was minimal on this lazy Saturday afternoon, and I was not delayed at any crossroads.

My time was thirteen minutes, twenty-one seconds. It had taken me a full minute and twenty-one seconds longer than what the Commission had calculated for Oswald. It was obviously going to take me more than a "brisk" walk to duplicate his pace.

When I clicked off the stopwatch, I noticed a young man underneath the hood of a car nearby. He was watching me closely. As I began to jot down some notes, he came over and asked what I was doing. When I told him, he graciously offered to drive me back to my starting point so I could try it a second time.

Back at the bus stop, I pressed the stopwatch again. On this attempt, I stepped up the pace, walking faster and occasionally breaking into a slow run. My time was twelve minutes, forty-six seconds. I was getting closer.

My chauffeur was at his car again. I walked over and asked him if he knew anyone still living in the neighborhood who had been a witness to the Tippit murder. He pointed to a house directly across the street from where the officer had been gunned down. Ask for Mrs. Higgins, he said.

Like many of the older homes in that neighborhood, the house at 417 East Tenth Street had been sectioned off into several apartments. I found Mr. and Mrs. Donald R. Higgins, co-managers, in Apartment B, which faced the scene of the crime. Mrs. Higgins came to the door at once but refused to talk with me when I mentioned my intent.

"Oh, let the young fella in," I heard a man say behind her. "He looks innocent enough." The voice belonged to Donald Higgins, who was seated in a reclining chair in the living room.

Mrs. Higgins had not been called to testify before the Warren Commission. She said neither the FBI nor the Dallas Police questioned her either. "Only some college kids came by shortly afterwards."[18]

I asked her what she remembered about that day.

"All I'll tell you is that I was sitting right there [pointing to where her husband now sat], watching the news about the assassination when I heard the shots outside. It was a warm day and the front door was open."

"How many shots did you hear?"

"I clearly remember three shots, but there could have been one or two more. Two seemed close together and there seemed to be a pause before the final one."

After the shots, Mrs. Higgins said she heard screaming and immediately jumped up and ran to the front door. She saw a police officer lying in the street slightly in front of the driver's side of the vehicle, and a man with a pistol in his right hand was moving in the direction of Patton Avenue, off to her right. "That's all I know," Mrs. Higgins added. So far, it sounded just as the Report had described it.

"Could you put a time to when you heard the shots?" I asked.

Mrs. Higgins glanced at her husband, who looked at me and then nodded to his wife. "Well, it doesn't fit with what they are saying," she said.

"I understand," I offered. "How much is it off?"

She hesitated again. "Well, it was 1:06."

This was considerably earlier than the 1:16 P.M. time that the Report said the shooting took place. If she was accurate, my efforts to duplicate Oswald's walk were moot. There is no way he could have left his rooming house at 1:03 and arrived here by foot at 1:06.

"How can you be so sure of the time?"

"Well, I was watching the news on television and for some reason the announcer turned and looked at the clock and said the time was 'six minutes after one,'" Mrs. Higgins explained. "He said it just like that, 'six minutes after one.' And you know how you always do, you hear the time and you automatically check your own watch. So I just looked up at the clock on my television to verify the time and it said 1:06. At that point I heard the shots."

"Are you positive of the time?"

"Yes, I am. I'd bet my life on it."

"Do you know what this means, then?" I persisted.

Mrs. Higgins looked at her husband and then back at me but said nothing. She knew.

"And the man you saw running away," I said. "What did he look like?"

Mrs. Higgins got noticeably upset and asked if I was writing a book. I assured her I was in Dallas only to satisfy my own curiosity. She remained quiet.

"Can you describe him in any way, tell me anything about him? Any description?" Finally, I asked, "Was that man Lee Oswald?"

Mrs. Higgins stared at me, not harshly, but more like my mother used to when she was trying to make a point. "He definitely was not the man they showed on television," she answered with a sigh. "Is that what you wanted to hear?"

It was, as long as it was the truth. I thanked Mrs. Higgins for her time and trouble.

"Be careful," she told me on my way out her front door.

My friend was still puttering around his car as I approached. He said he was heading toward downtown Dallas and would be happy to give me a ride back to the bus stop again, if I wanted. It was nearly an hour since my last walk. I was ready to try again.

Stopwatch poised, I pressed the start button for the third time. On this attempt, I walked noticeably faster, often at a trot. Like before, I encountered very little traffic at the intersections and did not have to alter my stride. But this one took its toll: by the time I reached my now-familiar destination, I had broken into a sweat. I was breathing heavily. My time was eleven minutes, fifty-eight seconds. I had proven it could be done.

But didn't Helen Markham say the man she saw was *walking*, not *running*, along Tenth Street? Didn't she describe that man as being calm, cool, and collected, not suffering the effects of a rapid hike?

Anyway, after a breather, I clicked on the stopwatch again and followed the path from the murder scene to the Texas Theatre, at 231 West Jefferson Boulevard. Along the way, I duplicated what Oswald did to discard his jacket, and I paused briefly at a storefront, something the fleeing suspect also did.

According to the Commission's watch, Tippit was killed at 1:16 and Oswald arrived at the theatre at 1:40. There was no explanation why the trip from the officer's slaying to the theatre, a distance of only six-tenths of a mile, took Oswald twenty-four minutes, when he had just completed nine-tenths of a mile in twelve.

The trip to the theatre took me ten minutes, walking the entire way.

I wanted to examine the interior of the theatre, so I purchased a ticket to *The Dirty Dozen* and went inside.[19] Immediately, I entered the lobby. Stairs to the balcony led up from there. And when my eyes became adjusted to the darkness, I sat down in the area where Oswald had been.

Pacifist, the ticket clerk must have thought when I left only moments later.

Back in the waning sunlight, I now strolled around the corner and behind the building, where I located a set of back doors. It was from here that arresting officer M. N. McDonald made his debut onto the theatre stage.

It was here that, according to Penn Jones, other Dallas policemen lay in wait, hoping to quiet Oswald for good when he fled out the back of the building.

For me, this was the culminating moment. I had read so much of Oswald's movements in the one-hour, twenty-minute period between assassination and arrest. I had analyzed it to death, so to speak, but only on paper. Now, I had seen it, walked it, felt it, experienced every foot of it. I may have failed to do it at Kent State, but on this project, I had clearly done my homework.

I was beat after more than a week of going nonstop. I had learned much. Yet now, on my last night in Dallas, I seemed to have more questions than when I'd arrived.

"No matter what your opinions, please don't give up on this," Penn Jones told me when I called to thank him and say goodbye.[20] I would miss him.

"The assassination is very broad, lots of names, lots of sub-events," he continued. "Focus on just one area and find out all you can about it."

It was late, and I knew I should have been in bed. My early-morning flight loomed just ahead. But in a last-ditch effort, I placed a call to Charles Brehm. I felt that Brehm, the closest witness to Kennedy when the fatal head shot hit its mark, could provide some insight.

At 11 P.M., he finally answered. He had just returned from a party, something I detected from the slur in his speech. He agreed to talk anyway.

Brehm and his five-year-old son were standing in the grass on the south side of Elm Street, almost directly across from Abraham Zapruder's camera position on the knoll. In *Rush to Judgment*, he was quoted as saying it was the second shot, not the third and final one, that caused Kennedy's head to explode.[21]

He also said that a portion of the president's skull flew to the rear and left of the automobile and toward the curb near where he was standing.

Brehm began with a detailed and vivid description of what he had witnessed.[22] He said that when the first shot was fired, the presidential limousine was slightly to his right, coming toward him down Elm. The car had slowed, nearly coming to a halt.

Immediately after it passed where he and his son were standing, a second shot rang out, he said. This was the one that struck the president in the head and caused "a piece of Kennedy's skull to fly back toward me." At this point, Brehm was "only ten feet from the vehicle."

"The car then sped up and the third shot missed completely."

The timing of the shots, according to Brehm, was the same as what others recalled: a pause of about three seconds between the first and second shots and the third shot "close to the second."

Surprisingly, Brehm had not been questioned by the Commission.[23]

I mentioned to him that some witnesses believed that more than three shots had been fired, and there was evidence of at least one missed shot. Brehm instantly became upset, severely criticizing conspiracy advocates, even accusing me of being one. Then he challenged me to meet him in Dealey Plaza "in no more than ten minutes."

It was a rare opportunity, too good to pass up even at this late hour.

It was nearly midnight when I saw a man approaching me, two children in tow. Brehm, in his early forties, politely introduced himself. His son, who was now ten, and daughter accompanied him. Nice children, I thought, until they both said, in unison, that I was "wasting my time" in Dallas.

I wondered where this opinion originated, the son having been only five when he saw the assassination and the daughter not a witness at all.

I assured the trio I was only seeking some truth.

Brehm led me to the exact spot where he had been standing on November 22. He then directed my eyesight to the sixth floor of the Depository and the close proximity of cars that continued to whiz by on Elm. He focused my attention on where the presidential car had been when he saw Kennedy's head explode.

Much of his anger, he explained, was due to Mark Lane. "He took my statements out of context and added a different meaning to them. Lane used my statement that a piece of the president's skull 'flew to the left' and that it 'came toward me' to imply that that shot had been fired from the knoll. I did not say that a shot came from there."

"But what you said about the piece of skull and how it moved toward you was correct, am I right?" I asked.

"Yes," Brehm admitted. "I did make those statements."

Still standing where Brehm had frozen me, I gazed at where he said Kennedy's car was positioned for the fatal head shot. In a direct line from there was the corner of the picket fence on the knoll. "What of the witnesses who claim they saw smoke from up there?" I pointed.

Brehm paused, gathering energy. "Come on over to my house," he bellowed, "and my wife will cook you a Mexican dinner that'll make *you* see smoke!"

I respectfully declined. His children snickered.

When I asked about the controversy concerning whether Kennedy's throat wound was one of entrance or exit, Brehm suddenly ripped open his buttoned shirt and challenged me to identify which of the wounds that he received "in the war" indicated a bullet's entry.

I respectfully declined. His children snickered.

"Why don't you think you were questioned by the Warren Commission?" I asked. "Could it have been because you said the skull fragment moved back and towards you, perhaps in contradiction to a shot from behind?"

"What difference does that make?" Brehm asked in return. "I figure they didn't need my testimony since the case was locked up anyway." With this, Brehm gathered his children and began to walk away. He had had enough.

"At least my conclusions agree with those of the Commission lawyers," he muttered over his shoulder, "and also those of Robert Kennedy."

I ran to catch up, thanking Brehm for his time and trouble and assuring him that his comments had not fallen on deaf ears. Brehm said nothing as he faded into the darkness.

It bothered me that I had been pigeon-holed so swiftly. Perhaps because of unsavory tactics by Lane, he simply became antagonistic with any who sought answers. Perhaps he was upset that, as the closest witness, he wasn't more in the limelight.

Perhaps he was soused.

Regardless, I thought a lot about him the rest of that night. As the plane took off later that morning from Love Field, I listed an explanatory letter to Brehm as one of the many things I would do in the weeks ahead. Then I finally fell asleep.

CHAPTER 9

April 1968

A mushrooming war in Vietnam, JFK and Martin Luther King murdered, then Bobby—what in the hell was going on from sea to shining sea?

Charles Brehm never replied to my letter. But Terry and I kept writing to each other, exchanging information, news clippings, and questions. I missed our nightly talks.

At least now I had the twenty-six volumes at my fingertips. And at least now I had time to search through them. I had joined the U.S. Naval Reserve—a less-likely group to end up in the war zone—and it was several months until I had to ship out for active duty.

Walther, Higgins, Brehm, Jarnagin, Holland,—the names kept haunting me. How many others were there? Who else should have been questioned but wasn't? What other clues had been cast aside? It seemed incredible that the Warren Commission—publishers of the 1938 dental records of Jack Ruby's mother[1] and the testimony of a woman whose only relevance was that she knew someone in 1942 who had once babysat an infant Lee Oswald[2]— did not attach more importance to these overlooked people.

This was particularly odd when other evidence, including Kennedy's backward head motion and the mass of people who ran to the knoll, so clearly indicated a need for further investigation. Take, for example, Margaret K. Hoover.

When the FBI interviewed her on November 28, 1963, she told agents about her discovery of a discarded piece of paper in her backyard. On that paper were the handwritten words *Lee Oswald, Jack Ruby, Rubenstein,* and *Dallas, Texas.*[3] The paper also held the name of a nightclub and a six-digit telephone number.

This may not have been unusual, considering the historic events that were then only a week old. The problem was, she had found the paper with those titillating words a month *before* the assassination, in October 1963.

The FBI quite naturally swarmed over Mrs. Hoover's residence in

Martinsburg, Pennsylvania, only twenty miles from my hometown. Mrs. Hoover's brother, Robert Steele, had tipped off authorities to his sister's discovery.[4]

During her interview, Mrs. Hoover told the FBI she had also found an envelope that held a used Seaboard Airline Railroad Company ticket for a coach seat on a trip that left Miami, Florida on September 25, 1963, arriving in Washington, D.C. the next day. All of the items, she said, were discovered near where trash was routinely burned by the resident of an apartment in the same building where Mrs. Hoover lived. That resident was Dr. Julio Fernandez, a Cuban refugee and a local junior high school Spanish teacher.

Mrs. Hoover furnished the FBI with the actual envelope and ticket stub but, according to the interviewing agent, she was unable to locate the scrap of paper holding the names. She suggested that the FBI contact her daughter, who had also seen the paper.

Margaret Kay Kauffman, also of Martinsburg, confirmed her mother's statement. She went so far as to detail the precise spot on the paper where the handwritten notations had appeared. Her description matched that given by Steele and Mrs. Hoover. But Mrs. Kauffman remembered more. The name of the nightclub, she thought, was the "Silver Bell or the Silver Slipper."[5]

The FBI then interviewed Mrs. Kauffman's husband, Gerald, who admitted being "very much concerned" about the goings-on regarding his wife and her mother.[6] He disclosed that Mrs. Hoover "has been under severe mental stress for many years" as a result of marital difficulties and probably had made up the entire thing. His wife's corroboration, he said, most likely was done simply to "pacify her mother." He also suggested that the FBI re-interview his wife after he had a chance to talk with her, so she "could clarify the situation and more accurately describe what she had or had not seen on the paper exhibited to her by her mother, now that she had given it more thought."[7]

When the FBI came knocking again, Mrs. Kauffman had indeed "given it more thought." She changed her story. She now told agents that after "considerable thought,"[8] she realized that the names *Lee Oswald* and *Rubenstein* were not written on the paper after all. The only thing she now was able to recall seeing was the name *Jack Ruby* and *Dallas, Texas*. She was no longer sure about seeing even that.[9]

After this flip-flop, the FBI wiped its hands of the whole matter and turned it over to the U.S. attorney's office, which declined to take legal action against the women "due to the emotional instability of the persons involved."[10]

The FBI also located Dr. Fernandez. He told agents on November 28, 1963, that he was definitely pro-American and anti-Castro, that while living in Cuba he had been the owner and editor of several magazines and newspapers, that he and his family had left the island in 1960 after becoming disenchanted with the Castro regime, and that when they first entered the United States they lived in Miami.[11]

He explained that the ticket Mrs. Hoover found was one used by his son to come north from Miami. Other than what he heard in the media, Dr. Fernandez said he knew nothing of Oswald or Ruby and had never been to Dallas.

I wrote Mrs. Hoover a letter the same day I uncovered these details in the twenty-six volumes.

"They told me [the] whole FBI force was in an uproar over my finding that paper," she responded.[12] "To say it upset me is putting it very mildly . . . I had so much fear at first that I only told my brother and my one daughter that saw the paper when I found it."

Mrs. Hoover said she turned all the material she discovered over to the FBI, *including* the paper with the names on it. She had no clue why the FBI said she hadn't done that. "I sure *never* [her emphasis] could believe Ruby and Oswald did not know each other as they said," she wrote me, "or their names wouldn't been on that paper together!"

She also discussed Dr. Fernandez. "He had worked in Washington, D.C. then moved here," she said, "then later taught in high school here. He also said he had worked at CIA."

Mrs. Hoover felt guilty about giving his name to the FBI, because his family "was so very nice to me," she admitted. "I felt they were innocent of the murder, but sure felt they knew something about it. Especially by him being in Washington awhile and working for CIA and Florida also." Curiously, nothing was mentioned in the FBI report of Fernandez once having worked in Washington, let alone in the intelligence community.

In the ensuing weeks, I sent Mrs. Hoover copies of the statements she had made to the FBI. Then suddenly, my letters, follow-up phone calls, and finally knocks on her door all went unanswered. So did my attempts to reach her daughter. Everyone had decided to stop talking.

But that wasn't the end to the story.

Not long after my conversations with Margaret Hoover, the mailman delivered something strange.

"I am one of a group of independent investigators who has each been working on the case since 1964 and who cooperate occasionally for particular pieces of investigating. We are all cooperating fully with Jim Garrison and helping him in every way possible. . . . "[13]

The letter came from the University of Minnesota in Minneapolis. Its author was Gary Schoener, a Ph.D. candidate in clinical psychology and a serious researcher of the Kennedy assassination. He said he wrote because of my interest in Mrs. Hoover, whom he too had interviewed. Mrs. Hoover had told him about me.

Schoener offered ideas on what I should do, "since you seem interested in becoming active in investigating the case." One was to get in touch with Vincent Salandria, a Philadelphia attorney. I had read about Salandria in several magazines. His interest centered on the medical evidence and Commission Exhibit 399. That was the famous "single bullet" credited with inflicting seven wounds to both Kennedy and Connally while remaining virtually pristine in appearance.

Schoener also requested copies of my personal research papers to determine how I could assist the growing number of independent researchers across the country. His letter was an open invitation to join an underground network of likeminded individuals, organized and working toward finding truths. I was flattered and immediately wrote to accept the deal.

A week later, Schoener replied. "Enclosed is the envelope in which your last letter came. Please examine it and drop me a note if it looks like it was opened after you sent it—i.e. if the sloppy sealing and tape was not yours. This is just a precaution since I have had many troubles with opened mail."[14]

The sloppy sealing was definitely not mine.[15]

"I'm glad that you would like to continue to take an active part in the investigation," Schoener went on. He suggested I do research at the National Archives in Washington, D.C. and, while there, spend time viewing Abraham Zapruder's film of the assassination. He also wanted me to read books by Harold Weisberg.

I had already read several and admired Weisberg because he was different from the others. He offered no theories or speculations about the crime, relying instead on showing contradictions that existed between the evidence and the Warren Report's conclusions. I associated his style of research with my own.

Schoener provided me with Weisberg's address and telephone number in Frederick, Maryland. "If you are passing that way on the way to Washington, you might drop by his house . . . perhaps getting a chance to meet the man who is doing the most work on the case. If you do drop in on him, please use my letter for identification. He might be able to give you a number of important leads to check out in the Archives, so that it would be very mutually rewarding.

"When at the Archives, do not tell them that you know either me or Weisberg, so that you will have the opportunity to learn more information," Schoener continued. "It's best to portray yourself as a student rather than a critic of the Warren Commission. My name and Weisberg's name are well known in the Archives."

I wrote about this development to Terry, who expressed suspicion. But I felt heady with the prospects of working with a discreet band of brothers, searching out history's meanings. I was young, motivated by a strong sense of idealism, of patriotism, of discovering the unknown.

At times, I could be very naïve.

CHAPTER 10

July 1968

Terry and I were led into a small room where a table with two chairs had been set up in front of a large movie screen. At the back of the room sat the projector and a National Archives staff member, waiting for us to settle in. What we were about to see, he whispered, was a copy of the Abraham Zapruder film made by the FBI from the original, which, for preservation's sake, was not available to researchers.

The copy was in color, silent, and, because the original was a mere twenty-six seconds in length, appeared three times in succession on this film to avoid unnecessary rewinding. He could show the segments at normal running speed and in slow motion, as many times as we wanted.

"Are we ready?" he asked.

"Yes," I answered.

Nothing could have prepared me for the horror of the next half-minute.

The room was darkened. The film flickered on the screen six feet in front of us.

In the beginning, the Dallas Police motorcycle escort turns left from Houston Street onto Elm Street in advance of the motorcade. It is a beautiful day. The sun shines brightly in a late November sky.

The motorcycles move slowly. Suddenly, because Zapruder briefly stopped then restarted filming, the presidential limousine appears. President Kennedy, sitting in the rear passenger-side seat, faces the camera and raises his right arm to wave to an obviously enthused audience. Mrs. Kennedy, in her distinctive pink dress and hat, sits to his left, gazing at those on her side of the street. My eyes are drawn to a young girl in the background wearing a red dress and white-hooded jacket as she merrily runs to keep pace with the passing car. On the same side of the car as President Kennedy and directly in front of him sits Texas governor John Connally, in a jump seat. To the governor's immediate left is his wife, Nellie.

The car glides behind a road sign, which temporarily obscures its occupants. As it reappears, Kennedy is noticeably distressed. He has been shot.

The young girl has stopped running and looks backward. Both of the president's arms splay awkwardly upward, with clenched fists in front of his chin. Mrs. Kennedy has turned toward her husband, wearing a quizzical look. She attempts to help her stricken husband, putting her hands on his upraised left arm.

Connally has turned sharply to his right to look backward, then pivots toward the front of the car. His mouth opens wide, as if to scream. His cheeks are puffed. He is in obvious pain.

The governor's wife begins to pull him down onto her lap. Figures in the background pass by: there is Charles Brehm, clapping his hands as his son stands beside him; and Jean Hill in her red coat, staring at the president, then looking up the street to her right; next is Mary Moorman and farther along is James Altgens, each with cameras to their eyes, taking what will become world-famous and controversial photographs. The car seems to coast leisurely down Elm, as if on snow, almost surreal in its quiet motion.

I want to reach out and somehow turn the steering wheel, push this vehicle from the road and avoid the awful scene that I know, I just know, is coming next. But I am helpless, as helpless as the young and vulnerable president. Kennedy appears to drift slightly forward and then, in a most sickening explosion of blood and brain matter, a chilling halo of crimson red appears above him. The right front side of his head has burst open, exposing a large gaping hole and a hanging flap of skin and still-attached skull bone. The shock of hair is disrupted. His once easily identifiable and handsome face suddenly looks monsterish, unrecognizable, severely altered. Strangely, his head moves backward and to his left with tremendous force, his body now limp and slamming into the back of the seat, then bouncing forward into his wife's arms.

Bystanders in the background at once run and duck for cover. In shock, Mrs. Kennedy crawls onto the trunk lid. Secret Service Agent Clint Hill, from the left running board of the follow-up car, jumps onto the rear bumper of the limousine and forces her back into her seat. The car accelerates, is consumed by the blackness of the Triple Underpass, and disappears, and the film mercifully ends.

President Kennedy was shot from the front.

How could it be denied?

His head had snapped *backward*. His body was slammed *backward* into the seat. How was that possible if Oswald fired from behind?

I pounded my fist onto the table. Why hadn't the Warren Commission investigated this? In its massive final Report and accompanying twenty-six volumes, not a single word was written about this sickening and frightening motion, this *contradictory* backward motion.

Commission members had viewed this film. Surely they must have seen this phenomenon. Why had they ignored it?

The first image that came to my mind was that of Walter Cronkite, who had told unsuspecting viewers in 1967 that the fatal shot in the Zapruder film "appears to move the President's head back." His sidekick, Dan Rather, described that same shot as causing a "minor explosion."[1]

After what I had just seen, there could never be more colossal understatements.

No wonder Gary Schoener insisted I spend time with this film during my venture into the bowels of the National Archives. The sad thing was, the film was only available to researchers. Reservations were required—in advance.

America was not otherwise privy. It would have to wait seven more years for that privilege.

"Shall I show it again?" the projectionist was asking.

I could not speak.

"Yes," I heard Terry say. "Yes, please."

The film was run again, and again, each time in triplicate, sometimes at regular speed, sometimes in slow motion. We watched it a hundred times if not more. Then we watched it in reverse, eerily inverting this blot on America's history. As I gradually gained my composure, I began focusing on single aspects of the film: the responses of the Secret Service agents; the movements of Mrs. Kennedy and Governor Connally and his wife; the bystanders and their reactions; and, of course, a closer examination of the president.

Four hours later, I had seen all I needed. Terry went off to lunch. I had long since lost my appetite. It was only when the Archives was about to close at nine that night that I noticed he had never returned.

"Aren't you going to ask me whether I still believe the Warren Report?" I teased him later in the hotel. It was a question he had asked a hundred times, if not more.

He looked up at me but was silent.

"I've grown tired of it," he finally admitted. "We're never going to know the truth anyway. That film proved it."

I had known this was coming. In the letters he wrote to me first weekly, then monthly, then only on occasion, I sensed his draining interest. He didn't want to go to Dallas. I had to practically beg him to come with me to Washington.

Maybe it was a lack of time or the frustrations of this game. Maybe it was the real world or the Zapruder film itself. Somewhere along the way, Terry had given up.

Maybe he was the smart one.

Examining Some Physical Evidence

I was alone now at the National Archives, staring at the many boxes of documents on the table in front of me, the boxes I had hoped Terry would help explore.

Minutes after I checked in that day, a staff member approached and motioned me to the door. I was escorted to a private area down the hall. Inside was a table that had several large cartons on it containing the physical evidence I wanted to examine: Oswald's rifle and pistol, his clothing, and Commission Exhibit 399. Look at it; carefully handle it; take as long as you like, said a monitor seated nearby.

So I began with the rifle, the Mannlicher-Carcano 6.5-millimeter Italian-made weapon Oswald fired three times.[2] It had been found stashed beneath some boxes during a police search on the sixth floor shortly after the assassination. According to the Report, the rifle had "an inexpensive four-power telescopic sight" and a sling that was "not a standard rifle sling but appears to be a musical instrument strap or a sling from a carrying case or camera bag."[3]

Two police officials simultaneously discovered the weapon. Deputy Constable Seymour Weitzman, in an affidavit filed on November 23, 1963, said, "This rifle was a 7.65 Mauser bolt action equipped with a 4x18 scope, a thick leather brownish-black sling on it."[4] Deputy Sheriff Eugene Boone, in a Sheriff's Department report filed on the day of the assassination, said, "The rifle appeared to be a 7.65mm Mauser with a telescopic sight."[5]

Boone was not asked about his "Mauser" label when Commission counsel questioned him in March 1964. However, he was shown the 6.5-millimeter Carcano for purposes of identification. After examining it, Boone testified, "It looks like the same rifle. I have no way of being positive."[6]

Weitzman, who admitted being "fairly familiar" with guns, *was* asked about his statement that the gun was a 7.65 German Mauser. "In a glance, that's what it looked like," he said.[7] The Commission, however, neglected to show him Oswald's rifle.

A third official, Deputy Sheriff Luke Mooney, was nearby when Weitzman and Boone found the rifle. He, too, had observed the weapon in its hiding place. But in a report to the Sheriff's Department filed on November 23, 1963,[8] and in his Commission testimony,[9] he was not asked nor did he volunteer anything about the make or model of the rifle.

Mooney also was not shown the weapon.[10]

Weitzman and Boone may simply have been mistaken when they described the rifle as a 7.65 German Mauser. In its secreted position, the rifle was hard to see and neither one of them actually held it.[11] Had they done so, the confusion might have ended there, since the notations *MADE ITALY* and *CAL. 6.5* were conspicuously stamped on the underside of the weapon.

That inscription *was* observed by Lt. Carl Day of the Dallas Police crime lab after he picked up the rifle and held it as his boss, Capt. Will Fritz, ejected a live cartridge from the chamber. Day, the Warren Report stated, "promptly noted that stamped on the rifle itself was the serial number 'C2766' as well as the markings '1940' 'MADE ITALY' and 'CAL. 6.5.'"[12]

The question then is why, despite Day's identification of the weapon as a 6.5-caliber Italian rifle, it continued to be labeled by authorities as a 7.65-caliber German Mauser throughout the remainder of the day.[13] It was even described as "a Mauser, I believe" by District Attorney Henry Wade in a press conference during the early-morning hours of November 23.[14]

How was it that the description being fed to a copy-crazed media was based on casual "glimpses" made by Weitzman and Boone, rather than the more authoritative identification the Report cites Lieutenant Day as making?

In any event, one thing *I* determined after nearly an hour examining the Carcano was that, even at the $19.95 purchase price, Oswald had paid too much for this thing. It was cheap in cost and looked even cheaper. From its worn wooden stock and scratched metal right down to the flimsy sling attached to its side, this thing was a throwaway. In its present state, it appeared better suited as a club to thwack its intended victim rather than shoot him. According to the date of its manufacture, it was twenty-three years old when the government said it was used so effectively in Dallas. It had not aged gracefully.

If Oswald was as talented with a rifle as the Commission claimed, whatever would compel him to invest in such an inferior firearm?

After I had carefully checked every square inch of the rifle, I held it up and looked through its telescopic sight. I put my finger on the trigger and hesitated. The room monitor was watching my every move. I expected him to stop me from doing what I was about to do, but he merely smiled.

So I did it.

I pulled the trigger and heard the distinctive click as metal met metal in the empty chamber.

As weapons experts testified in 1964, the trigger was tricky. At first it was easy to pull back but then became increasingly more difficult until the firing pin was released. The bolt action was no better.

In the dozen times I operated it, I found it to be sluggish and sticky. Even the Commission's experts had agreed that working the bolt was not the smooth operation it should have been and often required having to sight the weapon on its target again before firing another time. Perhaps the accuracy as displayed on November 22 far outweighed its poor appearance and operational quirks.

I rooted around in another box and located the three 6.5-millimeter shell casings found beneath the sixth-floor window.[15] Then I pulled out and examined the .38-caliber Smith & Wesson revolver allegedly used in the murder of Officer J. D. Tippit.[16]

I next asked my host about Commission Exhibit 399, the bullet assigned by the Commission the task of injuring both Kennedy and Connally. He slowly reached into his coat pocket and brought out a small hinged case, which he opened with the kind of fanfare usually reserved for presentation of an engagement ring.

Inside was the so-called "magic bullet." I picked it up gingerly and held this famous and extremely controversial piece of metal in my hand. Only through touch and firsthand examination can one realize what little deformity it actually had suffered, even though it had shattered Governor Connally's rib and pulverized his wrist bone.

Had it not been for a slight flattening at the rear, a small piece of its nose removed by the FBI for spectrographic testing, and striation marks along its sides, this bullet would have looked as it had when it was sold new. It was definitely no match for the damaged condition of other bullets test fired in attempts to duplicate its feat.[17]

Next I found Oswald's clothing: the shirt he wore on the day of the assassination and the discarded jacket found in Oak Cliff. I had also asked to see the suit coat and dress shirt worn by President Kennedy, to verify distances between the collar and bullet hole in each item. That request was denied. Their historic value and bloodstained appearance prevented release.

Oswald's shirt was rust colored with a tweed-type design to its fabric, long sleeved, and "small" in size and had several buttons missing from its front.[18] In its present condition, it looked surprisingly similar to the one worn by a man captured in a photograph by James Altgens who was standing in the Depository's front doorway as Kennedy passed. Critics said that man was Oswald. The Commission said it was employee Billy Lovelady.

The zippered jacket was light gray in color and manufactured by a clothing company in Los Angeles. It still had the much-questioned laundry tag labeled *B 9738* pinned to it. A separate laundry mark, *30 030*, was stamped onto the jacket and clearly visible.[19] Even though Oswald's shirt was sized "small," the jacket was tagged *M* for medium.[20]

I would be lying if I said I wasn't awed by this evidence. I was holding in my own hands the clothing worn by the assassin, the guns he used on that terrible day, and *the* bullet. It was an opportunity afforded to few others.

I thanked my by-now dozing host, then hurried back to the research room. There was still much to be done.

New Leads and Mr. Weisberg

The Zapruder film and the physical evidence were both reasons why I went to the Archives. The real motive, though, was to search through the reams of Commission Documents for any information I could find about Victoria Adams.[21] As I groped through box upon box of this mostly disorganized paperwork, I came across some tidbits.

One was a two-page interview of Miss Adams conducted by the FBI on November 24, 1963. Taken only two days after the assassination, it appeared to be her first official "on-the-record" statement. It was my first fresh lead in a while.

Miss Adams' story to the FBI then was virtually the same as what she related to David Belin some five months later. The report was written in a third-person format that the FBI routinely used to summarize its interviews.

"Vickie [*sic*] Adams, 3651 Fontana Street, Dallas, Texas, furnished the following information:

"She is employed as office service representative by the Scott Foresman and Company, with offices located on the fourth floor of the Texas School Book Depository Company, Dallas.

"On November 22, 1963, she was on duty at her place of employment and at about 12:20 PM on that date she went to the second window from the left of the building on the fourth floor and opened same in order to watch out of this window to observe the passing of the motorcade, bearing President Kennedy and group. She took her lunch with her at this time and stationed herself there with a fellow employee, Sandra Styles, 2102 Grauwyler Street, Dallas. They observed the motorcade as it approached and began passing in front of her window and at about 12:30 PM, as the car containing President Kennedy, Governor Connally and his wife, was passing, she heard three loud reports which she first thought to be fire crackers of a crank and she believed the sound came from toward the right of the building, rather than from the left and above as it must have been according to subsequent information disseminated by the news services."[22]

Now here was something new: the FBI relying on the news media to determine the source of the shots. Curious too was that in the right-hand margin of this document, next to where Miss Adams said she felt the sounds came from the "right of the building," someone had drawn an arrow to emphasize that comment.

"After the third shot, she observed the car containing President Kennedy to speed up and rush away. She had not been able to fully observe the President at the exact moment he was shot, inasmuch as her view was partially obstructed. She and her friend then ran immediately to the back of the building to where the stairs were located and ran down the stairs. No one else was observed on the stairs at this time, and she is sure that this would be the only means of escape from the building from the sixth floor. She and her friends [*sic*] ran out of the building, turned to the left and ran across the railroad tracks in the direction where they observed other people running, inasmuch as they felt that an attempt had been made on the life of the President, and they wanted to find out more about this situation. They had not gone far until they were stopped by a police officer who instructed them to return to the building. Consequently, they returned to the building and re-entered it.

"She did estimate that the time between her departure from the building and her return to the building was about four or five minutes. She stated that she did not observe anything or anybody during this time or immediately before or after, which would cause her place [*sic*] a connection with the attempted assassination of the President.

"Miss Adams was shown a photograph of Lee Harvey Oswald, bearing New Orleans, Louisiana number 112 723. She stated that she saw this individual only on one occasion which was about two or three weeks ago while he was in the company of other individuals at the building. At that time she did not know who he was and did not speak with him. She recalled only after seeing his photograph in the current newspapers that this was the individual suspected of having shot President Kennedy. She stated that she is rather sure that she did not see this individual on the day of President Kennedy's assassination."[23]

Odd, but again Miss Adams did not mention seeing Shelley and Lovelady. Other than that missing detail, there was remarkable consistency between what she said on November 24, what she told the FBI on March 23, and what she testified to before Commission staff on April 7.

This was unlike the inconsistencies shown by a number of other witnesses. She was certainly no Howard Brennan or Helen Markham in that respect.

The FBI returned December 19, 1963, this time regarding a different matter.

"Vickie Adams, 3651 Fontana, Dallas, Texas, employed by Scott-Foresman Company, Texas School Book Depository Building, was recontacted to determine if she had any knowledge as to acquaintanceship and/or association between Lee Harvey Oswald and Jack Ruby. Miss Adams stated she had been only slightly acquainted by sight with Lee Harvey Oswald. She is not acquainted with Jack Ruby and has no knowledge regarding Ruby's activities or associates. She has no knowledge of any connection between Jack Ruby and Lee Harvey Oswald."[24]

In still another box of documents, I found more. On February 17, 1964, Dallas Police Detective James R. Leavelle knocked on Miss Adams' door. Leavelle was the cop handcuffed to Oswald who gazed in shock as his prisoner was murdered by Ruby. According to Leavelle's report:

I talked with Vickie Adams at 8:10 PM this date, February 17, 1964.

The following statement is what she said happened on November 22, 1963.

"My name is Vickie Adams, 3909 Cole, Apt. D., no phone. My job is office service representative. I reported to work that day about 8:30 am, and I worked in that capacity until noon.

"A friend of mine, Elsie Darmon [sic] who lives in Oak Cliff and works in the office, wanted to take some moving pictures of the motorcade. I opened a third floor window [sic] about the third one from the front of the building. She took pictures of the motorcade. When the President got in front of us I heard someone call him, and he turned. That is when I heard the first shot. I thought it was a firecracker. Then the second shot I saw the Secret Service man run to the back of the President's car. After the third shot I went out the back door. I said, 'I think someone has been shot.' The elevator was not running and there was no one on the stairs. I went down to the first floor. I saw Mr. Shelly [sic] and another employee named Bill. The freight elevator had not moved, and I still did not see anyone on the stairs.

"I ran out the back door of the depository and around to the front. I started down toward the railroad tracks when an officer stopped me and turned me back. I asked the officer if the President was shot, and he said he did not know. As I turned back I saw another employee Molena [Joe Molina] standing by the front of the building facing Elm Street. I stopped and talked with Avery Davis another employee. I saw two men in street clothes, one was gesturing with his hands and asking questions. I asked Mr. Davis who he was. I later saw Jack Ruby on TV and thought it was the same man. No one had surrounded the building at that time. I went back into the building and to the passenger elevator, but the power was off. I went to the back to the freight elevator. There was two plainclothes men on it. However, the power on it also was turned off. I walked up the stairs to the fourth floor to my office. We were later told to leave."

This concludes Miss Adams' statement to me.[25]

Curiously, this rather casual interview nearly three months beyond the assassination, and taken after several other more detailed FBI reports, was the first one to include the names Shelley and Lovelady, an admission that later would be used to discredit Miss Adams.

There certainly seemed to be a lot of official interest in this woman.

As I tried to substantiate exactly when Miss Adams left the window,

I was struck by how little investigators had done on the record to nail down this crucial timing issue. Did she leave immediately after the last shot, or did she dillydally? With her that day were fellow workers Elsie Dorman, Dorothy Garner, and Sandra Styles. Anyone in that trio could have confirmed Miss Adams' actions, had they been asked. But they weren't. The Warren Commission didn't question a one of them about anything.

The absence of any documentation on Sandra Styles was particularly disturbing. After all, she had accompanied Miss Adams throughout the ordeal. If any of those women needed to be questioned, it was her.

Striking out with Victoria Adams was becoming the norm. It had happened in Dallas; now in Washington too. But I began to hit pay dirt with others.

On the fifth floor of the Depository, the floor between Victoria Adams and the assassin, three others watched the passing motorcade. Bonnie Ray Williams, Harold Norman, and James Jarman, Jr., were positioned directly under the window where the Commission placed Oswald.

Williams was interesting. He said he ate his lunch near the infamous sixth-floor window between noon and 12:20 P.M. but saw and heard no one there.[26] If that time is accurate, it would have given Oswald only a precious few minutes to prepare for his feat, since news reports indicated Kennedy was scheduled to pass the building at 12:25 P.M. Oswald would have had no way of knowing the motorcade was running five minutes late.

Norman claimed he had such a keen sense of hearing, he was able to hear the bolt action of the rifle being used and the expended cartridge cases hit the floor over his head.[27] Yet neither he nor his companions heard other sounds from above, such as the noise of someone running or even a hint of hurried footsteps.[28]

This is especially peculiar since the sixth floor had been undergoing repairs that week. The floor was so thin at spots that daylight could be seen through it.[29] Even more unusual, the three said that immediately after the shots, they moved to the west side of the building, closer to the back staircase Oswald descended, yet they *still* heard nothing.

It was only when Officer Baker suddenly emerged onto the fifth floor, on his way to the roof after his second-floor encounter with Oswald, that Williams, Norman, and Jarman noticed anyone in the direction of the staircase.[30]

Whether Oswald could have done all he was supposed to within the allotted time was, of course, invaluable to the Commission's conclusions. From the moment the final shot sounded, he was on an extremely tight schedule. He had to move quickly from the sixth-floor, *southeast*-corner window along an obstacle course of cluttered book cartons to hide his gun and escape down the back stairs at the *northwest* corner of the building in less time than it took Roy Truly and Officer Baker to run into the building and up a single flight of stairs to confront him within the second-floor lunchroom.

The reader will be more out of breath from reciting the above sentence than was Oswald after his four-flight dash.

On November 29, 1963, the FBI conducted what it called a "survey" to determine the possible ways Oswald might have escaped. It used ten different scenarios that involved the back stairs, the freight elevator, or combinations of both. After the "survey" was completed, agents settled on a scenario that had Oswald "walking from window on sixth floor to stairway, walking down stairway to second floor, walking on second floor from stairway to lunch room, spending 30 seconds in lunch room, and then walking to front stairway and walking downstairs to first floor and then walking to front door: 2 minutes 25 seconds."[31] It was the only scenario capable of putting Oswald in the lunchroom in enough time to greet Truly and Baker.

Timed tests were then conducted. Using a stopwatch, FBI Agent John Howlett reenacted Oswald's actions from the sixth to the second floor. He completed the feat in one minute eighteen seconds the first time, one minute fourteen seconds the second.[32]

Truly and Baker were also asked to reconstruct their run up to the second floor. Two tests were made, timed again by the FBI. They completed the trip in one minute thirty seconds the first time, one minute fifteen seconds the second.[33]

Based on these calculations, Oswald must have reached the lunchroom only seconds in advance of the showdown, all calm, cool, and collected.

The Secret Service performed additional time trials on December 5, 1963. It picked up Oswald's trail from the Depository's front steps. It clocked his movements from there to where he boarded the bus seven blocks away (four and one-half minutes); the time he was on the bus until it became stalled in traffic and he got off two blocks later (four minutes); his four-block walk to a waiting cab (three minutes); his 2.6-mile cab ride to a location beyond his rooming house (seven minutes); his four-tenths of a mile walk back to the rooming house (six minutes); his departure from there and his wait for a bus back to the city (thirty seconds); his eight-tenths of a mile hike to the Tippit murder scene (twelve minutes); and his six-tenths of a mile walk to the Texas Theatre, where he was finally captured (ten minutes).[34]

The Commission remained steadfast in its efforts to show that all of the actions attributed to Oswald in the hour following the assassination could, in fact, have been accomplished by him. If it intended to prove its case against him in a truthful and unbiased manner, that is exactly how the Commission should have handled those matters. Why, then, did it lack the same resolve with Victoria Adams?

The Commission knew how important she was; it admitted as much in its final Report. Why then didn't the FBI, Secret Service, or a Commission attorney grab a stopwatch and accompany her as she retraced her steps down the back stairs? Why wasn't her timing compared with that of Oswald's?

This oversight seemed inexcusable since Commission staffers Joseph Ball and David Belin, in charge of identifying the assassin, specifically listed Miss Adams' time conflict as one of the *key* areas they intended to closely examine.

They addressed that issue in a February 25, 1964, internal report. Under the heading, "The Time Sequence," Ball and Belin admitted, "If he [Oswald] were the assassin, he had to descend to the second floor in a short space of time in order to meet Truly and Baker."[35] The duo then cited Miss Adams:

"Vickie Adams, employed on the fourth floor of the TSBD Building, when interviewed on November 24, stated that she went to the second window from the left of the building on the fourth floor and opened same in order to see the motorcade and was there with a fellow employee, Sandra Styles. As the motorcade passed, she heard three loud reports that she first thought to be firecrackers and what she believed came from toward the right of the building rather than from the left and above. After the third shot, she observed the Presidential car speed up and rush away. She then ran immediately to the back of the building to where the stairs were located and ran down the stairs. No one else was observed at the stairs at this time and she said she was sure that this would be the only means of escape from the building from the sixth floor. She and her friends [*sic*] ran out of the building, turned to the left and ran across the railroad tracks. Five minutes later, they were directed to return to the building. We should pin down this time sequence of her running down the stairs."[36]

We should pin down this time sequence.

Why then didn't they?

As the days wore on and I continued to slowly gather information from my readings at the Archives, the faces of employees and other long-term researchers became familiar to me. One afternoon I noticed someone different. Yet I had seen him before, somewhere. Was it on television or the back of a dust jacket?

I inched my way to his table. "Mr. Weisberg?" I asked timidly.

He glanced up over the top of his narrow glasses. I introduced myself.

"Oh, yes," he said. He smiled and reached up to shake my hand. "Gary [Schoener] told me you might be here. He speaks highly of you. Pull up a chair and let's talk a bit. And please call me 'Harold.'"[37]

He was in his early fifties then, with short hair and a close-trimmed moustache. Wrinkles crossed his forehead and emanated from the corners of his tired eyes. He had a soft voice and gave the impression of a wizened warrior, a grandfather, the source of it all.

He wore the customary outfit of the times: baggy pants, leather shoes, a loud and large-checkered shirt with *two* breast pockets. He immediately made me feel at ease.

Weisberg asked what I was doing. I brought him up to date on my efforts and told him I had watched the Zapruder film.

"It's important for you to see that," he said. He asked about my trip to Dallas and told me that his time was spent laboriously searching through documents at the Archives. He drove there almost daily from his home forty-five minutes away.

He was here today, he explained, gathering some records to take to Jim Garrison.

I told him that I had read his *Whitewash* series of books[38] and that I greatly admired and respected his style of using facts rather than speculation to support his analysis.

He was generous with his time, and we chatted quietly for nearly an hour. I knew he was busy. So was I. As I got up, he told me he would look for me before leaving.

Two hours later, we were ambling down Pennsylvania Avenue to his parked car. Weisberg asked what hotel I was staying at and whether I intended to pursue research into the assassination. I assured him I did.

"Would you like to do some work for me?"

I stopped as if a bottomless chasm had suddenly opened in the sidewalk ahead. Had the most respected name in JFK assassination research just offered me a job?

"Well . . . ah . . . sure . . . I guess . . . I mean, of course . . . if I'm able."

He chuckled. "You'll do just fine. I'll be in touch."

Quick to honor his word, Weisberg called my room that night in front of a disbelieving Terry, who had spent his day touring monuments. While reviewing his papers at home, Weisberg found he needed some additional materials from the Archives. Would I mind getting copies of what he was missing and mail them to him, in care of Jim Garrison's office?

The next morning, I retrieved what Weisberg wanted and sent the records to the address he specified. I half-expected to be followed from the post office, based on Garrison's name on the mailing label and the intense attention his investigation had been attracting from the media.

The clerk simply tossed the parcel into a large, open bin with barely a look. It was merely the beginning of my long association with Harold Weisberg.

A day later, Terry decided to leave early for home. We exchanged goodbyes at the downtown bus depot. The one who got me involved in all of this promised to keep in touch.

But I would never hear from him again.

CHAPTER 11

July 1968

It was nearly 100 degrees on the streets that day. The cool air gushing from the Criminal Courts Building felt refreshing as I entered, searching for Dallas County Sheriff Bill Decker's office.

I couldn't seem to stay away from this city. I had some new questions and some new leads on Victoria Adams. I hoped to get some answers before I had to leave at the end of the month for the navy. Plus, I had my first assignment from Weisberg.

Echoing Penn Jones, Weisberg wrote me at home one day saying, "I wonder if there is not the possibility doors may open to you that close to Penn and the rest of us."[1] That's why he wanted me to interview Sheriff Decker on this, my latest trip. Weisberg was interested in files and photographs the sheriff supposedly never turned over to the Warren Commission.

As I entered the Sheriff's Department, a kindly secretary asked if I had an appointment. When I told her I didn't but explained I was a long way from home and doing some innocent research, she asked me to wait.

Three hours and a dozen magazines later, I was finally escorted by the secretary through the hallways to Decker's private sanctum. Weisberg was right about the doors, despite the delay in their opening.

Decker was not the person I had imagined. I had read that as a younger man, he had been a tough cop, very opinionated and very courageous. At times and while unarmed himself, he was able to convince criminals to throw down their weapons by the authority of his voice alone.[2]

But as he lifted himself up from behind his large desk to greet me, I noticed he had become frail after seventy years of life. His handshake was weak. He had moved beyond those Wild West ways.

He motioned me to a nearby seat. He studied me momentarily from behind thick lenses in his spectacles. I was, in his eyes, like the suspect of a crime not yet committed.

Another man sat silently in the shadows behind me in the corner of the office. He was not introduced. I could feel *his* eyes crawling up my back.

"What can I do for you?" Decker finally asked. "I only have a few moments."[3] The ground rules had been set.

I explained that I was doing research, as a student, into the JFK assassination and that I had a few simple questions. His only reply was a nod, indicating that he understood and was expecting me to go on without prompting. I decided to ease into it, even though my time was limited.

"Why did you direct your men to the grassy-knoll area when the shots were first fired?"[4]

He smiled slightly. He had heard that one many times. "A mistake" was all he said.

"I don't understand what you mean," I answered.

"Police Chief Curry was telling his men to go there. So did I, based on his initial response. But obviously, we both were wrong. The shots didn't come from there, did they?"[5]

He was still smiling, so I took his question to be rhetorical.

"Did you place a deputy by the name of Harry Weatherford on the roof of the County Records Building with a rifle during the assassination?" This was another of Penn Jones' ideas. He had accused Weatherford— had actually written editorials about it—of firing on the president from that rooftop position. Jones' source for that scenario was none other than Deputy Sheriff Roger Craig, who claimed that Weatherford let slip his rooftop location and that Decker had placed him there, for security reasons.

"No," Decker replied.

"But Roger Craig said you did."

"Roger Craig is a liar." It sounded spiteful, but Decker said it in a gentle manner, still with that sly smile on his face.

"You do not believe anything Craig has said?"

"Nothing."

It was obvious Decker had heard this line of questioning before too. He seemed to be humoring me with his succinct responses. It was time for what Weisberg had sent me here for in the first place.

"I know you have some personal papers or files regarding your end of the investigation into the president's assassination," I began, with all the casualness I could muster. "I wonder if I might be able to set up a time to examine them, maybe to read them and take some notes."

The smile immediately left Decker's face. He shot a glance toward the man in the corner. I was tempted to look around but didn't, figuring I'd feel the guy's hands around my neck soon enough.

Apparently, this was a new question, possibly from somewhere out in deep left field. Decker hesitated before replying. "I turned everything I had over to the Warren Commission."

When Weisberg first asked me to interview Decker, I spent some time reviewing the nintey-two pages of documents submitted by the sheriff to the Commission and printed in the twenty-six volumes.[6] The majority were voluntary statements that witnesses had made to members of the Sheriff's Office. Some were supplemental statements filed by deputies in which they reported their own locations at the time of the shooting and what they did immediately after.

Included also was a nine-page statement by Decker himself, describing in his words what actions he took on that day, plus copies of two interviews of the sheriff conducted by the FBI. The content of those interviews concerned Decker's unsuccessful attempt at transferring Oswald from the city to the county jail on the Sunday morning after the assassination.

Was what the Warren Commission published all that Decker had in his possession? Wouldn't the sheriff, whose own office figured prominently in the early stages of the investigation and whose deputies were present during many of the key moments that later became controversial, have had more? Weisberg thought so.

And so I persisted. "You are saying that all of your personal files and papers, working files and notes, everything that you kept during your involvement in the investigation, every bit of that was turned over to the Warren Commission?"

"All of it," Decker replied.

"What about any files you had containing photographs taken by sheriff's deputies, or photos you may have acquired from witnesses? Were they also turned over to the Commission?"

"Yes, they went to Washington too."

"Did you keep copies?"

Decker stared hard at me, expressionless, now realizing what direction I was headed in. He glanced at his watch. "I'm really rather busy this afternoon and I've extended what little I had available," he said. "I'm afraid we'll have to end this here."[7]

I could do nothing other than thank him for his time. He came around from behind his desk and offered his limp hand again. Then he showed me to the door and told me to have a nice time while in town, as if I were a tourist admiring the city's sights.

The man in the corner moved only his eyes as he watched me leave.

Sorry, Harold. I failed.

"It Was Oswald"

It wasn't much better when I knocked at another office. The response I got was meek. "Come in."

When I did, Carroll Jarnagin glanced up from his desk with a smile. His pleasantness left when he recognized who had entered.

"Remember me?"

He reached into his desk drawer and quickly removed and opened a pack of cigarettes, extracting and then igniting a cigarette. I certainly brought out a most unhealthy reaction in this guy.

He waved his free hand toward the chair, indicating I should sit. Jarnagin had done nothing to redecorate the place. It smelled and looked the same as it had when I was here last, five months ago.

"I remember you," he said.[8] He proceeded to tell me my name, where I was from, and the exact date and time of our previous meeting. He brought forth details of my past I had not remembered telling him during the idle chatter I apparently had lapsed into while we had talked last March. Then he gave me a verbatim recitation of the questions I had asked him back then, and the answers he had provided, all without benefit of notes.

The man had total recall.

"So," I began, "can I get you to talk a bit about seeing Oswald at the Carousel Club?"

Jarnagin returned to his shell, puffing profusely on what seemed like an endless supply of cancer sticks.

"How many deaths now?" he suddenly blurted out.

"What?"

"How many deaths of witnesses does Jones show now?"

"I don't really know," I said honestly. "I haven't been in touch with him yet."

"I'm sure it's higher than the forty-five you mentioned the last time you were here."

I had forgotten the number.

As usual, Jarnagin refused to answer my questions. He even declined my idea of simply nodding yes or no in lieu of a verbal response. After fifteen minutes of this nonsense, I got up to leave. Jarnagin raised his index finger and coughed out a plea.

"Wait," he gasped. "Please sit down." He studied me a bit longer, then broke his silence.

"It was Oswald I saw that night at the club."

I asked how he could be so sure. Was his eyesight as sharp as his memory?

He said he was able to see the man distinctly, since Oswald occupied the booth next to where Jarnagin was sitting, and based on the tantalizing conversation he heard, the attorney had begun to pay close attention. That was on October 4, 1963. When Oswald's picture appeared on television and in the papers nearly seven weeks later, Jarnagin said he immediately recognized him as the man he had seen with Ruby.

"Were there any other witnesses to what was being said?" I asked.

"I was accompanied by a young woman," he answered. "Her name was Shirley Mauldin, but she denies it now."[9]

Jarnagin said much of the conversation he overheard centered on a plot by Chicago gangsters to eliminate Kennedy. The plot was successful, he felt, because of Ruby's connections to organized crime.

"You're not writing a book, am I right?" he asked.

"No," I said. "I'm here strictly for my own curiosity."

"Good," he said, "because I'm afraid that if I talk publicly about it, they will get me too." Jarnagin was concerned for his life because of a previous incident. During Jack Ruby's trial in early 1964, Jarnagin said he was awakened in the middle of the night by a car idling just outside his bedroom window. As he drew the curtains aside to investigate, he noticed a hose attached to the exhaust pipe of the vehicle. The hose snaked its way over to the air-conditioning unit he had running in his window.

Carbon-monoxide gas was filling his room.

Whoever had set up the contraption must have discovered he was awake, Jarnagin said, because seconds later the car sped away, dragging the hose behind it.

The next morning, Jarnagin found an empty can of ether sitting outside the window. He discovered that it too had been poured into his air-conditioning fan. Had he not been awakened, he would have been overcome by the combined fumes.

Fortunately, the only consequence was a three-day headache.

Did he associate the attempt on his life with what he had seen at the Carousel Club?

"Most definitely," he replied. "I have absolutely no other reason for why it occurred."

"And you never told any of this to the Warren Commission?"

"They never contacted me," Jarnagin answered. "I notified the FBI right after the assassination about what I had seen and heard at Ruby's club, but I guess they weren't interested either. Other than Penn Jones, you're the only person I've really talked to."

On December 5, 1963, Jarnagin sent the FBI an eight-page statement of his encounter. It ended up in the twenty-six volumes.[10] Even though the Commission refused to question Jarnagin, it was still interested in what he had to say.

On June 8, 1964, the Commission asked Dallas District Attorney Henry Wade if he remembered the name of an attorney he had previously met who claimed to have seen Oswald and Ruby together.

Wade: That, I can't think of his name, some of you all may know it, but he is a lawyer there in Dallas.[11] . . .

[Commission General Counsel J. Lee] *Rankin:* Is the lawyer that you referred to . . . Carroll Jarnegan [*sic*]?

Wade: Carroll Jarnegan is his name; yes sir.[12]

Wade said he met Jarnagin while prosecuting Ruby for Oswald's murder. He described him as one of "some 8 to 10 witnesses" who came forward with information about a possible connection between the two.[13] According to Wade, Jarnagin had approached him with an offer to serve as a witness during the trial.

Wade: He told me this is what happened, and I said, "I can't put you on the stand without I am satisfied you are telling the truth because," I said, "We have got a good case here, and if they prove we are putting a lying witness on the stand, we might hurt us," and I said, "The only thing I know to do I won't put you on the stand but to take a polygraph to see if you are telling the truth or not."

He said, "I would be glad to." . . .

This was during the trial actually, and then when the man called me he took a lie detector. There was no truth in it. That he was in the place. He was in the place, in Ruby's Carousel, but that none of this conversation took place.[14] . . .

Rankin: You found that was not anything you could rely on.

Wade: I didn't use him as a witness and after giving him the polygraph I was satisfied that he was imagining it. I think he was sincere, I don't think he was trying—I don't think he was trying to be a hero or anything. I think he really thought about it so much I think he thought that it happened, but the polygraph indicated otherwise.[15]

I asked Jarnagin why he chose to talk to the district attorney if he feared for his life.

"I thought I could help," Jarnagin replied. "And the attempt on my life did not occur until after I had offered my information to Henry Wade."

"And the polygraph test?" I asked. "Wade told the Commission it showed you were not telling the truth."

Jarnagin shrugged. "What can I say? The polygraph is notoriously unreliable . . . and I was very nervous. I was aware of how the government was describing the relationship between Ruby and Oswald, and I knew different."

Suddenly, Jarnagin went mute, perhaps sensing he had said enough, or too much. I decided to leave after one final question.

"How do you know, in all honesty and with such certainty, without any doubt at all, that the man you saw talking with Jack Ruby that night was Lee Oswald? Could you possibly have been mistaken?"

The attorney took a final, long puff on his cigarette, then slowly snuffed out what remained of it in the ashtray. He leaned back in his chair, clasped his hands behind his head, and, without expression, looked me squarely in the eyes for what seemed like several minutes.

"It *was* Oswald," he answered. "I know it was him."

Penn Jones answered his phone on the first ring. I told him I was back snooping around again and brought him up to date. Then I asked if he knew where I could find Roger Craig.

"He's standing right here," Jones answered. "Let me put him on."[16]

Within seconds, I was talking with the man who was at the center of a controversy over what he had seen on the day of the assassination. I asked for an interview. He covered the mouthpiece, mumbled something, and, in a few moments, came back on the line.

"Penn says you're OK," Craig said, "so how about this Sunday?"

He agreed to meet me in the lobby of my hotel at noon.

Then I called Austin Miller. Never summoned as a witness, he was another of those who claimed he observed smoke on the grassy knoll.

"I have discussed this with so many people," he told me, moments into our conversation, "and I'm getting very tired of doing so."[17]

After I convinced him I was different, Miller sighed. He said it definitely was smoke he saw "around the trees in the corner of the picket fence on the grassy knoll."

"Could it have been steam or some kind of exhaust, as some think?"

"No," he firmly replied.

Miller said he felt that there had been three shots and that he saw the smoke just as he heard the third shot. Like S. M. Holland, Miller said he ran behind the fence on the knoll and up to where he had seen the smoke. He said it took him no more than a minute to get there, and although there were plenty of private cars in the parking lot, he saw no one behind the fence.

"Did you find any footprints there?"

Miller was silent. If it weren't for his steady breathing, I'd have thought he left the phone.

"Do you have a problem with that question?" Miller remained quiet. His silence was eerie.

I quickly started telling him that I had spoken to Holland and that he and I may be getting together to retrace Holland's steps. I invited Miller to accompany us.

He refused my offer. Then he hung up.

The Groundskeeper of Dealey Plaza

When I phoned Holland the next day, he remembered who I was and agreed to meet me on the Triple Underpass during his lunch hour.

As I stood watching traffic in Dealey Plaza an hour before Holland was to arrive, my attention was drawn to a man in the distance raking the lawn along the side of the grassy knoll. Solitary, he wore the overalls of a gardener and a wide-brimmed hat to ward off the hot rays of the sun. As I made my way closer, his overalls became the uniform of a city worker. I met his eyes and said hello.

"Are you Emmett Hudson?" I asked.

He stared at me for a moment, wondering no doubt how a young punk like me would know the name of the groundskeeper of Dealey Plaza.

"Do I know you?" he answered.

Hudson revealed in his July 22, 1964, Commission testimony that something strange had happened in Dealey Plaza after the assassination. Certain road signs once positioned along Elm Street had been mysteriously removed or relocated. Critics felt this was deliberately done to make accurate reconstructions of the assassination more difficult, if not impossible.

Of more interest to me was where this man stood as the shots rang out.

Hudson was watching from an elevated position on the steps leading from the sidewalk along the north side of Elm Street up to the monument where Zapruder took his famous film. If a shot were fired from the knoll, it would have passed directly over his head.

In a photograph taken by bystander Mary Moorman, Hudson can be seen standing in the background, overlooking the stricken president. The corner of the picket fence, where Holland and Miller had seen drifting smoke, is directly behind and slightly above Hudson's left shoulder.

On November 22, 1963, Hudson submitted a signed affidavit to the Sheriff's Department. He stated he heard three shots and they "definitely came from behind and above me."[18]

There was the rub. "Behind and above me" implied the knoll.

The FBI interviewed him again on November 25, at which time "Hudson said the shots sounded as if they were fired over his head and from some position to the left of where he was standing." The report continued, "In other words, the shots sounded as if they were fired by someone at a position which was behind him, which was above him, and which was to his left."[19]

When Commission attorney Wesley Liebeler questioned him in Dallas on July 22, 1964, Hudson reiterated what he had told the FBI eight months earlier.

Hudson: And when that third shot rung out and when I was close to the ground—you could tell the shot was coming from above and kind of behind.

Liebeler: How could you tell that?

Hudson: Well, just the sound of it.

Liebeler: You heard it come from sort of behind the motorcade and then above?

Hudson: Yes; I don't know if you have ever laid down close to the ground, you know, when you heard the reports coming, but it's a whole lot plainer than it is when you are standing up in the air.[20]

Suddenly, the source of gunfire was no longer *behind and above* Hudson but *behind and above* the motorcade.

Liebeler: After you heard these three shots and saw the President get hit in the head, you turned around and you ran up on the little knoll there and you got away.
Hudson: Yes.
Liebeler: While you were standing there, did you ever look up towards the railroad tracks there where they went across the triple underpass?
Hudson: No, sir; while I was laying there I didn't—I was looking down towards Elm Street.
Liebeler: So, you never looked up towards the railroad tracks that went across the underpass?
Hudson: No, sir.
Liebeler: But you are quite sure in your own mind that the shots came from the rear of the President's car and above it; is that correct?
Hudson: Yes.
Liebeler: Did you have any idea that they might have come from the Texas School Book Depository Building?
Hudson: Well, it sounded like it was high, you know, from above and kind of behind like—in other words, to the left.
Liebeler: And that would have fit in with the Texas School Book Depository, wouldn't it?
Hudson: Yes.
Liebeler: Did you look up there and see if you could see anybody?
Hudson: No, sir; I didn't. I never thought about looking up that way, to tell you the truth about it.[21]

Notwithstanding Liebeler's leading comment as to where the shots "would have fit in," it seemed clear Hudson had changed his initial thinking about the direction of the shots.

With all that in mind, I approached Hudson that morning in hopes he would clarify this very point. As with most other witnesses, the assassination had made an indelible impression on his memory.

"Can you spare a moment to show me where you were standing that day?" I asked, after explaining how I knew him.[22]

Hudson seemed to relish the opportunity for a break. He mopped his wet forehead with his handkerchief and slowly walked over to the steps leading up the knoll. He stopped exactly where the Moorman photograph showed him standing. He told me of the excitement of seeing the president, then the horror of watching as Kennedy's skull exploded a mere sixty feet in front of him.

When I inquired about the shots, he repeated what he had said to the Commission: they sounded as if they came from above, behind, and to the left.

"Above, behind, and to the left of what?" I asked.

"Above and behind the motorcade, and to the left of me," Hudson replied.

"But on the day of the assassination, you signed an affidavit that said the shots seemed to come from above and behind *you*. You said, 'Behind and above *me.*' And in your FBI interview, you said you felt the shots came from over *your* head."

Hudson remained silent.

"You said you heard three shots," I continued. "Would you tell me about them?"

"Well, there were definitely three that I heard," he explained. "But one of them was a bit unusual."

"What do you mean, 'unusual'?"

"Well, it sounded different from the others. It was louder, sharper, cleaner than the others. And two of them was close together, like, bang . . . bang, bang."

"Is that what you told the Commission lawyer?"

Hudson gave me a knowing smile. I'm sure he sensed by now that I already knew what he had told the Commission: that the three shots had been evenly spaced.[23]

"I stand by what I just said," he replied.

"So, during your testimony you clarified your earlier statements to say you felt the shots were actually coming from above and behind the president's car. Does that mean from the Depository?"

"No, but that is what the Commission wanted me to say," Hudson answered quickly.

"The Commission *wanted* you to say?"

"I never said it was from the Depository building," Hudson explained. "All I said was 'behind, above, and to the left.' That lawyer put those other words in there. He said something about what I was saying would include the Depository, wouldn't it? And I said, 'Right, it would include it.' But I never said they actually came from that building."

"And you got the impression the lawyer for some reason wanted you to say the shots came from the Depository?"

"Definitely," Hudson answered. "He didn't come out and say that, but you could tell by his tone and the way he asked his questions. I said they *sounded* like they came from above, behind, and to the left. We were off the record so many times on this . . . and other things.[24] He's the one who brought up the Depository. They could've come from there, I don't know, but I never said they did."

"Could a shot have come from the picket fence?" I ventured.

"I don't know," Hudson replied, after a pause. "I really don't. There was so much excitement and it all happened so fast, I'm just not sure."

I nodded my head and met his gaze.

"I'm getting old, son," he said, resignedly. "Almost retired now. I don't need all this." He smiled at me for a long moment and stared hard into my eyes, as if trying to convey something telepathically. Then he ambled off to continue his simple job, and his quiet life.

As I sat on the knoll pondering Hudson's words, I heard my name called from the sidewalk below. It was Holland. He was alone, his bodyguards either having the day off or no longer deemed necessary.

We walked to the top of the Triple Underpass. He positioned me at the exact spot he stood that warm November day. He had a commanding panorama: the motorcade coming directly at him, the Depository looming behind, the picket fence and grassy knoll to his immediate left. He had a box seat for sure.

Holland said he watched as the wounded president passed directly beneath him into the Triple Underpass. He had seen a puff of smoke on the knoll when Kennedy was shot in the head. He was curious. So he turned in that direction—to his left—and ran from the bridge, around the corner to his right, and onto the knoll, working his way behind the fence line.

I asked if he would reconstruct his actions for me. He agreed, and I set my stopwatch, following his every move.

Within seconds, at a sprint, he had reached the westernmost end of the picket fence, a position that offered a view of the parking area atop the knoll. He then deliberately slowed down, trying to duplicate the amount of extra time it had taken him to circumvent the large volume of cars parked in that lot on the day of the assassination.

In just under a minute, we had reached the corner of the fence where

Holland said he had seen smoke. I noticed during our entire reenactment that Holland had kept his eyes glued to his final destination. I asked if he had done the same thing on November 22.

"I did," he replied. "As soon as I could get a full view of that corner, my eyes were on it."[25]

"What did you see?"

"Nothing," he said. "No one was there, so I started scanning over the cars and railroad yards beyond. No one was there either. Then as I got closer to the corner, the policemen started piling in and all the spectators came running up."[26]

"As quickly as you got here," I asked, "don't you find it surprising that no one was around?"

"Not really," he answered. "It just means whoever it was got away quickly, perhaps by blending in with the crowd, but more likely, by being hidden in one of these cars."

"And they did so without leaving a single piece of physical evidence?"

"There weren't any fingerprints or shells that I know of, if that's what you're talking about," he said. "But someone had been here."

He marked off about a five-foot area directly behind the fence and slightly west of the corner. This, he said, was where he found numerous footprints in the soft mud, and the remains of recently smoked cigarettes. "Someone had been here," Holland repeated. "Do you know of anyone in everything you've read so far who has come forward to say they witnessed the assassination from behind this fence?"

I stared over the fence to the street below, lost in thought. The lines all seemed to converge here: Holland, Miller, and others looking from the underpass; Lee Bowers staring from where he was on duty in the railroad tower above and behind this fence, seeing two men at this precise spot; Mary Moorman's camera, capturing what appeared to be someone's head peeking over the fence as Kennedy was hit in the foreground; the mass of people who ran here after the shooting.[27] In there too was Emmett Hudson.

Holland briefly broke the spell, saying something about being late for work. I heard myself thanking him.[28]

Was it all just coincidence?

Deputy Sheriff Roger Craig

As he walked into the lobby that Sunday, I recognized him instantly, despite his casual attire. Roger Craig refused to talk with me in the hotel. In fact, he wanted out of the city limits of Dallas . . . ASAP. Therefore, we'd have to take a ride.

I didn't question his judgment; I merely slid into the front seat of his car. Craig got behind the wheel, started the engine, and furtively looked into the rearview mirror. Then he scanned the front as if expecting something—or someone—to suddenly pop up.

What had I gotten myself into now?

Thirty minutes later, after a cat-and-mouse ride through the city and who knows how many suburbs, we pulled up in front of a nice home on a quiet, treelined street. It was his sister's. We would be safe here, he said. Safe from what? I wondered.

Sis apparently had advance warning. She wasn't surprised as we entered the front door unannounced. She offered me a fleeting hello as she hurried out of the room, not to be seen again that afternoon.

Craig and I ended up at the kitchen table. I pulled out my tape recorder.

The first thing I wanted was an explanation for the secretiveness. Craig said he was "not well liked anymore" by many members of the Dallas Police and Sheriff's departments. He was, in their eyes, a traitor. He had to be cautious.[29]

"My *troubles*," he emphasized, "really started about the latter part of 1965, when my name came out in several books critical of the Warren Commission. The newspaper reporters and various people had come down and wanted to talk to me, and [Sheriff Bill] Decker gave me strict orders not to talk to anybody about it, to keep my mouth shut."

His problems with Decker involved "just little petty things that didn't amount to anything," Craig said. "And [on] July 4, 1967, he fired me."

Three months later, at the urging of Penn Jones, Craig was in New Orleans helping Jim Garrison. He returned to Dallas in late October.

"On the first day of November, I got a call from a friend of mine who was a nightclub owner," Craig said. The friend wanted to meet Craig in east Dallas at nine that morning. "So I went to the location and waited till about 10 or 10:15 and he finally showed up."

Craig said two vehicles followed him to the meeting site.

"The so-called friend of mine arrived and we went over and had coffee at a coffee shop just across the street from his club. One of the men [tailing Craig] followed us into the café and when we got ready to leave, he got up and left before us. We walked outside—this was about 10:30— and we walked to the corner and the light was red against us, so we couldn't cross. And I stepped down from the curb and into the street and as I stepped down my friend fell on the ground and then a shot rang out from behind. I didn't look around. I just got in my car and drove off."

What I really wanted to know about was Oswald's "escape."

"In regards to Oswald getting into the light green Rambler station wagon, I guess it was about twelve to fifteen minutes after the first shot was fired. Oswald came running down the grassy knoll from the direction of the School Book Depository, and there was a light green Rambler station wagon coming west on Elm Street, driven by a dark-complected Latin American, wearing a tan jacket. Oswald whistled and the car pulled over to the curb, stopped, Oswald got in it, and the two of them drove off west on Elm Street.

"I attempted to stop the car, but due to the traffic, I couldn't get across the street." At its closest point, Craig said the car was seven or eight feet away from him.

Several hours later that day, Craig stated he saw Oswald again. "Approximately 5 P.M. . . . I went to Captain Fritz's office to identify the suspect as the one I saw enter the Rambler station wagon. Captain Fritz and myself entered the room. Oswald was sitting behind the desk to our right. Fritz said, 'Is this the man?' pointing to Oswald. And I replied it was. And Fritz, directing his question to Oswald, said, 'This man,' pointing to me, 'saw you leave the building.' Oswald replied to Fritz, 'I told you people I did.' Fritz, trying to calm Oswald down, said to him, 'Now take it easy, son. We're just trying to find out what happened. What about the car?'

"Now Fritz distinctly said 'car,' at which time Oswald became very excited and replied, 'That station wagon belongs to Mrs. Paine—don't try to drag her into this.'[30] And then he very disgustedly sat back in his chair and said, 'Everybody will know who I am now.' And that was the end of my conversation with Will Fritz and Lee Harvey Oswald."

I asked Craig if he was sure the running man was Oswald.

"It *was* Oswald," he replied. "He was wearing a faded light-blue work shirt and medium-blue work pants, and his hair was very blown. It was a fairly windy day; it was kind of bushy."[31]

After Craig identified the car to several sheriff's deputies, one of them "went over to Ruth Paine's house to check it out, and in the driveway was parked a light-green Rambler station wagon, identical to the one I had described," he said. "And this, of course, was not accepted by the Warren Commission. I don't know why."

Part of the Commission's problem with Craig stemmed from his claim that both he and Captain Fritz confronted Oswald in Fritz's office. Fritz denied Craig was present. In a June 9, 1964, signed affidavit submitted to the Commission, Fritz said he recalled a man coming to his *outer* office on the afternoon of the assassination and "telling me a story about seeing Oswald leaving the building."[32] At the time, according to Fritz, Oswald was seated behind a closed door in his adjacent office.

But Fritz said he did not remember inviting that man in to take a look at Oswald, a decision hard to imagine in light of the "story" that man had just told.

"The Commission could not accept important elements of Craig's testimony," the Warren Report concluded.[33]

According to the Report, Craig may well have seen a man get into a "white Rambler station wagon 15 or 20 minutes after the shooting and travel west on Elm Street, but the Commission concluded that this man was not Lee Harvey Oswald, because of the overwhelming evidence that Oswald was far away from the building by that time."[34]

Craig told me that when he read his testimony in the twenty-six volumes, he discovered it had been "altered and key words have been taken out to make it read different than it should." He continued, "When [Commission attorney David] Belin interviewed me, he asked me if the car had out-of-state plates or Texas plates. And I said that they were *not* the same color as Texas plates. And he took the word 'not' out, so this completely changes that particular sentence. And what makes this so important is that [at] Ruth Paine's house, the Rambler station wagon parked in her yard *did* have out-of-state plates, at that time. And then he changed the color of the car from green to white, changed the color of the man's jacket driving the car from tan to green, so he just rearranged the car and the jacket, and just several things like that. I believe fourteen times is what I counted in the twenty-six volumes that they had changed my testimony and just by leaving out key words or changing colors and so forth."

If true, this was amazing stuff. But was it true?

"When Belin interrogated me in reference to my testimony, he would ask me certain questions and, whenever an important question would come up, such as a description of clothing or a time element or something that he had to know what my answer was beforehand, he would turn off the recorder and instruct the stenographer to stop taking notes. Then he would ask the question, and if the answer satisfied him, he would turn the recorder back on, instruct the stenographer to start writing again, and he would ask me the same question, and I would answer it. However, while the recorder was off, if the answer did *not* satisfy him or he wasn't happy with it, he would turn the recorder back on and instruct the stenographer to start writing again and then he would ask me a completely different question.

"In my testimony, there is no notation, 'off the record.' These were simply done at Belin's own will. He just took it upon himself apparently, but there's no notation on there that says, 'off-the-record conversation' or 'off-the-record questions.'"

A man who seemed to be everywhere, Craig also participated in a search of the sixth floor. He was present when the spent cartridge cases and rifle were found. "The cartridges were found in the southeast corner of the building, approximately five feet from the window," he explained. "They were lined up uniformly, no more than two and one-half to three inches from each other . . . all facing the same direction."

Craig said the neat and consistent positioning indicated to him that the shells had been *placed* there rather than ejected from a rifle.

"There also were no black marks around the opening of the cartridges, which is usually left when a cartridge is fired from any kind of weapon. You get powder burns on the edge. There were no powder burns on these cartridges."

In the sniper's nest, the cartons had been arranged to "rest something, such as a rifle, on these boxes and possibly steady yourself," Craig said. "There were no other boxes directly behind until, oh, for fifteen or twenty feet. Lying in the far east corner was a sack containing some chicken bones."

Did he see the large paper bag beneath the sniper's window?

"I never saw the rifle bag," Craig admitted, "and I was one of the first to arrive when that area was discovered. It just wasn't there. I could not have overlooked it if it was in there."

According to Craig, the rifle was hidden between stacks of boxes in the northwest corner of the sixth floor, near the back stairway entrance. "Deputy Sheriff Eugene Boone was the first to discover the rifle. I was about eight feet from him. And I rushed over and looked over the boxes down in the middle where there was an opening and there was a rifle lying down there with the bolt facing upward. I could see the scope. Capt. Will Fritz and the identification man from the city of Dallas then came over. The identification man lifted the rifle out by the strap, pulled the bolt back, and a live round came out of the chamber. The rifle was then taken downstairs and that's the last I saw of it.

"I felt then and I still feel now that the weapon was a 7.65 German Mauser and not the 6.5 Carcano the Commission says it was. I was there. I saw it when it was first pulled from its hiding place, and I am not alone in describing it as a Mauser."

What about Harry Weatherford being on the roof of the County Records Building?

"This came about after all the confusion was over with and the investigation was continuing, but I had withdrawn somewhat from it. Harry and I were talking on the front steps of the Records Building and I told him how windy it was, and just general conversation, and he said he didn't get to see the motorcade or anything because he was on the roof of the Records Building. Decker had put him up there with a rifle, supposedly for security reasons. And he liked to frozed to death because it was so windy up there and it was kind of cold that day. And that was the end of the conversation. Harry just left and went back in the Sheriff's Office. But it was casual and involuntary on his part. He just brought it up and told me about it."

Craig was yawning. I looked at the clock. Had three hours really passed?

Minutes later, we were heading west on Elm Street on our way back to my hotel. The traffic lights were with us, and Craig was talking about Arnold Rowland. "Why would a young kid like that make up a story about seeing two men on the sixth floor? There comes a point when you have to start believing what some of these people saw. They can't all be wrong."

It was perhaps this thought-provoking line that caused his defenses to relax. Almost as if it had dropped from the sky, a Dallas Police cruiser appeared on Craig's rear bumper, lights flashing and siren sounding. Craig had been caught.

We pulled to the curb. Two big and well-armed officers approached Craig's window and asked for his driver's license. After glancing at it, they headed back to their car. In a moment, they were again hovering over the driver's-side door.

"Do you know why we stopped you?" one of them asked.

"No sir," Craig replied.

"You went through a red light back there," the officer snapped.

We had done no such thing. By coincidence, I had been glancing at street signs as we traveled down Elm, closely watching for the corner of Elm and Murphy, where Oswald had boarded a bus after the assassination. The traffic lights were positioned within the same line of sight as the intersection markings. I knew that the previous light had been emerald green as we passed.

"That's not right, officer," I blurted out in Craig's defense. "That light was definitely green."

Both officers leaned down for a better look. Craig grabbed my forearm with his right hand and squeezed tightly. It was too late.

One of the officers walked around the front of the car and came up to my window. "Got identification?" he barked.

I fumbled with my wallet and handed him my Pennsylvania driver's license.

"What are you doing in Dallas?" he asked.

I hesitated for a moment, then told him I was here visiting friends.

"Is that right?" he persisted. It was an *I-think-not* kind of question.

After jotting my name down on his notepad, the officer threw the license into my lap and walked back to his partner. Both stood near the front bumper, talking softly and occasionally glancing through the windshield at us.

"We're going to let it go this time," one then said to Craig. "Don't let it happen again." He turned his eyes my way, perhaps expecting me to comment. By now I had learned my lesson.

We pulled away. Craig loudly sucked in some fresh air, then slowly let it out. He was quiet the rest of the way. The encounter had clearly disturbed him. After he dropped me off, I watched his taillights recede in the distance. I expected to see a car move out after him, but none did.

Then I glanced around to see if anyone was watching me.

"Craig has got to be more careful," Jones said when I called him later that night. "He's lucky you were with him. They wouldn't do anything with someone else around. And you're going to have to be careful as well, because if they didn't have your name already from you snooping around, they sure have it by now."

I double-locked my hotel-room door that night. Thanks, Penn.

CHAPTER 12

August 1968

By the time the Kennedy motorcade entered Dealey Plaza, J. C. Price had made his way to the roof of the Terminal Annex building, where he worked. From that vantage point, he had an overhead, unobstructed view of Elm Street, two short blocks away. "I saw one man run towards the passenger cars on the railroad siding after the volley of shots," Price told the Sheriff's Department later that day.[1] "This man had a white dress shirt, no tie and khaki colored trousers. His hair appeared to be long and dark and his agility running could be about 25 yrs of age. He had something in his hand. I couldn't be sure but it may have been a head piece."

Price "was on the roof watching the parade, heard the shot, and saw President Kennedy slump over," the FBI wrote two days later, on November 24. "He assumed the shot had come from the overpass and looked in that direction, but saw nothing pertinent."[2] There was no mention of a fleeing man.

Two years later, in a filmed interview with Mark Lane, Price reverted to what he had told the Sheriff's Department, adding that the man he saw was "about 145 pounds in weight and not too tall." He continued, "I'd say five-six or seven. He was bareheaded, and he was running very fast."[3]

As to the "head piece," Price now said it "could have been a gun."[4]

Why wasn't any of this in his FBI statement?

"Actually, I started to tell the agents about the man I saw," Price told me over the phone one day, "but they just didn't seem interested. They were only concerned with where I thought the shots had come from, and as soon as I said over near the underpass, they ended the interview.[5]

"By the time the FBI got to me," he continued, "it was the end of the weekend and it was pretty much on the TV that Oswald was the only assassin, and that he had been firing from the Depository building over there. So when the FBI dropped their interest in what I was saying about the man I saw, I figured what I had seen wasn't important at all. Maybe some spectator or something."

The fleeing man hardly fit a spectator's profile.

"He distinctly looked like he was running away from something," Price said, "unlike those who seemed to be running towards something, if you know what I mean. He looked like he was trying . . . well . . . to escape, looking back over his shoulders as he ran and everything. He wasn't acting like any spectator."

I asked about the "head piece."

"It appeared to be some kind of radio device," Price said, "like a walkie-talkie or something. That's what it looked like to me anyway."

When I asked why he told Lane it may have been a gun, Price explained. "I told him what I just told you: it looked like some kind of a radio device. Lane said to me, 'Could it have been a gun?' I could tell he was kind of pushing me to say that. And I said, 'I guess it could have been.' But it really looked like a radio device to me. If it was a gun, and I honestly don't believe it was, then it certainly wasn't as long as any rifle."

Near the end of our brief conversation, I inquired if Price would be kind enough to show me the view he had from the roof. "I'd be happy to. Stop by around noon tomorrow."

It was his next line that was the stunner.

"And don't forget your checkbook."

He hung up. Moments later, so did I.

I didn't bother going to see him the next day.

"He was a highly excitable man—*highly* excitable." Wes Wise, a reporter for KRLD-TV in Dallas, was describing for me his former friend, Jack Ruby. At boxing matches, Wise explained, "if Ruby did not like the decision, he went over to the press table and seemed to be agitated and seemed to have a quick temper and would say, 'You think that was an awful decision, Wes?' and, 'Wasn't that a terrible way they gave that decision to so-and-so?,' who would usually be the fighter that he probably had not put money on or was not in favor of.[6]

"He was the kind who liked to hang around with the police and the law people and the radio and TV people and was pretty well liked. As I've often said, if I had been in the basement of the City Hall, the Dallas police station, waiting for Oswald to be put into the wagon to be taken to County Jail and Jack Ruby had been standing right next to me, I would have turned and said, 'Hello, Jack,' or 'How you doing, Jack?' or something like that. I would have thought it was not unusual his being there because he was on the scene so much."

What caused me to look up Wise was the fact that he had noticed Ruby in Dealey Plaza on Saturday, November 23. That's not so strange, when one recalls that many migrated to that spot that weekend. But Ruby's appearance may have been beyond paying homage to a slain president.

"This was the day after the assassination," Wise explained, "at sometime around two o'clock in the afternoon or something like that, which of course was the day before he shot Lee Harvey Oswald."

Wise said he was on assignment to film the route taken the day before by Oswald from downtown to the Texas Theatre. He was sitting in a mobile news unit parked against a police barricade along the east side of the Depository. "Jack Ruby came running up and knocked on the window. And I rolled the window down, more or less annoyed at his disturbing me as I was trying to make transmission with the station, and [he] said something to the effect of, 'Wasn't it a terrible thing that had happened?' and, 'Wasn't it awful that the kids were going to be without . . . a father?' And I said, you know, I agreed with him that it was an awful thing. And I detected a sign of tears in his eyes. He didn't actually weep or anything like that. But there were, I thought, tears in his eyes.[7] And he pointed out to me that Will Fritz and Chief of Police Curry were over on the assassination site . . . in front of the School Book Depository building, in case I wanted to shoot pictures of them. And I thanked him for informing me of this; I hadn't seen them. And with that, I said goodbye to him."

Ruby approached him "from back in the direction of the railroad yards," Wise stated. "I remember this very briefly, for a moment, that it seemed sort of strange that he was coming from back there, because all of the activity, all of the crowd, was around in front of the building."

Ruby claimed he went to Dealey Plaza that Saturday to observe the many sympathy wreaths placed on the grassy knoll.[8] There are indications, however, that Ruby may have been there to stalk Oswald, who was initially scheduled to be transferred to the county jail in Dealey Plaza that afternoon.

The idea of Ruby plotting Oswald's murder in advance did not sit well with the Warren Commission, which felt more comfortable with the idea that Ruby committed the act not only alone, but strictly on impulse.

Garnett Hallmark, an attendant at Nichols Brothers Parking Garage, said Ruby drove in that Saturday and parked his car in his usual spot. He then walked into Hallmark's office to use the phone. Hallmark said:

> He was—he told this person who he had established as being Ken, that he had been to the city hall and was following this thing, and he had information to the effect that the transfer was to take place that afternoon. I got the impression that he had some information and possibly wanted corroboration. In other words, he just was not 100 percent sure, but he had—he thought he knew that the thing was to take place then, but was not 100 percent sure. Then, he remarked that people started strewing flowers at the scene of the assassination, which is in the immediate locale of the county jail, so that possibly because of the congestion they would not transfer Oswald that afternoon.[9]

Ruby neglected to mention his Saturday visit to Dealey Plaza in an otherwise detailed chronology of his weekend activities furnished to his lawyers prior to trial. He also failed to tell the FBI about it during a lengthy jailhouse interview on December 21, 1963.[10]

But Saturday was not the first time Ruby gave indications of shadowing Oswald. He was also seen, notebook in hand and acting like a reporter, at Dallas Police headquarters Friday night when Oswald was paraded to a news conference.[11]

Dallas Police Officer D. V. Harkness saw Ruby that Saturday too.

Belin: What did you do on Saturday?

Harkness: Saturday I was assigned to traffic at Elm and Houston, between Elm and Main.

Belin: Is there anything else that you did on Saturday or on Sunday that might in any way be relevant to this area of inquiry?

Harkness: On Saturday had a large crowd down there, and I observed Jack Ruby at the entrance of the jail down there on Saturday.

Belin: You saw Jack Ruby near the entrance of the jail on Saturday?

Harkness: Yes sir.

Belin: Has your statement already been taken by anyone before on the President's Commission?

Harkness: Yes sir.

Belin: But you did see Jack Ruby?

Harkness: I testified in Ruby's trial to that effect.[12]

Belin: Anyone else or anything else that might be in any way relevant here?[13]

Wasn't it "relevant" that Ruby, who twenty-four hours later would shoot Oswald in a similar situation and environment, was hovering over this earlier planned transfer?

If it didn't seem to warrant further questioning on Belin's part, this oddity certainly did stick in Harkness's mind. In response to Belin's concluding request for any other noteworthy information, the officer explained that, while on a family outing that following Sunday and after hearing on the radio that Oswald had been shot, he immediately telephoned Captain Fritz to report he had seen Ruby during the planned Saturday transfer.

The fact that Harkness thought his earlier sighting of Ruby was suspicious enough to call it to the attention of his boss still did not pique Belin.

Belin: Anything else?
Harkness: That is all.[14]

Officer Harkness was dismissed.

So why was Ruby in Dealey Plaza? "I really don't know," Wise told me during our interview. "He said he came to look at the wreaths and flowers, and I believe he did do that. But I don't feel that was his real reason. I think he came because of the scheduled Oswald transfer . . . for whatever reason."[15]

The Still-Missing Miss Adams

In the background of everything I was doing lingered my search for the still-missing Victoria Adams. On my first trip to Dallas, I had found nothing. No one knew about her. She had left her job. There were no telephone records. The address she had provided to the Warren Commission on April 7, 1964—4906 Wenonah—proved fruitless. She no longer lived there, and no one knew where she went.

But I had uncovered some new clues at the National Archives. During an interview with the FBI on November 24, 1963, Miss Adams had provided an address of 3651 Fontana Street. Although this was not her most current residence—Wenonah coming later—perhaps someone there knew of her current whereabouts.

Again, I had no such luck.

Then on February 17, 1964, when she was questioned by J. R. Leavelle of the Dallas Police, she gave her address as 3909 Cole, Apartment D. My taxi driver had trouble finding it, but when he did, no one there had a clue about her either. This woman had literally disappeared.

"Can you do me a favor?" I asked when I revisited Roy Truly at the Depository one morning. I didn't expect him to remember me. But he did and immediately rose from his desk to shake my hand.

I explained that I was looking for someone who had once worked in his building. Her former employer had been unable to assist me. As superintendent of the Depository, could he help, perhaps casually ask a few questions about her?

"I'll do what I can," he replied. I gave him my hotel phone number. He assured me he would call, one way or the other.

Truly was true to his word. That evening he telephoned to report he had found nothing. All he was able to determine was that Miss Adams had left her job unexpectedly and had not provided a forwarding address. She could still be in Dallas, or thousands of miles away. Truly did not know.

And neither did I.

Late on one of my last evenings, when very few others were around and business offices had all closed, I walked behind the Depository. I climbed the loading-dock steps to the back door, the one Miss Adams and Miss Styles had used. Clicking my stopwatch, I retraced their steps, as closely as possible to what Miss Adams had described doing: walking west just shy of the railroad yards, pausing as I recited under my breath the words she testified were used with the policemen she met there, walking down the west side of the building toward Elm Street, turning east, and heading back to the Depository's front steps.

I repeated this route five times. It took me anywhere from four minutes forty-three seconds to five minutes eighteen seconds. This fit with what Miss Adams had told the FBI on November 24, 1963: "She did estimate that the time between her departure from the building and her return to the building was about four or five minutes."[16]

Then I did some backpedaling. The shooting occurred at 12:30 P.M. Miss Adams testified it was somewhere between fifteen and thirty seconds after she heard the final shot that she left the fourth-floor window. She estimated she spent about one minute getting from her office window to the first floor. Allowing a few moments for when she said she spoke to William Shelley and the time it took to get to the back door, Miss Adams' timing would have put her outside by about 12:32 P.M.

Coupled with the four or five minutes she said she spent outside the building, that meant she would have been near the front entrance to the Depository approximately six or seven minutes after the assassination, or about 12:36 or 12:37.

Miss Adams testified that when she arrived there, she saw fellow employees Avery Davis and Joe Molina. Molina and Mrs. Davis told the FBI they remained outside the Depository for only a short while before going back inside.[17] If Miss Adams saw those two, she would have had to get to the front entrance before they reentered the building.

Even more interesting was what Miss Adams said she heard when she arrived at the front steps. A police radio was squawking out a broadcast that the shots may have come from the second or fourth floor of the Depository. Those words startled her, she said, because she had been standing behind an open fourth-floor window.

One has only to check a transcript of the police radio log printed in the twenty-six volumes to find this intriguing notation: "We have information the shots came from the fifth or fourth floor of the book Depository Store."[18] That broadcast was made at 12:38 P.M.

That was the transmission Miss Adams heard. No other police broadcast either before or after 12:38 mentions the fourth floor.

Although the Commission gave the impression of indifference to Miss Adams and the timing of her trek down the stairs—failing to conduct the necessary tests, failing to interview others who easily could have resolved the matter, dismissing her words in such a cavalier way—she did generate some behind-the-scenes concern. In his internal memorandum listing things to be done in his assigned area of investigation, David Belin wrote that he planned to "pin down" the timing of Miss Adams' descent. Then, less than three weeks before the Warren Report was publicly issued in September 1964, Commission staffer Wesley Liebeler played devil's advocate. He wrote a controversial and stinging twenty-six-page memorandum, taking jabs at the evidence used to tie Oswald to the crime.

One of his swipes involved the way the Commission had handled Miss Adams. "After two paragraphs of excellent analysis I am convinced that Victoria Adams either came down the stairs before or after Oswald did and it is clear that that is so because we know that Oswald came down the stairs and not the elevator," Liebeler wrote. "I still do not understand, however, how the fact that Victoria Adams came down the stairs before or after Oswald did show that Oswald came down the stairs. If the idea is to show that Adams was not on the stairway when Oswald was, I am not convinced by the analysis or speculation in these two paragraphs. Furthermore, if that is the idea it is not clearly set forth."[19]

Liebeler then offered a revision he thought might clarify the point. "How about a first sentence like: 'Victoria Adams testified that she came down the stairway, within about 1 minute after the shots, from the fourth floor to the first floor where she encountered two Depository employees—Bill Shelley and Billy Lovelady. If Miss Adams was on the stairway at that time, the question is raised as to why she did not see Oswald.'"[20]

That was in fact *the* key question. It was the one I personally wanted to ask. But after two trips to Dallas, I was no closer to finding the woman who could help me answer it.

CHAPTER 13

September 1966-August 1975

It was while living in California that Miss Adams decided to go back to school and acquire a degree in general education. She graduated with high honors. Then she elected to move into the real-estate field. She worked full time while continuing her undergraduate studies at night. Eventually, she would graduate summa cum laude with a bachelor's degree in business administration.

It had taken a lot of hard work and personal sacrifice, but she had finally pulled herself up.

It was not quite as easy to shake the memories of Dallas, however. Thoughts of what she had witnessed in Dealey Plaza still haunted her.

One day, while wandering along the bookshelves of a local public library, she spied a set of the twenty-six volumes. Curiosity prevailed once again. Turning to the sixth volume, she read the words she had offered—what was it now, some two or three years ago?—to that visiting Commission lawyer.

She could not believe what she saw.

She remembered being given the opportunity in Dallas to make corrections to any spelling or grammatical errors she found in her official testimony. In fact, someone had hand-delivered a copy of it right to her office, just for that very purpose. A wordsmith and nitpicker with the English language, she had found several typographical mistakes and had made the necessary changes.

She now discovered that each one of the errors had gone uncorrected. The mistakes left standing, she now realized, made her look stupid.

And why did it say at the end of her testimony that she waived her right to review her testimony when that is not what had happened? She *did* review her statement. She *did* make corrections, even if it had been for naught.

There was that Shelley and Lovelady stuff again too. Not only had there been a reference made to them in the Warren Report—saying that she had seen them on the first floor—but now words to the same effect were mysteriously in her own testimony. She was quoted in her testimony as saying to those two men, "The president has been shot."

She thought back, long and hard, but she was certain neither Shelley nor Lovelady were on the first floor when she arrived there. There was a guy—a black guy standing near the elevators—to whom she had made that comment as she and Sandra Styles ran out the back door. But Shelley and Lovelady? No, that just wasn't right.

Why were they saying she talked with two men who weren't there?

She didn't even recall seeing the Shelley/Lovelady passage in the copy of the testimony she had been given to review back in Dallas that day.

What was going on here?

Her husband by now had become an avid reader of all things assassination. He convinced her that she should remain quiet about her background. Too many people were dying. It would be much safer.

That attitude changed when Mark Lane came to town.

Miss Adams had not read Lane's book. But she had heard of him. So she and her husband decided to attend a lecture Lane was giving at the Hotel del Coronado. Her husband thought she should introduce herself to Lane afterward.

At that meeting, Lane seemed nice, interested, and apologetic that he hadn't found her early enough to include her story in his video version of *Rush to Judgment*. Yet Lane was concerned only with her sighting of the man she thought had been Jack Ruby, not her trip down the stairs—or even when it had occurred. He showed her a picture of Ruby standing in Dealey Plaza and told her the government had purposely cropped that picture so that only a part of him could be seen in the photograph.

Miss Adams could not figure out why that was so important.

Then he invited her to accompany him onto the Mort Sahl television show in Los Angeles. Sahl had a fascination with the assassination, Lane said, and would be interested in hearing her story.

Miss Adams felt somewhat safe, enough so to reason that this perhaps was her opportunity. This was her chance to rid herself of the spirits that had haunted her for all these years, to finally square things with the truth, to tell it like it really was. And so she agreed.

On camera a few weeks later, she went through the story one more time: how she left the window after the shots were fired, how she heard no one on the stairs; how she thought she saw Ruby in the crowds. But Lane and Sahl were concerned only with the latter and why Ruby happened to be where he said he wasn't. They didn't want to know about anything else, constantly interrupting her and bringing her back to Ruby.

She couldn't wait to get off the show. Meeting them both had not impressed Miss Adams. They didn't want her story; neither did the government. She vowed to not let herself fall into a trap like this ever again.

And so, she simply stopped talking.

CHAPTER 14

August 1968-March 1969

The first thing I noticed as Gary Schoener approached was that he still suffered the effects of the mugging he had endured in a Minneapolis alley months earlier. He walked with a slight limp, his one eye remained puffy, and his face was bruised and scarred. He otherwise looked like the academic he was: elbow patches on his sport coat and hair that hid his ears and touched his shirt collar.

Schoener was at home in Philadelphia, recuperating. Despite what others were saying, he felt there was no connection between the attack on him and the publicity his assassination research was generating.

I, on the other hand, was spending my first month of active duty in the naval yards there. We decided to finally get together one evening to discuss our mutual interest.

He gave me a pile of documents to examine, rattled off a list of areas that I should continue researching, and suggested I visit Vincent Salandria, a local attorney. But he knew nothing of the whereabouts of Victoria Adams.

He listened intently as I detailed my search for her. You'll find her one day, he told me, if you keep trying. I wasn't so sure.

I admired Schoener a great deal. He was intelligent, detail oriented, careful in his analysis, and caring enough to gently correct me when I made errors of fact during our conversations. He certainly was not a "kook," as many Commission critics were being labeled.

The next night I took a bus to the street Salandria lived on, not far from center city. The sidewalk was crowded by fashionable red-brick townhomes that seemed connected in an endless chain, and I began searching for numbers on doors. When I came to the one that was penciled on my slip of paper, I walked up the steps and knocked.

There was no answer. As I turned to leave, I noticed a man watching me from under a neighboring tree against which the dog he was walking was relieving himself. Unaccustomed I'm sure to seeing someone in a sailor suit standing on any of these doorsteps, he asked if he could be of assistance. I told him I was looking for Vince Salandria's residence. I had found it, he informed me, but he knew for a fact the homeowner had stepped out.

"Are you a friend of his?" the man inquired.

I told him I wouldn't know Salandria if I saw him standing on the sidewalk.[1] "A friend of mine actually recommended I stop by and visit."

"And would that friend of yours be Gary Schoener?" I must have been looking at him with narrowed eyes by now, for he laughed slightly and said, "I'm Vince Salandria. Nowadays, you can never be too sure."[2]

I tagged along as he and his dog meandered through the neighborhood streets. He continued his questioning, only now not as double-edged. He was curious about my background, whom I had interviewed, and what areas I was researching. He spoke favorably of Weisberg and Jones and seemed especially fascinated when I brought up my interviews with Roger Craig, Carroll Jarnagin, and S. M. Holland.

But he knew nothing of the whereabouts of Victoria Adams.

In his book-lined study an hour later, we drank iced teas and discussed his work. He said he had no doubt that Kennedy was eliminated as the result of a very sophisticated conspiracy and cover-up and that elements of our own government were involved. An event like this was not unusual in other countries, he continued, but was foreign on American soil.

This country, he emphasized, was no longer controlled by the populace but, rather, by the elite.

Salandria was different from Weisberg and Jones. He was dogmatic and unrelenting. He had made up his mind already, and he had no time for those who disagreed. And he was vitriolic about Arlen Specter, another Philadelphia lawyer. Specter served on the Warren Commission staff and was credited with originating the highly controversial "single-bullet" theory.

As I left at 1 A.M., Salandria handed me a stack of reprints of magazine articles he had written. He wanted me to read them, then return to discuss what I thought. I assured him I would.

But I never got the chance.

In one of his earlier letters, Weisberg informed me of his long and frustrating search for President Kennedy's official death certificate. He couldn't find it at the National Archives, and he felt that its absence was suspicious. Since the autopsy on Kennedy had been performed at the

Bethesda Naval Hospital, Weisberg thought the certificate might be on file there. Since I was in the navy, he believed I'd have better luck finding out.

It was all I needed to pursue this, his latest assignment.

I too inquired at the Archives. I was told the document could not be found and was not listed in the official index of available papers. Next, I wrote to offices of the navy in the Department of Defense and to the Bethesda Naval Hospital.

I turned up nothing.

Those letters raised a few feathers on lapel clusters, however. Word of what I had done was passed through military channels.

One afternoon several weeks later, I was summoned to the Office of Personnel. A captain handed me copies of the letters I had sent to the DOD and Bethesda. When I admitted they were mine, I was told my behavior was "inappropriate" for a member of the armed services.

My face got red.

The captain was more interested in my nose. Keep it, he said, out of something that is none of my business. It would be in my best interests, he advised, to cease such efforts—immediately!

And by the way, he continued, my stay in Philadelphia was being cut short. My orders had been expedited. I would be leaving the next morning for an aircraft carrier berthed in Portsmouth, Virginia. The meeting was over.

"Possibly you'd better have a different extra-curricular activity for a while," Weisberg wrote when I updated him.[3] Thanks, Harold.

By the fall of 1968, the underground network of fellow researchers was spreading. There were Salandria in Pennsylvania, Schoener in Minnesota, Weisberg in Maryland, and Jones in Texas. I was corresponding too with a young UCLA graduate student named David Lifton, who was part of the grapevine and was seeking my help in the Archives.

We were freely sharing information, exchanging copies of our personal papers, comparing notes and ideas, and helping each other. There was no competition amongst us; rather just a collective goal of seeking truths. It felt good to be involved.

The mail mischief was continuing, however, with the occasional letters to and from fellow researchers being opened and crudely resealed during transit. A car had followed me as I walked home from a camera shop after picking up copies of an important photograph uncovered in yet another Weisberg assignment. Even my telephone had been tapped. I picked up the receiver one day and briefly heard a recording of a previous conversation I'd had with Weisberg. Someone had pressed the wrong button.

If it weren't for the fact these events were real, I'd have thought I'd slipped into paranoia.

I was gaining some fame as well. When my hometown paper, the *Altoona Mirror*, began publishing my letters to the editor about the assassination, I attracted a local following. Invitations to radio talk shows began to arrive.

The experience was exhilarating, and I did not want to be out of this loop. So when Captain Bligh as much as told me to cease and desist in his Philadelphia office that day, it took me only seconds to reach a decision.

Damn the torpedoes. My "extracurricular activities" were my business, and I would continue them, even while still in the navy.

Yet the National Archives was a long haul from Portsmouth, Virginia. So sometimes I'd use the bus to get there. Occasionally I'd travel with shipmates heading in that direction. More often, it was by predawn hitchhiking on northbound I-95. I'd pay to have somebody stand my duty. I'd work double duty just to get the next day off. I'd use up accumulated leave.

But somehow, someway, I'd get to my destination, if only for a few hours of research. There were secrets hidden in the Archives, and I intended to keep looking for them.

Birth of a Notion: The Single-Bullet Theory

The Warren Report concluded that President Kennedy received a nonfatal wound by a bullet that entered the lower portion of the back of his neck, passed through his neck, and exited from just below the Adam's apple of his throat. This bullet went on to shatter bones and inflict five additional wounds in Governor Connally before coming to rest in his thigh. From there it popped out and was discovered on a stretcher. The bullet, later known as Commission Exhibit 399, had minimal deformity or loss of substance.

The timing of the shots based on analysis of the Zapruder film, the fact that only three empty cartridge cases were found on the sixth floor, and the knowledge that one shot missed the president and wounded a bystander made it quite simple. If Oswald was the sole assassin, the first bullet that hit Kennedy had to also cause all of Connally's wounds.

Yet there was considerable evidence that the nonfatal wound to Kennedy had actually struck the president lower on his body, in his back rather than his neck.

The Warren Report placed the wound in the rear of Kennedy's neck at "approximately 5½ inches (14 centimeters) from the tip of the right shoulder joint and approximately the same distance below the tip of the right mastoid process, the bony point immediately behind the ear."[4]

A head-and-shoulders diagram of Kennedy in the twenty-six volumes clearly places that bullet hole at the base of the neck, slightly to the right of the spinal column.[5] An accompanying drawing indicates the bullet took a downward path to exit his throat and hit Connally, as it would have had to do if it had been fired from above and behind the motorcade.[6] A lower entrance wound in Kennedy, such as one positioned in his back, would have required an upward path for it to exit at the hole in his neck. But that meant the emerging bullet would likely have missed the other occupants of the car entirely, necessitating a separate shot to the governor.

An FBI investigative report on January 13, 1964, stated, "Examination of the President's clothing by the FBI Laboratory disclosed that there was a small hole in the back of his coat and shirt approximately six inches below the top of the collar and two inches to the right of the middle seam of the coat."[7] It went on to say that "minute traces of copper" from the full copper alloy jacket of the penetrating bullet were found "on the fabric surrounding the hole" of both the coat and the shirt.[8] A "slit" was found on the front of Kennedy's shirt just beneath the collar button that "has the characteristics of an exit hole for a projectile," and a "nick" was discovered on the left side of the knot in the president's tie, "which possibly was caused by the same projectile as it passed through the shirt."[9]

The FBI said nothing about whether copper traces were also found surrounding the "slit" in the shirt or the "nick" in the tie. In testimony, FBI firearms expert Robert Frazier cleared up the question.

Specter: Is the nick consistent with a 6.5 millimeter bullet having caused the nick?

Frazier: Yes. Any projectile could have caused the nick. In this connection there was no metallic residue found on the tie, and for that matter there was no metallic residue found on the shirt at the holes in the front. However, there was in the back.[10]

Why weren't copper traces found on the front? That question was never asked.

Frazier's use of the word "projectile" is revealing and shows his inability to categorically say it was a bullet that caused the "slit" in the collar. The "slit," he said, "is not specifically characteristic of a bullet hole to the extent that you could say it was to the exclusion of being a piece of bone or some other type of projectile."[11]

J. Edgar Hoover made a similarly guarded reference to the coat and shirt holes in a March 23, 1964, reply to J. Lee Rankin, who had asked the FBI whether those holes were of entrance or exit. Hoover wrote:

> The hole in the back of the coat and the hole in the back of the shirt were in general, circular in shape and the ends of the torn threads around the holes were bent inward. These characteristics are typical of bullet entrance holes.
>
> The hole in the front of the shirt was a ragged slitlike hole and the ends of the torn threads around the hole were bent outward. These characteristics are typical of an exit hole for a projectile.[12]

It is interesting to note that it was termed a "bullet" going in, yet a "projectile" coming out. The two are not synonymous. If, for instance, a fragment from the president's exploding skull caused the throat wound, what happened to the bullet that entered his back? The FBI wrote, "Medical examination of the President's body had revealed that the bullet which entered his back had penetrated to a distance of less than a finger length."[13]

Was that the bullet that worked its way out of the wound to be later found on a stretcher?

Two photographs of Kennedy's coat and shirt reveal the location of the rear bullet holes. Those pictures were published by the FBI[14] but not included in the Warren Report or its twenty-six volumes.[15] Both graphically show the dark coat and blood-drenched white dress shirt Kennedy was wearing, and both clearly reveal bullet holes that on first glance appear considerably lower than what the Commission concluded.

Cmdr. James J. Humes, who with Cmdr. J. Thornton Boswell and Lt. Col. Pierre A. Finck performed the autopsy on the night of the assassination, confirmed the bullet-hole locations in Kennedy's clothing during his testimony. Under questioning by Arlen Specter, Humes admitted the holes were at a distance of "approximately 6 inches below the top of the collar and 2 inches to the right of the middle seam" on both garments.[16]

Seemingly in contradiction with himself, the doctor then stated the holes in the coat and shirt "conform quite well" with the location of the wound as shown in Commission Exhibit 386, a drawing that strangely depicts that wound as being much higher than what Humes had just described, actually at the base of Kennedy's neck.[17]

Humes attempted to clarify the discrepancy by saying because Kennedy was "an extremely well developed, muscular young man..." both his coat and shirt likely were bunched or pushed up high on his back.[18] Therefore, a shot through the bunched clothing at a height depicted by the Commission would appear lower on the coat when the garment was stretched out. This bunching effect, he explained, would be accentuated if the president had been waving to the crowd with an upraised right arm at the time the shot hit him from behind. Humes then cited a single frame from the Zapruder film showing Kennedy "just prior to the wounding" with a slightly raised right arm, waving to onlookers.[19]

In that photograph, Kennedy has not yet moved out of view of Zapruder's camera lens to a position behind the Stemmons Freeway street sign, where it was determined the first shot actually struck him. A timelier picture Humes should have examined was one taken by bystander Phil Willis, who was emphatic when he testified that he snapped it at precisely the moment he heard the first shot.[20] Taken from behind the presidential limousine and looking down Elm Street, the picture clearly shows Kennedy, his right arm no longer in the air and now lowered from the earlier waving motion captured in the Zapruder frame.[21]

And there appears to be no irregularity in the way Kennedy's coat lies across his shoulders.

Additional testimony also supports a shot hitting Kennedy lower in the back. On the flight back to Washington five hours after the assassination, Secret Service Agent Glen Bennett jotted down in his notebook that he actually saw the first shot strike Kennedy "about 4 inches down from the right shoulder."[22] Bennett was in the car directly behind the presidential limousine.

He reinforced that statement, giving the same measurement and description, when he prepared a follow-up report of his activities the next day.[23] Despite the agent's account being in conflict with the Commission's placement of the wound, the Report still gave him credit when it wrote, "Substantial weight may be given Bennett's observation."[24]

Secret Service Agent Clinton Hill, summoned to the morgue specifically to observe Kennedy's wounds, testified he "saw an opening in the back, about 6 inches below the neckline to the right-hand side of the spinal column."[25]

In contrast also was the November 26, 1963, report of FBI Agents James W. Sibert and Francis X. O'Neill. This report was available only at the Archives. Both agents witnessed the autopsy and stated the bullet hole in Kennedy's back "was below the shoulders."[26] During the autopsy, the attending doctors probed that wound, the agents wrote, but determined the bullet had not penetrated very far into Kennedy's body since "the end of the opening could be felt with the finger."[27]

This version of events is reinforced by Secret Service Agent Roy Kellerman, who testified he was standing beside Finck as he probed the wound "with his instrument and I said, 'Colonel, where did it go?'" Kellerman continued, "He said, 'There are no lanes for an outlet of this entry in this man's shoulder.'"[28] Kellerman also described the wound as "a hole in his shoulder."[29]

During the autopsy, Commander Boswell completed a "face sheet" that showed front and rear body diagrams, typically used in these instances to mark wound locations. On the rearward diagram he drew a bullet hole low on the back, in a spot that matched the clothing holes and where others had observed the wound. It is in sharp contrast to the higher position presented by the Commission.[30]

Perhaps all the witnesses had been wrong. Perhaps the position of the wound on the autopsy diagram had been placed incorrectly. Perhaps the coat and shirt had indeed "bunched."

One thing was certain, though: the question of exactly where that bullet had entered was of critical importance. The entire lone-assassin theory hinged on it.

It was a question easily answered. All that was necessary were the autopsy X-rays and photographs.

The Commission's Reenactment

But the Warren Commission never officially examined those critical pieces of evidence. Remarkably, it never allowed doctors on the witness stand to view them either, even though those doctors hinted at the inexactitude of their testimony without them.

The wound-location problem caused internal concerns as well. One of those bothered was Norman Redlich, a special assistant to J. Lee Rankin.

In an April 27, 1964, memorandum to Rankin, less than five weeks before the government's investigation was scheduled to end, Redlich discussed the confusion over this fundamental issue.

"The purpose of this memorandum," Redlich wrote, "is to explain the reasons why certain members of the staff feel that it is important to take certain on-site photographs in connection with the location of the approximate points at which the three bullets struck the occupants of the Presidential limousine."[31]

When Redlich referred to three bullets striking Kennedy and Connally, he was citing the FBI Summary Report issued on December 9, 1963, which stated Kennedy had been struck in the back by one shot, Connally a separate second shot, and Kennedy the third and final bullet. Although that scenario eliminated the "single-bullet" problems, it did not account for the shot that missed and caused the cheek wound to bystander James Tague. Nor was it possible to fire Oswald's rifle three times within the timeframe shown by the Zapruder film and necessary to make the FBI's theory work.

The FBI's solution, therefore, implied a case for conspiracy.

"Our report presumably will state that the President was hit by the first bullet, Governor Connally by the second, and the President by the third and fatal bullet," Redlich continued. "The report will also conclude that the bullets were fired by one person located in the sixth floor southeast corner window of the TSBD building."[32]

This paragraph contradicted itself. If the first sentence was accurate, the second could not be, under the constraints already described.

"As our investigation now stands, however, we have not shown that these events could possibly have occurred in the manner suggested above. All we have is a reasonable hypothesis which appears to be supported by the medical testimony but which has not been checked out against the physical facts at the scene of the assassination."[33]

Redlich recognized the importance of determining where the first shot struck Kennedy but, incredibly, told his boss, "Our intention is not to establish the point with complete accuracy, but merely to substantiate the hypothesis which underlies the conclusions that Oswald was the sole assassin."[34]

Accuracy seemed not the issue. Showing Oswald did it alone was.

Even though what he was writing—three shots, three hits—was in agreement with the FBI's conclusion, Redlich still felt that the FBI was wrong: "I should add that the facts which we now have in our possession, submitted to us in separate reports from the FBI and Secret Service, are totally incorrect and, if left uncorrected, will present a completely misleading picture."[35]

How Redlich knew in advance that the "facts" were "totally incorrect" and would provide "a completely misleading picture" is unknown. This is especially odd since his recommendation for on-site testing to verify or invalidate those "facts" was the purpose of his April memorandum to Rankin in the first place.

Regardless, Redlich felt that the two agencies he was criticizing should still be the ones to conduct the tests. "It may well be that this project should be undertaken by the FBI and Secret Service with our [the Commission's] assistance instead of being done as a staff project," he wrote. "The important thing is that the project be undertaken expeditiously."[36]

It took a month. On May 24, 1964, a simulated presidential limousine slowly rolled down Elm Street in Dealey Plaza, the curious watching from the sidelines. The FBI and Secret Service were doing their best to recreate "as precisely as possible what happened on November 22, 1963."[37]

Nothing was left to chance: the sixth floor had been restored to its sinister appearance, and an FBI agent crouched there at a half-open window and peered into the telescopic sight of Oswald's rifle, which was mounted to a tripod and now with a camera atop it, recording "the view as was seen by the assassin."[38] Two other agents "with approximately the same physical characteristics sat in the car in the same relative positions as President Kennedy and Governor Connally had occupied."[39] Even the old oak tree in front of the Depository was checked but spared pruning, since it "was approximately the same as on the day of the assassination."[40]

The Connally stand-in was wearing the coat the governor had worn, its back bullet hole circled in chalk. The Kennedy stand-in was not wearing the president's coat. The back of the suit coat he did have on also was marked in chalk at the location where the bullet had entered.

And there it was, clear in the Commission's own published record of this reconstruction. The chalk mark on the Kennedy stand-in's back was much lower than where the Commission ultimately put it. It was right where witnesses described it as being, exactly where Dr. Boswell had put it on his autopsy face sheet.[41]

The FBI and Secret Service had placed that mark on the stand-in where both agencies felt it belonged—in the back, not the neck.

In describing the reenactment, the Warren Report stated, "The back of the stand-in for the President was marked with chalk at the point where the bullet entered."[42]

If that were so, it meant the entrance wound to Kennedy was lower than the exit. It could not have gone on to strike Connally.

Enter Philadelphia attorney and Commission Assistant Counsel Arlen Specter. On the very afternoon the reenactment was completed, Specter was seen holding a trajectory rod between the two stand-ins, arbitrarily creating the only path that would allow a bullet to pass through Kennedy and still hit Connally. That path was higher on the Kennedy stand-in's back, well above the chalk mark and now in the neck.[43]

A week later, Specter officially adopted this notion, in effect saying the witnesses, the doctors, and even the FBI and Secret Service were all wrong. The wound was now higher on Kennedy's body. The same bullet had then gone on to hit Connally.

Oswald therefore did it and he did it alone. The single-bullet theory had been created.

Sometimes at the Archives, you can just plain get lucky. There is no other way of describing it.

On my researcher's table that day were boxes of files containing the official galley proofs of selected testimony sent to the Government Printing Office for inclusion in the twenty-six volumes. Based on Roger Craig telling me his testimony had been changed, I was looking for what Victoria Adams had said under oath—her official transcript of testimony—versus what had been printed in the twenty-six volumes, checking for any substantial changes between the two. The boxes were dusty, apparently never opened since 1964.

What I found was a photocopy of the court reporter's transcription of Miss Adams' testimony given in Dallas on the afternoon of April 7, 1964, before David Belin. Formerly stamped *Top Secret,* as all testimonies once had been, that classification on hers was now crossed out and marked *canceled* as of November 21, 1967. The court reporter was listed as Helen Laidrich.

I remembered from reading Miss Adams' testimony in the twenty-six volumes that she had agreed to waive her right to examine and sign her transcript before having it sent to Washington. The copy I was now holding must have been that version, for it had no signature, corrections, or notations on any of its twenty-three typewritten pages. The wording was identical to what was printed in the twenty-six volumes.

I was casually flipping through another one of the boxes when, in the middle and between two brown government folders, the white pages of a document flashed by. Closer examination revealed the inscription *Certificate of Death, NAVMED N (Rev. 4-58) Front.* It was President Kennedy's official death certificate.

It was not the often-confused one signed by Parkland Hospital's Dr. Kemp Clark, who released Kennedy's body for transport back to Washington.[44] This was the *federal* certificate of death for the president of the United States—the one signed the day after the assassination by Kennedy's personal physician, Rear Adm. George Gregory Burkley; the one Weisberg had been searching for; the one the Archives said it did not have. Yet here it was, buried in a box of documents that had been earmarked for publication in the twenty-six volumes of evidence.

I tried to be nonchalant, gazing at the words as if I was reading nothing more than a copy of Oswald's high-school truancy records. I felt as if all eyes were on me, though, mindful of my illicit discovery. When I serenely turned to look, life in the research room was as normal.

Page one was perfunctory. President Kennedy had died at forty-six years, six months of age with blue eyes, auburn hair, and a ruddy complexion and at a height of seventy-two inches and a weight of 172 pounds. The cause of death was listed as "gunshot wound, skull."[45]

If the certificate held nothing more than this—no graphic pictures or words—why had it been kept out of the Warren Report and the twenty-six volumes? What was it doing stuffed in a box of papers, all others of which *had* been published?

Perhaps it was because of page two. Under line item thirty, "Summary of Facts Relating to Death," Burkley wrote the following: "President John Fitzgerald Kennedy, while riding in the motorcade in Dallas, Texas on November 22, 1963, and at approximately 12:30 p.m., was struck in the head by an assassin's bullet and a second wound occurred in the posterior back at about the level of the third thoracic vertebra."[46]

Had it not been for my studies of human anatomy to better understand all the medical jargon by the doctors, I would never have caught the significance of this statement. A wound "at about the level of the third thoracic vertebra" was considerably lower on the back than where the Commission placed it. In fact, "at about the . . . third thoracic vertebra" was consistent with the evidence: where the FBI and Secret Service had placed it with a chalk mark during their reenactment tests, where the FBI had said it was in all their investigative reports, where witnesses had testified they saw it, where the bullet holes were in Kennedy's coat and shirt, and where Dr. Boswell had drawn it on his autopsy face sheet.

Coincidentally, and despite Dr. Boswell's later comment that he erred when he drew that face sheet, the *original* face sheet he had prepared had been verified and signed by Admiral Burkley. Yet a copy of that very face sheet as published by the Warren Commission failed to show Burkley's handwritten notation, "Verified" and his signature, "G.G. Burkley." As the face sheet appeared in the Commission's own evidence, the admiral's handwritten and corroborative notations had been covered over.

But Burkley's admission on the death certificate was specific and, based on every other bit of existing evidence, confirming. The wound in Kennedy's back was lower than the wound in the front.

That bullet could not have been the one that went on to hit Connally.[47]

Burkley accompanied Kennedy to Dallas, was with him in the emergency room at Parkland Hospital, was with the body on the way back to Washington, and was present at his autopsy. He signed the death certificate that clearly described the wounds, and he verified the position of those wounds on the controversial face sheet. Yet he was never called as a Commission witness.[48]

I needed a copy of this, especially for Weisberg, since he had assigned me the task of finding the death certificate. I waited for my opportunity, then approached a clerk behind the main desk who was obviously new to all this and momentarily alone. I explained that I was in the navy and there for the day and hoped for some quick copies to take with me.

I handed him a stack of about twenty papers, the death certificate tucked into the middle of the bunch. As was the custom, he glanced at each page. I figured he would look up at me with a knowing eye as he came upon the only document I really wanted, but he passed by it without hesitation.

"Be right back," he said.

Moments later, he returned. I expected to see an army of security guards flanking him, but he was alone. He gave me the originals first and watched carefully as I put them back in the open box on the table in front of me. As I reached for my copies, he suddenly pulled them away with a smile.

I had been caught.

"That'll be four fifty," he said.

I laughed nervously. "Here's ten; keep the change." Had I only found a fifty-dollar bill in my wallet, he would have been that much richer.

Not long after, I casually left the building, glancing over my shoulders, waiting for the alarm bells to sound and the massive exit doors to clang shut in front of me, locking me inside until my copies could be confiscated. But nothing happened. It was the dreaded paranoia, I agree. But at least I hadn't failed Weisberg on this one.[49]

CHAPTER 15

April–December 1969

Every turn, sign, and pothole along I-95 became a part of my mind. I was killing myself from lack of sleep. But I was gaining ground in my research at the Archives.

For instance, no one believed Roger Craig when he said he saw a man thought to be Oswald get into a Nash station wagon fifteen minutes after the assassination. But as so often happens in the Archives, an otherwise innocuous document came to light. This one told the story of Marvin Robinson, who happened to be driving through Dealey Plaza moments after the shooting when "a light colored Nash station wagon suddenly appeared before him."[1] As he related to the FBI on November 23, "this vehicle stopped and a white male came down the grass covered incline between the building and the street and entered the station wagon after which it drove away in the direction of the Oak Cliff section of Dallas."

To anyone unfamiliar with Roger Craig's story, Robinson's observations served little purpose. Yet it verified what the deputy sheriff had seen.

But was the man who got into the station wagon Lee Oswald?

No one believed Craig either when he said he went to Capt. Will Fritz's office to identify Oswald later that afternoon.

One day I received a package from Craig. Inside was a book written by Dallas Police Chief Jesse Curry. On an attached note, Craig had written, "Recognize the man on pg. 72?" The picture I turned to showed Fritz's outer office, under heavy guard while Oswald sat inside.

Standing in that office was Roger Craig.[2]

If it wasn't the real Oswald whom Craig saw running from the scene, could it have been the infamous "second" Oswald? There were numerous instances of someone portraying himself as Oswald in the weeks before the assassination. This body double appeared at rifle ranges, a furniture store, a gun-repair shop, a Selective Service office, a used-car lot—even the doorstep of a Dallas resident's home. This mysterious person always

155

drew attention to himself, with what would later turn out to be self-incriminating actions or comments.

The Commission dismissed these oddities, saying it could not have been the real Oswald. It never once wondered why so many independent and guilt-associating sightings had occurred in the weeks prior to the assassination and suddenly stopped immediately thereafter.

Then there was Carolyn Arnold. The Warren Commission published in the twenty-six volumes her March 18, 1964, statement to the FBI that she left her office at the Depository and went outside "at about 12:25 p.m." to stand on the front steps. It also included her remark she "did not see Oswald at the time President Kennedy was shot."[3]

Yet it completely brushed off a November 26, 1963, FBI interview in which Mrs. Arnold said she left her office "between 12:00 and 12:15 PM" and "thought she caught a fleeting glimpse of Lee Harvey Oswald standing in the hallway between the front door and the double doors leading to the warehouse, located on the first floor." The document continued, "She could not be sure that this was Oswald, but said she felt it was and believed the time to be a few minutes before 12:15 PM."[4]

At that same moment, others in Dealey Plaza, including Arnold Rowland and Carolyn Walther, were observing at least one gunman in the sixth-floor window. It obviously could not have been Oswald up there if Carolyn Arnold was right. Was this why her November 26 FBI interview was ignored?

Questions arose too about the physical evidence used against Oswald. According to the Warren Report, "A handmade bag of wrapping paper and tape was found in the southeast corner of the sixth floor alongside the window from which the shots were fired."[5] The Report concluded the bag was linked to Oswald in three ways: by fingerprints found on it, by fibers found in it, and by materials that had been used to make it.

But was the bag even on the sixth floor?

In order to preserve evidence, photographs were immediately taken upon discovery of the "sniper's nest." Those pictures, however, do not show the paper bag. They do reveal the arrangement of boxes around the window and what appear to be three spent rifle hulls on the floor.

The paper bag, however, is missing, even though the field of vision in those initial crime-scene photos includes the corner where the Report says the bag was located.[6] The Commission therefore had to use dotted lines on those pictures to indicate what it called the "approximate location" of the bag.[7]

Sheriff's Deputy Luke Mooney, the first person to discover and examine the sniper's nest, related in detail what he saw and how he took great care to preserve the area. He said nothing about a paper sack.

Mooney was specifically asked during his testimony if he had noticed "anything" lying on the floor in the corner, the spot where the bag was to be. He replied, "No sir; I didn't see anything over in the corner."[8]

Several Dallas Police officers who arrived shortly after Mooney made similar statements. They too had not observed a paper bag.[9]

This is the same thing Roger Craig had told me months earlier.[10]

Considering its large size and its placement in a conspicuous and open spot, it is odd no one noticed it.

Although the Report did not mention names, it apparently relied on Dallas Police Detectives Marvin Johnson and L. D. Montgomery to settle the mystery, at least somewhat.

Belin: Did you find anything else up in the southeast corner of the sixth floor? We have talked about the rifle, we have talked about the shells, we have talked about the chicken bones and the lunch sack and the pop bottle by that second pair of windows. Anything else?

Johnson: Yes, sir. We found this brown paper sack or case. It was made out of heavy wrapping paper. Actually, it looked similar to the paper that those books was wrapped in. It was just a long narrow paper bag.

Belin: Where was this found?

Johnson: Right in the corner of the building.[11]

Montgomery testified he also saw the paper bag lying in the corner.[12] It is strange that both Johnson and Montgomery saw the bag where others before them had not. This is especially odd when one considers Johnson's comment that nothing in that area had been moved prior to when the police pictures were snapped, pictures that did not show the paper bag.[13]

Regardless, a suspicious-looking sack was turned over to the Dallas Police Crime Lab, and officers were seen carrying it from the building. The outside of it was later dusted with powder, but no legible fingerprints emerged.[14] Later that night, the bag was sent to an FBI laboratory in Washington. Two legible prints were uncovered there, one of a left index finger and the other of a right palm.

Both prints belonged to Oswald.

The palm print was in such a position that it supported Buell Wesley Frazier's recollection of how he had seen Oswald carrying the package on the morning of November 22, as Oswald walked toward the Depository. Frazier said he observed Oswald carrying the bag with the butt end of the package in his palm and the other end tucked neatly under his armpit.

The discovery of the palm print and its location on the bag therefore verified Frazier's recollection. That fact was not disclosed within the Warren Report, however, which said only that the palm print "was from Oswald's right hand, in which he had carried the long package as he walked from Frazier's car to the building."[15]

That wording may have been carefully chosen because, only one page earlier, the Report had *discounted* Frazier's claim that he saw Oswald carry the package with one end in his palm and the other *in his armpit*—a physical impossibility based on Oswald's arm size if that package contained the disassembled rifle.[16]

The Report gives further assurance of an Oswald/paper bag link in a clipped subheading, "Fibers in paper bag matched fibers in blanket."[17] The evidence for that declaration, however, is not very convincing. When asked if fibers found in the bag came from the blanket in which the weapon had been stored, FBI hair-and-fiber expert Paul M. Stombaugh was guarded in his response: "All I would say here is that it is possible that these fibers could have come from this blanket."[18]

His caution resulted from the fact that not all of the fibers present in the blanket were found inside the paper bag. Since the blanket fibers were commonly used in many different fabrics, Stombaugh admitted that even if he had found every single one of the blanket fibers in the paper bag instead of the "so few" he did find, the best he could then say was those fibers "probably had come from this blanket."[19]

Noticeably absent from the Report was what FBI questioned-documents expert James Cadigan disclosed *wasn't* found on or in the paper bag.

Cadigan: I was also requested at that time to examine the bag to determine if there were any significant markings or scratches or abrasions or anything by which it could be associated with the rifle . . . that is, could I find any markings that I could tie to that rifle.

[Commission Counsel Melvin A.] *Eisenberg:* Yes?

Cadigan: And I couldn't find any such markings.[20]

Moments later, the agent was more emphatic, saying, "There were no marks on this bag that I could say were caused by that rifle or any other rifle or any other given instrument."[21] Eisenberg then used a lawyer's trick, reversing the question and asking Cadigan if the *absence* of marks would preclude the rifle from having been in the bag. The agent did not budge, telling Eisenberg the absence meant very little to him. More important, he emphasized, would be the *presence* of such markings, the abrasions that *could* be directly associated with the rifle. And he had found none.[22]

Nor did Cadigan find any oil on the inside surfaces of the paper bag, unusual since the rifle was described by the FBI as being in "well-oiled condition."[23]

Cadigan also conducted physical tests on the bag when questions arose about the origin of materials used to construct it.

On the day of the assassination, Dallas police confiscated samples of the heavy brown wrapping paper and tape found in the shipping room at the Depository. Those samples were turned over to Dallas FBI agent Vincent Drain, who then immediately forwarded them to Washington. Following comparison tests, Cadigan said he was able to determine that the paper from the bag and the wrapping paper from the Depository's shipping room were identical. The Report cited a portion of his testimony, in which he said, "In all of the observations and physical tests that I made I found . . . the bag . . . and the paper sample . . . were the same."[24]

That is exactly what Drain wrote in his November 29, 1963, follow-up report. He said the sample paper from the Depository "was examined by the FBI Laboratory and found to have the same observable characteristics as the brown paper bag shaped like a gun case which was found near the scene of the shooting on the sixth floor of the Texas School Book Depository."[25] Yet something was strange.

What appeared to be an identical copy of that report was put into the files of Dallas Lt. Carl Day, mentioned by Drain as the one who took custody of the paper bag. Drain's November 29 report and the copy found in Day's file had the same information: the date of release, date of dictation, city of origin, agent's name, and FBI file number. The details were the same, as they should have been if it were merely a copy of Drain's report. There was, however, one exception.

In Drain's copy, it states the sample paper from the Depository "was examined by the FBI Laboratory and *found to have the same* [author's emphasis] observable characteristics as the brown paper bag shaped like a gun case which was found near the scene of the shooting. . . . " But the version in Day's file read "was examined by the FBI Laboratory and *found not to be identical* [author's emphasis] with the paper gun case found at the scene of the shooting." The inclusion of the word "not" changed its entire meaning. Was it a simple typographical error?

When I brought that question to the FBI's attention, the agency never responded.

If the Commission accepted Cadigan's laboratory results and Drain's report indicating that paper from the Depository and the paper used to make the sack were the same, then why almost four months later was the Commission *still* asking the FBI to obtain paper samples from two of Oswald's previous employers, including where he worked in New Orleans during the summer of 1963, to see if those samples matched the bag from the sixth floor?[26]

Then came this intriguing document. Postal authorities in Irving, where Oswald stayed on the weekends, found on December 4, 1963, a partially opened parcel that, upon inspection because of its damaged and undeliverable condition, contained "a brown paper bag made of fairly heavy brown paper which bag was open at both ends."[27] The package had been addressed to a "Mr. Lee Oswald at a non-existent address in Dallas, Texas."[28]

The Warren Report said absolutely nothing about this one either.

"Why Would the Government Lie?"

Burton Cummings of The Guess Who was singing "No Time" as I entered the radio station a little before midnight that cold December evening. I was home on leave for a week, a full seven days before that behemoth of a boat I was assigned to—the USS *Franklin D. Roosevelt*—set sail for a seven-month sojourn in the Mediterranean Sea. The program I had been invited to this night was a live call-in show. Listeners could phone direct to the studio and ask whatever questions they wanted. A call-in program was a first for me. I had been reluctant about this, assuming the audience for late-night fare would lean more toward a discussion of aliens, the Loch Ness monster, and perhaps the spirit world.

Tim Burns, the overnight disc jockey and congenial host, told me he would start by asking a few general questions. Then he'd open the phone lines at about 12:30. "You should be out of here by one thirty—two at the latest."

Six hours later, we had to abruptly cut off callers when time limits ended the program. People were genuinely interested. For the most part, they were polite, hungry for knowledge, sincerely concerned, and, in many cases, making educated inquiries.

But one of my callers was a ringer. Knowing few would be aware of the story of Victoria Adams, I convinced my father to stay awake and telephone the studio, posing a question about her. I wanted to introduce listeners to her name and mention my search.

I had another motive too. At 50,000 watts and with some atmospheric skip and good propagation, I was hoping someone out there on that dark night might hear and help me. I was willing to try anything.

Around two o'clock, an older gentleman called. He insisted I was wrong to raise doubts about our government. Doing so, he said, was tantamount to treason.

His voice went an octave higher. "You are a disgrace to my country!" he shouted. Then he hung up.

An hour later he was back. "Why would the government lie about something like this?" was all he asked me.

The words hit hard. They were exactly what I had asked in response to Terry's long-ago question of why I believed the Warren Report. They were the words that started all this, put me in this very chair this very night.

"Well, why would it lie?" the man pressed, impatient at my silence.

"I don't know. . . . I don't know why," I heard myself say. "But I feel it may have." Now it was my turn. "Have you ever read the Warren Report?" I asked him.

He hesitated. "No. I don't have to."

"I suggest you do," I offered.

"This is unbelievable," he sputtered.

"Yes, yes it is," I replied. "I find it hard to believe myself." I'm sure he never understood what I really meant. His was an unfortunate attitude but one I would encounter often as the years rolled on.

Yet for now, it had been an exhilarating exchange.[29] I loved the spontaneity, the give and take, the challenge of not knowing what was coming next, the realization I had become more knowledgeable than even I imagined. I relished the opportunity of helping others better understand the growing confusion over the assassination. Many authors by now had introduced their own theories and solutions to the murder, whether evidence supported such wild ideas or not. It was fun to clarify those issues.

It felt good. It felt right. And then, it ended.

Not long after, the *Roosevelt* eased from its berth and turned eastward. I watched America recede and slip over the horizon. My active research into the Kennedy assassination was over, at least for a while.

The Guess Who had been right that night. There was no time.

CHAPTER 16

January 1970-February 1981

There was nothing else to do but read the books on the assassination I had brought along, plus the material sent to me overseas by my fellow researchers. I remember the Europeans who, to a person, said they could never understand why Americans naively believed that their government did not lie to its people. I remember the lieutenant who, spying the dust jackets of the books next to me on the mess-hall table late one night, arrogantly commented that I was wasting my time reading such garbage.

"But I'm reading the Warren Report . . . sir." He was not amused.

By the time I returned home, things had changed. Jim Garrison in New Orleans by now had lost his bid to prove conspiracy. The ripple effects, especially from an *I-told-you-so* media, made legitimate researchers look like fools.

"We are now in a difficult period," Weisberg wrote me. "Several of us have exercised very poor judgment, and some, without evil motive but quite erroneously, are recriminating. Some, also, are inclined to shoot from the hip. This addresses their personalities and judgment more than their integrity, and I suggest tolerance and an effort at understanding. We will survive it."[1]

Even the once-cohesive underground network was coming apart, unraveling because many of its members were now fearful their tireless and original research would be stolen for the thief's own lucrative book deal.

Weisberg had recently called his former good friend Penn Jones "miserable" and "shameful" and "straight out crooked" over a difference of opinion involving Garrison's investigation. Jones in turn accused Weisberg of being a CIA agent. A scathing letter from Weisberg replying to that charge effectively ended their long relationship.

The once-unified band of truth seekers was collapsing, a lack of time for research and a loss of trust for each other to blame.

The sixties were over. America was leaving Vietnam in disgrace. Gas lines were longer than those to see the hit movie, *Jaws*. Nixon resigned for lying. Former Warren Commission member Gerald Ford, who had pilfered classified information about Lee Oswald for his own book deal, suddenly became president.[2]

I went back to college, marrying halfway through. Then came a job, a mortgage, monthly bills, a son. Life had caught up with me too.

But Victoria Adams still haunted my mind. I could never let go of that search.

Yet the lack of results was frustrating. I thought for sure, in all the literature on the assassination, after all these years, someone by now would have found her, questioned her in more detail, determined the real story, or, at the least, provided a clue as to her current whereabouts. But there was nothing, not a word I had not read before, nothing fresh in any of the growing supply of books.

That is, until David Belin wrote his in 1973. In *November 22, 1963: You Are the Jury*, Belin asked his faithful readers to become the panel of peers never formally mustered to judge the guilt of Oswald.[3]

He brought nothing new to the mix. Unlike practically every other author who was ignoring Victoria Adams, though, the man who conducted the official questioning of her did not. "If her testimony was correct that she started running down the stairs when she did," Belin re-explained, "this conflicted with the other evidence that seemed to indicate that Oswald immediately came down the stairway from the southeast corner of the sixth floor to the second floor."[4]

Echoing the Warren Report, Belin discounted Miss Adams on the grounds she had seen William Shelley and Billy Lovelady on the first floor. "It is obvious that the human mind is far more accurate on identification of known persons than it is on estimates of time," Belin analyzed. "This is particularly true in this case because Miss Adams is so definite about whom she saw when she got to the first floor, and her observations are *confirmed* by the testimony of Billy Lovelady, who *believed* that he saw Miss Adams when they got back into the building [author's emphasis]."[5]

How can observations be "confirmed" by someone who merely "believed" what was seen? Belin didn't explain. Nor did he provide his "jury" of readers with the impromptu and suspicious passage of Lovelady's testimony—"I saw a girl but I wouldn't swear to it it's Vickie"—made before Miss Adams' name had even been mentioned.[6]

Shelley's testimony is even less "confirming," which is perhaps why Belin failed to cite it at all in regards to Miss Adams.[7]

And once again, where was Sandra Styles in all this? Belin, as a Commission attorney, failed to summon her for questioning. As an author, he neglected to even cite her name.

"The testimony of Victoria Adams, in summary, does not rebut the other facts," Belin concluded, "which indicate that the assassin, shortly after the time of the shooting, came down the stairway from the sixth floor. Rather, these facts seem to show that Victoria Adams was mistaken in her time estimate and that she did not get down to the first floor as soon as she thought she had, unless she ran down the stairs at the time of the lunchroom encounter when Oswald, Truly and Baker would not have been in view of anyone coming down the stairs."[8]

Even if that last possibility were the case, Miss Adams would have heard Oswald ahead of her on the stairs, as the Warren Report admitted years earlier.

To his credit, Belin took three pages to reject Miss Adams. The Warren Report had done it in two paragraphs. Yet what seemed curious about Belin's exposé was the fact that a decade after the assassination, despite most having never even heard of someone named Victoria Adams, he chose to spend this much time on a witness deemed from the very start to have simply been mistaken.[9]

Belin seemed to be beating a dead horse.

"By now," he related after bidding Miss Adams adieu, "you have an insight into the method of our investigation."[10]

A pivotal moment in this madness occurred in March 1975 when, for the first time, the Abraham Zapruder film was shown on national television. The program was "Goodnight America," hosted by Geraldo Rivera. "I'm telling you right straight out," he warned, "that if you are at all sensitive, if you're at all queasy, then don't watch this film—put on the late-night movie because this is very heavy."[11]

And there it was again, fuzzy now in its televised format but certainly clear enough to bring to the public eye the supreme horror of it all, proving Rivera accurate in his admonition. The studio audience audibly gasped as Kennedy's head exploded. "That's the most horrifying thing I've ever seen in a movie," Rivera responded. "That's the most upsetting thing I've seen."

"Goodnight America" woke up the country.

Early in 1975, Pres. Gerald Ford directed that an inquiry be made into alleged illegal activities by the CIA within the United States. The result was the Rockefeller Commission. David Belin was appointed its executive director.

Its findings were startling. The CIA had engaged in domestic break-ins and had been spying on, while illegally opening the mail of, thousands of American citizens. Something sounded familiar about that.

Fascinating also were two other conclusions. The CIA did *not* have a hand in the death of President Kennedy. And Kennedy's backward motion shown in the Zapruder film was *not* caused by a frontal shot, as many by now suspected, but by a seizure-like reaction from instantaneous and massive damage to his brain.

Next came a Senate inquiry headed by Idaho senator Frank Church. The Church Committee began delving more deeply into the CIA's illegal activities. A special JFK Subcommittee, headed jointly by Pennsylvania senator Richard Schweiker and Colorado senator Gary Hart, was charged with taking a closer look at whether those activities might have had connections to Kennedy's murder.

Surfacing at this point too was the unusual disclosure that a Dallas FBI agent, James Hosty, Jr., had received a letter from Oswald only days before the assassination and had been ordered by his boss, Gordon Shanklin, to destroy it following Oswald's murder. Hosty flushed the letter down the toilet.[12]

Hosty's name, office address, telephone number, and license-plate number had appeared in Oswald's address book.[13] Oswald had made the notation after Hosty repeatedly tried to interview him in Dallas following Oswald's return from Russia. Curiously, the FBI removed the page containing the Hosty information before Oswald's address book was given to the Warren Commission. The Commission also was not made aware of Hosty's destruction of evidence.

Whether it was that disclosure, Watergate, sinister activities by the CIA, or the public revelation that even then-Pres. Lyndon Johnson did not fully believe the Warren Report, things started to boil in Washington. The Church Committee concluded its review and voted without objection on May 13, 1976, to recommend formation of a special congressional panel to once more probe the John Kennedy assassination. The Committee found that the CIA had more irons in the fire than first imagined.

Foremost, it had been involved with the Mafia in secret attempts to eliminate Cuban dictator Fidel Castro and had financed several anti-Castro organizations planning a second invasion of that island, against the explicit orders of President Kennedy that had been issued in the wake of the Cuban Missile Crisis. Not only did the CIA keep Kennedy in the dark about many of these operations, it also failed to disclose these secrets to an inquiring Warren Commission. This was especially disturbing since one of the Commission's members, Allen Dulles, had been director of the CIA during the period in question.[14]

Less than a month later, the Senate's JFK Subcommittee issued its report, which strongly suggested that a conspiracy had taken Kennedy's life.

In September 1976, after combining two formal resolutions that called for such, the House Select Committee on Assassinations (HSCA) was established, to once more investigate the death of President Kennedy. It would use the Warren Commission's earlier treatise as its benchmark.

When that announcement hit the headlines, it gave me hope. I quickly wrote a letter to the Committee. I brought up Victoria Adams, shared what I had discovered about her over the years, and pleaded for them to resolve once and for all her important timing questions. I suggested they also locate Sandra Styles.

I never received a reply.

Most of the Committee's efforts were conducted behind closed doors. But in late 1978, television sets across the nation began glowing with live broadcasts of selected public hearings. One of the more interesting people questioned was Marina Oswald.

Looking older than her thirty-seven years and sporting a new name by marriage, Mrs. Porter told the Committee that her former husband greatly admired President Kennedy and never once said anything bad about him.[15] "That is very hard for me to comprehend," she said, when asked why Oswald would shoot a man he respected.[16]

Oswald's unexpected visit to the Paine residence the evening before the assassination, she explained, was an attempt on his part to patch up an earlier argument between the couple. He seemed relaxed and calm that night, she said, and they talked about moving into their own apartment in Dallas. When Kennedy's impending visit came up, Mrs. Porter said Oswald appeared to know very little about it, changing the subject back to family matters.

Oswald went to bed before her, she said, and was asleep by the time she retired. She said she never saw him enter the garage during the evening, where the rifle was stored.

Oswald was occasionally abusive toward her, she admitted, and he did not have many friends. He read books profusely, admired Fidel Castro, and had, in fact, told her he was the one who shot at General Walker, comparing his intended victim to Adolf Hitler. She said, "He thought he was really doing good service to a country by eliminating a person like Mr. Walker."[17]

When asked if she thought her former husband killed Kennedy, she said she believed Oswald was capable of doing so. She also felt he was alone when he did it.

The Telltale Tape

One of the more interesting witnesses before the HSCA was J. Lee Rankin, the former general counsel for the Warren Commission. He expressed disappointment over "some of the things that have been revealed" about the FBI and the CIA—two agencies the Commission had depended on.[18]

From the beginning, he said, the Commission was under pressure to finish its investigation quickly for an "anxious" America. He said Earl Warren had initially told him the job would take "2 or 3 months at the outside."[19]

There was never any attempt by the Commission, he explained, to hide or withhold information concerning a possible conspiracy. Nor, for instance, did the Commission have concerns about where Oswald was heading when he left his rooming house, the assumption being he was merely trying to escape.[20] The Commission, he assured, made accurate conclusions, despite the criticism prevalent throughout the intervening years.

Next came Richard Helms, who was downright indignant at having to answer questions about his role as deputy director of covert operations for the CIA during 1962-65. Despite Church Committee revelations, Helms said that the CIA "did everything in its power to cooperate with the Warren Commission"[21] and that it "made a major effort to be as cooperative and prompt and helpful as possible."[22]

This spirit of teamwork, however, had its limits. Helms explained to the HSCA that when he appeared before the Commission in 1964, he was mute about the CIA's illegal activities toward Cuba:[23]

> I don't know what the Warren Commission knew. . . . I didn't inform them of these things, but they had among them as members Mr. Allen Dulles, who was certainly aware of what had been going on with respect

to Cuba; Senator [Richard] Russell of Georgia, the chairman of the Oversight Committee, who was also aware of what was going on with respect to Cuba; Mr. McCone who was director at the time, also knew what was happening. What the Commission knew from those gentlemen I don't know. I never spoke to them myself about it.[24]

In hindsight, keeping the Commission in the dark was "a mistake, no doubt about it," he admitted. "I think we should have shoved the whole thing over. I would have backed up a truck and taken all the documents down and put them on the Warren Commission's desk."[25]

Mysterious deaths also became an HSCA agenda item. After careful examination, the Committee found no basis to rumors those deaths were related to the assassination.[26]

It found nothing suspicious about the recent death of Mafia henchman Johnny Roselli, who had testified in June 1975 before the Church Committee that he was the go-between for CIA contacts with organized crime in the Castro assassination plots. What was left of his body was found stuffed into a drum and floating off the coast of Florida not long after.

Nor did the HSCA think it unusual that Mafia boss Sam Giancana died shortly before *he* was scheduled to appear at the Church Committee to discuss the CIA/Mafia working relationship. While fixing a meal in his home, he was shot once in the back of the head and six more times in and around his mouth.

Then there was George De Mohrenschildt, who supposedly committed suicide shortly after he was told of the Committee's interest in questioning him about his relationship with Oswald.[27] De Mohrenschildt, a former CIA contact at opposite ends of the social and financial spectrum from Oswald, nevertheless befriended the aloof and impoverished assassin and kept in regular contact with him after Oswald returned to Dallas from Russia.[28] Regarding De Mohrenschildt's sudden demise, the Committee acknowledged it required "further investigation."[29]

Up to this point, the Committee was reinforcing the Warren Commission's conclusions. The severe backward head motion experienced by Kennedy was attributed to a "neuromuscular reaction" and not a gunshot.[30] Neutron-activation analysis on Commission Exhibit 399 and other ballistics evidence showed a "high probability" Kennedy was struck by only two bullets and Connally by one, all coming from above and behind and all "most likely" from Oswald's rifle.[31] Even the bullet found in General Walker's home, unable to be traced to a source up to this point, became an "extremely likely" match with Oswald's ammunition.[32]

By December 1978, near the end of its existence, the Committee seemed poised to render a verdict that Oswald remained the sole guilty party. Then the other shoe dropped.

On December 29, one of the most controversial aspects of the HSCA investigation reared its ugly head. The deadly sounds of the assassination in Dealey Plaza may have been inadvertently recorded onto a Dallas Police tape when a microphone on a motorcycle in the motorcade became stuck in the "on" position.

Gary Mack, an assassination researcher in Dallas, already had done work in this area. In 1976, he had obtained a multi-generation copy of the Dallas Police radio transmissions for November 22. He began analyzing the tape to determine what was on it. What he found was an approximately eight-minute gap produced when the transmitter button on one of the motorcycle police radios became stuck.

Thinking the open microphone may have been in Dealey Plaza and perhaps had picked up the sounds of gunfire, Mack began to study the tape and enhance its sound qualities. A year later, his suspicions were confirmed. There were at least a half-dozen instances on the tape where he felt gunfire might have occurred.

Mack wrote about his findings in an August 1977 article published by Penn Jones, who had sold the *Midlothian Mirror* by then and started up a research newsletter called *The Continuing Inquiry*.[33] That article caught the attention of the HSCA, which found the *original* dispatch tape kept during the intervening years by a retired Dallas police officer. After extensive searching "for the best people in the acoustics field," the Committee hired the Cambridge, Massachusetts, firm of Bolt, Beranek & Newman (BBN) to conduct scientific analysis of the tape.[34]

That same firm had been responsible for analyzing a tape recording made during the Kent State shootings. BBN was able to determine from that study precisely which National Guardsman was the first to fire his rifle that day. BBN also was selected to assist in the examination of Watergate tapes made by President Nixon.

Under supervision by Dr. James E. Barger, BBN's chief scientist, Mack's efforts were confirmed. Preliminary analysis indicated there were six instances of impulses on the tape that might be attributable to recorded gunshots. Barger recommended onsite testing.

Just as the Warren Commission had done fourteen years earlier, the

Committee closed traffic to Dealey Plaza on August 20, 1978, as riflemen in the Depository and on the knoll fired live rounds into sandbags placed on Elm Street. Four target locations had been set up based on the Zapruder film. Thirty-six microphone positions spaced eighteen feet apart along the motorcade route recorded the sounds of 432 test shots. The objective was to see if any of these shooting patterns matched the pattern thought to be that of gunshots on the police tape.

Barger testified before the Committee on September 11 that although pattern matches did occur, the question remained whether the impulses on the police tape represented gunfire or some other noise. Barger could therefore only estimate that there was a fifty-fifty chance one of those impulses represented a shot from the grassy knoll.[35]

Realizing its importance, the Committee sought further analysis of the tape from two independent experts who had been recommended by the Acoustical Society of America. Prof. Mark Weiss and his assistant, Ernest Aschkenasy, were asked to refine Dr. Barger's work. Three months later, Weiss provided his results: "It is our conclusion that as a result of very careful analysis, it appears that with a probability of 95 percent or better, there was indeed a shot fired from the grassy knoll."[36]

His words had the effect of a lightning bolt.

Analysis indicated that four shots had been fired. The first originated from the Depository at 47 seconds past 12:30 P.M. Only 1.6 seconds later, a second shot was fired from the same building. Then 5.9 seconds elapsed before a third shot took place, this one from a position near the corner of the fence on the grassy knoll. A mere half-second later, a fourth shot occurred, again from the Depository.

Four shots indicated conspiracy. The 1.6-second gap between the first and second shots, compared with earlier FBI tests showing at least 2.3 seconds were necessary to fire two shots from Oswald's rifle, meant another shooter may have been in the Depository. The half-second between the third and fourth shots coincided with statements by numerous witnesses that two shots took place almost simultaneously.

Ironically, the sequence of shots based on the tape recording was precisely how S. M. Holland had described it to me in 1968.

Scientific study of the tape revealed that the motorcycle with the stuck microphone was about 120 feet behind the presidential limousine during the shooting. The two-wheeler was moving at eleven miles per hour, the speed of the motorcade. Analysis of photographs revealed the rider to be Officer H. B. McLain.[37]

Weiss told the Committee his work had been thorough. He and his partner had taken into consideration such variables as temperature and humidity, whether architectural changes had occurred between the date of the assassination and when the acoustical tests were performed, and possible distortions from either the transmitting microphone on the motorcycle or the recording machine at police headquarters. Even the windshield on the motorcycle and its effect at altering echoes of sound waves was factored into the analysis.

Weiss: Now, if there is any weakness in the results of our analysis, it has to be in some consideration that has escaped us entirely, and that, contrary to anything I can imagine, would have significant impact on the measurements we have made. We, in fact, in performing this work, made every single measurement there many times, each of us made the measurements on the map, checked the results of the other fellow's measurement, checked the calculations out many times, and just to be sure that there were no errors that had crept in and then propagated through this analysis. Otherwise, I really cannot see a basis for finding significant fault with the acoustical analysis as described.

[HSCA] *Chairman* [Louis] *Stokes:* Then as a scientist, you are comfortable with the statement to this Committee that beyond a reasonable doubt, and to a degree of 95 percent or better, there were four shots in Dealey Plaza?

Weiss: Well, I would agree with that, with the somewhat clarification, that since our work concentrated primarily on the third shot, the one from the grassy knoll area, I would imply for the moment, limit the statement to that, with a, again, a confidence level of 95 percent or higher, which I guess if I were a lawyer, I might well express as beyond a reasonable doubt, that shot took place.[38]

A Shot from the Knoll?

Weiss and Aschkenasy were, of course, questioned extensively by the Committee. They were granite. They reiterated that the four impulses were definitely gunshots and could not have been confused, for instance, with backfire from a passing vehicle, firecrackers, two cars colliding in a nearby parking lot, or a train going by in the railroad yards behind the knoll. When asked about abnormalities in other police conversations being heard during the gunshots, the scientists said audible clicks indicated others had been attempting to communicate at the same time. Also heard on the tape were the eerie and morbid sounds of a carillon, a bell not present in Dealey Plaza. The conversations by other officers located either in or outside Dealey Plaza, one of whom may have been near the ringing bell, could have resulted in the "crossover" sounds, Aschkenasy explained.

Weiss stated:

> But there are a number of times where you do hear other voices coming on, other people communicating, sometimes very distorted sounds of the voices, sometimes quite clear and intelligible, and it is all during the time that this one transmitter has been on. In fact, as you go on in time past the point at which the shots occur, the ability of other transmitters to come into the channel becomes increasingly—it occurs more frequently. You hear more people coming in. You hear comments to the effect that somebody has his microphone button stuck, and it is all audible and understandable so there are indeed several transmitters being received simultaneously during that period, and therefore it could very well have been that there was another motorcycle who happened to key on at just that point in time and picked up the sound of a bell.[39]

Could the sounds of gunfire have come from anywhere other than Dealey Plaza? The only other possibility, Aschkenasy said, was if those sounds were created at a site with *exact* replication of everything in and surrounding the real Dealey Plaza. "That is the only way it can come out," he emphasized.[40]

Aschkenasy assured everyone both he and Weiss "were totally independent of the Committee."[41] They had no preconceived notions about what they would find, they were not coerced or influenced in any way by any members of the Committee, and when they first sat down to listen to the tape, they felt "somebody has got to be kidding; this can't be gunshots."[42]

Aschkenasy continued:

> If I may say just one line, it's that the numbers could not be refuted. That was our problem. The numbers just came back again and again the same way, pointing only in one direction, as to what these findings were. There just didn't seem to be any way to make those numbers go away, no matter how hard we tried. It was not a question of interpretation of the

numbers; it was a question of what the analysis yielded, the mechanical analysis . . . and it all just came out the same way.[43]

Dr. James Barger of BBN, who months earlier gave a knoll shot a fifty-fifty possibility, was called back. After further review, Barger judged "the likelihood of there having been a gun shot from that knoll and received at that point now to be about 95 percent or possibly better."[44]

When asked if he was confident the tape contained the sound of gunfire, Barger replied unhesitatingly, "Quite confident, yes."[45]

As if this were not startling enough, the public hearings were brought to a close on December 28 with a cinematic coup de grace: another televised showing of the Zapruder film. This time, the film had a dubbed soundtrack of gunfire, timed to occur at the precise moments indicated on the Dallas Police tape.

Before the lights were dimmed in the Committee room, Chief Counsel G. Robert Blakey announced to those seated both there and in their homes that the film they were about to see "may be offensive to people of special sensitivity."[46] He was right. There had, in a way, been a false serenity to the earlier silence of the original Zapruder film. Now, with audio, the scene became all too real.

The sounds of four gunshots reverberating in Dealey Plaza matched perfectly with the reactions of Kennedy and Connally, the president's head snapping backward at the exact moment of the third and fourth shots, one determined by experts to have come from the knoll. Visually, at least, it now made sense.

With this bombshell in place, the Committee reexamined its previous medical and ballistics evidence, trying hard to make sense of it all. In the end, it came up with a new scenario for history, a *second* government version of how President Kennedy had been killed.

It placed Oswald in the window, alone. It said he fired the first shot, missing Kennedy entirely and failing even to hit the vehicle in which his target rode. It said he fired the second shot only 1.6 seconds later. The Committee made that assertion based on new testing showing the gun actually *could* be re-fired that fast if the shooter relied on the iron sights at the end of the barrel to key in on his mark rather than the telescopic sight. It had no way of knowing, of course, but it presumed Oswald did just that.

This second shot hit both Kennedy and Connally, going on to become the single bullet of "single-bullet theory" fame.

Then a third shot came from the knoll. It missed everybody. The Committee did not discuss this close-range incompetence or the possible identity of the shooter. It conceded, however, that Oswald and the knoll shooter had to know each other, since the chances were "extremely remote" that two strangers would unknowingly choose the same location at the same time on the same day to shoot the president of the United States.[47]

A half-second later, Oswald fired the fourth and final bullet, snuffing the breath out of Kennedy.

Because it had reached the end of its federally funded life, the Committee recommended that the U.S. Justice Department pick up the trail and seek out the identity of the elusive grassy-knoll shooter.

In the years that followed, the Committee's controversial conclusions underwent serious scrutiny and severe criticism. One of the oddest twists occurred in 1979 when a musician named Steve Barber bought an adult magazine that, as part of that month's featured highlights, had a recording of the Dallas Police tape included on a plastic insert. After listening to it, Barber somehow detected something the Committee's experts had missed.

He heard Sheriff Bill Decker. Decker was talking on a separate police channel from the motorcade's lead car, telling his men, "Hold everything secure." He uttered those words approximately one minute after the assassination, raising the question of how his voice could appear as "cross-talk" on the tape at the same time the impulses of shots were being recorded in Dealey Plaza some sixty seconds earlier.

The Justice Department eventually entered the fray when it pulled together twelve distinguished individuals from the National Academy of Sciences (NAS) to study the Committee's acoustical work and check out Barber's discovery. Called the Ramsey Panel after its chairman, Harvard professor Norman Ramsey, the group ultimately issued a ninety-six-page report confirming Barber's analysis and condemning the Committee's. It reached three unanimous conclusions: 1) Weiss, Aschkenasy, and Barger committed "serious errors" in their work. 2) The impulses attributed to gunshots were actually from other unknown sounds recorded a minute *after* the assassination from an unspecified location other than Dealey Plaza. 3) "Reliable acoustical data" thus negated there being a second gunman.[48]

Although the NAS suggested other avenues where still further studies of the police tape could be made, it felt because the evidence against there being a grassy-knoll shooter was so strong that "the results to be expected from such studies would not justify their cost."[49]

Because the NAS was a congressionally chartered agency, critics charged its study with bias and said those who conducted the NAS tests were not qualified acoustic experts. In addition, critics felt the NAS had not conclusively explained how Sheriff Decker's voice had gotten on the Dallas Police tape in the first place or why other cross-talk also on the tape contradicted the NAS results. Left unanswered too, they said, was how the timing and sequencing of the impulses on the tape matched with other corroborating evidence—the Zapruder film, the three rifle casings in the Depository, the exact location and speed of the suspected motorcycle, the testimony of witnesses—and precisely represented a blueprint of echo patterns unique only to Dealey Plaza.

Nevertheless, the Justice Department accepted the NAS findings. It refused to look into the matter further. Its huge metal doors in Washington, above which still reads the motto, *The Place of Justice is a Hallowed Place*, would clang shut as far as President Kennedy's assassination was concerned.

Suddenly, America was confronted with *two* official solutions to the murder.

I remembered the words of Rep. Richardson Preyer as he questioned J. Lee Rankin about the corner the Warren Commission had been boxed into.

Preyer: But you were somewhat in the position of asking the FBI to investigate itself, or going to the innkeeper to ask whether the wine was good or not.

Rankin: Well, back at that time, Congressman, that did not seem so impossible as it might today.

Preyer: Yes, I think your answer to an earlier question has demonstrated a certain fall from innocence that we have all had since that time. Things are now believable which we would not have thought believable at that time.

Rankin: That is correct.[50]

Indeed, many of us had suffered a "fall from innocence."

Like the parlor game where facts of a story are altered the more times it is whispered into the ears of those participating, the layers of disagreement and disparity were gradually obscuring the truth to

Kennedy's death, whatever that truth may have been at the start. Was finding the truth even possible anymore?

It was at this point that I felt that I'd seen and heard enough. I felt as Terry had those many years ago after seeing the Zapruder film in Washington.

And then came still another death. Penn Jones would not chronicle this one, for this time it was not a witness to the assassination. It was someone else, someone more important to me.

He had been the one to provide continual encouragement, the only one who knew me well enough to understand my true motives in all this, the one who pushed me to keep going, keep growing, keep searching for the truth. I watched numbly as my father was put into the ground.

Mortality suddenly became an issue.

It was 1981, approaching two decades beyond the assassination. The country had two government-conceded solutions to the crime. No one seemed to care.

The research community lacked luster, cohesiveness, and the mutual support I had once been proud it possessed, proud actually to be a part of. All that seemed to remain in these days were the pseudo-researchers, who expounded on ridiculous and wild-eyed theories to the crime, branding not only themselves but everyone else as kooks.

Victoria Adams was lost, my efforts to find her fruitless and wasted. There were no leads. At this point, I had lost my focus, perhaps even my determination.

Maybe Terry had been right after all. I began to wonder if any of this was really worth it anymore.

Then, when I stopped wondering, I quit.

CHAPTER 17

February 1981–October 1998

Victoria Adams had settled down. The memories of Dallas—and the fears those memories generated—had all but vanished. Like tossing an extra blanket over the bed on a cold winter's night, she buried them deep, out of sight.

She didn't even have dreams about that day anymore.

She was in the Great Northwest now, even farther removed than before. First it was Spokane, then Seattle. She liked this part of the country. It was clean here, safe, even peaceful.

It was a place where one could establish roots, if one chose. And she did, for nearly a decade.

She'd stuck it out with her real-estate career too, making the kinds of business decisions that would gain her listings in *Who's Who of American Women* and *Who's Who in the World*. She had found her niche.

Then one day she got the urge to move again. Only this time, it was different. No longer was it that sudden impulse to flee; now it was simply a desire to see.

She was getting older, approaching midlife. She wanted to travel America's highways, view the country up close and personal, drink in its sights and feast on its diversity. For the next six years, she and her husband did just that and only that. They moved about from coast to coast in a five-wheel trailer. She enjoyed every minute of it.

She had always wanted to be a writer, getting a taste of it during her high-school years when she worked and wrote for the *Monitor*, a small Catholic newspaper in San Francisco. Now on the road, she wrote and published a newsletter called *Principles in Action*. It was a diary of sorts, a chronicle of the people and stories she met and heard along the way.

Next came the idea of writing a cookbook. The result was a collection of simple but appealing recipes gathered from those who lived beside the blue roads of the land. The title was *No More Than 4 Ingredients*, and it sold well along the way, providing the extra income that kept this pair of gypsies going.

She loved seeing her country, traveling through nearly all of the contiguous states. By 1997, she had made her way east to Pennsylvania, where the rolling farmland of the central region appealed to her eyes and the simple lives of the Amish appealed to her sense of balance. She became so enamored with the area that she remained there for several months, living near Harrisburg, the state capital, dining in that city and savoring its surrounding attractions.

Then it was over, the journey finished. Reality returned, and so did the itinerant duo—back to the Northwest and the utility bills, the mortgage, the car payments, the humdrum of everyday life.

That would suit Victoria Adams just fine. There would be few changes, few interruptions, few things to remind her of her past, at least for a few more years.

CHAPTER 18

January 1991–March 1994

I had finally settled down and moved to a bucolic place called Harrisburg, the capital of Pennsylvania. During this period came the uproar over Oliver's Stone's latest film, *JFK—The Movie*. It was his version of a heroic but still defeated Jim Garrison. Although Stone said he based his storyline on the historical record, there were plenty of Hollywood exceptions. Yet the film generated excitement, not only in the media but also with uninformed citizens swayed by its sensationalism.[1]

A friend of mine who knew of my past even asked that I conduct a seminar to discuss what was and wasn't accurate in the movie. When he advertised that event, the local press was on me with questions. I had come home once more.

If nothing else, *JFK* quickly attracted a large number of outspoken but temporary adherents. Like the market for literary morbidity opened by the House Select Committee's conclusion that Kennedy was likely killed by conspiracy, Stone's portrayal opened the doors to even more authors bent on contributing their most outlandish "solutions" to the crime. Television networks showed renewed interest, and the writings of many "pioneer" critics were reprinted. This wave of questioning would not last long, but while it did, an unexpected change in the government's attitude took place.

All at once, previously withheld Kennedy assassination documents started to be released. On October 26, 1992, then-Pres. George Bush affixed his name to the liberating legislation, officially called the President John F. Kennedy Assassination Records Collection Act.

Less than a year earlier, if he was to be believed, the same President Bush was unsure which government body had locked away the information in the first place. Bush had not read "the speculation about this new movie," he told *People* magazine when asked in December 1991 about Stone's *JFK*. "Nobody has come into this office with serious— with any—questions about the findings of the, what was it, the Warren Commission? So I don't spend any time thinking about it."[2]

The movie encouraged me to visit Harold Weisberg. I had kept in touch with him over the years but only by letter and telephone. For the first time in years, I looked at the man in a different way, realizing how old he had suddenly become.

Aware of my disillusionment with assassination research, he nevertheless encouraged me to get back into the saddle. Much needed to be done, he said, especially since more and more documents were being released. Health concerns prevented him from traveling to the Archives.

He wanted me to wear his shoes.

Weisberg could talk me into anything: an interview with Bill Decker, assignments that got me followed and my phone tapped, a search for Kennedy's death certificate. That evening I began to pull some dusty books from my shelves.

As I had done earlier—what was it now, twenty-four years ago?—I started with the government's version, this time the House Select Committee's final report. Like the Warren Commission, the HSCA had compiled its own set of accompanying volumes of evidence, but fortunately only twelve of them.

The HSCA Report was impressive. It tackled many of the questions left hanging by the Warren Commission. It also created a few of its own.

Unlike its predecessor, the Committee used "scientific analysis of physical evidence" to place Oswald on the sixth floor of the Depository.[3] That evidence, the Committee said, was substantial. For instance, fingerprint experts confirmed that the paper sack found near the southeast corner window, and "suitable for containing a rifle, showed a latent palmprint and fingerprint of Oswald."[4] Several cartons stacked next to that window also revealed incriminating evidence, one holding a palm print and fingerprint and another just a palm print. All of them belonged to Oswald.[5]

"The Committee was aware that Oswald's access to the sixth floor during the normal course of his duties would have provided the opportunity to handle these items at any time before the assassination," the HSCA Report conceded. "Nevertheless, the Committee believed that the way the boxes were stacked at the window and the proximity of the paper sack to the window from which the shots were fired must be considered as evidence indicating that he handled the boxes in the process of preparing the so-called sniper's nest and that he had used the paper sack to carry the rifle into the Depository."[6]

Other fingerprints were found there too. Speaking little of the care exhibited by police, the majority of those prints belonged to Dallas Police Detective Robert Studebaker.[7] Strangely, additional prints remained unidentifiable, despite comparison fingerprints taken from more than a dozen Depository employees and other policemen.[8]

This was not unusual, the Warren Report concluded years earlier, "since these cartons contained commercial products which had been handled by many people throughout the normal course of manufacturing, warehousing, and shipping."[9] But the Report contradicted itself on this issue when it stated some three hundred pages later that because cardboard is an absorbent material, "Tests run by the FBI show that usually a latent impression on such cardboard cannot be developed by powder more than 24 hours after it is made."[10]

This latter conclusion was the one used to confirm that Oswald had handled the boxes recently.

HSCA handwriting analysis established it was Oswald who had ordered and purchased the murder weapon through the mail.[11] Photographic analysis established it was Oswald holding that weapon in a picture taken by his wife prior to the assassination.[12] Similar analysis confirmed it was Oswald's rifle, not a 7.65 German Mauser, that was stashed on the sixth floor.[13] Neutron-activation analysis linked his weapon to a recovered whole bullet and fragments.[14]

Evidence seemed strong that Oswald's rifle was the one used and that he was, at some point at least, on the sixth floor. Absent, however, was substantiation that Oswald actually fired the gun that day. Missing too was any evidence putting Oswald on the sixth floor at the crucial time of 12:30 P.M.

The Committee was faced with conflicting witnesses who said they had seen Oswald on the first, fifth, and sixth floors shortly before noon on November 22. It resolved this touchy matter simply by deciding "not to try to reconcile the testimony of these witnesses."[15] Instead, it admitted that since no one said they saw Oswald at the exact moment of the assassination, and no one claimed to have been on the sixth floor during the shooting, then no one really knew exactly where Oswald was. Therefore, "he could have still been on the sixth floor at 12:30."[16]

Despite that kind of logic, one thing was for certain. Oswald wasn't watching the assassination from the front steps of the building, as many critics continued to claim. The Committee cited forensic anthropologists who said photographs of lookalikes Billy Lovelady and Oswald confirmed "the man in the doorway bore a much stronger resemblance to Lovelady than to Oswald."[17] The pattern of the shirt worn by the doorway man "corresponded more closely with the shirt worn that day by Lovelady."[18]

Plus, Lovelady admitted to being there.[19]

The most questionable part about putting Oswald behind the rifle on the sixth floor was the Committee's use of testimony that said he was spotted afterward in the second-floor lunchroom. How his presence in the lunchroom proved he was four flights above as the president drove by was not made clear. The Committee cited three "particularly significant" witnesses in an attempt to justify its odd reasoning.[20]

"Depository Superintendent Roy Truly and Dallas Police Officer M. L. Baker both entered the Depository right after the shots were fired," the HSCA explained. "They encountered Oswald on the second floor, and in testimony to the Warren Commission, they gave the time as 2 to 3 minutes after the shots."[21]

As a footnote to that "2 to 3 minutes" reference, the reader is directed to the Warren Commission testimony of both Baker and Truly. Yet the footnote does not pinpoint where in the combined fifty-eight pages of testimony of those men that the actual "2 to 3 minutes" reference is made.

That is because it doesn't exist. Baker's only mention of timing refers to the FBI reconstructions of his movements from outside the Depository to the second-floor lunchroom: one minute thirty seconds on the first attempt, one minute fifteen seconds on the second.[22] Truly gave times as one minute eighteen seconds and one minute fifteen seconds.[23]

Neither one referred to a window of "2 to 3 minutes." Even the Warren Report did not offer a "2 to 3 minutes" timeframe.

Why the Committee added more time onto what Baker and Truly said took place is a mystery. That exaggeration is even more confusing when the HSCA Report cites its third "significant" witness: "A witness who personally knew Oswald, Mrs. Robert A. Reid, also a Depository employee, testified to the Warren Commission that she also saw him on the second floor approximately 2 minutes after the assassination."[24]

Mrs. Reid had, in fact, used that two-minute figure in her Warren Commission testimony.[25] But her sighting occurred *after* Oswald paused to purchase a Coca-Cola from a soda machine, according to the Warren Report; *after* Oswald's confrontation with Baker; and *after* he then walked into her office down the hall from the lunchroom. If she saw him two minutes *after* the assassination, her timing actually fits better with Baker's and Truly's initial estimates before the Commission that they encountered Oswald in the lunchroom some ninety seconds or less after the shooting and not the Committee's "2 to 3 minute" remark.

Forgetting this obvious contradiction, the HSCA Report concluded, "The testimony of these three witnesses was mutually corroborating. Since all were outside the Depository when the shots were fired, their statements that it took them about 2 minutes to get to the second floor were reasonable. It appeared equally reasonable that in those same 2 minutes Oswald could have walked from the sixth floor window to the rear stairway and down four flights of stairs to the second floor."[26]

"The conclusion with respect to this evidence alone was not that Lee Harvey Oswald was the assassin," the HSCA summed up, "but merely that the testimony of these witnesses appeared credible and was probative on the question of Oswald's whereabouts at the time of the assassination."[27]

The HSCA Report admitted its awareness of contrary arguments as to when and how the paths of Oswald, Baker, and Truly crossed. (Was this a veiled reference to Victoria Adams?) But on-site tests, it explained, support the Committee's contention Oswald arrived on the second floor from the sixth floor.

"The Committee traveled to Dallas and toured the Texas state book Depository building [sic]. During those visits, the times required to reach the second floor from both the street and the sixth floor were determined. The Committee found that the testimony of Truly and Baker does not preclude a finding that Oswald was on the sixth floor at the time the shots were fired."[28]

The times the Committee "determined" or the methods used to conduct those tests were not included in its published evidence.

Curious also was the complete absence of inquiry into Victoria Adams. Yet the Committee was clearly aware of who she was, what she had said, and what she had done. Based on internal working papers, the HSCA was also interested in the timing of her trip down the stairs.

For instance, it reprinted in full Wesley Liebeler's critiquing memorandum, which discussed the confusion over how the Warren Report had handled Miss Adams.[29] It also possessed an August 8, 1964, memo written by Warren Commission staffer Howard Willens, who, commenting on how the matter of Oswald's descent from the sixth floor could be handled, suggested, "the Commission could rely on some witnesses and *reject the testimony of others, such as Victoria Adams* [author's emphasis]."[30]

Despite its apparent disregard in the printed record, at least someone on the HSCA staff showed more than just a passing interest in Miss Adams. That person requested copies of her original testimony before the Warren Commission. And the copies that had been requested were only of that portion where she discussed when she left the window and the timing of her descent.[31]

The HSCA Is "Deeply Troubled"

"The Committee found that while most of the Depository employees were outside of the building at the time of the assassination and returned inside afterwards, Oswald did the reverse; he was inside before the assassination and afterward he went outside," the HSCA observed. "Every other Depository employee either had an alibi for the time of the assassination or returned to the building immediately thereafter. Oswald alone neither remained nor had an alibi."[32]

Actually, he did have an alibi. He told police he was eating lunch on the first floor when the shots were fired, then went up the stairs to get a drink in the second-floor lunchroom. Of course, no one believed him.

"That Oswald left the building within minutes after the assassination was significant," the Committee concluded.[33]

The HSCA Report neglected Roger Craig's statement of seeing a man similar to Oswald fleeing in a station wagon.[34] Nor did it address the many inconsistencies in Oswald's outbound journey. Instead, it merely said Oswald boarded a bus, took a taxi to his rooming house, changed clothes, and then walked nine-tenths of a mile to his encounter with Tippit.

Scientific analysis by the HSCA "determined positively" that the four cartridge cases found in the bushes near where Officer Tippit was slain had all been fired from the pistol removed from Oswald's possession when he was arrested thirty-five minutes later in the Texas Theatre.[35] As it turned out, those shell casings—the ones tossed aside in front of several gaping witnesses—were the only ballistics link between Oswald's gun and the shooting. Since Oswald's revolver had been "partially modified" to use different ammunition, scientific analysis of the bullets recovered from Tippit's body was *not* able to conclude they had been fired from Oswald's gun. All the Committee could do was say those bullets "were consistent with their having been fired from Oswald's revolver."[36]

Did Oswald possess a capacity for violence? "The presence of such a trait would not, in and of itself, prove much," the Committee reasoned, but the absence of that character flaw "would be inconsistent" with what Oswald was accused of.[37]

The Committee said Oswald shot Tippit with a display of extreme overkill, tried to shoot other officers during his arrest, and attempted to kill Gen. Edwin Walker.[38] He seemed fully capable of assassinating the president.

But the Walker matter begged for more clarification. Despite scientific analysis, examination of the "bullet fragment" removed from the wall in Walker's home showed only "characteristics similar to bullets fired from Oswald's Mannlicher-Carcano rifle."[39] The Committee's use of the term "bullet fragment" implied that only a small portion of the projectile had been recovered. But a check of the final report of the Committee's Firearms Panel reveals that what was actually examined was a nearly whole "full metal jacketed, lead core bullet" that weighed "147.1" of the 162 grains usually found in 6.5 Mannlicher-Carcano ammunition.[40]

"In addition," the Committee continued, "neutron activation analysis of this fragment confirmed that it was probably a Mannlicher- bullet [*sic*]."[41]

How could sophisticated neutron-activation testing of a nearly whole bullet *confirm* only that it was *probably* from Oswald's gun?

The Committee admitted it was aware that two people were seen driving around Walker's home in a suspicious manner two days before the shooting, and more than one person was seen leaving after the shot was fired. "These statements have never been substantiated, and the case remains unsolved," the Committee said.[42] As to whether Oswald may have had associates in the Walker matter, the Committee acknowledged, "No leads were developed, and this line of inquiry was abandoned."[43]

There was even more. As mentioned, S. M. Holland's description of the shots fit nicely with the Committee's acoustical sequence. Yet the Committee could not verify his sighting of smoke, stating, "None of the photographs of the grassy knoll that were analyzed by the photographic evidence panel revealed any evidence of a puff of smoke or flash of light, as reported by several people in the crowd."[44]

The Committee admitted to being "deeply troubled" by Oswald's murder and, after investigating it, disagreed with the Warren Commission's conclusion as to how Ruby gained access to the Dallas Police basement. According to the Warren Report, Ruby entered without assistance, "probably" by walking down the Main Street ramp.[45] It based that conclusion solely on Ruby's own version of events, while ignoring, according to the HSCA, the "eyewitness testimony of every witness in the relevant area."[46]

The conclusion of the HSCA was that Ruby entered the police station, with aid from a mysterious helper, by way of a less conspicuous doorway from an adjacent alley, then headed down to the basement area, where the shooting took place. Although who provided the aid was not made clear, the HSCA Report implied it came from police personnel, adding "the assistance may have been provided with no knowledge of Ruby's intentions."[47]

The Committee went on to say it did not believe Ruby's act of vengeance was a burst of spontaneity but rather "involved at least some premeditation."[48]

The Committee also was "troubled" by Ruby's close proximity to Oswald during a press conference at the police station on Friday night and by his appearance Saturday in Dealey Plaza when Oswald originally was scheduled for transfer to the county jail. "These sightings . . . could indicate that Ruby was pursuing Oswald's movements throughout the weekend."[49]

Was Lee Oswald a spy? The HSCA found "no credible evidence" he was connected with the FBI or CIA. Jack Ruby, however, was a different matter.

On nine separate occasions prior to the assassination, the FBI made contact with the nightclub owner in an attempt to enlist him as an agency informant, because of his knowledge of "criminal elements in Dallas."[50] Those attempts apparently failed.[51]

The Committee did level some criticism at the FBI, though. It said the FBI's limited efforts to determine if a conspiracy existed were "seriously flawed"[52] and "deficient."[53] The Committee found that, even though the bureau had specialists on Cuban affairs, the FBI hardly examined Oswald's much-publicized activities along that line.[54] And the agency focused its efforts too narrowly on Oswald, and "the critical early period of the FBI's investigation was conducted in an atmosphere of considerable haste and pressure from Hoover to conclude the investigation in an unreasonably short period of time," the Committee determined. "The committee also noted that Hoover's personal predisposition that Oswald had been a lone assassin affected the course of the investigation, adding to the momentum to conclude the investigation after limited consideration of possible conspiratorial areas."[55]

In addition, the Committee described the relationship between the Warren Commission and the FBI as being "distinctly adversarial and that there were limited areas in which the FBI did not provide complete information to the Commission and other areas in which the bureau's information was misleading."[56]

The CIA wasn't off the hook either. Overall, the Committee described the CIA's assistance to the Commission as "inconsistent with the spirit of" the investigation,[57] mainly because of that agency's don't-say-a-word-unless-specifically-asked attitude. That policy, for example, was how the CIA justified silence about its super-secret alliance with the Mafia over a plan to get rid of Fidel Castro.[58]

The Secret Service, according to the Committee, failed to adequately respond to threatening information it possessed prior to the Dallas trip, was not prepared to defend the president against sniper attack, and relinquished its role too quickly when the FBI took over the Commission's investigative work.

The Committee also found "regrettable" the fact that the Department of Justice did not take on a more supervisory role over the FBI. "The promise of what the department might have realized in fact was great," the Committee wrote, "particularly in the use of such evidence-gathering tools such [sic] as a grand jury and grants of immunity."[59]

Government agencies had, in fact, performed poorly.

As for the Warren Commission, the Committee concluded it had shown little initiative. It relied too heavily on the FBI and CIA, the very agencies that ended up deceiving it.

The Commission's inquiry "was conducted in good faith, competently, and with high integrity, but . . . the Warren Report was not, in some respects, an accurate presentation of all the evidence available to the Commission or a true reflection of the scope of the Commission's work, particularly on the issue of possible conspiracy in the assassination," the Committee determined. "It is a reality to be regretted that the Commission failed to live up to its promise."[60]

Did the HSCA live up to its own promise? When formed, the Committee established three questions it felt obligated to answer to fulfill its legislative mandate: What kind of a job did federal agencies do in their investigation of the assassination? Was there a conspiracy? Who murdered Kennedy?

Federal agencies, the Committee found, did not do well. In practically every instance, there appeared to be deception and disguise, not only in information presented to the Warren Commission but also in what the Warren Commission presented to the public.

As to question two, the Committee agreed there was a near certainty that a conspiracy existed.

Who did it? The Committee still declared it to be Oswald, a crazed little man bounced around like a pinball in life's game, seeking nothing but notoriety. He was proficient enough to kill Kennedy from his sixth-floor perch. The grassy-knoll gunman simply missed.

The question remains, however, that if Oswald sought only stardom—his personal fifteen minutes of fame, so to speak—wouldn't he have wanted to do his deed alone? Wouldn't a knoll shooter have negated Oswald's selfish and solitary attempt at self-aggrandizement, especially if the knoll shooter was accurate and Oswald was not?

Where was the evidence that Oswald actually pulled the trigger or was even on the sixth floor at the time of the shooting? Try as they might, the Warren Commission and now the HSCA could at best only surmise he had been there and done that. Every bit of evidence used to place Oswald on the sixth floor, as a Warren Commission attorney frankly admitted years earlier, was merely "circumstantial."[61]

CHAPTER 19

April 1994–April 1999

"The Commission's first client is the public," wrote Alfred Goldberg, a historian charged with helping compose what would soon become the Warren Report, the official and, as it turned out, the first of the government's versions of who shot John Kennedy.[1] Those were lofty words and among the first I read as I found myself journeying back to the National Archives to examine some of the newly released documents.

Goldberg's pledge opened a four-page memorandum to General Counsel J. Lee Rankin. Rankin had asked Goldberg for his thoughts on how to pull together into readable form the mass of evidence the Warren Commission was acquiring. He also wanted Goldberg's feelings on how the final product might be received.

"This public," Goldberg thought, "consists primarily of some millions of intelligent and reasonably educated people in the United States and abroad who are waiting to be informed of the facts of the assassination of President Kennedy and the conclusion of the Commission as to who did it and why."[2] Goldberg predicted the Report was destined to become "a major historical document" and "the definitive history of the event."[3] Therefore, its value "will rest ultimately on the extent to which the information is complete and on the skill and judgement [sic] with which it is evaluated," he said. "Clear evidence is the only means by which to establish historical facts, and this report must speak to the public through facts that are arranged, emphasized, and generalized to give meaning to confused and confusing happenings.

"It is the professional and patriotic duty, and the announced intention, of the Commission Staff to tell the whole truth about the assassination of President Kennedy. There is complete agreement that the report must be as honest, accurate, and objective as it is humanly possible to make it. It must include both sides of issues and clearly distinguish fact from hypothesis.[4]

"The requirement for accuracy," he emphasized, "is so paramount that it cannot be exaggerated."[5]

190

Goldberg's noble words were written in April 1964, five months before the Warren Report went to print. What, then, happened to those well-intentioned goals during that intervening period? Why did the Commission's crowning work contain unclear evidence and inaccuracies, the exact opposite of what should have been its hallmark? Why had it not become the "definitive history of the event"?

Was it because the "skill and judgement" of the Commission and its staff were lacking? How could that be, though? These were trained and honorable men, selected specifically because they were among the best and brightest in their chosen fields, clear thinkers and very responsible too.

There were a couple of laxities, such as when Commission member Gerald Ford took classified documents to include in the first chapter of his upcoming book, or when member Hale Boggs carelessly left top-secret papers exposed on the front seat of his car. Those were but minor improprieties.

Goldberg's prophecy for a "definitive history of the event" was attainable only if *all* the information was available for the Commission to judge and evaluate. An outburst by Sen. Richard Russell at an early Commission meeting, however, seemed prophetic:

> I have never been able to understand why it is that every agency acts like it's the sole agency in the Government. There is very little interchange of information between the departments in the United States Government. The entire view is that they are a separate, closed department, and there is no interchange of information.[6]

Russell would be proven correct. Both the CIA and FBI, for example, considered activities of the Fair Play for Cuba Committee (FPCC) to be a serious threat to the internal security of the United States. Both agencies were conducting active investigations into that faction. The FBI, in particular, singled out the FPCC as requiring "intensive coverage" because it was "the principal outlet of pro-Castro propaganda and agitation."[7]

Yet neither the CIA nor FBI exchanged notes or compared their individual results.

Was Oswald a member of the FPCC? He said he was. Authorities and the media certainly used that fact against him. Yet if he had such an allegiance and the FBI knew of it, why wasn't he included on that agency's list of security risks, as every other member of the FPCC had been?

This is an odd omission, since Oswald's background included a lengthy stay in Russia, a conspicuous detail of which the Communist-hating FBI was aware. And during the summer of 1963, the FBI also knew he was in New Orleans, a vitriolic hotbed of *anti*-Castro activities, proclaiming himself to be the head of the FPCC's local chapter.

When it came to Pres. Lyndon Johnson, the FBI had no problem sharing what it knew about Oswald only hours after the assassination. In an unsigned memo addressed modestly to "Mr. Johnson" on November 22, 1963, the bureau listed five points concerning the suspected assassin, including the error that Oswald had visited the Soviet Embassy in Washington, D.C.,[8] had been arrested for disturbing the peace in New Orleans, and had received a dishonorable military discharge. It also noted the following:

"4. Reported to drink to excess and to be wife beater.

5. Present Status: Arrested in connection with killing of Dallas policeman. *No direct link with assassination* [author's emphasis]."[9]

FBI Director J. Edgar Hoover certainly did not feel that Oswald had "no direct link" to the president's murder. Upon learning Kennedy had died, Hoover told Dallas Special Agent in Charge Gordon Shanklin to "go all out on this and find out who did it."[10] Less than an hour later, however, Hoover was on the phone to Attorney General Robert Kennedy, telling him he "thought we had the man who killed the President" and adding, "we have had a case on Oswald as he has been involved in the Fair Play for Cuba Committee."[11]

If Hoover knew of Oswald's FPCC involvement, why wasn't Oswald listed as a security risk? Why wasn't that information passed along to the Secret Service and local police authorities in advance of the president's trip to Dallas?

Not long after that, Hoover described Oswald as being "in the category of a nut and the extremist pro-Castro crowd."[12]

And when an FBI agent only hours after the assassination suggested the bureau look into the possibility that a member of the National States Rights Party was involved, Hoover responded, "Not necessary to cover as true subject located."[13] However, at that time, Oswald had not yet been charged with the crime.

J. Edgar Hoover, of course, wanted his own agency to singly investigate and write the final chapter on Kennedy's murder. He wanted to tout the fact that his men had quickly solved the case. He was therefore not pleased to hear on November 25, the day of Kennedy's funeral, of a planned *Washington Post* editorial calling for a "Presidential Commission" to probe the assassination.

One of his assistant directors quickly telephoned the *Post*'s managing editor, advising him that such an opinionated piece would "muddy the waters and would create further confusion and hysteria."[14] The FBI, the caller explained to the *Post*, was conducting a "swift and intensive" investigation in which "no stone is to be left unturned," and the results would be shared with the public and would "lay to rest any rumors of substance that had been flying around."[15]

When the *Post* remained unconvinced and said it was moving ahead with the story anyway, Assistant Attorney General Nicholas deB. Katzenbach intervened, going directly to the paper's editor. He asked that the story be quashed. This time it worked.

The next day, Hoover relayed to the White House his success at having "killed the editorial in the *Post*."[16] He also said his FBI had turned up evidence of only three shots, adding, "We have one complete bullet found on the stretcher on which the President was carried into the hospital, which apparently fell out of the President's head."[17]

According to Hoover, the only question remaining was who should publicly issue the FBI's conclusions—the Justice Department or the White House. President Johnson's thoughts, at that moment, were elsewhere. He was considering turning the whole mess over to the State of Texas.

Hoover quite naturally was aghast.

Curiously, Katzenbach was perhaps the earliest and strongest proponent of a Presidential Commission, despite his influence in "killing" the *Post* editorial.

During his HSCA appearance years later, Katzenbach said he "thought very early that such a Commission was essential . . . that such a Commission should be formed of people of impeccable integrity, people who would search for the truth and who would make that truth public because I did not believe that if it remained entirely within the executive branch that that effect could ever be achieved as far as the general public here or abroad was concerned."[18]

He "never intended at any point that the investigation done by the FBI would be a substitute for the kind of investigation of President Kennedy's assassination."[19]

Katzenbach was in a tough spot, though. In Robert Kennedy's absence, he was running the show at Justice, the supposed overseers of the FBI.

"My awkwardness," he explained, "was because it was perfectly obvious to anybody who knew anything about the Federal Bureau of Investigation that they were certain to resent the appointment of any such commission . . . and if I were thought to be the source of that or to recommend that, then it would very seriously affect my relations with Mr. Hoover and the Bureau."[20]

Nevertheless, on November 25, Katzenbach penned a two-page memorandum to Johnson aide Bill Moyers, "exerting tremendous pressure,"[21] as the HSCA would later describe it, to form "a Presidential Commission of unimpeachable personnel to review and examine the evidence and announce its conclusions."[22]

Katzenbach said, "The public must be satisfied that *Oswald was the assassin*; that he did not have confederates who are still at large; and that the evidence was such that he would have been convicted at trial [author's emphasis].

"Speculation about Oswald's motivation ought to be cut off . . . ," he went on. "Unfortunately the facts on Oswald seem about too pat—too obvious (Marxist, Cuba, Russian wife, etc). . . . The matter has been handled thus far with neither dignity nor conviction."[23] He suggested a quick response "to head off public speculation or Congressional hearings of the wrong sort."[24]

Critics later charged that this memo signaled a rush to judgment against Oswald.

While the White House secretly considered Katzenbach's proposal, Hoover continued his own agenda.

"Seems to me we have the basic facts now," he wrote four days after the assassination.[25]

Two weeks later, the FBI Summary Report was born, with its conclusion that Oswald was the sole assassin. Instead of laying rumors to rest, as promised, it generated its own, especially with the conclusion that Kennedy was hit by two bullets and Connally by a separate third.

That three-for-three logic disregarded two questions: how James Tague, the bystander, was wounded by a missed shot, and how Kennedy and Connally could have been hit by separate bullets in less time than it took to fire Oswald's rifle twice. The FBI's Summary Report, therefore, implied a second assassin.

The dilemma over who would release that report became moot.

Johnson by now had been swayed into creating the Warren Commission. Adding insult to injury, one of the Commission's first moves was to reject going public with Hoover's Summary Report, choosing instead to use it only as a foundation to the Commission's inquiry.

It was clear in the beginning that the Commission had serious doubts about the FBI's three-shots, three-hits scenario.

[John] *McCloy:* This bullet business leaves me confused.

Chairman [Warren]: It's totally inconclusive.

[Sen. Richard] *Russell:* They couldn't find where one bullet came out that struck the President and yet they found a bullet in the stretcher.[26] . . .

[Rep. Hale] *Boggs:* And this business about where the bullets penetrated the President's body, speculation about the wound in the throat, the hole in the windshield.

McCloy: That is very unsatisfactory.

[Rep. Gerald] *Ford:* I thought it was a narrative that was interesting to read but it did not have the depth that it ought to have.[27] . . .

Boggs: Well, this FBI report doesn't clear it up.

Chairman: It doesn't do anything.

Boggs: It raises a lot of new questions in my mind.[28]

Ironically, the FBI was called on to resolve the very problems it was accused of creating. In hindsight, it became in HSCA member Richardson Preyer's eyes the "innkeeper" summoned to appraise his own wine.

As expected, the innkeeper objected. The Commission asked the FBI, for example, to determine how fast the presidential automobile was traveling while it was under fire. When an agent alerted Hoover to the request, Hoover replied, "O.K. It seems like a lot of poppy cock to me."[29]

Even though the Commission rejected the FBI's version of events, Hoover never changed his mind about the bureau's conclusion that all three shots found their mark.

Years later, a line in a newspaper article discussing the Commission's rebuff caught Hoover's eye. It read, "Confusion on this point has been caused by a preliminary FBI report that apparently was erroneous." Hoover, ever the diligent one, underlined those words and wrote as marginalia, "What about this?"[30]

The Warren Commission depended on the FBI as its investigative right arm. Yet in Hoover's eyes, the Warren Commission was a waste of time. It was nothing more than "poppy cock," since, in his opinion, the case already had been solved—by *his* own men.

What leads were missed—what clues were overlooked—as a result?

The CIA's Battle Plan

The CIA was even worse.

The super sleuths had their own conduit sitting right at the Warren Commission's table—former CIA director Allen Dulles. He had been head of that agency during the critical period of 1953 through 1961. Dulles took his Commission job seriously, attending the testimony of nearly two-thirds of all the witnesses summoned.

But like any good spy, he worked both sides. According to an internal agency document, for example, Dulles spent a slow Saturday in April 1964 talking shop with an unknown individual (that name being "sanitized" from the document) at the CIA. Dulles's purpose was to alert his contact to questions the Commission intended to ask Richard M. Helms, deputy director for CIA planning, when Helms appeared the following month.[31]

Dulles also relayed advice on how those queries should be answered. Of utmost concern, according to Dulles, was a potential query on whether Oswald had been a CIA agent.

"Mr. Dulles felt the reply should be straightforward and to the point," this contact wrote in a follow-up memo to Helms. "He thought language which made it clear that Lee Harvey Oswald was never an employee or agent of CIA would suffice. We should also state that neither CIA nor anyone acting on CIA's behalf was ever in contact or communication with Oswald."[32]

Helms also was instructed not to volunteer information regarding the agency's method for selecting and handling agents since, even though "it would have been unlikely for Oswald to have been chosen as a CIA agent to enter Russia," there were "always exceptions to every rule and this might be misunderstood by members of the Commission with little background in activity of this sort."[33]

The contact then offered his own advice to Helms. "I agreed with him that a *carefully phrased denial* [author's emphasis] of the charges of involvement with Oswald seemed most appropriate."[34]

Helms appeared before the Commission on May 14, 1964. As predicted, one of the first questions he was asked concerned whether a relationship had existed between his agency and Oswald. His reply was a "carefully phrased denial":

> I had all of our records searched to see if there had been any contacts at any time prior to President Kennedy's assassination by anyone in the Central Intelligence Agency with Lee Harvey Oswald. We checked our card files and our personnel files and all our records.
>
> Now, this check turned out to be negative. In addition, I got in touch with those officers who were in positions of responsibility at the times in question to see if anybody had any recollection of any contact having even been suggested with this man. This also turned out to be negative, so there is no material in the Central Intelligence Agency, either in the records or in the mind of any of the individuals, that there was any contact had or even contemplated with him.[35]

In March 1964, prior to Helms' appearance, Rankin had sent a letter to the CIA requesting some routine information. What was being sought was not remarkable. How the CIA reacted was.

In typical fashion, an unnamed person drafted an internal memo advising an unnamed recipient:

> We have a problem here for your determination.[36]
>
> This is responsive to paragraph 3 of Rankin's letter. Staff officer does not desire to respond directly to paragraph 2 of that letter which made a levy for our material which had gotten into the hands of the Secret Service since 23 November.[37]
>
> Unless you feel otherwise, staff officer would prefer to wait out the Commission on the matter covered by paragraph 2.[38]

In other words, the CIA wanted to delay its response, trusting that the Commission would close up shop before the request was renewed.

Similar guidance was provided to then-director of the CIA John McCone prior to his own appearance before the Commission. In eighteen pages of written briefing material, McCone was advised of several touchy areas that might be raised during his testimony. Recommended responses were provided, including what to say if McCone was "challenged by anyone on the Commission" regarding his affidavit that said Oswald was not a CIA agent.[39] McCone was also advised to "not respond on the record to queries" involving Oswald's activities while he was in Mexico in September 1963 or his possible relationship with the "Cuban Intelligence Service."[40]

If the CIA was reluctant to offer assistance during the Commission's existence, it certainly had no problem lending support to the Commission's ultimate conclusion that Oswald was the sole assassin.

The CIA's in-house newsletter, "Propaganda Notes," announced on September 22, 1964, that "the long awaited Warren Commission Report, on its exhaustive investigation into the assassination," would soon be presented to the public.[41] Included was the warning that "Communist regimes" would use the Report to "denigrate American society."[42]

"Covert assets should explain the tragedy wherever it is genuinely misunderstood, and counter all efforts to misconstrue it intentionally— provided the depth of impact warrants such action."[43]

In an April 1, 1967, dispatch to "Chiefs, Certain Stations and Bases," the CIA termed itself at "war" with critics of the government's version of the crime.[44] Titled "Countering Criticism of the Warren Report," recipients were advised of several options in its battle with the disbelievers. One in particular asked them "to discuss the publicity problem with liaison and friendly elite contacts (especially politicians and editors), pointing out that the Warren Commission made as thorough an investigation as humanly possible, that the charges of the critics are without serious foundation, and that further speculative discussion only plays into the hands of the opposition."[45]

Another option was "to employ propaganda assets to answer and refute the attacks of the critics." The dispatch continued:

> Book reviews and feature articles are particularly appropriate for this purpose. The unclassified attachments to this guidance should provide useful background material for passage to assets. Our play should point out, as applicable, that the critics are (i) wedded to theories adopted before the evidence was in, (ii) politically interested, (iii) financially interested, (iv) hasty and inaccurate in their research, or (v) infatuated with their own theories.[46]

Along those lines, the CIA's battle plan suggested that if "friendly" book reviewers were doing their job, they "might be encouraged to add to their account the idea that, checking back with the [Warren] Report itself, they found it far superior to the work of its critics."[47]

By no means, the dispatch warned, should agents initiate commentary about "the assassination question" where it was not already being discussed.

But other games were being played as well. In August 1975, several well-known critics, including Weisberg and Jones, opened their mailboxes to find a mysterious letter, postmarked Mexico City, which contained a copy of a note supposedly handwritten by Lee Oswald on November 8, 1963. In its entirety, that note read:

> Dear Mr. Hunt,
> I would like information concerning my position.
> I am asking only for information. I am suggesting that we discuss the matter fully before any steps are taken by me or anyone else.
> Thank you.
> Lee Harvey Oswald.

Written two weeks before the assassination, the wording held sinister implications. Jones thought "Mr. Hunt" was Dallas billionaire H. L. Hunt, whose "association" with Oswald implicated the superrich, rightwing element in the crime. Others felt "Mr. Hunt" was E. Howard Hunt, a CIA agent whose name was current dinner talk as a result of the mushrooming Watergate fiasco.

Weisberg thought the whole thing fishy.[48] "I think there is little doubt—this is a fake," he wrote to attorney and friend Jim Lesar. "Of course the FBI is going to decline comment. They want all the nonsensical stuff to receive all the attention possible. This is an essential of the continuing disinformation operations."[49]

The solution surfaced in 1999 in documents accompanying a KGB archivist who defected from Russia. According to those papers, the KGB had deliberately concocted the "Hunt" letter, forging Oswald's handwriting and signature so well that even HSCA experts couldn't tell the difference.[50]

The "Mr. Hunt" reference was intended all along to be E. Howard Hunt. The KGB designed the note solely as a prank to implicate the CIA in Kennedy's murder.[51] The episode was nothing more than another example of Cold War capers.

CHAPTER 20

May-June 1999

It is a "sordid situation," Earl Warren bemoaned. He was not referring to the KGB's "Hunt" escapades. Warren uttered that remark in front of his Commission's personnel on December 5, 1963, the first of several behind-closed-doors, members-only meetings. He was commenting on the terribleness of that Dallas day two weeks earlier and the duty that now confronted them all.

"Reviewing these details . . . is really sickening to me."[1]

Knowing what the HSCA said years later, I found it fascinating to read now the once-secret but recently released transcripts of the thirteen Executive Session meetings of the Warren Commission. It was a revealing study of the chronological thought processes of the men at the taproot.

During that initial gathering, Warren had a vision. He felt that the Commission's job should be "essentially one for the evaluation of evidence as distinguished from being one of gathering evidence."[2] He was under the mistaken assumption "that we can rely upon the reports of the various agencies that have been engaged in investigating the matter," and he felt there would be no need "for a staff of investigators."[3]

"If we can't rely on them," Warren commented, referring to the FBI, CIA, and Secret Service, "I couldn't think of any investigators we can get to do it anyway. So I would hope that we could hold our meetings and take any evidence or any statements that we want in camera, and eventually make our report without any great fanfare throughout the country."[4]

Warren's dream was actually delusion. Commission members came to grips with that fact by December 16, at the third Executive Session meeting.

"Everyone has all kinds of questions," Hale Boggs announced. "Reading that FBI report [FBI Summary Report of December 9, 1963] leaves a million questions."[5]

Even J. Lee Rankin, the just-hired general counsel, had to agree. He told those present that he may call upon them "for some investigative

200

help, too, to examine special situations, because we might not get all we needed by just going back to the FBI and other agencies because the [FBI Summary] report has so many holes in it." He continued, "Anybody can look at it and see that it just doesn't seem like they're looking for things that this Commission has to look for in order to get the answers that it wants and it's entitled to."[6]

There were other concerns, too, such as who was releasing tidbits of the FBI's Summary Report to the press. It hindered the Commission's work. And what about the touchy situation of interviewing Mrs. Kennedy—"that little woman," as Warren would call her?[7] Members also began asking about seeing the film taken by Abraham Zapruder.

"We've got to put this show on the road," Warren declared.[8]

By January 1964, deadlines had been set. Rankin proposed that a final report be completed by mid-May, four months hence. He wanted it handed to President Johnson by June 1.[9]

Commenting on the "tremendous mass" of files expected to be examined in such a short period of time, Allen Dulles suggested the staff save energy and simply "pick out what they think is essential," with the option that "we can browse around if we have time."[10]

Then, things hit the proverbial fan.

"This is a serious thing," Boggs lamented at a hastily called meeting on January 22.[11] The focus was the scintillating message from Waggoner Carr, district attorney of Texas, who informed the Commission "that the word had come out . . . that Oswald was acting as an FBI undercover agent."[12]

"It is going to be very difficult for us to be able to establish the fact in it," Rankin admitted to his hushed audience.[13] "I am confident that the FBI would never admit it, and I presume their records will never show it, or if their records do show anything, I would think their records would show some kind of a number that could be assigned to a dozen different people according to how they wanted to describe them."

Dulles, no stranger to this topic, explained, "I mean when they hire somebody they hire somebody for a purpose. It is either . . . Was it to penetrate the Fair Play for Cuba Committee? That is the only thing I can think of where they might have used this man [Oswald]."[14]

Rankin expressed deeper thoughts.

Secondly, there is this factor . . . that is somewhat an issue in this case, and I suppose you are all aware of it. That is that the FBI is very explicit that Oswald is the assassin or was the assassin, and they are very explicit that there was no conspiracy, and they are also saying in the same place that they are continuing their investigation. Now in my experience of almost nine years, in the first place it is hard to get them to say when you think you have got a case tight enough to convict somebody, that that is the person that committed the crime. In my experience with the FBI they don't do that. They claim that they don't evaluate, and it is uniform prior experience that they don't do that.[15]

The question was asked why, if the FBI traditionally remains neutral, it broke the mold and took such an adamant stance against Oswald as early as the agency did in its investigation. One member said he didn't have a clue. Rankin, however, did.

"They would like to have us fold up and quit . . . ," he suggested. "They found the man. There is nothing more to do. The Commission supports their conclusions, and we can go on home and that is the end of it."[16]

"[The] implications of this are fantastic, don't you think so?" Boggs chimed in.[17]

"Terrific," Rankin replied.

"I think this record ought to be destroyed," Dulles opined. "Do you think we need a record of this?"[18]

At the January 27 Executive Session five days later, discussion of Oswald's possible intelligence connections continued.

Boggs inquired about the method of hiring government agents, especially if there were no "signed contract" to prove actual employment.

Boggs: The man who recruited him would know, wouldn't he?
Dulles: Yes, but he wouldn't tell.
Chairman Warren: Wouldn't tell it under oath?
Dulles: I wouldn't think he would tell it under oath, no.
Chairman Warren: Why?
Dulles: He ought not tell it under oath. Maybe not tell it [*sic*] to his own government but wouldn't tell it any other way.
McCloy: Wouldn't he tell it to his own chief?
Dulles: He might or might not. If he was a bad one then he wouldn't.[19]

Dulles labeled Oswald "a stupid fellow," a most unlikely candidate for intelligence work.[20] This was from the head of an agency whose plots to kill Castro read like the pranks of a renegade fraternity house. There was the CIA's idea of placing a bomb in Castro's cigar, triggered to ignite when his stogie was lit. Or an underwater device lodged in a seashell and timed to explode should Castro be enticed by its beauty during one of his routine swims. Or a powder to be spilled on Castro that would quickly dissolve his beard, rendering him so foolish looking he would be dethroned in shame. Or an offshore Fourth of July fireworks display so grand it would signal to credulous Cubans the Second Coming of Christ, who was pre-portrayed by the CIA as being a devout anti-Castroite.

Several Commission members then began to put two and two together. Why, for instance, since Oswald had once lived in a Communist country, didn't the Secret Service consider him a possible threat when Kennedy visited Dallas?

"If he was on the payroll of the FBI," John McCloy ventured, "they would think he was all right, they would not think of his being a defector."[21]

Next was this exchange:

Rankin: Part of our difficulty in regard to it is that they have no problem. They have decided that it is Oswald who committed the assassination, they have decided that no one else was involved, they have decided—

Russell: They have tried the case and reached a verdict on every aspect.

Boggs: You have put your finger on it.[22]

Doubts then arose over whether the FBI had forwarded to the Commission everything it had on Oswald. "That has always been a queer thing to me before this rumor came up," Russell said. "I couldn't understand why they went to Mrs. Payne [*sic*] and Mrs. Oswald, but didn't go to him."[23]

Along those lines, Rankin cited a "two-hour" meeting between Oswald and the FBI in August 1962, the results of which had been submitted to the Commission in a mere two-page report.[24] "We don't have any report that would cover anything like a two hour conversation," he said. "It is a relatively short report. Now, what occupied the rest of the time?"[25]

He had additional concerns. "Then there is a great range of material in regard to the wounds, and the autopsy and this point of exit or entrance of the bullet in the front of the neck, and that all has to be developed much more than we have at the present time. We have an explanation there in the autopsy that probably a fragment came out the front of the neck, but with the elevation the shot must have come from, and the angle, it seems quite apparent now, since we have the picture of where the bullet entered in the back, that the bullet entered below the shoulder blade to the right of the backbone, which is below the place where the picture shows the bullet came out in the neckband of the shirt in front."[26]

Russell offered two possible solutions. "One is we can just accept the FBI's report and go on and write the report based on their findings and supported by the raw materials they have given us, or else we can go and try to run down some of these collateral rumors that have just not been dealt with directly in this raw material that we have."[27]

"The plot thickens, doesn't it?" McCloy noted.[28]

"That Little Woman"

By the spring of 1964, the Oswald/FBI rumor had dried up. The principals to the rumor in Dallas had been investigated, with negative results. Several at the FBI, including Hoover himself, had submitted affidavits affirming Oswald was not on the agency's books. It was forgotten, and the Commission moved on.

As late as April, the deadline for putting the conclusions into President Johnson's hands remained June, even though Commission members at that point had not yet visited the scene of the crime. They intended to do just that, in order to avoid criticism if they didn't.[29]

There also was debate over the physical appearance of their Report and the need to avoid "a very cumbersome size to be circulated to the public."[30]

"If historians later want to read it over and work on it, well and good," Dulles said in another classic understatement, "but I don't think anybody would pay any attention to it to begin with."[31]

The Commission failed to meet its June 1 deadline. In fact, if Gerald Ford can be believed, the Commission had not at that point even decided whether Oswald was the sole guilty party. "Any statement that Commission members have come to this or that conclusion is obviously false, because the Commission has not discussed these matters as a Commission to my knowledge," Ford explained in the June 4 Executive Session. "I don't like being quoted when I have not made any final judgment."[32]

This was an amazing statement in light of a draft outline for the

Warren Report circulated on January 11, 1964, five months prior. In that outline, which remained virtually identical to what appeared in the finished product, one of the main section headings read, "Lee H. Oswald as the Assassin."[33]

"Now, I have checked a little bit with some of my newspaper friends, and they tell me that any time AP or UP have a story with the same dateline, there is no doubt that it was a leaked story by a government official, or by anybody else who was involved," Ford persisted. "And ever since that time, and in a growing intensity, and in growing volume now, there is this kind of newspaper propaganda with the same intent in mind. I have some personal conclusions, but I cannot prove them, so I don't want to make any allegations. But it disturbs me."[34]

Warren had the solution. A press release was written explaining that testimony was almost completed and a final report was forthcoming. But under no circumstances had any final conclusions been drawn. Ford was pleased.

Ironically, it was Ford who, two months later, would be accused of leaking to *Life* magazine details from a diary Oswald kept while in Russia. Ford admitted to the FBI he "did previously talk" with representatives of that magazine but not about Oswald's diary.[35]

Years later, the HSCA determined that Ford may have been keeping the FBI abreast of Commission activities and discussions, especially those detrimental to that agency.[36] Then-President Ford denied the charge.[37]

But Cartha D. DeLoach, an assistant director of the FBI whose internal memos helped link Ford to that accusation,[38] wrote about the matter in his 1997 book, *Hoover's FBI: The Inside Story by Hoover's Trusted Lieutenant.* "For a while," DeLoach said, "it appeared as if the Warren Commission report would treat the FBI respectfully, or so we heard from Congressman Gerald Ford, our chief contact on the seven-man commission."[39]

Late on the afternoon of Friday, June 5, Warren and Rankin finally got around to interviewing "that little woman," Jacqueline Kennedy. Robert Kennedy sat in the shadows for moral support.[40]

Conspicuously absent was Arlen Specter, who by this time already had completed his work concerning the very topic of which Mrs. Kennedy's observations were an integral part. Specter did, however, submit a list of ninety questions to Rankin, from which those "deemed irrelevant or too specific" could be deleted.[41] Most of them were.

Mrs. Kennedy's deposition lasted ten minutes and took up only three pages in the twenty-six volumes.[42] When it came time for her to discuss her husband's injuries, this terse line appeared in her published testimony: "[Reference to wounds deleted.]"[43]

Early critics felt that something sinister was going on—that what Mrs. Kennedy said at that point may have offered some sort of proof of a second gunman and therefore was stricken from the public record. The passage of time, however, filled the gap. With her testimony now declassified, her missing words became known:

> I was trying to hold his hair on. But from the front there was nothing. I suppose there must have been. But from the back you could see, you know, you were trying to hold his hair on, and his skull on.[44]

Why had these words been deleted from her testimony in the twenty-six volumes? They seemed innocuous, no more offensive than this sentence that did end up being published in the Warren Report: "At that point, both Governor and Mrs. Connally observed brain tissue splattered over the interior of the car."[45] Or this line, referring to one of the attending doctors at Parkland: "He observed shredded brain tissue and 'considerable slow oozing' from the latter wound, followed by 'more profuse bleeding' after some circulation was established."[46]

Perhaps the deletion resulted from nothing more than what Howard Willens, the Commission's administrative assistant, had proposed back in December 1963. In a memorandum to Rankin regarding a proposed interview with Mrs. Kennedy, Willens said, "In order to insure the privacy of Mrs. Kennedy's personal recollections and feelings, it might be desirable to seal the recording of this conversation for a stated number of years. After some sensitive editing of this transcript, most of the information desired by the Commission would probably be supplied by such a statement."[47]

Evidence of such "sensitive editing" has been found. According to the twenty-six volumes, Mrs. Kennedy said, "And Governor Connally screamed."[48] But what she told the Commission in full that day was: "And Governor Connally screamed like a stuck pig."[49]

July and August passed quietly as the members left behind in Washington scurried to finish writing the Report. By the time the final Executive Session meeting rolled around in September, few chores remained.

Each Commission member became responsible for proofreading several pages of the Report's first chapter, "Summary and Conclusions." Care was taken to make sure no conflicts occurred between the conclusions in that chapter and the evidence presented in chapter 3, "The Shots From The Texas School Book Depository," and chapter 4, "The Assassin."

Commission members were informed each would receive copies of the Report and its twenty-six volumes for personal use, plus a leather-bound set for their own bookshelves.[50]

Group portraits were also scheduled.

Arrangements were made "to liquidate and close up the affairs of the Commission."[51] Final expenditures were to be tabulated and shared with members. All documents and records were to be "delivered to the National Archives to be held in perpetuity for the use and benefit of the people of the Unites States."[52]

"There being nothing further to come before the Commission, the meeting was adjourned," the stenographer typed.[53]

Six days later, after clearing their busy schedules, all seven members collectively handed over the 888-page Warren Report to President Johnson.

"It's pretty heavy," was Johnson's first impression.[54]

And with that, the Warren Commission ceased to exist.

But the hits would keep on coming.

It was November 22, 1963. Like many others, Navy Cmdr. John Ebersole never expected his week to end the way it did. Yet there he was, late into this Friday night and on into early Saturday, standing in for his temporarily absent boss as acting chief of radiology at the Bethesda Naval Hospital.

Before him lay the lifeless body of the former president.

Ebersole had been summoned to shoot what would become the controversial X-rays, one of the most hotly debated byproducts of the crime. The sole purpose of his job that evening was to locate the elusive bullet that had entered Kennedy's back. Since no lanes of passage through the body or any corresponding exit wounds had been detected, attending doctors felt that the missile must be somewhere inside.

Or so it was initially thought. Hours later, all Ebersole had discovered was the image of a small, circular pellet in Kennedy's stomach—he would call it "buckshot"—that he guessed resulted from previous consumption of a duck or rabbit whose meat had not been thoroughly cleaned.

Confusion over the bullet's whereabouts remained, until autopsy doctors learned quite unexpectedly from a phone call either to or from doctors in Dallas (Ebersole could not remember which) that the tracheotomy at the base of Kennedy's throat actually had been made over a preexisting bullet hole. Ebersole placed the time of this newsflash at 10 or 10:30 P.M., on Friday, November 22, perhaps a bit later but certainly before things had been tidied up by 3 A.M. Saturday.

Suddenly it all made sense. The bullet was not in the body after all. The X-rays had revealed nothing because that missile had exited from the throat.

Or so it was initially thought.

Confusion over the missing projectile had thus ended.[55] The radiologist was told to go home, his services no longer needed. Yet something strange would come up.

According to Ebersole's version of events, the doctors learned of the obscured bullet hole *during* the autopsy, maybe even as early as halfway through it. Yet autopsy surgeon Cmdr. James J. Humes said under oath to the Warren Commission that he wasn't informed of the bullet hole in Kennedy's throat until he spoke by phone with Dallas doctors from his home *at 8 A.M. Saturday*, up to ten hours *after* Ebersole said that conversation took place.

Humes implied that the Saturday revelation about the hidden throat wound was what caused him to write a second draft of his autopsy report. He then burned the first and apparently erroneous draft in his fireplace.

Yet if Ebersole was accurate and Humes had actually learned about the obscured bullet hole *during* the autopsy, what was it about the first draft of Humes' report that required revising it the next morning?[56] What exactly had Humes written on those enflamed papers?

Years later, while Ebersole served as chief of radiation therapy at a hospital in Lancaster, Pennsylvania, he was invited to testify before the HSCA about his late-night observations. A local newspaper reporter received a tip about Ebersole's upcoming appearance, interviewed him, and, on March 8, 1978, penned a story that quoted Ebersole as saying, among other things, that "the back of his [Kennedy's] head was blown off."[57]

Damage to the back indicated a shot from Kennedy's front.

Ebersole would later deny making that comment, saying he had been misquoted.

Yet on March 11, three days *after* that article appeared and while being officially queried about Kennedy's corpse, Ebersole essentially repeated what he had told the reporter, telling the HSCA medical panel, "The back of the head was missing."[58] The HSCA would exclude

Ebersole's sixty-eight-page deposition from its published twelve volumes of evidence.

The Committee was nevertheless still interested in Ebersole's mention of the strange Friday-night phone call. It sought clarification from FBI agents Francis O'Neill and James Sibert, both present during the autopsy. In a signed affidavit in 1978, O'Neill said he left the autopsy room only once, to quickly grab a bite to eat. He stated:

> When Humes and [Navy Cmdr. and autopsy assistant J. Thornton] Boswell couldn't locate an outlet for the bullet that entered the back, Sibert left to call SA Charles Killion (FBI Laboratory) to determine if any extra bullets existed. He was advised of the finding of a bullet on a stretcher at Parkland Hospital in Dallas and relayed this information to the autopsy surgeons. I know for a fact that when the autopsy was complete, there was no doubt in anyone's mind in attendance at the autopsy that the bullet found on the stretcher in Dallas came out of JFK's body.[59]

In the margin to the left of this statement, someone wrote the following cryptic words: "Unless he got his sandwich when Humes phoned Perry [Dr. Malcolm Perry at Parkland Hospital] he knew Humes called Perry before 11 P.M. 11/22/63."[60]

On the coversheet of this document, someone also wrote and circled the line, "Autopsy room had a phone," a detail also mentioned by O'Neill in his affidavit.[61]

An Adams by a Different Name

On January 12, 1977, two staff members of the HSCA interviewed Thomas Evan Robinson, the funeral director who had been responsible for embalming the president after the autopsy. He told them he saw a small, quarter-inch-wide wound on Kennedy's right temple , just at the hairline. Was it evidence of a shot from the front?

He also recalled dialogue between autopsy doctors regarding discovery of a piece of metal or a bullet fragment within the victim's chest.

And he said there had been a ragged, somewhat circular wound about the size of an orange, "directly behind the back of his head."[62] The wound was so large, Robinson said, that "a piece of heavy duty rubber" had to be used to fill the void during the embalming process.[63]

"It had to be all dried out, packed and the rubber placed in the hair and the skin pulled back over it as much as possible and stitched into that piece of rubber," Robinson continued. "They were afraid again of leaks, once the body is moved or shaken in the casket and carried up the Capitol steps and opened again, we had to be very careful, there would have been blood on the pillow.[64]

"Putting the head into the pillow of the casket would have hidden everything," Robinson added.[65]

Robinson also explained he did not draw any autopsy face sheets or sketches of the body, something he routinely did, because, "like I said everything was done to protect the family as far as we were concerned."[66]

At the conclusion of his HSCA interview, however, he made a rough drawing depicting the rear of Kennedy's head. On that sketch, Robinson placed the large, gaping wound he had observed in the center and lower portion *on the back of the skull.*

It was right where other doctors had observed it; right where the government said it wasn't.

Robinson's interview also was not published by the HSCA. Neither was his illuminating drawing.

The comments of both Ebersole and Robinson were scheduled to be locked tight for fifty years. The JFK Act interrupted their hibernation. But the story doesn't end there.

In 1992, after the country turned passive as a result of all the confusion, the prestigious *Journal of the American Medical Association* (JAMA) published a ten-page interview with autopsy surgeons Humes and Boswell.[67] Both quickly labeled their critics "conspiracy buffs" whose theories were nothing but "hogwash."[68]

Nevertheless, Humes did admit to burning his "original notes," saying he did so simply to avoid having them turn into "a collector's item," since they were stained by the president's blood.[69]

Boswell admitted to his lack of care when he erroneously placed the back wound as low as he did on Kennedy's body chart, saying if he had seen the bullet holes in the president's clothing first, he would have realized his mistake.

In actuality, the holes in Kennedy's clothes corresponded precisely with the hole location depicted on Boswell's drawing.

During the interview, Humes made the extraordinary statement, "I believe in the single-bullet theory that it struck Governor Connally immediately after exiting the President's throat."[70]

Only someone who had read Humes' testimony to the Warren

Commission could have realized this comment was the *opposite* of what he had said in 1964. Back then, after being shown the bullet of "single-bullet" fame, Humes was asked if he felt that projectile could have caused all the damage to both men. "Most unlikely," he had responded.[71]

I brought this contradiction to JAMA's attention and also asked why nothing had been said about the death certificate signed by Admiral Burkley that confirmed Boswell's placement of the back wound. I'm still awaiting a reply.

In the meantime, I hadn't forgotten about Victoria Adams. There just weren't any new clues to pursue. But I must have had a penchant for those with that last name.

Somewhere in my journey, I became fascinated with Francis W. H. Adams, distinct in more ways than his dual middle names (William Holbrook). Adams was a senior Warren Commission attorney teamed with Arlen Specter to head what many considered the most important aspect of the investigation: the source of the shots.

He was touted as the perfect candidate for the job: wise at fifty-nine years, a former police commissioner of New York City, a leader in the community, someone who was genuinely interested in working for the Commission.[72] He was honest too, revealing in his application for federal employment that his only scrape with the law came when he was questioned by police on a violation of the New York State prohibition act—as a teenager some forty years earlier. The offense was so minor that official records weren't kept.[73]

So why, when J. Lee Rankin was questioned by the HSCA years later, did he make the comment he should have fired Adams from the very beginning?[74] Adams was certainly conscientious, at least early on in his Commission job. He diligently wrote detailed and lengthy memos to his boss, explaining his expected course of action. His goals were lofty.

He said he fully intended to resolve the confusion over the location of Kennedy's back wound. He also wanted to closely examine films of the assassination, especially Zapruder's, and solve that nagging three-shots, three-hits timing problem presented by the FBI.[75] But suddenly, all that ended.

Records indicate that by February, only a month after being hired, Adams was gone. Well, not gone literally, but there was a noticeable change in his work habits.

He just no longer showed up.

He'd pop in every once in a while to exchange pleasantries, but as far as work for the Commission went, it was virtually nil. The most important aspect of the investigation—the source of the shots—was therefore left squarely on the shoulders of thirty-three-year-old junior attorney Arlen Specter.

Adams' behavior remained a question mark. There was no resignation letter; no quibbling "memos to file" indicating dissention, as several others had written; no outward signs of dissatisfaction. He just quit working.

Indeed, the only thing he was on record as saying about the matter was his quote to an author in 1966 that he simply was too busy at his law firm—his real job—and that "he had a different concept of the investigation."[76]

I was curious what he meant by "different concept," so I wrote Francis Adams often at his law office and residence in New York. I left telephone messages with his secretary.

He never replied. Yet I had this strange feeling about the man. That feeling became stronger when I spoke with his daughter many years later.

From an obituary in the *New York Times*, I discovered that Francis Adams had died on April 20, 1990, at a convalescent home in Devon, Pennsylvania, near Philadelphia. His wife, Katherine, and two daughters, Judith Clifford and Joyce Adams, were listed as survivors.

I addressed a letter to his wife, mentioning my intentions and interest in her husband. Five days later, on a lazy Sunday afternoon, the telephone rang at my home. It was Joyce Adams.

She explained her mother had recently turned ninety-five and "doesn't remember things."[77] Her sister, Judith, had intercepted and read my letter, became frightened by the nature of its contents, and turned the matter over to Joyce. She apparently was the more unruffled sibling.

"So, what's up?" she asked me, rather offhandedly after introducing herself. Before I could answer, she began a long-distance grilling of my interest in the assassination, my background as a researcher, and whether or not I had spoken with "Specter," using a condescending tone with his name and assuming I knew whom she meant. The line of personal questions made me wonder if she had ever been associated with S. M. Holland.

I explained I had tried on several occasions to reach "Specter," but he refused to return my calls or answer my letters.[78]

"What is it about my father that makes you so curious?" she inquired.

I explained I suspected Francis Adams had discovered something amiss in the way the Warren Commission was handling the investigation, and rather than take part in it, he chose to back away.

"That sounds just like my father," she replied. "Are you sure you didn't know him? If he didn't think it was right, he'd quit immediately—no hesitations. If he didn't think it was being run properly, he would be the type to leave."

Some had felt, I explained to Joyce, that her father had dropped out of the Commission because he was too busy at his own law firm.

"I read that somewhere," she responded, with a bit of sardonic laughter. She obviously did not believe that excuse. "Why would he have accepted the position in the first place if that were the case?"

In no uncertain terms, she explained that her father definitely would have considered his duties investigating a presidential assassination to be of paramount importance—the highest priority—and certainly would not have abandoned them because of his law firm. That, she said, could not have been the reason.[79]

Then I broached my big question. I inquired if her father had made any kind of notes or kept any personal papers concerning his days with the Commission.

She hesitated. Yes, I heard her whisper, he had. But it was her sister, Judith—the timid one alarmed by my letter—who maintained possession of those "private" files.

"My father was opinionated and wrote his notes in longhand," Joyce said, adding he had once confided to her that the area of investigation he was assigned to oversee—the source of the shots—"was the most important area" of the entire case.

"Perhaps if I could review your father's files, I may be able to clarify his actions, strictly for the historical record," I suggested.

She paused again. "Just what do you expect to find in there?"

I told her I didn't have a clue but would know if I found it.

"Well, you probably will not find the smoking-gun, midnight memo listing everything," she said. "But I'll get in touch with Judy and tell her that I have no problem with this. Let me call you back in two or three days."

Two or three days passed, then two or three weeks. A month later, I wrote a follow-up letter to Katherine Adams, knowing it would end up in Joyce's lap once again.

There was only silence. I didn't seem to be having any luck with anyone named Adams.

CHAPTER 21

May-September 1999

Sometimes it is simply a matter of luck when you're at the Archives. Occasionally, out of all those hundreds of thousands of documents and millions upon millions of words—out of all that verbal rubble—all it takes is a single innocuous sentence. Sometimes that sentence is so innocent and simple in content that, to the uninformed eye, it means absolutely nothing.

Yet to one crazy enough to keep tabs on the evolving evidence, one bedeviled with the pursuit of time-consuming details, that simple sentence can snatch the breath away. It had happened to me before. It was about to happen again.

It was getting late on this particular afternoon. I was rushing to finish reviewing an otherwise boring box full of files sent to the Warren Commission in 1964 by the U.S. attorney's office in Dallas. Only fifteen minutes remained before I had to leave for dinner and a hockey game with my son, who worked in downtown Washington.

That's when I found it.

My habit was to thumb through files looking for documents concerning Victoria Adams, hoping to discover something—anything— either overlooked in the past or perhaps newly released. Usually, I found nothing. But as I took a parting glance that day at these papers out of Dallas, a page caught my eye.

Across its top was the handwritten notation, "Adams, Vicki." The single sheet was a copy of a registered letter sent by airmail to J. Lee Rankin in Washington. It was signed by Martha Joe Stroud, an assistant U.S. attorney, on behalf of Barefoot Sanders, the U.S. attorney for Dallas.[1]

The date typed under its Department of Justice letterhead was June 2, 1964. Miss Stroud was forwarding to Rankin a copy of Miss Adams' signed deposition, taken less than two months earlier, on April 7, in that same office by Commission counsel David Belin. During the intervening

214

time, the official transcript of her questioning had been prepared and then shown to Miss Adams. In her letter to Rankin, Miss Stroud listed half a dozen errors Miss Adams had identified in her testimony and wanted corrected.[2]

As a way of refreshing Rankin's memory, Miss Stroud wrote, "Mr. Bellin [*sic*] was questioning Miss Adams about whether or not she saw anyone as she was running down the stairs."[3]

It was Miss Stroud's next sentence, the final one in the text, that punched me in the gut. "Miss Garner, Miss Adams' supervisor, stated this morning that after Miss Adams went downstairs she (Miss Garner) saw Mr. Truly and the policeman come up."[4]

After Miss Adams went down the stairs, Dorothy Ann Garner saw Roy Truly and Officer Marrion Baker come up. I could not have been more stunned had someone tapped me on the shoulder at that moment and announced, "Hi. I'm Victoria Adams and I heard you've been looking for me."

All along, the Commission discredited Miss Adams. All along it said she could not have come down the stairs when she said she did. The Commission's logic was simple. Oswald fired the shots. Oswald came down the stairs. If Miss Adams was on the stairs when she said she was and didn't see or hear him, then obviously she was the one who was wrong.

Based on the Commission's reasoning, she therefore had to have come down the staircase *after* Oswald did, *after* the escaping assassin already had passed by the fourth floor in his descent, and *after* Officer Baker and Roy Truly had passed by the fourth floor as they headed up to the roof. Thus, she had to come down later than she thought.

The Commission admitted that if Miss Adams was correct with her timing, she "would probably have seen or heard" Oswald either above or below her.[5]

The only alternative was if Miss Adams happened to pass by as Oswald, Truly, and Baker were already in the second-floor lunchroom. Even under those circumstances, with Oswald getting to the lunchroom only seconds ahead of Truly and Baker, plus the brevity of the encounter there, Miss Adams *still* should have heard Oswald somewhere on the stairs. Yet she had seen and heard no one.

As the Commission concluded, "she actually came down the stairs several minutes after Oswald and after Truly and Baker as well."[6]

In order for the Commission's conclusion to be accurate, Miss Adams would have had to descend the stairs *after* Truly and Baker had continued their path up those same stairs from the second floor and *after* they had both passed the fourth floor, where Miss Adams' trek originated.

I stared at Miss Stroud's letter again and reread those important words: *Miss Garner, Miss Adams' supervisor, stated this morning that after Miss Adams went downstairs she (Miss Garner) saw Mr. Truly and the policeman come up.*

It was *after* Miss Adams had gone down the stairs that Dorothy Garner, who remained behind, saw Truly and Baker emerge onto the fourth floor. Miss Garner's impromptu verification of this detail confirmed what Miss Adams had been saying all along. Miss Garner's statement showed that Miss Adams *did* in fact descend the stairs when she said she had—not when the Commission surmised.

Why then didn't Victoria Adams see or hear Lee Oswald?

And to whom was Miss Garner making this statement? Was it to David Belin? Was Belin troubled by what Miss Adams told him in her testimony nearly two months earlier? Was Belin seeking clarification from Dorothy Garner, Miss Adams' boss? If the Commission attorney was that conscientious, why then hadn't he sought out Sandra Styles?

If Miss Garner was being officially examined, as the wording of Martha Stroud's letter implied, where then was that interview or testimony? The National Archives, the Dallas D.A.'s office, and the U.S. Department of Justice had no record of it. The Warren Commission never officially called Miss Garner as a witness. There is no official record of her ever having been questioned by Belin or anyone else on the Commission's staff.

Nothing other than Miss Stroud's reference exists. But the bottom line was that Miss Adams had been telling the truth.

"So she *was* telling the truth!" Weisberg eerily echoed my thoughts as he read my copy of Martha Joe Stroud's letter.[7]

It had taken me a while to find him this time. Normally, as I drove up the long driveway to his home, I'd spy him typing at his desk behind the large corner window to his office. After I'd break his concentration by tapping on the glass, he would look up, smile, and wave for me to enter the back door.

The house was dark and locked this day and more unkempt than usual. I became worried. Neighbors told me Weisberg and his wife, Lil, had taken up temporary residence in a rehabilitation center. They were recuperating from recent illnesses.

I hated to visit him there. It reminded me of my father.

"What I can't figure out," I told Weisberg, "is why Sandra Styles was never questioned."

"The Commission didn't want any confirmations," he answered. "Having one was enough; two was worse. They both would have had to see Oswald."

I was thinking about that when he made a suggestion.

"You need to write a book on this."

In all these years, I had never given it a thought. Never once had I entertained the idea of writing extensively on my research. To have the discipline, time, and organizational skills necessary to put into readable form the results of my decades-long efforts, to me, sounded impossible.

Who would want to read it anyway?

"Who would want to read something by me?" I asked. "And wasn't it you who always liked the fact I stayed in the background with my work?"

"That was when *you* were helping *me* and *I* was writing the books," Weisberg replied. "But I can't do that anymore. You need to put your material down, if for nothing more than the historical record. Use my files, anything I've written. If I'm able, I'd be happy to edit it for you."

"Ah, I think I'll pass on that one," I joked. Then I got serious. "Anyway, there are way too many books on this subject out there already. The world doesn't need another one."

"Write about your search for Vicki Adams," he said. "That's new; that's fresh. And yes, there is a lot of trash out there. That's why you'd have to do yours differently. You'd have to write the truth."

Now there was a novel idea. But I knew what he meant.

I had come a long way with this man, once described by the government as knowing more about the assassination than even the FBI.[8] He had displayed that knowledge and precise detail so many times. I always paid close attention, followed his suggestions, and ended up in some fixes because of it.

But putting down 100,000 words was a lot different from composing an occasional letter to my hometown-newspaper editor. I told him I would think about it, although I never really intended to.

Then he called me at home one afternoon a couple of weeks later and reminded me to bring along my tape recorder the next time I visited him. He had some things he wanted to say.

What he had to say turned into a three-hour interview. We talked about everything regarding the assassination: witnesses, Garrison, the government, and the gullible. He discussed the frustrations of having to self-publish his own books; how deception, disguise, and disgrace had replaced truthfulness, fact, and honor; how wild-eyed conjecture and tabloid speculations had become the accepted staple of publishers and, therefore, readers; how the sum of it all—every last bit of it—still mattered to this country, whether people realized it or not; and how no one seemed to care about that anymore.

There was bitterness in his voice, a consuming sense of failure that he had not, after these many years, been able to get to the bottom of this mystery. He was discouraged. But at the same time, he realized that had he done nothing—had he not at least tried to figure it all out—he could not have lived with himself.

At that moment I saw Weisberg as the father I no longer had, the man whose humility belied his deep wisdom. Over the years, he had been labeled a lunatic, a money-hungry opportunist out for his own gain, a charlatan. Maybe it was from jealousy. Maybe it was just from the way things had become in this country.

He was none of those. I knew that.

His words to me on that day were hardly what you'd call motivational, certainly not for what he wanted me to do, or maybe expected me to do.

Looking back now, I think it was then—as I drove home from his modest home in Frederick late that day—that I reached my decision. Somewhere along Route 15 North, as James Taylor crooned "Fire and Rain" from the dashboard, I realized it. I might be able to do this. At least I should try. Weisberg had given me a message, a sense of purpose. In some small way, it was his latest assignment for me.

I would try to put my past on paper, if only for the sake of the historical record. There were so many holes to fill, though. Never intending to write about this subject, I had left countless voids in the chronology.

And the source of it all, Victoria Adams, was still nowhere to be found.

CHAPTER 22

October 1999

From nearly twenty miles out, I could see the approaching skyline, massive in its beauty against the clear blue sky and rising high above the low, flat land ahead of me. The weather was perfect, much different from that rainy day when I first set foot in Dallas with Eugene Aldredge way back in 1968. Now I was doing the driving, alone and stuck in horrendous inbound traffic along Interstate 30 on an early Sunday afternoon.

After what seemed like hours, I made my way onto the Commerce Street exit ramp, through the Triple Underpass, and up into Dealey Plaza. It was crowded with the curious.

Had more than thirty years really passed since I was here last?

I parked the car at the first available meter and walked back a few blocks, getting my first look at the place in over three decades. As always, I was struck by its beauty and historical significance. I had to stand motionless for a long while as the past and present washed over me. Visually, very little had changed.

The U.S. Post Office, on the roof of which stood J. C. Price, was now the Federal Building. "Old Red," the Dallas County Courthouse where Ruby was convicted, now housed the Dallas Convention and Visitors Bureau. The County Records Building looked the same. The Dal-Tex Building was now more stylishly called "501 Elm Street."

Then there was the Texas School Book Depository, no longer known as that, its former title cleanly removed from above the front entrance. It was now the Dallas County Administrative Building. The famous sixth floor had been turned into a public showpiece, aptly titled "The Sixth Floor Museum," open daily. No longer present was the large yellow-and-black Hertz Rent-A-Car sign once prominently perched at an angle on the roof. Its absence gave the building a stark, boxlike look.

In morbid irony, a sign posted now on the front door read, *No weapons or explosives are allowed in the building. All persons will be subject to search.* Too bad such a policy didn't exist in 1963.

Beside the front steps was a plaque proclaiming the structure a national landmark, the site where Lee Harvey Oswald "allegedly" fired shots to kill the president. Someone had underlined the word *allegedly* with white chalk.

The loading docks where Oswald routinely entered—where Victoria Adams and Sandra Styles had hurried from—had now disappeared. In their place was an oversized, brick-enclosed elevator that took paying customers up six flights to the new museum. Ground level now housed a lobby and souvenir store, where one could purchase JFK T-shirts; "Jack and Jackie" pens, key rings, and coffee mugs; and countless other tourist staples related to this particular attraction.

The old railroad tower sitting atop the grassy knoll, from where Lee Bowers had spotted two men, was still there but vacated. The nearby picket fence was in shambles, the majority of its pointed slats broken or missing, the victim of theft, time, and abuse. On the wooden slats that remained, hundreds had written messages to the world, poetic and emotional notes etched after viewing this otherwise peaceful part of town.

Behind the fence, the once-dirt parking lot was now professionally paved and lined. Most of the railroad tracks were removed, those left behind currently accommodating part of the city's gleaming rapid-transit system. From here, it ferried people to the new Reunion Center, a series of ultramodern, black-glassed office buildings with an eye-catching spherical tower where one could get an overhead view of this former killing field.

A block away, actors were gearing up for their "world premiere" of a stage play called *The Life and Death of John F. Kennedy,* in which the young president "reveals his innermost feelings and thoughts, and finally watches his own death," according to a mass-produced handout. It went on, "Both funny and moving, this work is a remarkable addition to the Kennedy legend."

The Kennedy legend? I wondered. I decided to forgo this cultural highlight. Nor would I pay for yet another vendor's offering—"the opportunity of a lifetime," as the driver announced to onlookers—a slow ride down Elm Street in an open-top black limousine, sitting just as Kennedy did in his final moments.

Dealey Plaza had transformed itself into an out-of-towner's dream, a major and apparently profitable fixture of the now-fashionable West End Historic District of Dallas. It had become a circus.

On this sunny Sunday, "Smitty's" was selling hot dogs to the hungry from a sidewalk meat wagon. A fast-talking sales kid was peddling four-dollar copies of *JFK News,* a tabloid dealing with the lore of this land. Guided walking tours that were guaranteed to "stimulate" and "rivet" the paying customer, or so the hosts promised, were starting to assemble.

And some guy was standing behind a card table, charts on tripods surrounding him, as he conversed with a half-dozen onlookers. As I approached, I recognized him as Robert Groden. He had been the one who supplied the Zapruder film to Geraldo Rivera. Groden had also served as a photographic analyst for the HSCA.

Now he was peddling his books from a street corner.

Groden and Weisberg once had been friends. That ended when Groden took sides with Oliver Stone and helped the producer while *JFK—The Movie* was being filmed in Dallas. The two had not been on speaking terms since 1993, when Weisberg wrote Groden, criticizing his relationship with Stone and saying of the producer, "The man and truth cannot even be in the same room at the same time."[1]

"Hi. I'm a friend of Harold Weisberg," I said to Groden when he was finally alone.

Groden was momentarily taken aback, but then smiled and politely asked about Weisberg's health. "I heard he has been quite ill," he said.[2]

We chatted for a bit about the mundane, then I asked him why he chose to spend Sundays selling his books along Elm Street in Dealey Plaza.

"I do it to keep the issue alive," he replied. "I'm here every weekend, weather permitting."

Groden was selling a thirty-eight-page highly condensed version of his twenty-five-dollar-plus book, *The Killing of a President,* for a mere five dollars a copy. This shortened account was labeled the "Dealey Plaza Memorial Edition." While I had been walking around earlier, I noticed a woman named Diane Allen hawking the same pamphlet from a table on the grassy knoll. She was listed as a coauthor, so I asked Groden about her.

"Diane helped me with it," he said, with a sneer in her direction and contempt in his voice. "But she stole my photo collection in the process."

When I asked why, if he knew this, he didn't go to the police, he responded, "The Dallas Police won't do anything for me."[3]

As we were talking, a young couple approached and inquired about Groden's earlier comments to them concerning an observable bullet mark made by a shot that apparently had missed Kennedy.

"See it now before it's gone forever," Groden told them while pointing to a distant sewer cover two-thirds of the way down the left side of Elm. He then pocketed the money the two gave him for a copy of his pamphlet. This place had turned into a virtual sideshow.

"And where did that shot come from?" I asked, after the tourists had walked away.

"The roof of the Records Building," he answered.

"You're sure?"

"Indeed. The angle proves it."

"Was that the one fired by Harry Weatherford?" I asked, echoing a belief of Penn Jones, with whom Groden had become good friends after he had relocated to Dallas from New York.

"I believe it was him," he said. "I don't know it, but I believe it. It was an awfully poor shot regardless."

Near the end of our brief chat, a Dallas Police cruiser slowly pulled up and came to rest on the side street about fifty feet away. The sole officer inside began watching us.

"Stick around a minute, can you?" Groden whispered to me.

In a moment, the officer eased out of the car and made his way down Elm to where Groden and I were standing. He was a giant.

"Look what you're doing to the grass," he blurted out, dragging his foot along the trampled ground, flattened and muddy under Groden's feet.

Groden immediately apologized and moved himself and his table to the concrete sidewalk. "Is this ok?" he inquired. He had suddenly become timid.

The officer said nothing, instead turning the solid black lenses of his sunglasses in my direction. Not knowing if he actually had me in his sights or was just looking at the surrounding landscape, I smiled slightly and nodded my head, feeling as I had when Roger Craig was pulled over by Dallas's finest.

"Better," he snorted.

He stood around for a while, his presence scaring others from coming near. Apparently they too were familiar with the bad-cop theories. Then he got back into his patrol car and left.

"I've been arrested several times for being here," Groden explained. "Probably would have been again if you weren't around."

Groden suggested we talk privately at a later time. I told him where I was staying, and he promised to call. I never heard from him. The last

I saw of Groden was when he beeped the horn of his van and waved as he drove toward the Triple Underpass about an hour later, the thinning crowds apparently putting an end to his book sales.[4]

As usual, my evenings in Dallas were spent roaming around and sitting in Dealey Plaza. There was something about this place, as the day wound down and the lights popped on in the surrounding city, that allowed me to better reflect on things and see them more clearly. Even the occasional shrill and initially startling blasts of an air horn to scare nesting sparrows from the trees did not diminish the feeling.

As I sat at the base of the colonnade where Zapruder had once stood, a huckster walked up with his overpriced tabloid and began his spiel about how, if I really wanted to know the truth about what happened here, I needed to buy his paper. "See this?" he asked, leafing through his product and excitedly explaining the story behind several of the more controversial pictures inside. "The shots came from everywhere, even the trees."

Then he turned to the famous James Altgens photograph, the one depicting the person many thought was Oswald standing on the Depository's front steps. He thrust the page into my face. "Who is that man?" he asked.

I had had enough. "That man is Billy Lovelady," I replied.

"Oh . . . you've heard this already, huh?"

"You might say that."

Sorry, buddy, no sale.

CHAPTER 23

June 1999

Prior to this trip to Dallas, I had met with Weisberg and told him of my plans. He suggested I get in touch with Gary Mack, a well-known researcher and an archivist at the new Sixth Floor Museum. I wrote to Mack, using Weisberg's name as a reference, telling him of my upcoming visit, and seeking information regarding Victoria Adams, Sandra Styles, or Dorothy Ann Garner.

I also inquired about Kenneth Cody, the bus driver whose name appeared in Oswald's notebook and a man I had made nervous, and vice versa, many years ago.

Mack replied shortly after, saying he could be of no help with any of the three women I had mentioned. "I never spoke with them and know nothing of their whereabouts, " he wrote.[1] But he did provide me with the name and address of Joe Cody, the nephew of Kenneth and a retired Dallas police officer. I decided to write Joe a letter.

"He [Kenneth] died about 15 years ago," Joe replied a week later. "We all believe that the reason for my uncle's name and telephone number in Oswald's effects is that my uncle owned a duplex in the vicinity where Oswald lived and he might possibly wanted to rent it. My uncle had his name on a sign in front of the duplex exactly like Oswald had it written in his notes."[2]

Strangely, Oswald had not included Kenneth's name. All that had appeared in his notes was a telephone number.

Coincidentally, Joe Cody had been good friends with Jack Ruby. In fact, Joe's name had been jotted down in a notebook kept for Ruby at his Carousel Club.

So *Kenneth* Cody's number was in Lee Oswald's notebook; *Joe* Cody's name was in Ruby's. Ruby kills Oswald. . . . Nothing in this case seemed too strange anymore.

"I knew Jack Ruby well since the day he moved to Dallas," Cody wrote. "If you come to Dallas I will tell you a lot about Ruby."[3]

And that is how, the morning after my encounter with Groden, I found myself driving to DeSoto, a little bedroom community about fifteen miles south of Dallas where Cody and his wife owned a nicely kept and furnished ranch house. He gave me a quick tour before sitting down for a taped interview.

Cody had known Ruby since 1950, meeting him in one of Ruby's former south Dallas nightclubs. Once they became better acquainted, the two often went ice skating. "He was pretty fair," Cody said, when I inquired about Ruby's abilities on the rink.[4]

Cody was working Burglary and Theft when he saw Oswald the day of the assassination. "They tried to get him [Oswald] into Homicide and they couldn't so they took him over to Burglary and Theft. They put him into an interrogating room and I'm talking to him and I said, 'What's your name?' He said, 'Lee Harvey Oswald.' 'Where do you work?' 'Texas School Book Depository.' I said, 'Did you work today?' He said, 'Yes.' So I called an officer in and said, 'Kill him if he moves.'"

It was Joe Cody who had purchased as a present for Ruby the $62.50 Cobra pistol that the club owner later used to gun down Oswald. Cody said the weapon remained registered in the police officer's name, which caused him some embarrassment when investigators traced the gun following Ruby's arrest.

I asked Cody if he felt that his former friend could commit such a murder.

"No, I did not," he answered. "Oh, I knew he was capable, but I didn't think he'd go and, you know . . . I never thought Jack Ruby would shoot Lee Oswald."

Did Ruby ever express admiration for President Kennedy?

"I didn't even know that he knew who the president of the United States was," Cody answered. "Now when Kennedy got *killed,* he was down there at the Burglary and Theft and he was in the hall down there and I said, 'Get your ass in here, Ruby.' So I opened the door and let him in so Ruby could conduct his business and wouldn't have all them people . . . But anyway, we get in there and he [Ruby] said, 'Aw, wasn't that terrible?'"

What about the mood of the Dallas Police?

"Here's the thing: Oswald shot the president, then he went home, changed clothes, and shot Tippit. We got him out of the theatre and brought him down. They've got Oswald; they've got witnesses; they've got a hidden rifle. Friday evening, by eight o'clock at night, we all went home. It was over with, as far as we were concerned."

When the Warren Report confirmed Oswald as the sole assassin,

Cody said it was no surprise to the Dallas Police. "They knew it," he stated. He added that the police "don't even pay attention" to the wild theories that continue to surround the assassination.

I then inquired about Kenneth Cody, telling my host of my encounter with him in 1968.

"He was my dad's younger brother, born in Shamrock, Texas, and he came to Dallas probably in the thirties. Kenneth went to work for the bus company. He'd buy some little houses over there, a duplex, he had two or three of those, and he had a sign in the yard that said, 'Call Kenneth Cody' and the phone number, you know, if you want to rent it. And that's where Oswald got his phone number, and he wrote it down and put it in there. It was just a few blocks from where Oswald lived."

Cody admitted he talked with his uncle about the matter, but he said Kenneth claimed he did not know Oswald and never received a telephone call from him regarding the property.

I found out too it was *Joe* Cody, and not Kenneth, who had the private pilot's license and his own plane, a further clarification to Penn Jones' theory that Kenneth had aided the escaping shooter or shooters.

Joe told me he never flew assassins out of Dallas that day.

When I left DeSoto hours later, I headed south fifteen miles to Midlothian. The town was much the same as I remembered it: small, slow, a bit dusty, sort of the Mayberry of Texas. The *Midlothian Mirror* had moved a block away from its old location to a newer and smaller office. Gone were the posters of Batman and Robin and the pictures of John Kennedy. Gone too was the flavor—the gritty character and the smells—it once held.

Still up the street was Penn Jones' old home, the trees now round and full and much taller. I stepped onto the wooden porch and peeked through drape-free windows into the living room where I had sat and talked often with the former owner. The room was bare now, the house vacant. It was up for sale.

The man who had chronicled the deaths of others had himself died a year earlier of Alzheimer's. Many had known him, but little would be written about him, save for the glowing obituary in the weekly paper he once owned.

Who would I now share my notes with in the evenings?

The next day I walked over to the Dallas Municipal Archives in the large and architecturally odd looking City Hall building. Its small office was the city's version of the National Archives. Files maintained by the Dallas Police had recently become available there to researchers.

Yet there was still nothing on Victoria Adams except a copy of her February 17, 1964, interview with Detective James Leavelle.[5] There were no reports on Sandra Styles and none on Dorothy Garner, a woman of particular interest due to my recent discovery of the Stroud letter at the National Archives.

Over the next several days, I called every *V* or *VE* or *Victoria* Adams in the phonebook—again. As before, it was a futile effort. I figured it would be. But I did find a listing for *Leavelle, Jas R.*

Like Cody, James Leavelle had been a colorful Dallas cop. For instance, during his Warren Commission testimony, he described for counsel Joseph Ball how hectic things were at headquarters on the afternoon of the assassination: "If you ever slopped hogs and throw down a pail of slop and saw them rush after it you would understand what that was like up there—about the same situation."[6]

Ball was so enamored with the comparison that he suggested to Alfred Goldberg, one of the writers of the Warren Report, that this "colorful extract" from Leavelle's testimony be included when the Commission critiqued media activities during the assassination weekend.[7] Goldberg thought better of it.

Then in 1992, Leavelle, who had been handcuffed to Oswald when Ruby jumped from the crowd, was demonstrating how another officer had grabbed Ruby's pistol. Forgetting he was using a loaded gun as a prop, Leavelle ended up accidentally shooting the photographer who was there to record the action.[8]

"You once questioned a witness by the name of Victoria Adams?" I inquired when Leavelle answered the phone that evening in 1999. "Do you remember her?"

He thought for a moment. "No, I don't recall that name."[9]

I summarized her story, mentioning the fact that she claimed to have come down the stairs immediately after the shooting and had heard no one during her descent.

The cobwebs began to clear from his memory. "I vaguely recall interviewing a young woman who said that," he replied. "But it wasn't germane to what we were looking for."

"Wasn't germane?" I echoed. "What *were* you looking for?"

"We were preparing for trial," Leavelle explained, "and if the witness couldn't provide anything we could use against Oswald, it wasn't important."

Miss Adams apparently had not fit the bill.

Carl Day had become a controversial figure over the years. As head of the Dallas Police Crime Lab, he was among the first to arrive on the sixth floor and examine the rifle in its hiding place.

Day told me in a telephone conversation that he did not personally find the rifle, but he was called over to view it immediately after its discovery and before anyone had touched it.[10] When he first saw the gun, he explained, it was hidden underneath and between several boxes. Scraps of paper covered up much of it. When he took the police photographs, shown in the twenty-six volumes, the paper had been removed to provide a better view of the weapon, he said.[11] "I just took the pictures of what I saw at the time."

Day personally took charge of the weapon after it was lifted from its hiding place. He made a special trip to police headquarters and put it behind lock and key. Then he returned to the Depository.

It was later that afternoon, he said, when he met Roy Truly, who related the story of "running up to the second floor right after the shots" and seeing Oswald "standing at the Coke machine."

Back at headquarters that evening, Day said he examined the rifle more carefully and discovered a palm print on the protected underside of the gun barrel. The print was later identified as belonging to Lee Oswald.

"This [print] was an old one," Day admitted. "Fresh ones, you can rub your finger over and it will rub off. Older prints you can rub your finger over and the print will still be there."

Day said he used powder and tape to lift the print.

By 10:30 P.M., he recalled, he was instructed "from upstairs" to immediately turn the rifle over to the FBI. "It caught me midstream," he said, but at least he had finished examining the weapon.

Day added he also saw "fragments" of "fresher prints" on the trigger housing of the rifle, but "none were identifiable."

"It was an older rifle," he said. "It could still shoot, but it wouldn't hold prints. There was no telling how long any of those prints had been on there. My job was to identify whose they were—not when they were put on."

I asked how the Dallas Police reacted to the FBI's intrusion.

"Some in the department were upset the way the FBI handled it, but it didn't affect me. You have to remember that it was really *our* crime—at that time it wasn't a federal crime to murder the president."

Day said the rifle was returned to Dallas on Sunday as part of "the condition of us releasing it to the FBI." Three or four days later, he added, the FBI took everything, including the palm print Day had lifted from that weapon. Up until that point, he said, the print had remained in a box, undisturbed.

"There were just too many cooks in the kitchen," Day commented, referring to the multiple agencies—FBI, Secret Service, Dallas Police, and sheriff's office—who wove their individual ways through the investigation and the evidence that weekend. The result, he summarized, was confusion, a lot of misinformation, and incomplete details being released to the public.

The Doorway Man

Thirty years earlier, I had spoken by phone with Carolyn Walther. She had told the FBI she witnessed a man with a rifle leaning out a Depository window while a second man stood beside him. The Warren Commission ignored her.

I happened to see her name in the phone directory and decided to touch base. When she answered the phone, it was hard not to notice the advanced age in her voice. I explained who I was, and how I had made her cry three decades earlier.

She remembered.

"I have but one question to ask, if you don't mind," I said.

"I may or may not answer," she replied with a sigh. "I'm so tired of it."[12]

"After all these years," I asked carefully, "after thirty-six years, do you *still* stand by your statement of seeing a man with a gun and another man standing next to him in the Depository?"

"Yes, I do," she answered quickly. "Why wouldn't I? I know what I saw and nothing can change that."

After some coaxing, she recounted her story once again. The details she provided matched up exactly with what she had told the FBI, and what she had told me those many years ago. I asked if she had kept up with the subject. She replied that she had read a handful of books but became upset when several described her as being a liar.[13]

"I'm not a liar," she said. "I know what I saw. And it's the truth."

Early the next morning, after forking over six bucks and being offered an audio tour in my choice of seven different languages, I was among six others who boarded the highly polished elevator. Our destination was the sixth floor of the former Texas School Book Depository. I was on my way to what Roy Truly had denied me years ago. And I was obligated to pay for the privilege.

As the doors opened on arrival, I was greeted by a wave of emotions, good and bad. Emerging onto this most famous of all warehouse floors, I had, in a small way, reached a goal that had hung above me since day one.

The appearance, of course, was different now. The once dusty, messy, and dark book-storage area had turned into the clean, organized, and well-lit Sixth Floor Museum. The massive support posts were there, just as they had been when Oswald worked the floor. He probably glanced up at the black 6 on the post just outside the two freight elevators that remained against the back wall. The elevators had been inoperative for a long while but retained the original wood-slat gates, their smoothness a testament to decades of duty. How many times had Oswald touched them? How many times had he walked—or run—by where I now stood?

The floor was new, raised for public safety several inches above the original gapped and splintered boards beneath. Overhead, the huge, exposed wooden beams and the accompanying pipes had been left untouched. Between the beams, one could see the underside of the diagonally laid boards of the seventh floor, now used to store the old rooftop Hertz sign.

The once-mazelike layout of boxes holding school textbooks, the mainstay of this former business, had disappeared, replaced by another mazelike array of partition walls dividing the open floor into small display areas. Each area was named for its related subject matter and informed the uninformed of what had happened here. I could hear in the distance the voice of John Kennedy, echoing from a looped videotape.

I did not stop to listen. I was on my way directly to the southeast corner window.

My stomach churned. This display area was called "The Perch." Behind protective Plexiglas, I saw what could only be an educated guess as to how it looked when the shots were fired.[14] The original wood-plank flooring was visible beneath the simulated stacks of "Scott Foresman" book cartons. One carton had been carefully crafted to hide a camera that broadcasts continuous peeks out this window on the Internet.

Who had stood here that day? Was it Oswald? Or was it someone else?

Based on the imposed limits, the best I could do for a reenactment was crouch behind a set of windows a few feet to the right of "The Perch" and stare down into Dealey Plaza. I could imagine the parade going by and the cheering crowds and the feelings of excitement. And the first thought that hit me was why, why in the world would Oswald wait until the presidential limousine turned the corner onto Elm to shoot his victim?

It is a dilemma one can only experience from this vantage point: the shot he failed to take as the car approached the building on Houston Street; Kennedy, clearly vulnerable, as he looked straight ahead toward the assassin; the target getting closer and closer, looming larger and larger in the murderous rifle sights. This seemed so much easier and more likely than when the president's car traveled down Elm away from the shooter, with his head bobbling right to left. It didn't make sense, unless perhaps crossfire had been planned.

There was one place left to see. Over in the northwest corner of the building was another encased area, this one depicting where the rifle was discovered. Against the wall hung a black sign with white letters reading, "Stairway."

It was the sixth-floor entrance to the old wooden staircase. Was this really the start of Oswald's famed descent?

Back on the first floor, I inquired whether Gary Mack was available. I remembered Mack from several television documentaries. He was once a critic of the Warren Report but, in Robert Groden's estimation, had "gone to the other side" when he became curator of the Sixth Floor Museum.

He came up from below to greet me, then showed me the way to his nicely remodeled offices in the basement of the Depository. Coincidentally, he had been cueing up some related film on his computer. He showed me one of particular interest.

It was the movie shot by Elsie Dorman from the fourth-floor window of the Depository. She had been filming the event with her husband's camera, shooting out the open window as Victoria Adams and Sandra Styles stood beside her. I was watching the assassination through Miss Adams' eyes.

Kennedy was seconds from death as his car approached on Houston Street. The vehicle swung wide and turned left directly below, the camera giving a bird's-eye view down into the limousine. Its occupants were not centered in the frame. Owing to the photographer's inexperience, the images fluttered about rapidly. The film abruptly ended as the car entered Elm and became obscured behind tree limbs.[15]

Mack agreed to chat a bit. He began by telling me a story about Billy Lovelady and the never-ending confusion over whether it was Lovelady or Oswald on the Depository's front steps in James Altgens' photograph. "Back in the late seventies, I was hosting on occasion a Sunday-night talk show on the Kennedy assassination on one of the very popular stations in Dallas, and one of Billy's friends—personal friends, not from the Depository but a neighbor or something like that—listened to the shows and at the end of one of them, he called and, because we had been talking about Lovelady, said, 'If you'd like to interview Billy I'd be happy to set it up for you. Normally he doesn't do these things, but you seem like reasonable folks.'[16]

"So, within a few days we were on the phone, not recorded unfortunately. He was living in Aurora, Colorado, at the time, which I think is where he was when he died.[17] He told me that the shirt that he was wearing that day was purchased for him by his wife at a local Goodwill here in Dallas for fifty-nine cents, and he still had it—would never part with it. He'd been offered a lot of money for it—would not part with it for anything. He was fully aware of the controversy; he just thought it was kind of silly because not only was he the guy on the steps but all of his coworkers were on the steps, they all knew him, they all knew Lee, and they all were all saying, 'That was Billy. I know both guys.'

"He told me a funny story. He said he didn't know Oswald well at all—in fact, most of the guys didn't because he [Oswald] was relatively new—but they all recognized the physical similarities, and a couple of the guys purposely called Billy 'Lee' and Lee 'Billy,' just to tease them. He said, 'Oswald got a kick out of it. He thought it was funny, but I didn't. I didn't like it.'"

The shirt on the man in the doorway was open partway down the chest, just as was the shirt Oswald wore following his arrest. Buttons apparently missing from Lovelady's shirt were shown missing from Oswald's as well. Wasn't Mack curious about that?

"Well, yes and no," he answered. "This happens to be one of my areas of great interest. The pictures of Oswald after the arrest, of course, are after the struggle [with police officers in the Texas Theatre] when some buttons were torn, so pictures of him under arrest don't show the shirt the way it was at the time of the assassination.

"Most researchers have heard the name Robert Groden. No question that he is a pro-conspiracy guy. Groden did something that no one else was able to do when he worked for the House Assassinations Committee. He and I have been acquainted since '77 or '78. Groden got access to the original negative of that [Altgens] photograph and he made blowups of that for the House Committee and the photo panel and the photo panel couldn't really tell the pattern of the shirt either, so they made their own blowups and again, they were not able to make the image clear enough to be able to tell. The negative went back to Groden and he tried a different technique and he had a name for it. He called it 'variable density cynexing.' I have no idea what the hell that means. But he claimed it was a technique that was able to 'strengthen the contrast,' that is what he said, so that he could see the pattern in the shirt. And of course when you are looking at a black-and-white reproduction of a colored object, the tonal value tends to shift; you're not really sure what you're looking at. Once he had a clear blowup, where he could see the pattern, then he compared it with black-and-white blowups from two color home movies, and in black and white, the patterns were clearly the same. Now the shirt [Lovelady's] is actually a red and blue and white. It's just [that] the way it turns out in black and white can be confusing, so if you're not a photographer and you don't have that background, people don't think of these things. Robert Groden used to be on record as saying, 'That was Oswald in the doorway' until he did the work using the original materials, and he's been saying for twenty-one years now, 'It's Lovelady.' The Committee even flew Groden and a Committee member to Denver to meet Lovelady. Groden even took his own pictures of Lovelady wearing the shirt and those are published in the [HSCA] volumes too.[18] So, as far as I'm concerned, that's one of the stories that's been put to rest."

Except for the Dealey Plaza hucksters, I thought.

Billy Lovelady was incessantly hounded by the media and the critics due to confusion over the doorway man.

"Let me tell you a story," Mack continued. "And this is why he quit talking to people. It was so bad that there was a night in Dallas when, and I forget what the noise was that startled him, but something startled him in the bedroom—he had been asleep—and he sat up in bed and a flash went off *in the room*. Someone actually had gotten into the house and either rigged up something in the room or had a flash at the window to get a picture. That's how bad it had gotten; that's when he stopped talking. He was scared. That's the phrase he told me. He didn't have any personal confrontations with people—he said, 'Sometimes I'd talk to them and sometimes I wouldn't depending on whether they sounded normal or not.' He said, 'That was it when that happened. I was scared for my wife and my kid.'"

I asked Mack how accurate were the museum's depictions of the sniper's nest and where the rifle was found.

"Best we can do," he replied.

Mack also said the sixth-floor entrance to the wooden staircase was as it appeared originally. I told him the story of how I climbed those stairs to the second-floor lunchroom, unbeknownst to Roy Truly. He laughed and said I had been lucky to get away with it, since Truly was always very particular about whom he allowed into the building after the assassination.

That evening, I sat in my customary spot in Dealey Plaza, watching the tourists and the wandering pitchmen. I thought of how far I had traveled since Terry had asked me why I believed the Warren Report, now more than thirty years ago. I had come to this rather mystical place called Dallas and stood behind the window from where the Warren Commission said the shots originated; behind the fence where the House Select Committee placed a second shooter; and in the middle of Elm Street, where a white-painted X marks for sightseers the exact spot of the final horror. Was it from a convergence of bullets? There was certainly a convergence of theories.

The next morning as I left town for the long ride home, I did something I always wanted to do. I pointed my car into the center lane of Elm and slowed to a crawl as I drove through Dealey Plaza, past the former Depository, over the X in the street, alongside the grassy knoll and the gawking tourists, and on into the darkness of the Triple Underpass. A chill ran down my back. I stared into the rearview mirror until I could see the spot no longer.

All I had to do now was try to explain this on paper.

CHAPTER 24

February 2-3, 2002

She sat quietly in her chair on that cool Saturday evening, mystified by the single line in the e-mail that had popped up on her computer screen.

"Are you the Vickie Adams who graduated from Presentation High School in San Francisco and once worked in Dallas, Texas?" It was signed, "Larry Roberge."

The name meant nothing to her. Who is this person who writes me out of the blue, and how does he know about me? she wondered. He couldn't be a former classmate. Presentation was an all-girls' school. And she hadn't known any Roberges in Dallas, or anywhere else for that matter.

She clicked the Reply button. "Yes, I am," she typed. "But I don't recognize this name. Who are you?"

There was no response the rest of the night.

When she awoke the next morning, another strange e-mail awaited her. This one was from somebody in Harrisburg, Pennsylvania—she remembered the place well—who told her Mr. Roberge was a friend who was following a lead. This latest missive asked if she was the Victoria Adams who had once worked for Scott Foresman and was a witness to the Kennedy assassination.

She froze.

"For the sake of this email," the mystery writer continued, "I will assume that you are that person."

As she went deeper into this electronic dispatch, determining its author to be a man, she became more and more intrigued by his tale of the lengths he had gone to in order to find a woman named Victoria Adams—to find *her*. He said he was writing a book, intending to focus on what she had witnessed, on what she had said and done so many years before, and on his seemingly unquenchable desire to hear her story, firsthand.

In a way, she was flattered.

"All the while," he wrote, "it has been your testimony, the sincerity of what you said during it, and the absence of further information about what you witnessed, that for some reason has fascinated and consumed me the most."

She read on, about his years of research, his trips to Dallas and Washington, his efforts to find truth in a sea of deception. He sounds honest, she thought—candid, forthright, if a bit verbose and perhaps melodramatic. But she had heard it all before.

They had wanted the truth from her back then, or so she thought. They had wanted her to tell them about what she did and what she saw, in her own words, sparing no details. She had done that, on numerous occasions.

Then they had called her a liar.

A long time ago, she had promised herself not to make that mistake again. But somehow, this seemed different. He wanted her help to right this wrong. He wanted to hear her side firsthand. He wanted her absolute truths.

She was swayed by those words. Was this the chance she had always wanted?

"You cannot imagine," she read on, "the excitement I felt when I first learned my search for Miss Adams may be over, nor the uncommon nervousness I have felt while writing this email to you, nor the anticipation and fear of what you may say in response as I now click the 'Send' button."

Her memories flashed before her. She had kept them bottled up for so long now, a mute testament to her past. She had stood at the precipice of no longer giving a damn about what had happened in Dallas that day, a city far away in more ways than one.

The truth had been told before, and she had told it. Why bother again?

It would be quite simple. She could write back and say she was not, after all, the one he was looking for. But that would be a lie. And she didn't lie.

Better yet, she could simply press the Delete key and end it right here. Based on the brick walls he said he already had hit in his search for her, that alternative could easily be perceived as just one more goose chase, one more wrong number, one more dead end.

But she began to type.

CHAPTER 25

January 2000–February 2002

It was my son who had convinced me to buy a computer for the writing job ahead. Little did I realize what else that gizmo could do.

It reconnected me to Gary Schoener, whom I had not heard from since 1970. He had remained in Minnesota, completing all the requirements for his Ph.D. in clinical psychology, except for his dissertation. He was now in charge of the Walk-In Counseling Center, a pet project of his back when I first met him.

Life's demands had forced Schoener to quit his assassination research in the mid-seventies.

And it reconnected me to Vincent Salandria, who stopped his studies of the assassination because his wife could no longer tolerate his obsession with that subject. Tired and frustrated at seventy-two and convinced that Kennedy was murdered at the hands of the U.S. military-intelligence system, Salandria had no patience with those who felt that "who did it" was still a mystery.

There was David Lifton. Since writing his bestseller, *Best Evidence*, he had persisted, researching and composing again for an upcoming volume about the many lives of Lee Oswald. Still in California, he once more asked for my assistance in obtaining documents for him from the Archives.

And of course, I would help him.

Reestablishing old ties by way of the computer made me think. Could this thing be used to find Victoria Adams? With its far and instantaneous reach, was it the perfect resource?

It proved as fruitless as everything else. When I typed her name into a search engine, all I found were pages devoted to spicy women's wear from Victoria's Secret or references to a dark-haired singer in an all-female band called the Spice Girls.

I e-mailed the Scott Foresman Company in Dallas, where she last worked. Then I queried the company's main offices in Chicago.

The immediacy of this techno-mail system allowed me to hit the proverbial brick wall much quicker than I had become accustomed to with the U.S. Postal Service.

I sent more such letters to places where she had worked between high school and Dallas. I scoured the Internet for birth records, death records, voter records, tax records, *any* records. The occasional and unknown "Victoria Adams" popped up, giving me encouragement. Closer inspection always led to dead ends and more frustration. Searches made by my son through his employer's extensive computer banks at a large Washington, D.C. law firm showed nothing on record nationwide. A private detective specializing in locating the lost told me that with no other information than what I possessed—especially with no idea of the state she may be residing in or if she had taken a married name—it would be a waste of time and money for him to continue.

I was losing hope, motivation, and even the desire to continue writing my story. Then, at the height of my despair, it happened. Isn't that the way things always seem to work?

CHAPTER 26

February 3, 2002

The words in Larry's e-mail struck me at full throttle. *"She said she is the one who graduated from Presentation High School in 1959 and used to work in Dallas, Texas. I think it would be too much of a coincidence not to be the same one."*

Victoria Adams mentioned during her Warren Commission testimony that she had graduated from high school in San Francisco. Weeks earlier I had begun an online search through what seemed like an endless list of schools in that city. I was exploring alumni pages for her name, hoping for a last-chapter reprieve from what seemed like the inevitable: an epilogue to my book that said all my efforts to find this woman, in the end, had failed.

Then, alphabetically, I came upon Presentation High School. Its site revealed a listing for a 1959 graduate named Victoria Adams. The name fit. So did the year. Despite numerous attempts, though, I was unable to access any more information. So I typed off an e-mail to the school, seeking assistance.

No one replied.

Then Larry Roberge, a computer-geek friend of mine, asked one day how I was progressing with my book and my search for the missing witness. I brought him up to date and explained how I lacked the technical knowhow to pursue my most recent online discovery. He offered to help.

I gladly dumped the job into his lap.

Somehow, within a week, he had ferreted out the woman's e-mail address and written her a note, asking if she had once lived in Dallas. When she replied yes, he immediately notified me.

I had been down this road before—so many times. Yet there was something about this one, something that finally seemed to lend this lead an aura of authenticity. So I drafted a lengthy e-mail, taking my time, explaining everything, sweating out every word. I knew if she were the *real* thing, I had to be careful with my words. I didn't want to scare her away.

Was it really "too much of a coincidence," as Larry said?

I clicked the Send button and waited, for three hours.

"Wow," this woman finally replied. "Hard to believe someone has been looking for me for over 30 years."

Had she really said "looking for *me*"?

"Yes, I am Victoria Adams, graduated from Presentation High School in 1959 and worked for Scott, Foresman in Dallas, as well as in Chicago."[1]

I had finally found her.

CHAPTER 27

February 3, 2002

Victoria Elizabeth Adams was sixty-one now and living on the West Coast. No longer the "Miss Adams" I had grown accustomed to, she had married during the intervening years. She chose to keep her maiden name but preferred the more contemporary "Ms. Adams." It was a subtle change.

"Too bad you didn't know my biography is in *Who's Who of American Women* and *Who's Who in the World*," she wrote that day. "Has been for years. But that is basically irrelevant except as a way of perhaps adding more credibility to what I saw and said at the time.[1]

"Remember, though, I was a very young woman at the time (22 years old) and believed in my government. Because of the strange circumstances and discounting of my statements, my multiple questioning by various government agencies and the Warren Commission's conclusions, I lost my starry eyed beliefs in the integrity of our government. And I was scared, too. I was a young lady alone with no family or friend support at the time."

I was absorbed by her words.

"Still, I saw what I saw and my testimony apparently didn't fit what the government wanted. That is too bad. Repeatedly I asked that my testimony be confirmed by another witness who was with me part of the time, but I was basically blown off."

She said she once spoke briefly with Mark Lane. And she appeared on the Mort Sahl television show, which Lane had arranged. But neither seemed interested in her real story. Other than that, and a few relatives, she had told her full story to no one.

"Essentially, however, things kind of died around it and I just gave up, figuring I would die with my own truth inside of me."

She refused to read much of anything regarding the assassination. "My husband is bored by the topic, and I had no desire to read someone's opinion of what happened when I was actually there and indirectly participated in the events of the day."

In subsequent conversations, she became careful with me, feeling out this person who had suddenly trespassed into her otherwise tranquil life. She sought details, writing samples, verifications. She queried me philosophically, closely examining my opinions and thoughts, trying hard to repress the fear she said she had felt so many times in the past.

"I don't have burly guys at my side and don't do investigations on people," she told me, referring to the experiences I had shared with her about S. M. Holland. "What I do have is a sense of trust that my Universe is operating exactly as it should if I operate in the same way. But, still, once in awhile, my old survival, and fight-or-flight fears surface."

I did my best to dampen her concerns. I didn't want to have to search for her anymore.

"Thanks for quelling those fears," she responded. "I'll help you in any way I can."

Permission granted, I bombarded her on an almost daily basis with the questions I had held in reserve. She answered. I checked the details she provided, then sought more. She answered. One day I inquired if this was the first time she had provided such particulars to anyone.

"Absolutely," she replied.

Why me? I wondered.

"The reason I chose to discuss it with you was, you convinced me that you were sincerely interested in knowing the truth. And most importantly, you seemed convinced that I had been consistent in telling the truth as I remember it. So often, people just give up . . . like me . . . and quit. You didn't."

Suddenly, the gaps in her story began to close. Victoria Adams had led a troubled early life. At the age of eleven, she became a ward of the State of California after her parents abruptly deserted her. She was raised in several foster homes until she finished high school.

"Much of my young life was spent in fear and I concentrated more on survival than anything else," she recalled. "I was afraid to speak, afraid of ridicule, afraid I couldn't defend myself. Fear was a constant companion."

After graduation, Ms. Adams entered the Novitiate at St. Martin, Ohio, in the Ursuline Order. She had gone to boarding school there when she was ten and considered it a stable environment. Two years later, she moved to Atlanta, where she worked briefly for a social-services organization and an attorney before becoming a sixth-grade teacher at the Immaculate Heart of Mary School. When the academic year ended in 1962, she was off again, this time to Dallas. Her first job there was in reservations at a Holiday Inn, and in the fall of that year, she taught a sixth-grade class at St. Monica's School.

It was at this point that she began to closely examine her religious convictions, pondering her past and becoming fearful of what might be her only future. She decided for the first time to take control.

"I realized I was no longer a believer," she admitted. "If I could not believe what I had been taught, I could not teach the concepts and beliefs, because I would be untrue to myself. Rather than subject children to any lies on my part, I chose to give up Catholicism and the Catholic school system. Those days were really confusing, but liberating in a sense."

When the school term ended at St. Monica's in mid-1963, Ms. Adams set her sights on something new and applied for what seemed like an interesting job at the Texas School Book Depository.

"My position with Scott Foresman in Dallas was a created one. They needed someone to be a customer service representative with the Catholic school system and the colleges in the southeast because they wanted to increase their market share in that arena. That was my job. And I always felt kind of out of the flow, since I was the only one who did that and I was the last hired, only working there for about a year."

That year, however, became a turning point for Ms. Adams, both professionally and philosophically. Her life was changing dramatically, unalterably, in many different ways. And right in the middle of it came November 22.

"The day was cold and looked like it was going to rain. I carried a huge purse, big enough to accommodate my shoes, and I wore a gray coat. These details seem rather insignificant until later when we were released to go home, because I remember thinking that the Secret Service wouldn't know if I had been carrying a weapon in my purse or the umbrella was a shotgun or some kind of rifle, which I had under my coat.

"I parked my car near the railroad tracks several blocks away, walked to the office in my tennis shoes, into the front of the building and took the elevator to the fourth floor, arriving ahead of time as I always did, took my high heels out of my purse and changed into them.

"Normally the office was quiet, but that day everyone was excited since the presidential motorcade was going to come right by our building. We were on the fourth floor and our windows would give us a good view, so I decided I would watch from the windows instead of trying to watch on the street. I am short, and figured I could see better, especially if the President and First Lady were in a convertible.[2]

"I remember some grumbling about JFK and someone showed me a black bordered statement or something in the newspaper, but I didn't care. It didn't affect me directly and I wasn't particularly political anyway. It was just exciting being able to see the President go by.

"The morning went as usual, with typical letters, phone calls and customer service activity. About 20 minutes before the motorcade was due, someone opened our windows (the old kind that lift up) so we could see well, and I think six of us gathered at the windows to watch. Some people who worked in my office went downstairs and became part of the crowd gathering on the corner.

"I stood with Sandra [Styles] and we strained toward where we knew the motorcade would be coming from. To us the Kennedys were like a fairy tale—one in which the rich and beautiful live a life of make believe. They didn't have to work like we did, doing the same things day after day with more of the same on the horizon. They had power, money and jewels and could jet here and there. In contrast, I could collect my $350 a month wages and go home and dream of what it must be like to be rich and married to a handsome powerful man.

"As I watched the motorcade proceed toward the Depository, the President and Mrs. Kennedy were clearly visible. I thought Mrs. Kennedy looked stunning with roses on her lap. As they rounded the corner, they turned toward our building, waving and smiling. The car continued moving slowly and a tree obstructed my view. That is when I heard what I thought was a firecracker go off. As the car came back into view I saw that something was wrong and watched as Mrs. Kennedy appeared to be trying to climb out of the car. I saw a Secret Service man jump in and the car began speeding up toward the triple underpass. Before it reached that I turned to Sandra and I said, 'I want to see what is going on.'

"We ran to the back of the office and down the stairs."

"We ran down the stairs," Ms. Adams continued. "We were both in high heels. No one was there. We would have heard other steps. The noise on those steps is very obvious. And remember, the elevator cables were not moving. It was quiet.

"We ran outside and noticed a lot of people running toward the railroad tracks. The railroad yard behind the grassy knoll was quite a distance away. I could not see anything other than people running toward the railroad cars and I tried to run that way, too. But a policeman stopped us. I didn't get very far—maybe 10 or 20 feet from the Depository building. So we turned back to Houston and to the front of the building.

"It was mass confusion. That was when I noticed Ruby."

How sure was she it was Jack Ruby?

"Supposedly Jack Ruby was a great admirer of President and Mrs. Kennedy," she answered. "What was peculiar was according to his testimony he was several blocks away at the newspaper office when the motorcade was passing by on Houston and Elm. But I saw him immediately after the gunshots on the corner of Houston and Elm and just happened to notice him since he was asking questions of people, like he was a reporter. He was rather distinctive in that he had on a suit and hat. I didn't see anyone else acting like that. I mentioned this in my testimony more than once, trying to give as much information as I could about what I saw that day. From what I know nothing ever was said about that.

"But when I met Mark Lane, he showed me a picture of Ruby dressed like I had seen him and where I said he was. He said the Warren Commission had cropped the photo.

"Now, remember, I wasn't into investigative reporting or anything and had no idea how important that information was about Ruby's whereabouts and I am not even sure it is important now. The reason I know it was Ruby was I saw him on TV after he shot Oswald and recognized the face as being the same one I had seen on that corner."

While she was standing in front of the Depository, observing all that was happening around her in the early moments following the assassination, Ms. Adams said she heard a police broadcast coming from a motorcycle parked nearby. I pressed her for more details about the nature of what she overheard.

"The only thing I remember about that was the fear it produced—that I might be implicated in some way. I do not recall what was said."

Even though she couldn't recollect the exact words, the "fear it produced" is consistent with what she told the Warren Commission she had heard: a police broadcast indicating the shots may have originated from the fourth floor, the very floor where Ms. Adams worked.

"Sandra went back inside. I stayed outside. I didn't care if I would be fired. I needed to know what was happening."

Only after satisfying her curiosity a bit longer did Ms. Adams return to the building, taking the front elevator to her office and her desk. She was sent home not long after being questioned by "several men." By then, it was shortly after 2 P.M.

"One of the things I did immediately after I got home," she continued, "was write a longhand, six-page letter to John O'Connor, who was the editor of *The Monitor*, a San Francisco Catholic newspaper. I detailed my moves and exactly what I did that day and especially what I witnessed. John never received that letter and I don't know what actually happened to it."

She wrote him, she said, because she had worked for O'Connor while in high school. I asked how she could be so sure he had not received her letter.

"I never spoke directly with O'Connor. My foster father, when I discussed the letter with him—he also worked at *The Monitor*—told me that John O'Connor had never received such a letter from me. My foster father was the advertising manager of the newspaper at the time and he and O'Connor spent a lot of time together."

Ms. Adams did not keep a copy of the letter for herself. She was at the time, she admitted, still "young and naïve."

"I suspect it was taken by someone in Dallas after I mailed it, but have no proof of that."

"Maybe I Was Key and Didn't Know It"

The initial statements Ms. Adams made to investigators in her office that Friday afternoon hoisted some red flags. Ms. Adams suddenly became a focus, questioned repeatedly by various agencies and always about the same thing: her trip down the stairs and exactly when she had made it.

"It really didn't dawn on me that my actions were pertinent to anything until much later," she said. "In Dallas, the people in my office were pretty chagrined that the secret police and CIA and all those others were interested in me. I think they were disappointed it wasn't them. And, quite frankly, I couldn't figure out why they were so interested. At least then."

She told me about the night she was startled to find Dallas police officer James Leavelle standing at her front doorstep. The date was February 17, 1964.

"One time, a detective from the Dallas police came to my apartment, showed his badge and asked to talk with me. I asked him why he needed to talk with me since I had already given my testimony to the Dallas police. 'Oh,' he responded, 'the records were all burned in a fire we had and we have to interview everyone again.'[3] Because the Dallas

Police Department had been much maligned in the weeks following the assassination, I guess nothing surprised me. But that did. So I once again said the same thing, which at that point felt like ad nauseam."

The officer's sudden appearance that evening was strange too because Ms. Adams had only the day before moved to this location, a new apartment. She had not yet notified anyone—not her boss, associates in her office, or even the post office—of her change of address. The apartment was even rented in her roommate's name.

Under those circumstances, Ms. Adams became nervous about how the police had found her and, in hindsight, figures she must somehow have been followed.

"I never felt like I was a key player in the drama, just a player. Maybe I was key and didn't know it. Maybe the government had already decided to reach a conclusion they wanted to reach and didn't bother with some girl on the fourth floor. And I sure didn't mind that.

"The whole thing was a pretty frightening ordeal and a devastating time to everyone. I had never witnessed anything like that and the horror of watching TV those days was awful. Seeing a real live murder occur before my eyes on TV was horrifying. And then there was always that niggling fear in the back of my mind that maybe why they were sending so many people to talk with me was they thought I knew something or someone that was involved.

"I was afraid of the implication of that.

"I was a young girl making about $400 a month at that time and I couldn't hire an attorney to help me if somehow the government decided I was involved more than I was. I had no adult to turn to. I was also concerned that I might be called to testify before the Warren Commission itself. I had no money to make such a trip. I had no income except from my job."

Ms. Adams was not summoned to Washington. She did, however, end up being questioned by Commission attorney David Belin in Dallas.

"When I gave my deposition to the Warren Commission attorney, he was another of those patronizing types," she remarked.

"When I went into the office he was using, he did not stand up, as was the custom in the South when a woman entered the room. He stayed seated. Then he told me he was going to ask me some questions and he wanted me to answer them without elaboration. So he went through all of the questions he had.

"I answered.

"He told me that all my answers and his questions were 'off the record,' and that he would invite a court reporter in to take my actual deposition and I was to answer exactly what I said to him—no variations. During the informal part, he leaned back in his chair, crossed his arms and looked at me straight. . . . 'Now Miss Adams, don't you think you could be wrong? Memory is a funny thing and tricks some people.'

"I looked him straight in the eye and said, 'I could be, but I'm not wrong. I know what I saw, what I did and what I heard.'

"He told me at the end of his questioning he would ask me if I had anything to add that I hadn't mentioned up to then. I was supposed to say, 'No,' as I had in the initial session. But I didn't.

"As I started speaking, he looked startled, especially when I talked about seeing Jack Ruby on the corner across the street from the Depository building.

"He ended the session, thanked me for my time and I left. That was the last contact I had with anyone regarding the events."

A transcript of her testimony was later delivered to her office for her review, she said. Ms. Adams made several spelling corrections and changed a few other inaccuracies. Not a single one of those corrections appeared in her final testimony printed in the twenty-six volumes. A self-admitted "word person," Ms. Adams said she was disturbed by the errors left standing.

"Perhaps the reason that bothered me is I saw it as just one more attempt at minimization of my credibility. You can imagine I felt stupid and like a fool when I read the book [the Warren Report] when it came out. The echoes of that attorney's words haunted me, 'Now, Miss Adams, don't you think you could be wrong?'

"They made me wrong, because they literally wanted to hang the murder on someone and do it quickly to stop the truth from being known, whatever the truth really was.

"Apparently the Warren Commission didn't think [what I told them] was true. Or if they did, they managed to make it appear wrong. What I said was true. I said it so many times I got tired of saying it. Quite frankly I didn't even know it was important to anything. I was just a young girl interested in what was going on and worried that something terrible had happened. I wanted to know and I couldn't know if I was standing around in some office talking with others who didn't know. Even today, looking back, I am amazed that it was important.

"But obviously it was."

CHAPTER 28

February 4-9, 2002

Gradually, the official inquiries stopped.

"When that Dallas detective lied to me [about the fire], I knew something wasn't right," Ms. Adams said. "I knew when John O'Connor didn't respond to my letter, something wasn't right. I knew when Ruby killed Oswald that something wasn't right. But the faith loss actually hit its finality when my testimony was discounted and I knew someone was trying to fit a puzzle together with lots of pieces from some other puzzle they had and create a story they wanted the public to believe.

"I felt like a fool, an idiot whose credibility would be challenged from that point on. To me, who I was was more important than what I did. At that point, both who I was was being denied, as well as what I did. I had been disparaged and felt ridiculed and minimized. This truly shook me to my core.

"I'm sure you can't imagine the feelings that coursed through me as I realized the possibilities of what was going on. I must say it was a great relief when I was offered a job at the Scott Foresman home office in Chicago."

I asked if she had expressed those fears to others.

"I never have written or discussed my situation with any researcher or reporter," she said. "One time about 10 years ago I offered to do it locally with the local newspaper, but there was no interest, so I dropped it. I kept no journals about the event, fearing that whatever I wrote might be stolen and misused. My husband was big into telling me to be quiet. Witnesses disappeared. Witnesses were killed.

"Perhaps you can imagine the state of mind of a young lady in her 20s who had been frightened about many things. This was one fear she didn't need. No researcher has ever gotten in touch with me about what I witnessed, at least until now.

"You're it."

Not long after David Belin questioned her, Ms. Adams moved from Dallas.

"When Scott Foresman offered me a transfer to their home office, I accepted it and moved the following year in July. I felt there was no place for me to go career-wise in Dallas and the home office offered more opportunity. At the same time I considered myself to be 'over the hill' and that my biological clock was rapidly going downhill. I was ready to get married. I did—to a man from a Chicago suburb and we moved to the West Coast. I desperately wanted to be a saleswoman with the company instead of into the editorial stuff. I asked if the company would provide a scholarship for me to be able to attend college at night, since I had no parents and no one else to help me. They said 'no,' although they provided scholarships to high school students. I was crushed.

"By that time I was the executive secretary to the vice president of sales, very efficient and very young. I had again reached my plateau. I left the company in 1966 and moved to San Diego and began working for a couple of surgeons as an office manager."

While living in California and continuing to work part time, Ms. Adams went back to college and acquired a degree in general education, graduating with honors. By 1970, she had her first child. Changing gears again in 1974, she turned her career interests toward real estate, working full time in that profession while continuing to pursue her education at night. She finally graduated summa cum laude with a bachelor's degree in business administration.

Still more changes were on the horizon. "A couple of years later my husband and I hit the road and traveled for six years until our money ran out. We returned to 'real' life and 'real' bills and 'real' responsibilities."

During that lengthy escape, she turned into a real "gypsy," as she often described herself. It was no wonder I had been unable to catch up with her.

During that period, Ms. Adams and her husband lived in a five-wheel trailer along the highways, traversing the country, seeing the sights, and experiencing mostly rural America at ground level. Ironically, part of her travels brought her to my backyard in 1997. She stayed in Pennsylvania for two months, visiting Harrisburg and its restaurants and tourist attractions. For two weeks, she lived only twenty-five miles from my home.

We could have passed each other, dined at the same eatery, been at the same museum at the same time. Wasn't that what Larry might consider too much of a coincidence?

When her journey was done, she returned home to live out her otherwise quiet life, until, that is, I found her.

I would, of course, quiz her often about her trek down the back staircase. I milked her story for every nuance and detail, initially asking if it were possible that her "clattering in our heels" descent, as she described it, may have drowned out other footsteps.

"No one else was on those stairs unless they were creeping down on tiptoe." She was always emphatic about that.

"We could not have drowned out the sound of other feet by our noise. Whenever anyone was on the stairs you could hear them on any floor. We would have heard someone on the stairs. Absolutely."

I inquired too about the timing: how fast it took from when she left the window until she reached the top of the stairs and how fast she descended those stairs to the first floor.

"I am sorry about this," she replied, "but I have no concept of how long. Remember, this was all done in the desire to get outside to see what was happening and to get out quickly before someone stopped me, which I thought they might have. If you asked me how many steps there were between floors, for example, I couldn't answer that either.

"None of that stuff interested me then nor later, because I really never saw it as relevant. I never really concerned myself with thinking about the implications of timing. I was so interested in getting out that I did the unthinkable—for a woman. I ran out without my purse."

Perhaps Ms. Adams had moved so quickly she was down the stairs before Oswald even started his descent.

"If Oswald was interested in getting away fast, you bet he would have hurried," she answered. "I was interested in getting to the action, too, but I didn't speed it up like a shooter would have. Actually what I think happened is that Oswald was where he said he was all the time."

Did she mean in the first-floor employees' lounge?

Ms. Adams never realized the implications of that thought on November 22. When she talked with investigators, she told them only what she knew: that she had gone down the steps moments after the shooting.

I asked when it first dawned on her that she should have heard or seen Oswald if the assassin was escaping from above.

"It was sometime during that week," she responded. "I am convinced that there was something funny going on, but I don't hold any more answers to the riddle than you do. Both Sandra and I were very nervous about the whole thing since we knew we had been where the killer reputedly was at approximately the same time. I cannot say much about what I believe happened, but I do suspect that Oswald was never on the sixth floor at the time of the assassination.

"I do think the government wanted people to get on with their lives and out of the drama of the assassination and they did what they wanted.

"And I don't believe my testimony was ignored. It was discounted, which is entirely different. And even in Sandra's deposition [to the FBI in March 1964, a copy of which I had sent her], I see there was nothing that suggests they really wanted to know the timing. I actually think the Warren Commission needed to bring an end to the investigation.

"It is hard to understand that Sandra and I were both young ladies and we weren't into political things. Instead we were into having fun, meeting young men and making a living. This was really scary for us. If you can put yourself into our shoes, we had high-powered people playing 'who dun it' and we were wanting to make sure they knew we didn't or didn't have a connection of any kind to anyone who did. That was pretty heady stuff for young women in those days."

I specifically asked if she remembered seeing Kennedy when she heard the first shot. "No," she answered, "because I did not see the limousine at that time. It was under the tree." As she gazed out the window, she said, the tree was "slightly to my right."

I then inquired about the sequence of shots. "As I remember," she wrote, "there was the first shot and then a pause and then the last two seemed very close together."

Ms. Adams told me she occasionally visited the second-floor lunchroom when she worked at the Depository, the scene of the Oswald/Baker/Truly encounter. She always got there, she said, by going down the back stairs.

Did she happen to notice any activity in or around that lunchroom when she passed by on November 22?

"I don't recall noticing anything or anyone on the second floor," she said. "But, remember, I wasn't looking for anything in the building. My intent was to get outside as quickly as possible. I can't answer whether anyone could have been in the lunchroom. If they were they should have been the ones doing the noticing. I mean, here were people running out of the building. For all anyone else knew, we could have been the ones who did it. Do you know what I mean?"

What about the layout of her office? What did she have to do to get to the top of the fourth-floor staircase?

"I am certainly not great with distances," she admitted, "but if I had to take a guess, I believe that from the window to the door I had to reach at the back of the office was no more than 50-70 feet. We had to run around a group of three tables, like banquet tables, and then out the door to the stairway."

Then I brought up my discovery of the transmittal letter at the National Archives—the shocker from Martha Joe Stroud stating Dorothy Garner made the startling comment she saw Roy Truly and Officer Marrion Baker arrive on the fourth floor *after* Victoria Adams had left. When I sent Ms. Adams a copy of that document for her response, she was not excited by the official confirmation.

"Dorothy merely corroborated what I know I did and when I know I did it."

Would Miss Garner have been that perceptive, under the circumstances, to notice such details?

"Dorothy Garner was the office manager at Scott Foresman and assistant to the regional manager," Ms. Adams explained. "She was an efficient, no nonsense kind of lady, demanded punctuality and a great job. She basically ran the branch by herself. The male figurehead, Joe Bergen, the regional sales manager, was gone most of the time and Dorothy handled whatever he needed for him, as well as overseeing the office production. Scott Foresman in Dallas was one of four regional offices.

"Quite frankly she intimidated me and I followed her orders and instructions to a 'tee,' because I was both scared of her and respected her. She demanded the best, watched the clock like a hawk and tolerated no nonsense nor talking when she ruled her kingdom.

"If you can picture an old fashioned prim librarian telling everyone to 'shush,' you have an idea of the power and demeanor of Dorothy Garner. Sandra and I were actually pretty nervy to sneak outside when we did. If I recall correctly, we were actually supposed to be back at work then. In fact, I roamed around outside while Sandra went back inside. I think she was more concerned about obedience than I was, especially in that situation.

"I remember thinking my job was at risk if I stayed outside, and I would probably get reprimanded by Dorothy Garner, but finding out what was going on was more important than potential repercussions to me in the moment.

"To my recollection, nothing ever slipped by Mrs. Garner, except us that day. She was extremely detail oriented and was very proud of what she did. She was both feared and respected by the staff."

Did Ms. Adams know Lee Oswald?

"I did know Oswald," she said.

"He was an unassuming dock worker at the Depository. I said hello to him whenever I saw him, smiled, and that kind of thing. I never had a conversation with him, however. I didn't with any of the dock workers, but I knew them by sight. There weren't that many of us who worked in the Texas School Book Depository."

I asked Ms. Adams about the scene in the movie *JFK* where a frenzied Oswald is shown squeezing between her and Miss Styles on his wild run down to the second-floor lunchroom. It depicts what would have occurred if the Warren Commission's timing was correct and Miss Adams was telling the truth. Had she seen the film?

"Yes," she said. "It's only a movie. Obviously I knew it was inaccurate, but I wasn't upset anymore. I think I just had finally accepted that people were going to believe what they wanted to believe, including the film makers and story tellers. But they weren't there. I was."

One day I played devil's advocate, purposely misquoting a portion of her testimony by saying she had told Belin the shots came from the direction of the grassy knoll. I wanted to see what she'd say.

"I didn't say that," she objected, her memory laser sharp.

"I said the shots sounded like they came from below me to my right. I didn't know where they had come from."

Then came my most important question of all.

CHAPTER 29

February 10-12, 2002

I was, quite naturally, always bothered by her statement that she saw and briefly spoke with William Shelley and Billy Lovelady on the first floor. After all, that was what the Warren Commission and others used to discredit Victoria Adams.

At first, it seemed clear to me. If she saw those men, who each claimed they didn't return to the building until several minutes after the shooting, then Ms. Adams descended the steps later than she figured. This was the preeminent point in her story.

"I honestly can't remember seeing them [on the first floor]," she told me one day. "No, I don't remember them being there."

Did she know those two well?

"Not at all, except to see them around. I doubt I could even recognize them today as they were then. I really did not associate with anyone who worked at the Depository, except for the people in my office and there was very little socializing with them."

My mention of the Shelley/Lovelady encounter, however, prompted Ms. Adams to ask that I send her a copy of her official testimony. She wanted to recheck what she actually said about the incident. She had not kept a duplicate of her deposition and had read it only once, in California some thirty-five years earlier.

"This makes me really wonder about that section in my testimony," she wrote after reviewing her words. "It sounds like the way I did in the rest of the testimony, but I am beginning to wonder if that [her statements regarding Shelley and Lovelady] was inserted into my testimony later."

Ms. Adams' testimony quoted her as saying she spoke in passing to both men, offering the thought that Kennedy may have been shot. She told me she did, in fact, recall making that comment to someone on the first floor. But it was not, she said, to Shelley or Lovelady.

"I remember saying to a fairly big black man inside the building right near the loading dock right after I got down the stairs that I thought the president may have been shot. I don't know what his name is. I do know that he worked for the Depository and I think he was a warehouse worker.[1]

"You would think that if I said that to them [Shelley and Lovelady], 'I believed the President was shot,' they would have said something or done something, instead of saying nothing, as I am quoted as saying.

"And, if they had been away for some time running around the railroad tracks, I can't imagine that they would have returned to the building and been standing in the back of the building when all the action was outside.

"And how could I have seen them on the first floor anyway if they were outside the building for that long. When I came down they wouldn't have returned yet.

"They weren't there," she emphasized.

Ms. Adams was clearly uneasy about this matter. "Also, Belin appears to make a big deal out of the Shelley and Lovelady encounter. Another thing—and this may seem really minor, but I think it is important—whenever I answer a question 'yes' or 'no,' by habit I always said 'sir.' Unless I happened to continue on with a sentence. If you will notice, my 'yes' in that section is not followed by 'sir.' At that time in my life, that was a habit with me. Just like simple Southern courtesy.

"There's something wrong with that whole section."

When I showed her a copy of Detective Leavelle's evening interview with her on February 17, 1964, she was equally mystified. Leavelle's report has her saying, "The elevator was not running and there was no one on the stairs. I went down to the first floor. I saw Mr. Shelly [*sic*] and another employee named Bill. The freight elevator had not moved, and I still did not see anyone on the stairs."

"That sentence about Mr. Shelley and Mr. Lovelady seems out of context to the rest of my statement," she noted. "Like it's been inserted. It doesn't seem to fit. And if I didn't see them, why would the police put that in there? Is this why the Dallas police lied to me about there being a fire, so they could interview me again?"

Ms. Adams also seemed concerned about the end of her Warren Commission testimony, where it stated she voluntarily waived her rights to review what she had said before having it sent to Washington. "If I waived my rights to sign my deposition," she remarked, "why did they send someone to my office to ask me to read my testimony and make corrections and then not include them in the final transcript?

"I suspect my testimony has been doctored, but I have no proof since I never had a copy of the original."

I asked if she remembered seeing the Shelley/Lovelady incident in the copy of testimony she was given to correct.

"I don't recall seeing that section at all," she answered. "If it had been in there, and since I didn't see them, I would have edited it out."

Still bothered, Ms. Adams brought up Sandra Styles. "Since Sandra was specific with other names and people, I would think she would have mentioned seeing them [Shelley and Lovelady], too, when she gave her deposition to the FBI." Miss Styles had not.

"I was pretty confused by all of this at the time, and for awhile didn't even know why what I had to say was important. However, once I realized it, I kept asking why the Warren Commission wasn't calling for Sandra Styles. In fact, during the initial briefing before my testimony was taken by the attorney [Belin], I asked him why didn't they call Sandra Styles. He said they didn't need her. They had me. That was enough. Looking backwards I think they didn't want to corroborate any evidence.

"I repeatedly asked all of the agencies that interviewed me to interview and question Sandra Styles. They kept saying they didn't need to. I always thought that very strange, since what I did and when I did it was so important to them, and Sandra was with me until we got outside. She returned to the building before I did, but her descent was at the same time as mine.

"What I kept saying over and over was that Sandra could affirm what we did immediately after the gunshots."

And then, another light bulb went on in my head.

CHAPTER 30

February 13, 2002

I had tried on several occasions to locate Sandra Styles. Admittedly, it was only with the hope that she could somehow lead me to Victoria Adams. But through the years, I found even less information on Miss Styles than on Ms. Adams.

The Warren Commission never questioned Miss Styles. Few others had either. Therefore, there were no records of her birthplace, the schools she had attended, or her former work experiences.

The end of her trail came quickly.

What would she have said to the Warren Commission? Would she have corroborated Ms. Adams? Did *she* happen to see Shelley and Lovelady?

"I liked Sandra Styles," Ms. Adams replied when I sought details about her former coworker. "As I remember, she went to a school in Waco. I'm pretty sure she graduated from a college there, but she wanted to get married and be a stay-at-home mom. Sandra and I did nothing together socially, nor do I remember the office having any social events, so there was little reason for a connection."

That was all interesting, but it was certainly not enough.

"Regarding Sandra Styles—I am not sure she was born in Waco," Ms. Adams added a few days later. "I think I remember she said she went to college there. She went to a Christian college. I think it was Baylor. She was right around my age—maybe a year older. That's basically all I know about her except she was concerned about bad hair days and always wore a pretty dress, hoping people would look at her dress instead of her hair. Women are always vain."

Cyberspace quickly took me to Baylor University. Either I was getting better, or this Web site was more "user friendly." In a matter of only minutes, a "Sandra Styles Butler" popped up as an alumna. I immediately wrote to the college for more information. Surprisingly, I received an answer within hours, giving me Mrs. Butler's current residence in Texas, her telephone number—even her e-mail address.

This one was just too easy.

"Yes, I remember Vicki Adams very well," Mrs. Butler said when I telephoned her that evening. "We worked together; we were buddies."[1]

Not wanting to influence her recollections, I didn't mention what Ms. Adams and I had been discussing. Instead, after she agreed to talk, I asked what Mrs. Butler remembered about the assassination. She spoke in general terms for several minutes. I narrowed the sights and asked if she recalled when she and Ms. Adams left the fourth-floor window.

"I can't remember exactly, but we moved away from the window fairly quickly," she replied. "And I'd say we moved quickly down the stairs too."

"Fairly quickly" was too vague.

Ms. Adams said she left the window as the presidential limousine was about to enter the Triple Underpass. Taking a different approach, I now asked Mrs. Butler what she could recall seeing that day.

"Well, I watched the motorcade as it approached and turned the corner," she said. "I saw Jackie's pink suit, and then it went behind a big tree in the front of the building. I heard the shots and thought they were firecrackers. The car was moving slowly and I saw Jackie get onto the trunk—there was lots of movement by Jackie. I saw the Secret Service agent get on the car and push her back in. I can't remember anymore."

"Mrs. Butler," I said, "think hard. Do you remember whether you actually saw Kennedy's car go into the underpass?"

She paused. "No, I don't remember seeing that at all," she answered. "That was when we left."

That was when we left. This was right when Victoria Adams said they had left the window, right before the car went into the underpass.

That was when we left. It was corroboration. And *that* was what others had ignored over the years, either from disregard or deceit. This woman had just confirmed what Ms. Adams had been saying all along. With Mrs. Butler in tow, Ms. Adams had left the window when she said she did, *certainly* before when the Warren Report said she did and *certainly* within a timeframe in which she should have seen or at least heard Oswald, *if* Oswald had been coming down from the sixth floor.

The implications were chilling.

"Are you still there?" I heard Mrs. Butler ask.

"Yes . . . yes, I am," I finally said. I cleared my throat. "It's been thirty-nine years since this happened, Mrs. Butler. Are you sure of what you saw and did?"

"It's a hard thing to forget," she replied, slowly.

I asked why she decided to leave the office in the first place.

"I don't know," she answered, hesitated, then laughed. "It just seemed like the thing to do at the time. Vicki wanted to go, so I went."

She told me she saw and heard no one on the back stairs, no sounds whatsoever. The stairs were old, wooden, and creaky, she explained. She would have heard some sounds if anyone else had been anywhere on them—above or below. There were, she repeated, "no other sounds."

"A few people were milling around on the first floor," she said. "One was a black man." That was apparently the same man Ms. Adams had mentioned. I casually asked her if William Shelley or Billy Lovelady were there.

"No," she said, emphasizing she would have recognized them, since she knew both men well.

Mrs. Butler said she went outside the rear of the Depository, then returned to the front of the building when a police officer told her and Ms. Adams they could go no farther. Before she went back inside, she said she heard a radio squawking on a parked motorcycle. She could not recall what was being said.

When I told her what Ms. Adams had heard—mention of where the shots may have originated—it still did not jog her memory.

"Vicki was more observant than I was," she admitted.

Over the next several days, I peppered her with more questions in e-mails, some fresh, some redundant, in hopes of eliciting more details. For instance, I asked again why she had left the building.

"The blind, unquenchable curiosity of youth?" she wrote rhetorically. "It was obvious that something was going on down there. Probably if I had been able to see and know more from where I was, I would have stayed put."[2]

I asked again whether she saw Shelley and Lovelady on the first floor.

"No, I didn't. I believe they were at the front entrance, and we went out the back door and around to the front of the building. I believe most of the Depository employees were watching from the front entrance. I have seen at least one picture in which Billy is with that group."

I told her that Ms. Adams' testimony referred to Shelley and Lovelady being on the first floor when both women arrived there.

"I can't imagine why Vicki would have said that—if she did," Mrs. Butler commented. "They definitely weren't there."

I explained that the Shelley/Lovelady sighting was the sole reason the Commission disbelieved Ms. Adams. I asked for her opinion on whether that incident might have been inserted into Ms. Adams' testimony for that express purpose. There was a long silence.

"All I can say," she finally answered, "is that Shelley and Lovelady were definitely not on the first floor when we got there."[3]

How many shots did she hear?

"Three shots; my first instinct was to look down to the left. I don't know whether that was because of the location of the shooter or because of reverberation."

What was it like in Dealey Plaza in those first moments?

"Lots of rushing around and chaos."

How fast did she move from her office and down the stairs?

"I was moving fast but not running. The stairs were not well lighted, and I was probably wearing high heels."

Who questioned her about what?

"I was never questioned outside the office and acknowledged that I had no information pertinent to the investigation. They [the FBI] mainly wanted to know whether I knew LHO [Lee Harvey Oswald] or recalled ever having seen him. I did not. I don't recall any questions re: the trip down the stairs. If the WC [Warren Commission] representative didn't interview me, he probably didn't feel I had anything to add."

Yet she *did* have something to add, something vitally important.

Ms. Adams' actions were so consequential that the Commission elected to comment on them in its final Report, even though it chose not to believe a single word she said. Why, then, comment at all? The Commission certainly had remained mute on more noteworthy matters than "some girl on the fourth floor."

The Commission had the means and opportunity to check out her story. It would have been so easy to question Mrs. Butler back then. It would have been so easy to conduct the necessary time tests.

An agent could have duplicated Oswald's moves by running from the sixth-floor window down the back stairs to the second-floor lunchroom. An agent could have duplicated Officer Baker's moves by running from the street outside the building and up the stairs to the same second-floor lunchroom. An agent could have duplicated what Ms. Adams did by running from the fourth-floor window to the first floor.

Where would those paths have crossed?

The Commission had conducted the first two tests—the movements of Oswald and the policeman—on several occasions. It had even gone so far as to time the actions of Mrs. Reid, her significance only being that she saw Oswald *after* the lunchroom encounter. Why had it failed to do one of the more important tests: the timing of Ms. Adams' descent?

The Commission never once sought answers from any supporting witness, as it in all honesty should have. It never diligently tried to resolve the timing questions, as it with all integrity should have. It never considered an alternative, as it with all objectivity should have.

Why not?

Ms. Adams was not surprised when I told her of Mrs. Butler's comments concerning when they had left the window and the absence of both Shelley and Lovelady on the first floor. Again, it was something she had known already. But she was happy that, for the first time, someone else now knew. Someone had finally talked with both her and Sandra Styles and had uncovered the truth.

"I just want someone to hear the truth and not just hear it, but recognize the truth," Ms. Adams told me one day. "I hope someone, somewhere, sometime will at least consider that maybe things were not really as they appeared to be, no matter how many degrees the person had who said they were such and such a way. Just because something is in print doesn't necessarily make it true.

"Each of us, in our own way, wants to make a lasting contribution to life. At this point, one lasting contribution I can make is to have my truth heard and eventually shared."

She would tell me she always wanted to be a writer and a teacher. She had been both, if only briefly. She would display over the ensuing months a piercing, dry sense of humor. She would say all she ever wanted to do, from the first moment on, was to let others know that what she had said a long time ago was the truth, had always been the truth, and was nothing but the truth.

"So, who am I today?" she asked. "I am a responsible, honest, supportive woman with a passion for learning to discern between perceived and factual truth. In short, I am just an ordinary woman living an ordinary life doing ordinary things."

Ms. Adams had grown up.

In this ever-expanding mess called the Kennedy assassination, she had turned out to be anything but ordinary. And somehow, I had known that all along. I just had to prove it, if to no one but myself.

CHAPTER 31

September 18-November 15, 2007

"Life isn't fair," she wrote to me one day, "and, oh yeah, neither is death."

The words were chilling. Never before in the nearly six years I had known her had the otherwise-upbeat Vicki Adams sounded like this. It was September 18, 2007, a Tuesday morning, and that was her way of introducing me to the news she was dying from cancer, the seriousness of which she had kept from me until now. Doctors days earlier had given her six months.

She lasted only two.

"If life isn't fair, how is death fair or how is anything fair," she had asked, but not in anger. That would have been unlike her. "Is there really justice? You know me . . . gotta have answers."

She had not even hinted at her illness to me because, she said, she did not want that unhappy news to influence the way I was writing about her. That was the real Victoria Adams.

Miss Adams, for that is how I will always remember her, was only sixty-six.

"No one really wants to know the truth, or at least that seems to be my sense of things," she wrote. "There is too much glamour in speculation and the concept of thrillers with open-ended questions."

This woman, alone for so long with those terrible memories from the past, had by now come to grips with all the fears that had once surrounded her every day. "Bravery, to me, has been acting heroically in spite of enormous fear," she wrote, a month before her death. "It is setting one's own needs and wants for comfort, ease, and convenience aside and sometimes reaching through the scared and fragmented parts of ourselves to help someone or something right now."[1]

Bravery was indeed what she had shown by her willingness to finally release the demons of Dallas.

"It does not take courage to grow old," she would say among her parting words. "It does not take courage to die. It takes courage to live in the moment. . . . To live is to be courageous.

"Perhaps it is really brave of the listener to listen to the dying."

CHAPTER 32

June 2011

After Miss Adams went downstairs she (Miss Garner) saw Mr. Truly and the policeman come up. Those words kept haunting me, even years after Vicki's death. So did all the associated questions.

Where was Dorothy Garner when she observed this? What made her go there? What else might she have seen? To whom had she made that comment?

When the shots rang out in Dealey Plaza, Mrs. Garner was at the fourth-floor window of the Depository. At thirty-five years of age, the last ten of which she spent with Scott Foresman, she had moved her way up to become the office supervisor.

She was there with three of her employees: Sandra Styles, Elsie Dorman, and Victoria Adams.

During routine interviews conducted of all Depository employees on duty that terrible day, Mrs. Garner told the FBI on March 20, 1964, that following the shooting, she "remained on the fourth floor of the building in the Scott Foresman offices until approximately 2:30 p.m."[1] The impact of that otherwise harmless comment would not become apparent until more than three decades later when the Martha Joe Stroud letter surfaced. For it was there that Mrs. Garner's quoted words put her into a position of not only proving Miss Adams to be truthful but also of challenging the Warren Commission's scenario of how, or even if, Oswald fled from the sixth floor.

Yet little was known about this woman, at least from the public record.

One of the good things about writing a controversial book such as this is that it solicits tips along the way. Often those tips are anonymous and lead nowhere. Occasionally, they are gems. I was following one of the latter when I caught up with Dorothy Ann (sometimes known as May) Garner, a woman who otherwise had become a ghost, flickering in and out of occasional written reports. Now in her eighties, she still couldn't shake the visions of that day in Dallas.

I introduced myself on the phone by telling her I had written a book and was now continuing my inquiry into Victoria Adams. She had absolutely no idea why I had taken the time to pen a volume about one of her former employees. It occurred to me at that point (which Mrs. Garner soon confirmed) that she was completely unaware of the implications surrounding what that former employee had done.

In my mind this was a good thing, since I felt that her comments might now lack any potential bias accumulated over the years and thus lend more credibility to anything she could tell me.

I began with preliminaries, asking her what things were like that day.

"It was total confusion," she said. "The Dallas Police, FBI, Secret Service were coming up the stairs, in the elevators, in all the offices. The news media and workers and outsiders were going everywhere."[2]

The Dallas Police Department, she said, "took over our phones." When I asked what that meant, she explained. "They wouldn't allow personal calls to go out. After the employees were allowed to leave, I went to a nearby diner and called my husband." It was her first opportunity for outside communications.

The focus of my call was threefold: what she knew about Victoria Adams, whether she was in a position to have seen Officer Baker and Roy Truly or anyone else on the back stairs, and to whom she had made the comment that appeared in the Stroud letter.

Did Miss Adams and Miss Styles leave the window right away? I asked her.

"The girls did," she responded. "I remember them being there and the next thing I knew, they were gone." They had left "very quickly . . . within a matter of moments," she added.

What did Mrs. Garner do after that?

"There was this warehouse or storage area behind our office, out by the freight elevators and the rear stairway, and I went out there."

Her move to that area clearly took her to a spot where she could have observed activity on the back stairs as well as on the elevators. But how fast had she arrived there?

Mrs. Garner said she immediately went to this area, following "shortly after . . . right behind" Miss Adams and Miss Styles. She couldn't remember exactly why she went there, other than "probably to get something." Mrs. Garner said she did not actually see "the girls" enter the stairway, though, arriving on the fourth-floor landing seconds later. When I asked how she knew they had gone down right away, Mrs.

Garner replied, "I remember hearing them, after they started down. I remember the stairs were very noisy."

Were the freight elevators in operation during this time?

"I don't recall that," she answered. "They were very noisy too!"

Mrs. Garner said she remained at that spot and was alone for a moment before "several came out back from the office to look out those windows there." The view from these windows, facing west and situated near the stairway, included the grassy knoll and railroad yards, where many people ran following the shooting.

The presence of other employees at the west windows was confirmed by Bonnie Ray Williams, who, with Harold Norman and James Jarman, had watched the motorcade from the fifth floor. The three had used the same stairs as they made their way down to the first floor. Williams testified he arrived on the fourth floor "where we saw these women looking out of the window."[3]

Mrs. Garner was now confirming how quickly Victoria Adams had entered the stairway. Perhaps it was so quick that Miss Adams was ahead of the lagging assassin. This possibility was actually addressed when the Warren Report wrote, "If her estimate of time is correct . . . she must have run down the stairs ahead of Oswald and would probably have seen or heard him."[4]

With Mrs. Garner being in the position she was as quickly as she was, I asked her if she happened to notice whether Lee Oswald came down the stairs after Miss Adams and Miss Styles entered the stairway.

She laughed at the question. "No, I don't remember that. I don't remember seeing him at all that day . . . except on TV."

Later in the interview, she would reflect back on the question she found so amusing, saying she felt sure she would have remembered if she had seen Oswald on the stairs, or anywhere that day for that matter, based on his later notoriety and the fact that it would have made a distinct impression on her mind.

Had she seen Roy Truly on November 22?

"I saw him several times that day," she said, "but I'm not sure when or where."

How about a policeman accompanied by Truly coming up the stairs?

"I remember I saw a policeman or police officers on the stairs, yes."

I pressed a bit more and asked the question again, recognizing that the passage of time, the "confusion of the moment" as she had called it, and the fact that its significance was lost on her may have made my query seem unimportant. Did she remember seeing Roy Truly and a police officer come up the stairs together?

"I could have," she answered, "but there was so much confusion. It was, after all, a few years ago!"

Mrs. Garner was providing two key pieces of evidence: one that corroborated Victoria Adams regarding how quickly she and Sandra Styles left the window and moved to the back staircase and a second that corroborated the Stroud letter by placing herself at a location where she could have observed activity on the stairs immediately after the shooting.

Like Sandra Styles before her, Dorothy Garner had been neglected by the Warren Commission. Or had she?

Although no public record exists of an interview or conversation between Mrs. Garner and the Commission or its staff, apparently one did take place. From the moment I discovered the Stroud letter, I was always intrigued as to whom Mrs. Garner had made her statement. Was it David Belin, charged with this area of the investigation? After all, he had been in Dallas not long before that, taking depositions from other Depository employees.

So I asked Mrs. Garner if she recalled someone from the Warren Commission talking with her.

"Yes, I do remember that," she replied quickly. According to her, the questioning occurred "several months later . . . quite a few months later," a timeframe that fit with the June date shown on the Stroud letter. She could not remember who the man was. The name David Belin did not ring a bell. She also could not recall where the questioning had taken place or specifically what had been asked. She did say, however, that the conversation, which she admitted could even have been by telephone, was "brief."

When I then asked if she was sure of the agency the questioner was from, she replied firmly, "Yes." When I inquired how she could be so definite the person had been from the Commission, she answered, "He identified himself as being from the Warren Commission."

In retrospect, I found Mrs. Garner to be an honest and forthright woman. She appeared credible and without any reason to embellish her story, which was evident from her lack of knowledge to its overall importance. The characteristics other employees attributed to her were evident throughout much of our discussion. She spoke well for her age and often asked me to repeat a question, not because she was hard of hearing, she assured me, but to ensure she had understood it correctly.

The intervening years had no doubt caused her to forget some specifics, but her memory seemed clear on when Miss Adams and Miss Styles left the window, how fast both women got to the stairs, where Mrs. Garner had gone after the shooting, and what she had or hadn't observed while there.

She was completely unaware of the significance of the story regarding Miss Adams or the role Mrs. Garner played in it, which may account for why some details did not make a more indelible mark on her memory.

The key points of the interview remain:

Coupled with Sandra Styles' story and the meaning behind her statement in the Stroud letter, Mrs. Garner is strong corroboration for what Miss Adams did and when she did it.

Mrs. Garner was indeed in a position to observe activity on the back stairs immediately after the assassination.

Mrs. Garner did not see Lee Oswald on the stairs but felt she would have had he been there. This is noteworthy regarding the idea that Oswald may have come down the stairs *after* Miss Adams had descended.

Mrs. Garner talked with someone from the Warren Commission.

Somewhere along the line, Mrs. Garner joined Sandra Styles and Victoria Adams, as well as a host of others, in having their actions and observations discredited or, even worse, ignored. This lack of further investigation on the part of those who had a duty to do so is unsettling in itself. It becomes worse when one considers how each of those slighted was so critical to the conclusions of the official inquiry.

And it continues to cast a dark and growing shadow over the guiding principle Earl Warren stressed to his staff, that "truth is our only client here."

Yesterday

This time I do not have to stop to get his mail from the oversized box along the side of the road, something I did each time I visited to save him an arduous trip down the driveway. The gesture is no longer necessary.

The tall pines have shed their old needles everywhere, littering the ground and contrasting starkly against the pure-white drifts of snow beneath. His well-worn automobile no longer sits in the carport, its former presence always a sign I would find him at home.

Deer still scurry about in the surrounding woods. Birds still drop down to an outdoor feeder. It is empty of nourishment.

To the left, water in his run-down swimming pool rests frozen. To the right is the large plate-glass window behind which he used to sit, hunched over his old Royal in such concentration that he would not notice me for several minutes as I stood outside and watched.

He is not there on this day. Nor are his typewriter, numerous filing cabinets, desk, books, papers, pictures, cushioned chair and footrest, or cane. They are all gone now.

Because so is Harold Weisberg.

He had died February 21, 2002, from "a kidney ailment and sepsis," so his obituary reported. He had been "a prolific writer and persistent critic of the official report that found a lone gunman responsible for the death of President John F. Kennedy."[1] More than that, he had been my mentor.

He took me under his wing when I was a mere fledgling. He taught me from the start how to do it the right way. He granted me liberties with his files, materials, and thoughts that he would few others.

And he encouraged me to start what I now seem to be trying to end.

What a journey this has been, this rite of passage no less bizarre or revealing than those of Holden Caulfield or Nick Adams. It started with Terry's persistent question. *Still believe the Warren Report?*

I could not answer him back then. My results had not as yet been tabulated.

I joined the ranks of fellow researchers, who, always maligned and often rightfully so, sought the same as I. Or so I once thought.

The places I had only read about sprang to life, becoming real in sight, sound, and smell. The witnesses—sometimes corrupted, occasionally crazy, more often courageous—turned into flesh and blood right in front of me.

And somewhere along the way, without warning, things were not the same for me anymore. My youthful innocence—some might say exuberance—had been lost, just as had America's when, whether he was loved or hated, John F. Kennedy was killed in a place called Dealey Plaza.

"Truth" is a word mentioned often and by many throughout these pages, from those who claimed to seek it to those who claimed they possessed it. Truths and fancies abound when one studies the Kennedy assassination. The Warren Report stated as early as 1964, for instance, that it "found no evidence of conspiracy." That is hardly the truth. The record clearly indicates that the Commission was aware of evidence in its possession that *did* indicate a conspiracy. It just chose to ignore it or, as Miss Adams would say, "disregard" it.

Oswald ordered the rifle. Handwriting tests confirm this. But who picked it up from his post-office box? Records routinely kept that would answer that question are strangely missing in this case.

So too are all his military files and a lot of other routine documentation that in any other circumstance would be readily available.

No fresh fingerprints belonging to Oswald were found on the rifle. No proof was established that Oswald fired the rifle that day, let alone that the rifle had even been discharged. Its barrel was not swabbed, a common police procedure.

Evidence that he actually used the weapon is weak, with what little there is conveniently coming from his wife, Marina, a woman the government otherwise considered to be unreliable. Evidence that he bought ammunition for that weapon, or even practiced firing live rounds with it, is simply nonexistent.

No one saw or heard Oswald as he hurriedly left the sixth floor—not the men on the floor below and not the women who should have heard or seen him on the stairs. He just suddenly appeared in the lunchroom, calm, collected, and exactly where he said he had gone after eating his noon meal on the first floor. No one believed him, of course. After all, he was the assassin. That was why he "escaped" from the Depository, acted so strange as he rushed home to grab his revolver, shot Tippit, fled to a darkened movie theatre, scuffled with police, and seemed so cocky and defiant while in custody.

The list goes on, *ad infinitum, ad nauseam.*

Facts of this case are still, to this day, being stretched to their limits. Misinformation has become routine.

Weeks before the fortieth anniversary of Kennedy's assassination, in one example, ABC News enticed audiences using this blurb about its upcoming documentary on the event: "One of the greatest crimes. One of the most respected reporters. And now, the truth."[2] There was that word again.

On the appointed night, host Peter Jennings quickly tipped his hand by charging that, one, Oswald was the only person absent from an employee roll call held shortly after the shooting, and two, Oswald was a "sharpshooter."[3]

The first accusation was provably false, as any respectable reporter should have known. The fact that Oswald was *not* the only one missing from the roll call had been confirmed years earlier.[4] The second accusation—Oswald the sharpshooter—was such a blatant stretching of the truth that even the Warren Commission had refused to use it.[5]

It should not be necessary to frame a guilty man.

Even Victoria Adams, rare though her appearances may be in published literature concerning the assassination, has not been spared the occasional glib remark. In his 1,600-page tome supporting the Warren Commission, author Vincent Bugliosi actually proposes that she might well have been Kennedy's assassin. "Why not?" he asks. "Women can pull triggers too, you know."[6]

In 1964, the Warren Commission wrote that there was no conspiracy. In 1979, the HSCA concluded there most likely had been. That supreme contradiction remains unresolved, even today.

When it comes to the JFK assassination, America is lost in guesses and garbage. America is lost in the mumbo jumbo that authors compose, publishers relish, and readers devour. America is lost.

A long time ago, I asked my mentor how one goes about digging out truths in a junk pile such as this. Truth is a tough nut in any area, especially here, he told me. It requires hard work, long hours, and verification from existing evidence and sources.

"What if all of that evidence is not available?" I asked.

He smiled in the knowing way he always did. "Then you find it," he answered.

The truth is out there, somewhere. I realize that now. It is being held by those who have no reason to be untruthful.

But I still have a bit of unfinished business.

In 1967, after I was roped into this, my friend Terry kept asking me if I still believed the Warren Report. I always hedged his question back then and have not seen or heard from him since our final day together in Washington. But I can answer you now, Terry, wherever you may be, for whatever any of this is worth.

No, Terry. I no longer believe the Warren Report.

Why the change? he would probably ask.

Well, I would answer, because I've reached four conclusions. Number one, the assassination did not happen the way the government says it did. Forget for a moment that vital evidence at the crime scene—the boxes surrounding the "sniper's nest," the three rifle hulls found on the floor, even the murder weapon itself—was disturbed and handled by inattentive police officers in disregard of proper forensic practices. Forget for a moment that upon discovery, the so-called "magic bullet" was not preserved as it should have been, thereby rendering its surface useless for blood and tissue sampling. Forget that the autopsy doctors were not qualified for authoritative examination of gunshot wounds, that records routinely made under similar circumstances were in this case absent or incorrect, and that the victim's brain was not dissected, even though the cause of death was a gunshot wound to the head.

Forget too the lack of fingerprints, the timing problems, what the films show, and what the witnesses claim they saw. Forget the absence of nitrates in paraffin tests performed on Oswald's cheek, the altered documents, the missing this and the missing that. Forget what he said and what she said.

Forget it all and think about just one thing. Why was there such haste on the part of the government to shut this investigation down? Why, on the very afternoon of the assassination and in the face of so much early evidence pointing toward conspiracy, was a single person fingered for the crime with such zeal, *before* any of that contrary evidence—whether it was right or wrong—had even been examined?[7] If nothing else convinces me that something here is all wrong, it is the urgency with which the government tried to convince us that everything was all right.

Number two, those responsible for writing the Warren Report

knew it was wrong when they wrote it. There was an agenda on the Commission's part, an immediate and unchanging urgency to reach a predetermined conclusion. The reader will recall that as early as January 11, 1964, in a "Tentative Outline" distributed by Earl Warren to the other Commission members, Section II was titled, "Lee Harvey Oswald as the Assassin of President Kennedy." This was little more than a month *after* the Commission was formed to investigate the murder and three weeks *before* hearings to examine any evidence linking Oswald to the crime had even begun.

As a result of that rush to judgment—for what else can it honestly be called?—contrary evidence was overlooked. Questions that should have been asked were not. Routine follow-ups were never made.

If a layman can recognize such failings, why couldn't they? Smart men like those sitting on the Warren Commission do not make these kinds of errors.

Number three, the assassination was beyond the capabilities of one man. There is nothing, not a shred of evidence, that shows that Oswald had the rifle competency he is credited with possessing. And multiple attempts to duplicate Oswald's alleged feat by far more talented riflemen than he have consistently failed. Efforts to prove his prowess have shown bullets fired into plywood, fiberboard, wood blocks, Styrofoam and a host of similar building products, human cadavers, dead goats, live goats and who knows how many innocent farm animals, gelatin blocks, water barrels, tubes of cotton, light bulbs, watermelons, grapefruit, pumpkins, and no doubt a large assortment of other suitable fruits and vegetables.

Posits abound to make it somehow work. A faulty telescopic sight that impeded FBI rifle experts testing the assassination weapon was instead deemed an "advantage" to Oswald; or, in lieu of that, he didn't use the damaged telescopic sight at all but relied on the end-of-the-barrel iron sights, not only for better accuracy but now to gain speed to overcome the problem that was discovered concerning the timing of the shots; or, in lieu of that, he lengthened that timeframe by shooting at the president through the old oak tree; or, in lieu of that, he wrapped the weapon's sling around his arm for more efficiency; or, in lieu of that, he didn't use the sling at all because, without it, he could reload the weapon faster.

The medical and physical evidence, under close examination, simply does not support the single-assassin, single-bullet scenario as proposed by the Warren Report. Not a single witness to the crime has described the assassination as occurring the way the Warren Report concluded it happened. We are left then with nothing but speculations, theories, conjectures, guesstimates, and beliefs.

Finally, number four, solving the mystery of who shot John Kennedy is beyond the capabilities of a private citizen. Studying this case has led me down a most unsettling path. Yet Victoria Adams turned out to be the beacon at the end of that road. And I would be remiss if I didn't seek some degree of closure in my investigation of her. Once again, I've arrived at four conclusions.

Number one, the Warren Report is wrong about Miss Adams; she *did* come down the stairs when she said she did.

Miss Adams was a model witness, consistent with virtually every detail she provided, from her early police and FBI questioning, through her Commission testimony, and into her lengthy discussions with me forty years later. The only hiccup has been her reference to Shelley and Lovelady, which, despite multiple previous official interviews, never came up until a curious meeting with Jim Leavelle in February 1964, three months after the assassination, and then again two months later during a more formal appearance before David Belin.

The timing of her trek down the stairs has been corroborated by not one but two other witnesses: Sandra Styles and Dorothy Garner. The June 2, 1964, letter from Martha Joe Stroud to J. Lee Rankin is strong support that Miss Adams descended those stairs when she said she did. It is a document that strangely remained under wraps until only recently. It took the JFK Act to finally pry it loose, but by then, who was left to recognize its significance other than someone obsessively familiar with the circumstances surrounding it?

Number two, those responsible for writing about Miss Adams in the Report knew that what they were saying was wrong when they wrote it. Again, the Martha Joe Stroud letter provides the proof.

The significance of these words—"that after Miss Adams went downstairs she (Miss Garner) saw Mr. Truly and the policeman come up"—cannot be overemphasized. Written June 2, three months prior to the Warren Report's publication, the letter was sent to the general counsel for the Commission, a man who was responsible for every single aspect of the investigation and who was fully aware of Miss Adams' importance. It was sent at a time when David Belin was actively pursuing this very line of inquiry. Its focus on what Miss Adams had told Belin and what Mrs. Garner was now saying implies more than just a casual interest in both women.

The Commission therefore knew, in advance, of Miss Adams' truthfulness. With the Stroud letter, that agency had to know that what was soon to be written about Miss Adams was blatantly wrong.

I'll remind the reader that it was Belin who had officially questioned Miss Adams two months earlier. It was Belin who was in charge of determining the identity of the assassin. It was Belin who wrote in a February 25, 1964, internal memo, "We should pin down this time sequence of her running down the stairs." It was Belin who had to know the monumental significance of what Mrs. Garner was quoted as saying in that letter. It was his job to understand what it meant. He had to know that Miss Adams was right or, at the very least, realize that further investigation was necessary.

And yet he did nothing.

In 1964, he allowed the Warren Report to say that she was wrong. Nine years later, in his book that asked the public to be the jury in this case, he hid from them what would prove *him* to be the one who was wrong and instead continued with the distortion that Miss Adams was "mistaken" and came down the stairs later than she thought. Honest men do not make these kinds of errors.

Number three, evidence indicates that efforts have been made to intentionally make Victoria Adams appear wrong. The reference to Shelley and Lovelady in Miss Adams' testimony was obviously the cornerstone used by Belin—and ultimately the Warren Commission— to discredit her. That supposed encounter has become the lynchpin cited even today by those who continue to debunk this woman.

But did that encounter take place?

The evidence is clear that Miss Adams was correct about when she descended the stairs. She has remained consistent throughout the years with her claim that she arrived on the first floor within a minute after the shooting. Two other women—the one who accompanied her and the other who observed the beginning of her descent—confirm that timing. The Stroud letter validates her as well.

How then does one explain her seeing Shelley and Lovelady on the first floor when both men were still outside the building?

It is interesting to note that the only evidence used by the Commission to back up its conclusion that Miss Adams was wrong are the words supposedly expressed by Miss Adams in two contested interviews, words she has steadfastly denied saying.

Shelley, for instance, did not remember seeing Miss Adams when he returned to the first floor. This is odd, because she supposedly spoke to him, uttering almost the exact same phrase—"the president has been shot"—as did Gloria Calvery, a woman whom Shelley *did* remember seeing only minutes earlier. In fact, he even described meeting Mrs. Calvery, in his police affidavit on the day of the assassination and then again five months later in his Commission deposition.

Lovelady's testimony, on the other hand, strongly suggests he was led into his response that he "saw a girl but I wouldn't swear to it it's Vickie." The Warren Report enriched that comment to read that he "saw a girl on the first floor who he believes was Victoria Adams," even though that's hardly what he had said.

While it may not be uncommon for a lawyer to rehearse questions and answers with a witness, it seems suspicious in this case since the resulting testimony was never presented in open court, where opposing counsel has the opportunity for cross examination. The maneuver instead creates the distinct impression that what ended up on the record are words previously filtered or encouraged, certainly not the hallmark of a fair and objective examination.

Miss Adams today says she did not see Shelley and Lovelady on the first floor. Neither did coworker Sandra Styles, who knew both men well. Marrion Baker and Roy Truly mentioned nothing about the two men either. If Baker and Truly started up the stairs after Miss Adams and Miss Styles came down them, as the Stroud letter implies, wouldn't those two have noticed Shelley and Lovelady, who each testified they stayed on the first floor for a while after returning to the building?

Baker should have spotted them, since he seemed observant and intent on confronting anyone in his path. Truly certainly knew Shelley, as his co-manager, and was very familiar with Lovelady as well.

But the women *did* see someone there. Miss Adams and Miss Styles independently corroborated each other when they told me they saw a black man near the back elevators on the first floor. That is the person Miss Adams spoke to, she said. Baker and Truly noticed the same man at the same place, Truly going so far as to identify him as being an employee.

All four of these witnesses, then, observed this lone individual. Substantiation regarding the presence of Shelley and Lovelady, however, is absent.

If Miss Adams came down the stairs when she said she did, and Shelley and Lovelady remained outside the building for as long as they say they did, what then is the alternative? Could the testimony of Victoria Adams have been altered?

During my interviews with Miss Adams, she revealed something never before known, something reinforced by the Stroud letter: that she had personally made changes to a transcript of her testimony that was unexpectedly hand delivered to her in Dallas. Until then, I was under the impression, based on what I had read in the Commission's own evidence, that she had waived her right to do so and therefore had not seen her statement prior to it being sent to Washington.

A lack of personal review could have opened up the possibility for testimony tampering. However, discovery of the Martha Joe Stroud letter, which listed six corrections Miss Adams had made to her testimony, confirmed that she had in fact seen her statement in advance and had made changes to it.

My first question was, why would she suddenly have been asked to review her words if she had already declined to do so? This didn't make sense to me, and it certainly didn't make sense to her.

My second question was, shouldn't those corrections, completed well before the Commission's publication deadline, have been made to and appeared on the transcript of her testimony sent to the Government Printing Office (GPO) instead of the one I had seen in 1968, the one that showed no corrections at all?

Based on this confusion, I went back to the National Archives with a request to examine once more the official testimony of Victoria Adams. And now I found something strange. It appears that *two* versions of Miss Adams' testimony currently exist: one from 1964 and a second one recently made available.

Both versions are word-for-word the same. Both contain the concluding line about her relinquishing the opportunity to review her deposition, and both have the questionable references to Shelley and Lovelady. Thus, both versions are identical with her testimony as it appears in the twenty-six volumes.

Yet there are differences.

Whereas the earlier version, the transcript I had examined in 1968 and the one sent to the GPO, bore no signature, no corrections, and no notations whatsoever, this later version now has an inked signature as well as inked corrections, all presumably in the handwriting of Miss Adams.[8]

If one version was an exact duplicate of the other, the "TOP SECRET" classification label displayed across the top and bottom on each page of both versions should also look the same. But they do not. The lettering of the classification label on the earlier version of her testimony is small, straight, and professional in its script. Lettering on this later version is slanted, often appearing to have been hand stamped, and is in a larger script style.

The unsigned version supports the official testimony of Miss Adams, where she is quoted as waiving her right to examine her statement. This later version supports the Stroud letter with its list of corrections and apparently represents the "Enclosure" typed at the bottom of that letter. It was not, however, attached to or included with the Stroud letter when I discovered that letter in 1999.

Whereas the 1964 version was declassified on November 21, 1967, this differing transcription shows an *additional* declassification stamp, bearing a more recent date of February 9, 2011. Coincidentally, that is two months after existence of the Martha Joe Stroud letter was disclosed for the first time in the self-published edition of *The Girl on the Stairs*.

To date, no one has been able to explain why this same document needed declassifying twice, the second official release occurring forty-four years later.

None of the corrections made by Miss Adams in Dallas appeared in her official Warren Commission testimony. This is strange, since the Commission had sufficient time to make those changes. It means the unsigned, uncorrected version of her testimony was indeed what was sent to the GPO.

Why that one? Maybe her corrections were considered inconsequential. But over the years, I have personally examined dozens of other witness transcriptions and seen a variety of seemingly trifling correctional notations made by those witnesses, practically all of which *did* show up in the final versions printed in the twenty-six volumes.

Equally unusual is that when the HSCA examined selected portions of Miss Adams' testimony a dozen years later, one of the pages it reviewed does not display the handwritten corrections that *do* show up on the same page in the more recent version. This indicates that either the HSCA did not have the corrected version in its possession or the corrected version was not available at that time.[9]

Miss Adams told me she did not see the names Shelley and Lovelady in the copy of her testimony she reviewed in Dallas. She said if she had, she would have removed those references.

How does one thus reconcile the fact that Shelley and Lovelady are mentioned in a transcript signed by Miss Adams? Could their names somehow have been inserted *after* Miss Adams made her corrections and affixed her signature?[10]

Had my college friend Terry suggested such a possibility back in 1968, I would have laughed uncontrollably. No longer does the thought seem so funny.

With these continuing questions, I next made a more formal request to the National Archives. I described the confusion over what Miss Adams had told me and what appeared in the two varying transcripts of her testimony. I said I hoped to resolve this conflict for the sake of historical accuracy.

This time, I wanted to see the official stenographer's tape of her testimony, not simply a typewritten copy made from that tape. I wanted to see precisely what had been taken down by court reporter Helen Laidrich, the only other person present as Belin questioned Miss Adams that day. Such tapes do exist. According to an inventory of JFK records available at the National Archives, they are contained in sixteen boxes under the title "Entry 39: Stenotype Notes of Proceedings."

Three weeks later, I received a reply.

"We searched our collection and exhibits database for the stenographer's tape, but were unable to locate the item."[11]

Remarks like that no longer surprise me.

In order for the Commission to sustain its scenario of how Oswald escaped from the sixth floor, it had to use the sighting of Shelley and Lovelady as a means of discrediting Miss Adams (which it ended up doing); say that Miss Adams was wrong about when she came down the stairs (which it did); ignore Sandra Styles and Mrs. Garner (which it did); suppress the Stroud letter (which it did); enhance the meaning of Lovelady's words (which it did); and neglect to conduct any tests that conceivably could have proven destructive to that scenario (which it also did).

As time passed and related documents surfaced, were more extreme steps necessary to support it as well?

"I am more convinced now that Belin or someone put those questions and answers in my testimony," Miss Adams replied after digesting a copy of the Stroud letter I had sent for her reaction. "Guess it takes a lot of creativity to build a case for a lone gunman and take the heat off the government."

And finally we reach my fourth conclusion from my investigation of Miss Adams. The truth about her has now provided a critical clue as to whether or not Oswald was on the sixth floor at the time of the assassination.

What evidence was used to put him there in the first place? The testimony of Howard Brennan, a fickle witness who could not pick him from a police lineup and gave a description that failed to match Oswald's appearance? The statements of others who merely saw "a man" there? His fingerprints on boxes he routinely handled during his job? His clipboard found on a floor he routinely visited in the course of that job?[12] His secreted rifle? The paper bag? His "escape"?

Someone *was* on the sixth floor during those fateful moments. And scientific evidence from the HSCA indicates that a shot or shots came from or near that location. But who pulled the trigger?

What, then, can be used to preclude Oswald's presence there? The innocent demeanor of a man confronted by a gun-toting policeman in the brief moments following the assassination? The possibility he may have arrived in the lunchroom by way of the first floor and not the sixth? His comment under questioning that he was eating lunch on the first floor when the shots were fired and that he walked upstairs to get a drink shortly after, a drink he said he was holding when confronted by police? His claim of innocence—of being a patsy—under the glare of television cameras? The fact that no one saw him on the sixth floor, including the man who ate his lunch there only minutes before the murder? The fact that three men standing on the fifth floor and in a position to see or hear someone on the back stairs saw and heard no one coming down from the sixth floor immediately after the shooting? The fact that two women on those stairs at the same time as Oswald would have been also saw and heard no one?

The fact that the government dealt the way it did with that last fact?

If nothing else convinces me that something here is wrong, it is the way the Warren Commission handled what turned out to be right.

What puts Oswald in a place other than the sixth floor is indeed circumstantial. Yet it is no more circumstantial than everything that has been used to put him on the sixth floor.

But Miss Adams told the truth, didn't she? The government chose not to believe her, for whatever reason. In fact, it went to great lengths to prove her wrong, for whatever reason.

But the bottom line is this: Victoria Adams told the truth. And that is what counts here. Isn't it?

I have done what Weisberg asked me to do. I have completed for the historical record what turned out to be his final assignment. The days have become slower now. People have reappeared around me and the air is fresh again. My work is over and I have survived in a guise most would describe as "one piece." I am no longer weighed down and oh so much wiser.

I started this journey a thousand or so years ago, unaware of its trials and its costs, its burdens and its blessings. It was taken deliberately, without regret, its goal only to find answers to who shot my president. In the end, I found Victoria Elizabeth Adams.

And in the end, I also found myself.

"We are not afraid to entrust the American people with unpleasant facts. . . . For a nation that is afraid to let its people judge the truth and falsehood in an open market is a nation that is afraid of its people."

John F. Kennedy
October 27, 1963,
twenty-six days before his death

APPENDIX 1

Testimony of Miss Victoria Elizabeth Adams

The testimony of Miss Victoria Elizabeth Adams was taken at 2:15 P.M. on April 7, 1964, in the office of the U.S. attorney, 301 Post Office Building, Bryan and Ervay streets, Dallas, Texas, by Mr. David W. Belin, assistant counsel of the President's Commission.

Belin: Do you want to stand and raise your right hand, please. Do you solemnly swear that the testimony you are about to give before the President's Commission on the Assassination of President Kennedy shall be the truth, the whole truth, and nothing but the truth, so help you God?
Miss Adams: I do.
Belin: All right. Would you please state your name?
Miss Adams: Victoria Elizabeth Adams.
Belin: Are you known as Vickie Adams?
Miss Adams: That's correct.
Belin: Where do you live?
Miss Adams: 4906 Wenonah, Dallas, Tex.
Belin: What is your occupation?
Miss Adams: I am employed as an office survey representative.
Belin: By whom?
Miss Adams: Scott Foresman Co.
Belin: Where do you work?
Miss Adams: On the fourth floor of the Texas School Book Depository.
Belin: Where?
Miss Adams: 411 Elm.
Belin: That is at the corner of Elm and Houston?
Miss Adams: That is correct.
Belin: I might ask how old are you?
Miss Adams: Twenty-three.
Belin: Where were you born originally? In Texas?

284

Miss Adams: San Francisco, Calif.

Belin: Did you go to school in San Francisco?

Miss Adams: I attended part of my grammar school and high school in San Francisco.

Belin: Were you graduated from high school?

Miss Adams: In San Francisco, that's correct.

Belin: Then what did you do?

Miss Adams: Following that I entered the Ursuline Order in St. Mary's, Ohio, and I left there as a novice in 1961.

Belin: Then what did you do from there?

Miss Adams: I went to Atlanta, Ga. and taught school at the Immaculate Heart of Mary School. And following that I came to Dallas and was employed by the Holiday Inn Central during the summer months, and I obtained a teaching position at St. Monica's School here.

Belin: And you taught at St. Monica for some period of time?

Miss Adams: Yes; for 1 year.

Belin: Then you went to work for Scott Foresman?

Miss Adams: I went to work for Scott Foresman.

Belin: Were you at work on November 22, 1963?

Miss Adams: That's correct.

Belin: Were you aware of the fact that the President's motorcade was going to go right by your building?

Miss Adams: Yes, sir.

Belin: How did you learn of this information?

Miss Adams: Through newspaper media and also conversation.

Belin: Do you remember when you first read about it in the papers?

Miss Adams: No, sir; I don't.

Belin: Would it have been before November 22nd?

Miss Adams: Yes.

Belin: Where were you when the motorcade passed?

Miss Adams: I was at the—

Belin: Were you inside or outside the building?

Miss Adams: I was inside the building.

Belin: What floor?

Miss Adams: Fourth floor.

Belin: Did you watch the motorcade through a window?

Miss Adams: Yes, sir.

Belin: Sometimes that is kind of complicated to try and pick out which window if you are counting from the right or left, so I am going to count from the east side of the building to the west side of the building. Now the windows are separate windows, but they are kind of in pairs, so to speak. Were you standing on the first pair of windows, either one of those two windows?

Miss Adams: No, sir.

Belin: Counting from the east side, were you standing in the second pair of windows?

Miss Adams: No, sir.

Belin: From the east side, were you standing in the third pair, of either of those windows?

Miss Adams: Yes, sir.

Belin: Now, of that third pair, from the east side, would it have been the east window or the west window?

Miss Adams: The west window.

Belin: So another way, if you don't count in pairs, but count in single units from the east side, you would have been in the sixth window from your left as you were facing out the window, is that correct?

Miss Adams: That's right.

Belin: Were you standing with anyone?

Miss Adams: Yes, sir.

Belin: With whom?

Miss Adams: I was standing with Sandra Styles, Elsie Dorman, and Dorothy May Garner.

Belin: Will you state what you saw, what you did, and what you heard?

Miss Adams: I watched the motorcade come down Main, as it turned from Main onto Houston, and watched it proceed around the corner on Elm, and apparently somebody in the crowd called to the late President, because he and his wife both turned abruptly and faced the building, so we had a very good view of both of them.

Belin: Where was their car as you got this good view, had it come directly opposite your window? Had it come to that point on Elm, or not, if you can remember.

Miss Adams: I believe it was prior, just a second or so prior to that.

Belin: All right.

Miss Adams: And from our vantage point we were able to see what the President's wife was wearing, the roses in the car, and things that would attract women's attention. Then we heard—then we were obstructed from the view.

Belin: By what?

Miss Adams: A tree, and we heard a shot, and it was a pause, and then a second shot, and then a third shot.

It sounded like a firecracker or a cannon at a football game, it seemed as if it came from the right below rather than from the left above. Possibly because of the report. And after the third shot, following that, the third shot, I went to the back of the building down the back stairs, and encountered Bill Shelley and Bill Lovelady on the first floor on the way out to the Houston Street dock.

Belin: When you say on the way out to the Houston Street dock, you mean now you were on the way out?

Miss Adams: While I was on the way out.

Belin: Was anyone going along with you?

Miss Adams: Yes, sir; Sandra Styles.

Belin: Sometime after the third shot, and I don't want to get into the actual period of time yet, you went back into the stockroom which would be to the north of where your offices are located on the fourth floor, is that correct?

Miss Adams: Yes, sir; that's correct.

Belin: When you got into the stockroom, where did you go?

Miss Adams: I went to the back stairs.

Belin: Are there any other stairs that lead down from the fourth floor other than those back stairs in the rear of the stockroom?

Miss Adams: No, sir.

Belin: Those stairs would be in the northwest corner of the building, is that correct?

Miss Adams: That's correct.

Belin: You took those stairs. Were you walking or running as you went down the stairs?

Miss Adams: I was running. We were running.

Belin: What kind of shoes did you have on?

Miss Adams: Three-inch heels.

Belin: You had heels. Now, as you were running down the stairs, did you encounter anyone?

Miss Adams: Not during the actual running down the stairs; no, sir.

Belin: After you left the Scott Foresman office and went into the stock-room, did you see anyone until you got to the stairs on the fourth floor other than the person you were with?

Miss Adams: Outside of our office employees; no.

Belin: Would these office employees that you might have seen, all be women?

Miss Adams: Yes, sir.

Belin: Then you got to the stairs and you started going down the stairs. You went from the fourth floor to the third floor?

Miss Adams: That's correct.

Belin: Anyone on the stairs then?

Miss Adams: No, sir.

Belin: Let me ask you this. As you got to the stairs on the fourth floor, did you notice whether or not the elevator was running?

Miss Adams: The elevator was not moving.

Belin: How do you know it was not moving on some other floor?

Miss Adams: Because the cables move when the elevator is moved, and this is evidenced because of a wooden grate.

Belin: By that you mean a wooden door with slats in it that you have to lift up to get on the elevator?

Miss Adams: Yes.

Belin: Did you look to see if the elevator was moving?

Miss Adams: It was not; no, sir.

Belin: It was not moving?

Miss Adams: No.

Belin: Did you happen to see where the elevator might have been located?

Miss Adams: No, sir.

Belin: As you got to the third floor, did you take a look at the elevator again at all, or not, if you remember?

Miss Adams: I can't recall.

Belin: As you got off the stairs on the third floor, did you see anyone on the third floor?

Miss Adams: No, sir.

Belin: Then you immediately went to the stairs going down from the third to the second?

Miss Adams: That's correct.

Belin: As you ran down the stairs, did you see anyone on the stairs?

Miss Adams: No, sir.

Belin: All right. You got down to the second floor. Did you see anyone by the second floor?

Miss Adams: No, sir.

Belin: Did you immediately turn and run and keep on running down the stairs towards the first floor?

Miss Adams: Yes.

Belin: When you got to the bottom of the first floor, did you see anyone there as you entered the first floor from the stairway?

Miss Adams: Yes, sir.

Belin: Who did you see?

Miss Adams: Mr. Bill Shelley and Billy Lovelady.

Belin: Where did you see them on the first floor?

Miss Adams: Well, this is the stairs, and this is the Houston Street dock that I went out. They were approximately in this position here, so I don't know how you would describe that.

Belin: You are looking now at a first floor plan or diagram of the Texas School Book Depository, and you have pointed to a position where you encountered Bill Lovelady and Mr. Bill Shelley?

Miss Adams: That's correct.

Belin: It would be slightly east of the front of the east elevator, and probably as far south as the length of the elevator, is that correct?

Miss Adams: Yes, sir.

Belin: I have a document here called Commission's Exhibit No. 496, which includes a diagram of the first floor, and there is a No. 7 and a circle on it, and I have pointed to a place marked No. 7 on the diagram. Is that correct?

Miss Adams: That is approximate.

Belin: Between the time you got off the stairs and the time you got to this point when you say you encountered them, which was somewhat to the south and a little bit east of the front of the east elevator, did you see any other employees there?

Miss Adams: No, sir.

Belin: Any other people prior to the time you saw them?

Miss Adams: No, sir.

Belin: Now when you were running down the stairs on your trip down the stairs, did you hear anyone using the stairs?

Miss Adams: No, sir.

Belin: Did you hear anyone calling for an elevator?

Miss Adams: No, sir.

Belin: Did you see the foreman, Roy Truly? Did you see the superintendent of the warehouse, Roy S. Truly?

Miss Adams: No, sir; I did not.

Belin: What about any motorcycle police officers?

Miss Adams: No, sir.

Belin: Now what did you do after you encountered Mr. Shelley and Mr. Lovelady?

Miss Adams: I said I believed the President was shot.

Belin: Do you remember what they said?

Miss Adams: Nothing.

Belin: Then what did you do?

Miss Adams: I proceeded out to the Houston Street dock.

Belin: That would be on this same diagram? It is marked Houston Street dock, and you went through what would be the north door, which is towards the rear of the first floor, is that correct?

And down some stairs towards the rear of the dock?

Miss Adams: That's correct.

Belin: Where did you go from there?

Miss Adams: I proceeded—which way is east and west?

Belin: East is here. East is towards Houston, and west is towards the railroad tracks. You went east or west? Towards the railroad tracks or towards Houston Street?

Miss Adams: I went west towards the tracks.

Belin: How far west did you go?

Miss Adams: I went approximately 2 yards within the tracks and there was an officer standing there, and he said, "Get back to the building." And I said, "But I work here."

And he said, "That is tough, get back." I said, "Well, was the President shot?" And he said, "I don't know. Go back." And I said, "All right."

Belin: Then what did you do?

Miss Adams: I went back, only I went southwest.

Belin: Well, did you come back by way of the street, or did you come back the same entrance you went out?

Miss Adams: No, sir.

Belin: You went back in through the front entrance, through the front of the building?

Miss Adams: Well, I didn't go back in right away.

Belin: What did you do then? There is a street that would be a continuation of Elm Street that goes in front of the building, and Elm Street itself angles into the freeway. Did you go back either of those streets?

Miss Adams: Yes, sir. I went by the one directly in front of the building.

Belin: What did you do when you got there?

Miss Adams: When I got there, I happened to look around and noticed several of the employees, and I noticed Joe Molina, for one, was standing in front of the building, and also Avery Davis, who works with me, and I said, "What do you think has happened?"

And she said, "I don't know."

And I said, "I want to find out." I think the President is shot.

There was a motorcycle that was parked on the corner of Houston and Elm directly in front of the east end of the building, and I paused there to listen to the report on the police radio, and they said that shots had been fired which apparently came either from the second floor or the fourth floor window, and so I panicked, as I was at the only open window on the fourth floor.

Belin: Did they say second floor or second floor from the top?

Miss Adams: It said second floor. So then I decided maybe I had better go back into the building, and going up the stairs—

Belin: Now at this time when you went back into the building, were there any policemen standing in front of the building keeping people out?

Miss Adams: There was an officer on the stairs itself, and he was prohibiting people from entering the building, that is correct. But I told him I worked there.

Belin: Did he let you come back in?

Miss Adams: Yes, sir.

Belin: Then what did you do?

Miss Adams: Following that, I pushed the button for the passenger elevator, but the power had been cut off on the elevator, so I took the stairs to the second floor.

Belin: You then went all the way back to the northwest corner of the building and took the same set of stairs you had previously taken to come down, or did you take the stairs by the passenger elevator?

Miss Adams: By the passenger elevator.

Belin: Do those stairs go above floor 2?

Miss Adams: No, sir; they didn't.

Belin: What did you do when you got to the second floor?

Miss Adams: I went into the Texas School Book Depository office and just listened for a few minutes to the people that were congregating there, and decided there wasn't anything interesting going on, and went out and walked around the hall to the freight elevator meaning the one on the northwest corner.

Belin: Would it have been the west or the east? The one nearest the stairs or the other one?

Miss Adams: Yes; the one nearest the stairs.

Belin: Then what did you do?

Miss Adams: I went into the elevator which was stopped on the second floor, with two men who were dressed in suit and hats, and I assumed they were plainclothesmen.

Belin: What did you do then?

Miss Adams: I tried to get the elevator to go to the fourth floor, but it wasn't operating, so the gentlemen lifted the elevator gate and we went out and ran up the stairs to the fourth floor.

Belin: Then you went back to the Scott Foresman Company offices?

Miss Adams: Yes, sir.

Belin: Now trying to reconstruct your actions insofar as the time sequence, which we haven't done, what is your best estimate of the time between the time the shots were fired and the time you got back to the building? How much time elapsed? If you have any estimate. Maybe you don't have one.

Miss Adams: I would estimate not more than 5 minutes elapsed.

Belin: Is there any particular reason why you make this estimation?

Miss Adams: Yes, sir; going down the stairs toward the back, I was running. I ran to the railroad tracks. I moved quickly to the front of the building, paused briefly to talk to someone, listened only to the report of the windows from which the shot supposedly was fired, and returned to the building.

Belin: How long do you think it was between the time the shots were fired and the time you left the window to start toward the stairway?

Miss Adams: Between 15 and 30 seconds, estimated, approximately.

Belin: How long do you think it was, or do you think it took you to get from the window to the top of the fourth floor stairs?

Miss Adams: I don't think I can answer that question accurately, because the time approximation, without a stopwatch, would be difficult.

Belin: How long do you think it took you to get from the window to the bottom of the stairs on the first floor?

Miss Adams: I would say no longer than a minute at the most.

Belin: So you think that from the time you left the window on the fourth floor until the time you got to the stairs at the bottom of the first floor, was approximately 1 minute?

Miss Adams: Yes, approximately.

Belin: As I understand your testimony previously, you saw neither Roy Truly nor any motorcycle police officer at any time?

Miss Adams: That's correct.

Belin: You heard no one else running down the stairs?

Miss Adams: Correct.

Belin: When you got to the first floor did you immediately proceed to this point where you say you encountered Mr. Shelley and Mr. Lovelady?

Well, you showed me on a diagram of the first floor that there was a place which was south and somewhat east of the front part of the east elevator that you encountered Truly [*sic*] and Lovelady?

Miss Adams: I saw them there.

Belin: I mean; you saw them?

Miss Adams: Yes.

Belin: Would that have been a matter of seconds after you got to the bottom of the first floor?

Miss Adams: Definitely.

Belin: Less than 30 seconds?

Miss Adams: Yes.

Belin: Do you know, or did you know Lee Harvey Oswald either by sight or by name?

Miss Adams: I didn't know Lee Harvey Oswald, per se. I didn't know his name. I recognized him after I saw him on television, as having been with some men, but I had no dealing with him.

Belin: By that, you mean having been employed with some men by the Texas School Book Depository?

Miss Adams: That's correct.

Belin: During the trip down the stairs on the way down did you ever encounter Lee Harvey Oswald?

Miss Adams: No, sir.

Belin: Is there any other information that you can think of that might be relevant to anything, connected with the assassination?

Miss Adams: At the time I left the building on the Houston Street dock, there was an officer standing about 2 yards from the curb, and about from the curb across the street from the Texas School Depository, and about 4 yards from the corner of Houston and Elm, and when we were running out the dock, going around the building, the officer was standing there, and he didn't encounter us or ask us what we were doing or where we were going, and I don't know if that is pertinent.

Belin: No one stopped you from getting out of the building when you left?

Miss Adams: That's correct.

Belin: That is helpful information. Is there any other information you have that could be relevant?

Miss Adams: There was a man that was standing on the corner of Houston and Elm asking questions there. He was dressed in a suit and a hat, and when I encountered Avery Davis going down, we asked who he was, because he was questioning people as if he were a police officer, and we noticed him take a colored boy away on a motorcycle, and this man was asking questions very efficaciously, and we said, "I guess he is maybe a reporter," and later on on television, there was a man that looked very similar to him, and he was identified as Ruby.

And on questioning some police officer, they said they had witnesses to the fact that he was in the Dallas Morning News at the time. And I don't know whether that is relevant or what.

Belin: That is all right, we want to get that information down. Was this before you got back in the front door of the building that you saw this?

Miss Adams: Yes, sir; while I was standing by the motorcycles.

Belin: Is there anything else?

Miss Adams: That is all, I believe.

Belin: Miss Adams, you have the opportunity if you would like, to read this deposition and sign it before it goes to Washington, or you can waive the signing of it and just let the court reporter send it directly to us. Do you have any preference?

Miss Adams: I think I will let you use your own discretion.

Belin: It doesn't make any difference to us. If it doesn't make any difference, we can waive it and you won't have to make another trip down here.

Miss Adams: That is all right.

Belin: We want to thank you for your cooperation. We know that it has taken time on your part. Would you also thank your employer?

Miss Adams: Yes, sir.

Relevant Testimony of Billy Nolan Lovelady

This testimony was taken at 3:50 P.M. on April 7, 1964, in Dallas by Commission assistant counsel Joseph A. Ball (6H340-41).

Ball: You came into the building from the west side?
Lovelady: Right.
Ball: Where did you go into the building?
Lovelady: Through that, those raised-up doors.
Ball: Through the raised-up doors?
Lovelady: Through that double door that we in the morning when we get there we raised. There's a fire door and they have two wooden doors between it.
Ball: You came in through the first floor?
Lovelady: Right.
Ball: Who did you see in the first floor?
Lovelady: I saw a girl but I wouldn't swear to it it's Vickie.
Ball: Who is Vickie?
Lovelady: The girl that works for Scott, Foresman.
Ball: What is her full name?
Lovelady: I wouldn't know.
Ball: Vickie Adams?
Lovelady: I believe so.
Ball: Would you say it was Vickie you saw?
Lovelady: I couldn't swear.
Ball: Where was the girl?
Lovelady: I don't remember what place she was but I remember seeing a girl and she was talking to Bill or saw Bill or something, then I went over and asked one of the guys what time it was and to see if we should continue working or what.
Ball: Did you see any other people on the first floor?
Lovelady: Oh, yes; by that time there were more; a few of the guys had come in.

Ball: And you stayed on the first floor then?

Lovelady: I would say 30 minutes. And one of the policemen asked me would I take them up on the sixth floor.

Ball: Did you take them up there?

Lovelady: Yes, sir; I sure did.

Relevant Testimony of William H. Shelley

This testimony was taken at 4:10 P.M. on April 7, 1964, in Dallas by Commission assistant counsel Joseph A. Ball (6H330).

Shelley: We walked on down to the first railroad track there on the dead-end street and stood there and watched them searching cars down there in the parking lots for a little while and then we came in through our parking lot at the west end.

Ball: At the west end?

Shelley: Yes; and then in the side door into the shipping room.

Ball: When you came into the shipping room did you see anybody?

Shelley: I saw Eddie Piper.

Ball: What was he doing?

Shelley: He was coming back from where he was watching the motorcade in the southwest corner of the shipping room.

Ball: Of the first floor of the building?

Shelley: Yes.

Ball: Who else did you see?

Shelley: That's all we saw immediately.

Ball: Did you ever see Vickie Adams?

Shelley: I saw her that day but I don't remember where I saw her.

Ball: You don't remember whether you saw her when you came back?

Shelley: It was after we entered the building.

Ball: You think you did see her after you entered the building?

Shelley: Yes sir; I thought it was on the fourth floor awhile after that.

Ball: Now, did the police come into the building?

APPENDIX 4

The Martha Joe Stroud Letter

PLEASE ADDRESS ALL MAIL TO
UNITED STATES ATTORNEY
P. O. BOX 152

United States Department of Justice *Adams   Vicki*

UNITED STATES ATTORNEY
NORTHERN DISTRICT OF TEXAS
DALLAS 1, TEXAS

75221

June 2, 1964

AIR MAIL - REGISTERED - RETURN RECEIPT REQUESTED

Mr. J. Lee Rankin
General Counsel
President's Commission on the
Assassination of President Kennedy
200 Maryland Avenue N.E.
Washington, D. C. 20002

Dear Mr. Rankin:

I am enclosing the signed deposition of:

Victoria E. Adams

The following corrections were made: page 59 line 19 changed to "service"; page 59 line 20 add "and"; page 60 line 18 to "Martin"; page 64, line 14 to "there"; page 75 line 5 add "and"; page 79 line 4 to "officiously."

Mr. Bellin was questioning Miss Adams about whether or not she saw anyone as she was running down the stairs. Miss Garner, Miss Adams' supervisor, stated this morning that after Miss Adams went downstairs she (Miss Garner) saw Mr. Truly and the policeman come up.

Sincerely yours

Barefoot Sanders
United States Attorney

Martha Joe Stroud, Assistant
United States Attorney

Enclosure

298

Notes

Foreword

1. Among those who did view the Zapruder motion picture back in 1965-66 were some of the "first generation" critics of the Warren Report: Vincent Salandria, Stewart Galanor, Thomas Stamm, and Josiah Thompson.

2. David S. Lifton, *Best Evidence: Disguise and Deception in the Assassination of John F. Kennedy* (New York: Macmillan, 1980), 7.

3. This writing provides a true account of my original perception of the "head-snap" controversy—that the sudden backwards motion represented critical evidence of a shot from the front. By 1970, based on my awareness that dozens of witnesses thought that the limousine briefly halted, I believed that the Zapruder film was altered and that the primary significance of the head-snap is that it represents evidence of editing (i.e., removal of frames) from the Zapruder film. See my essay "Pig on a Leash," which can be found on the Internet.

4. *Warren Report* (hereinafter listed as WR) (Washington, D.C.: U.S. Government Printing Office, 1964), 152.

5. Ibid., vol. 3, 362.

6. In his first FBI interview, on November 22, 1963, Truly described the situation after the president's car passed and he heard shots fired. "He then noticed a Dallas City police officer wearing a motorcycle helmet and boots running towards the entrance of the depository building, and he accompanied the officer in the front of the building. They saw no one there and he accompanied the officer immediately up the stairs to the second floor of the building, where the officer noticed a door and stepped through the door, gun in hand, and observed Oswald in a snack bar there, apparently alone" (Commission Document 5, 322, hereinafter listed as CD). Interviewed the next day, he described it this way: "As they reached the second floor landing, the officer opened a door to a small lunch room next to the business office on that floor, and stuck his gun in the door. Lee Oswald was in the lunch room" (CD 5, 324).

7. Commission Exhibit 1381 (hereinafter listed as CE).

8. The last half of the article was devoted to the issue of a grassy-knoll assassin and featured a detailed statement from UCLA physics professor James Riddle. Dr. Riddle noted that when one shoots at targets at a rifle range, the little ducks "fall away from you, not towards you."

9. Warren Commission Hearings, vol. 17, 48. Citations referring to the twenty-six volumes are listed as 17H48, for example, to indicate vol. 17, page 48.

10. The president's assassination occurred at 12:30 P.M. CST; the official "start time" for the autopsy was 8 P.M. EST.

11. This thesis is developed, in detail, in *Best Evidence:* specifically, that the character (i.e., size and shape) of the wounds in both the head and neck was dramatically altered between the time the president was pronounced dead and the time the autopsy officially began. The Dallas doctors reported an egg-sized wound, approximately 35 square centimeters, at the right rear of the head; at Bethesda, the defect was recorded at

170 square centimeters, i.e., the entire top of the head (the "skullcap") was recorded as "missing" in a diagram made by one of the autopsy surgeons. With regard to the neck wound: the Dallas doctors made a small (2-3 centimeters) horizontal tracheotomy incision. At Bethesda, Commander Humes listed that incision as "6.5 cm" (and testified that it was "7-8 cm.") and that it had "widely gaping irregular edges." These issues are in *Best Evidence* in chapter 13 ("The Head Wound: Dallas versus Bethesda") and chapter 11 ("The Tracheotomy Incision: Dallas vs. Bethesda").

12. See chapter 9 of *Best Evidence:* "October 24, 1966: A Confrontation with Liebeler."

13. Ibid.

14. Ibid., 224.

15. As I later learned, the chief autopsy surgeon made this statement—in front of the two FBI agents—because of the huge size of the hole in the president's head (a hole much larger than anything seen in Dallas). See chapter 12 of *Best Evidence,* "An Oral Utterance." So it looked to him as if a craniotomy had already been performed. This matter is discussed in detail in chapter 13 of *Best Evidence,* devoted to the head wounding.

16. I ascertained this information not only in telephone interviews with key personnel at Bethesda but in filmed interviews I conducted with these key witnesses in the fall of 1980, two months prior to the publication of my book.

17. The letter—dated June 2, 1964—was transmitting a corrected version of the Adams transcript. It volunteered that Dorothy Garner, Adams' supervisor, noted that Officer Baker and building superintendent Roy Truly appeared on the fourth floor *after* Vicki had descended the stairs. Garner's account didn't prove exactly when Adams descended the stairs—for that, we have to rely on Adams herself. When interviewed two days after the assassination, Adams said she and Sandra Styles "ran immediately to the back of the building to where the stairs were located and then ran down the stairs" (CD 5, 39). In her signed statement to the FBI dated March 23, 1964 (CE 1381), she said "after she observed the car carrying President Kennedy speed away," she and Styles "then ran out of the building, via the stairs." What the Martha Stroud letter does is rule out the notion that Vicki Adams had been in error by minutes, i.e., that she had descended the stairs not seconds later, as she claimed (remember, she used the word "immediately"), but several minutes later. Despite the importance of this letter, Dorothy Garner was not called to testify. But then, neither were Sandra Styles or Elsie Dorman. The probable reason for this lapse was the truly arrogant attitude of the late David Belin. Barry described the scene on April 7, 1964, when Adams gave her deposition in Dallas to Belin, who often behaved like a true believer. "Belin leaned back in his chair and said he didn't believe a word she was saying." Well then, asked Vicki, "Why don't you interview Sandra Styles?" "We don't need her, we have you," replied Belin. This was the sort of investigation conducted by the Warren Commission.

Chapter 1

1. Mark Lane, *Rush to Judgment* (New York: Holt, Rinehart & Winston, 1966), 110.

2. WR, 154.

Chapter 3

1. 6H388.

2. Ibid., 388-90.

3. Ibid., 391.

4. Ibid., 391-92.

5. Ibid., 393.

Chapter 4

1. CE 496 (as shown in 17H210).

2. A janitor, Piper was questioned by attorney Ball the next day, April 8, but was not asked a single question about whether he saw Shelley and Lovelady reenter the building or what time that may have been (6H382-86).

3. 6H330.

4. Ibid., 331.

5. Ibid., 340.

6. Ibid., 340-41.

7. 22H632.

8. Ibid., 644.

9. Ibid., 648.

10. Ibid., 676.

11. Ibid., 673.

12. Ibid., 662.

13. CE 2003 (as shown in 24H226).

14. Ibid., 214.

15. As an interesting aside, the September 28, 1960, edition of the *Washington Post* reported that eight airmen at Andrews Air Force Base had been arrested by the FBI for theft of government property. One of those charged was twenty-three-year-old Billy Nolan Lovelady, who later admitted to his participation in stealing and then reselling several .38-caliber revolvers. Part of the penalty assessed to Lovelady, in addition to a discharge, was a $200 fine. Lovelady paid $125 of it, then reneged on the balance due. The FBI caught up with him in Dallas in January 1963 and arrested him at his place of employment, the Texas School Book Depository. He was immediately taken to a local jail. Ochus V. Campbell, vice president of the Depository, advanced Lovelady the outstanding amount of his fine, and the case was officially closed. (See FBI Document No. 52-75836.)

Chapter 5

1. A cashier at an Irving grocery store told the FBI that on Thursday, October 31, 1963, she cashed a thirty-three-dollar Texas unemployment check for Lee Oswald (CE 1165, 6, as shown in 22H225). Without any explanation, the Commission changed the date and stated in its Report that the transaction occurred on Friday, November 1 (WR, 331).

2. Marina Oswald felt that there was a different reason for the unexpected Thursday visit. Because her husband had not been to Irving the previous weekend and did not intend to visit during the upcoming weekend of November 22-24, and since they had had a bitter argument over the telephone earlier that particular week, Marina told the Commission that Oswald made the Thursday evening visit to "make up" with her (18H638) and to "make his peace with me" (1H65). She also said that her husband talked with her that night about wanting them to live together again and "that if I want to he would rent an apartment in Dallas tomorrow—that he didn't want me to remain with Ruth [Paine] any longer, but wanted me to live with him in Dallas" (1H66).

3. WR, 130.

4. See CE 994, 43 (as shown in 18H639). See also the testimony of Marina Oswald, 1H69.

5. 2H243.

6. WR, 137.

7. 6H360.

8. 1H120.

9. 3H49.

10. 1H66.

11. 3H48.

12. 2H249.

13. Ibid., 226.

14. Coincidentally, Frazier once worked in a department store and often uncrated curtain rods as part of his duties. He told the Commission, "If you have seen when they come straight from the factory you know how they can bundle them up and put them in there pretty compact, so he [Oswald] told me it was curtain rods so I didn't think anymore about the package whatsoever" (2H229). The FBI's measurements are discussed in CE 2009 (as shown in 24H409).

15. WR, 134.

16. 6H377.

17. WR, 250.

18. CD 87.

19. 3H144-45.

20. 3H148. Brennan said he declined to make a positive identification (even after seeing Oswald's picture twice on television prior to the lineup) because he was afraid for himself and his family. It was only after Oswald was killed and fears of possible reprisal subsided that Brennan changed his mind and said he knew all along Oswald was the man in the window. But according to his testimony, Brennan did not notify authorities of this important flip-flop until December 17, more than three weeks after Oswald was murdered (see 3H155).

21. 6H351. See also WR, 143.

22. 6H383.

23. 6H328.

24. 2H173-76.

25. One can only appreciate the lengths to which the Commission went to prove Rowland wrong by reading the testimony of his wife, who, for lack of a better term, was verbally coerced into admitting her husband had once exaggerated about his school grades (see 6H189-90). Despite Commission attorney David Belin assuring Mrs. Rowland that his line of questioning would not "take away from the testimony of your husband as to what he saw in the building at the time," that is exactly what happened.

26. 6H263.

27. The sixth floor was used for storage of textbooks and routinely had hundreds of boxes strewn throughout. The area was even more disorganized on that day as the result of a new floor being laid by a crew of men who were working there during the morning hours and broke for lunch around noon.

28. WR, 149-56.

29. 3H246.

30. Ibid., 250.

31. Ibid.

32. Ibid.

33. Ibid., 225.

34. Ibid., 278-79.

35. WR, 157.

36. 6H409-10.

37. WR, 159.

38. Ibid. See also 2H280-81.

39. Ibid.

40. 6H412.

41. See CE 381-A (as shown in 16H974). The ticket indeed has the date of "Fri. Nov. 22, '63" on it, but the time is listed only generally as "P.M." Some critics later charged that the ticket was planted on the unsuspecting Oswald. Although the Warren Report does not say exactly when the transfer ticket was discovered—it mentions only that it was found "when Oswald was apprehended" (WR, 157)—the footnote it uses to support that statement takes the reader to the testimony of Dallas Police Detective Richard M. Sims,

who stated he actually found the ticket in Oswald's shirt pocket two hours after his arrest, at about 4 P.M. that Friday, during a search of the suspect shortly before the first lineup was held (7H173).

42. 2H256.

43. CE 370 (as shown in 16H966).

44. 6H429.

45. 6H428. The agent was John Howlett, who had been the stand-in for Oswald during the time tests of the assassin's escape to the second-floor lunchroom. Others in the car included Commission counsel Joseph Ball and a member of the Texas attorney general's office.

46. WR, 161.

47. 6H443.

48. Ibid.; 6H444.

49. WR, 253.

50. Ibid., 163.

51. See the December 5, 1963, affidavit of Mrs. Roberts in 7H439.

52. WR, 165.

53. Ibid.; WR, 166.

54. Ibid., 167.

55. Ibid.

56. 3H310-11.

57. 11H435.

58. CE 2523 (as shown in 25H731).

59. 11H438.

60. Bushes obscured his view of Tippit's police car, so Scoggins was not an eyewitness to the actual shooting.

61. WR, 166.

62. Ibid.

63. Ibid. See also 3H334.

64. 2H261. Interesting too was the testimony of W. E. Perry (7H234), Richard L. Clark (7H237-38), and Don R. Ables (7H241). Each was a Dallas Police Department employee who participated, with Oswald, in the police lineups. They explained that when called on during the lineup procedure, each gave a fictitious name and occupation. Oswald, however, gave his true name and where he worked—details by now in wide public circulation.

65. 6H447. The Report gives the distance as twenty-five feet (WR, 166).

66. Benavides was interviewed for a four-part series on the assassination that was broadcast by CBS News in June 1967. Asked then if there was any doubt in his mind that it was Oswald who shot Tippit, Benavides replied, "No, sir, there was no doubt at all. I could even tell you how he combed his hair and the clothes he wore and what have you, all the details. And if he had a scar on his face, I could probably have told you about it, but—you don't forget things like that." See Part III, 6, of the official transcript of "CBS News Inquiry, 'The Warren Report.'" Only someone who had read Benavides' testimony in 6H444-54 could appreciate what a startling reversal this was.

67. 6H451.

68. Ibid.

69. WR, 175.

70. CE 2003, 117 (as shown in 24H253).

71. CE 1843 (as shown in 23H521). As a curious aside, when Benavides was shown the jacket during his questioning by Commission counsel Belin, the lawyer blundered. Instead of displaying CE 162, the "light-beige" jacket found at the gas station and presumably the one worn by Tippit's murderer, Belin showed Benavides CE 163, a separate *blue* jacket of Oswald's found in the Depository:

Belin: I am handing you a jacket which has been marked as "Commission's Exhibit 163," and ask you to state whether this bears any similarity to the jacket you saw this man with the gun wearing?

Benavides: I would say this looks just like it (6H453).

The mistake went uncorrected.
72. 7H4.
73. 7H10-11.
74. Ibid., 15.
75. Ibid., 12.
76. Ibid., 10. Mrs. Postal couldn't be exact as to how many persons had purchased tickets because "everything was happening so fast."
77. 3H299. One Commission member was astonished by McDonald's relaxed manner, asking the officer if, despite Brewer's specific identification, he still intended to search the other patrons. "It was my intention—everybody I came to," the officer replied (3H303).
78. See, for instance, the testimony of Mrs. Postal, 7H12-13.
79. WR, 169.

Chapter 7
1. From handwritten notes made during a personal interview with Aldredge, March 19, 1968.
2. From handwritten notes made during a personal interview with Jones, March 19, 1968.
3. See CE 18 (as shown in 16H69-70).
4. I would verify this by checking a cross-reference telephone directory at the Dallas Public Library.
5. Penn Jones, Jr., *Forgive My Grief Volume I: A Critical Review of the Warren Commission Report on the Assassination of President John F. Kennedy* (Midlothian, TX: Midlothian Mirror, 1966).
6. Penn Jones, Jr., *Forgive My Grief II: A Further Critical Review of the Warren Commission Report on the Assassination of President John F. Kennedy* (Midlothian, TX: Midlothian Mirror, 1967).
7. From handwritten notes made during a personal interview with Truly, March 20, 1968.
8. Pauline E. Sanders, a Depository employee standing outside near the front steps of the building, told the FBI that a uniformed police officer wearing a white helmet ran up the steps and into the building "within a matter of ten seconds" following the shooting. See CE 1434 (as shown in 22H844-45).
9. Although Truly (3H225) and Baker (3H251) both testified that Oswald was holding nothing in his hands, Baker wrote in a signed statement on September 23, 1964 (the Warren Report was presented to President Johnson the next day), "On the second floor, where the lunchroom is located, I saw a man standing in the lunchroom drinking a coke." The words "drinking a coke" were then scratched out by the officer (see CE 3076, as shown in 26H679). It is strange that at that late date, and six months after testifying to the contrary, Baker spontaneously wrote that Oswald had a drink in his hand. Maybe Baker simply had made a mistake. But one thing is for certain: the additional time it would have taken Oswald to deposit money in the soda machine and select his drink before Baker got to him would have posed further headaches to a Commission already grappling with a strained schedule, not to mention the question as to why an escaping assassin, cops on his heels, would even bother to stop for a soda. There is evidence suggesting that Baker was accurate in his September description after all. Oswald was asked, during a Friday-night interrogation by Dallas Police Capt. Will Fritz, where he

was when Baker confronted him. According to Fritz, "He [Oswald] said he was on the second floor *drinking a coca cola* [author's emphasis] when the officer came in" (WR, 600).

10. See CE 1118, a diagram of the second floor, in 22H85 and reprinted in larger scale in WR, 150.

11. 3H255.

12. Ibid.

13. WR, 151.

14. Ibid.

15. 3H255.

16. 3H223.

17. 3H255.

18. 3H256. Mrs. Robert A. Reid testified, however, that Oswald occasionally came to her office on the second floor next to the lunchroom to "get change" for the soda machine and even to converse with others about his newborn girl (3H275-76).

19. This embarrassing line, including any others in Cody's presence, is taken from handwritten notes made during a personal interview with Cody, March 21, 1968.

Chapter 8

1. From a tape-recorded interview with Jones, March 22, 1968.

2. See 6H430-31 for Whaley's testimony describing this breach of police ethics. Whaley, sixty, was killed in a head-on collision in his cab on December 18, 1965. The other driver also died. Jones wrote, "Whaley had the opportunity to talk to Oswald; Oswald may have told Whaley nothing, but there was a chance." See Jones, *Forgive My Grief II*, 12.

3. Mrs. Roberts, sixty, died on January 10, 1966, after suffering "an apparent heart attack." Jones wrote, "Oswald may have told Mrs. Earlene Roberts nothing, but there was a possibility which could not afford [sic] to be overlooked by the plotters of the assassination." See Jones, *Forgive My Grief II*, 12.

4. Ibid., 19. Jones wrote that the brother looked so much like Domingo, his death may have been a case of mistaken identity. "Benevides [sic] described a man other than Oswald" and "was not asked to go down to the lineup to view Oswald," Jones said. After his brother's death, Benavides left the area for a few months but later returned and "now . . . cooperates completely with the Dallas Police Department" and "states positively now that the escaping person was Oswald."

5. From handwritten notes I was permitted to make during a personal interview with Holland, March 25, 1968.

6. Although police who also ran to the knoll would look through the windows of many of the cars parked behind the wooden fence, testimony reveals that the trunks of those vehicles were not searched. Veteran Dallas Police Officer Joe M. Smith testified he "looked into all the cars" during a twenty-minute search of the parking lot immediately following the shooting but saw nothing suspicious in any of the vehicles. As an aside, he said when he first entered the parking area with gun in hand, another man already there quickly flashed identification indicating he was a Secret Service agent (7H535).

7. Jones, *Forgive My Grief Volume I*, 54-60.

8. From handwritten notes made during a personal interview with Jarnagin, March 27, 1968.

9. FBI File No. DL 89-43, 24-25.

10. From handwritten notes made during a telephone interview with Walther, March 27, 1968.

11. Those critical of Mrs. Walther often cite this mistake in floor location as one of the reasons she is unreliable and therefore not to be trusted with any of her other observations. In *Reclaiming History: The Assassination of President John F. Kennedy* (New York: W. W. Norton, 2007), author Vincent Bugliosi does just that after chastising

"conspiracy theorists" for having the audacity to use such a dubious witness. Yet in his follow-up book on the same subject, Bugliosi defends a similar mistake made by Sgt. D. V. Harkness, who reported over the police radio that a shot "came from the fifth floor of the . . . Depository." In a footnote, Bugliosi justifies that miscue by saying, "Harkness's error is understandable in light of the fact that in 1963 the Depository's first-floor windows were covered with decorative masonry. Persons unfamiliar with the building could easily mistake the second floor for the first, third for the second, and so on—making the sixth floor appear as if it were the fifth floor. This is apparently what Harkness did during these initial confusing moments." See Bugliosi, *Four Days in November* (New York: W. W. Norton, 2007), 80.

12. Mrs. Walther is probably referring to the children of witnesses William and Gayle Newman, who were standing on the north side of Elm Street near the knoll. Immediately upon hearing gunshots, the couple pulled their children to the ground and covered them with their own bodies.

13. WR, 165.

14. Ibid.

15. My time tests were conducted on March 30, 1968.

16. WR, 165.

17. Ibid.

18. From handwritten notes made during a personal interview with Mrs. Donald R. Higgins, March 30, 1968.

19. The Texas Theatre must have had a penchant for war flicks: when Oswald was arrested there, the movies *Cry of Battle* and *War Is Hell* were playing.

20. From handwritten notes made during a telephone interview with Jones, March 30, 1968.

21. Lane, 56.

22. From handwritten notes made during a telephone and personal interview with Brehm, March 30 and into the wee hours of March 31, 1968.

23. Brehm's name was added to an accumulating number of witnesses never summoned to Washington to testify or even questioned in Dallas during the Commission's on-site investigation. His name was known, however. On the day of the assassination, he appeared on local television and was quoted in the city's evening newspaper. The FBI also interviewed him at length on November 24, 1963 (see FBI File No. DL 89-43, 28-29).

Chapter 9

1. CE 1281 (as shown in 22H395).

2. From the testimony of Anne Boudreaux, 8H36-37.

3. CE 3067 (as shown in 26H653-54).

4. Ibid., 652.

5. Ibid., 655. Coincidentally, Jack Ruby once operated a club in Dallas called the Silver Spur, which closed its doors to the public in the mid-1950s. He also was part owner of the Sovereign Club, before changing its name to the Carousel Club.

6. Ibid., 656.

7. Ibid.

8. I had to wonder exactly when Mrs. Kauffman, having been interviewed by the FBI twice in one day and providing obviously conflicting stories, found the time to give the matter "considerable thought" and whether her change of mind occurred as the result of her husband coaching her against becoming involved.

9. CE 3067 (as shown in 26H656).

10. Ibid., 657.

11. Ibid., 657-59.

12. Margaret K. Hoover, letter to author, April 25, 1968.

13. Gary Schoener, letter to author, June 10, 1968.

14. Ibid., June 17, 1968.

15. As time went by, several others would report damage to envelopes they received from me, and I too would occasionally observe similar problems with letters addressed in my name. In each and every case, the mail mischief involved correspondence regarding the JFK assassination.

Chapter 10

1. See Part II, 6, of the official transcript of "CBS News Inquiry: 'The Warren Report,'" which aired June 26, 1967.

2. CE 139 (as shown in 16H512).

3. WR, 84.

4. See CE 2003 (as shown in 24H228).

5. See Decker Exhibit 5323 (as shown in 19H507) (hereinafter listed as DE).

6. 3H294.

7. 7H108.

8. See DE 5323 (as shown in 19H528-29).

9. 3H281-90.

10. Ibid.

11. 7H107 (Weitzman) and 3H293 (Boone).

12. WR, 9.

13. See, for example, CE 3048 (as shown in 26H599). Note also that this news report states the rifle was found "in a staircase on the fifth floor of the building."

14. See CE 2169 (as shown in 24H831). It is interesting to note that Malcom H. Price, Jr., one of those who thought he saw Oswald at a rifle range in September 1963, told a Commission attorney that the gun he saw that man carry, and which Price actually handled, was "a Mauser-type rifle." When asked whether there was printing stamped on it, Price said he didn't notice any other than its serial number (see 10H373-74). By coincidence, Warren Caster testified that two days prior to the assassination, he brought two rifles he had purchased over his lunch hour into the Depository building, where he was employed. One of the guns he openly displayed to fellow workers was a Mauser (7H387).

15. CE 543-45 (as shown in 17H241). A busy man, Deputy Sheriff Luke Mooney found the shell casings about ten minutes before he observed the rifle.

16. CE 143 (as shown in 16H513).

17. See CE 853 and 856-58 (as shown in 17H849-51). The bullet I was holding actually looked remarkably like two bullets that had been test fired from Oswald's rifle in such a way, and presumably into a soft substance, that they would be undamaged, easily recovered, and capable of being used for comparison purposes (see 3H497 and CE 572, as shown in 17H258).

18. CE 150 (as shown in 16H515). See also Shaneyfelt Exhibit 24 (as shown in 21H467-70).

19. Although the Report diminished the significance of the laundry tag and mark by not mentioning them at all, these important clues still caused quite a stir. In *Six Seconds in Dallas* (New York: Bernard Geis Associates, 1967), author Josiah Thompson writes that an extensive FBI investigation of all laundry and dry-cleaning businesses in the Dallas-Ft. Worth area failed to uncover the originator of the labels. The FBI also struck out after conducting inquiries of 293 such establishments in the metropolitan New Orleans area. (See Thompson, 228-29.)

20. Much has been made of the fact that Oswald wore size-small shirts while the jacket supposedly discarded by the fleeing cop killer in Oak Cliff was a medium, the implication being that the jacket was the wrong size to be a part of Oswald's meager wardrobe and therefore it belonged to someone else. Oswald's only other jacket was a heavier blue one found in the first-floor lunchroom of the Texas School Book Depository after the

assassination (see 6H345 and CE 163, as shown in 16H521). It would have been revealing to determine the size of this jacket in comparison to the other, but as is symptomatic of research into the Kennedy assassination, no size labels appear on this item.

21. Commission Documents (CDs) are documents the Warren Commission examined during the course of its investigation but chose not to publish in its twenty-six volumes of evidence. CDs are only available for review at the National Archives.

22. CD 5, 39.

23. Ibid.

24. CD 105, 339.

25. "Key Persons Interviewed" file; Adams, Victoria E.

26. 3H173 and 178.

27. 3H191.

28. Consider, for example, the following exchange during Jarman's testimony (3H205-6):

Ball: Had you heard any person running upstairs?
Jarman: No, sir; I hadn't.
Ball: Or any steps upstairs?
Jarman: No, sir.
Ball: Any noise at all up there?
Jarman: None.

29. Ibid., 195.

30. WR, 153 and 3H180.

31. FBI File No. DL 89-43, 120-22.

32. WR, 152. According to the Report, Howlett "placed the rifle on the floor near where Oswald's rifle was actually found." In a March 20, 1964, affidavit, Howlett also says he "placed the rifle on the floor" (see "Key Persons Interviewed" file; Howlett, John Joe). Yet pictures taken when the rifle was discovered show that it had not been simply "placed" on the floor by the fleeing assassin but was rather carefully secreted between and under several boxes (see CE 514, as shown in 17H224, and CE 718, as shown in 17H501). This would have resulted in slightly longer reenactment times than what Howlett was able to achieve. Howlett may not have even been using a gun for his simulations. Many years later I would find a three-page Secret Service document titled "Explanation of Film Sequences: Reconstructing the Assassination of the President." The document provides an interpretation of several films taken by the government to duplicate key events of the assassination. One of these shows Agent Howlett on the sixth floor of the Depository, "fleeing the scene by the route which we believe Lee Oswald used, as it is the most direct route," the document states. "The end of this sequence shows Agent Howlett placing a *stick* [author's emphasis] at the point where the assassin [*sic*] weapon was found and exiting down the steps which we think Lee Oswald used." See CD 87, 233.

33. Ibid. Truly told me in a March 21, 1968, interview that he and Baker were actually moving "much faster" on the day of the assassination than what they did during the Commission's timed tests. Regarding those tests, Baker testified they were conducted in such a way that "we walked the first time and then we kind of run the second time" from his motorcycle into the building (3H253). Yet Baker's description of the actual event in his testimony reads as if his movements were in reality nothing short of an outright bolt into the building, knocking people out of the way and even colliding with Truly as they both hurriedly tried to enter the swinging front door. Photos published later clearly show Officer Baker running at full stride toward the Depository building. (See, for instance, Richard B. Trask, *Pictures of the Pain* [Danvers, MA: Yeoman Press, 1994], 424, and Robert J. Groden, *The Killing of a President* [New York: Viking Studio Books, 1993], 64.)

34. CD 87, 324. One day while reading through files marked "Staff Working Papers"

of the Commission, I came across a two-page unsigned, undated, and badly typed document titled "Memo To Files Re: Movements of Oswald after the Assassination." The anonymous author had discovered that if the times furnished by the Secret Service were accurate, Oswald could not have been Tippit's murderer. Concluding with a look at how long it would have taken Oswald to walk from his rooming house to where Tippit was slain, the memo states, "According to the Secret Service Report, this takes 12 minutes putting him at that spot 1:19. Tippit was killed at 1:18." (See Staff Working Papers, Box 6.) The Commission actually made matters worse when it stated on page 165 of its Report that Tippit was killed sometime prior to 1:16 P.M.

35. Staff Working Papers, "Outline of Ball-Belin Report #1," 116.

36. Ibid., 117-18.

37. From handwritten notes made after my first meeting with Weisberg, June 27, 1968.

38. *Whitewash—The Report on the Warren Report* (1965) and his subsequent *Whitewash II—The FBI-Secret Service Cover-up* (1966) were privately published by Harold Weisberg at Hyattstown, Maryland. Both titles were later picked up and distributed by Dell Publishing Company.

Chapter 11

1. Harold Weisberg, letter to author, July 26, 1968.

2. See, for instance, Melvin M. Belli, *Dallas Justice: The Real Story of Jack Ruby and His Trial* (New York: David McKay, 1964), 43.

3. From handwritten notes made during a personal interview with Decker, July 31, 1968.

4. Decker was riding in the backseat of the motorcade's lead car, which was being driven by Dallas Police Chief Jesse Curry. At the moment shots were fired, Curry got on his police radio to say, "Get men on top of the underpass; see what happened up there." Decker, grabbing the microphone from Curry, is quoted as telling the radio dispatcher, "I'm sure it's going to take some time to get your men in there. Put every one of my men there." (See Sawyer Exhibit A, as shown in 21H390-91.) It is not clear what Decker meant by "there." Was he referring to putting his men on the underpass, as Curry had just directed, or having them report to Dealey Plaza in general? In a nine-page statement of his activities that day, Decker elaborated on his radio order by saying that he wanted his deputies advised "to immediately get over to the area where shooting occurred and saturate the area of the park, railroad and all buildings." (See DE 5323, as shown in 19H458.) Unfortunately, he was never asked for further clarification of the orders to his men when Commission counsel questioned him on April 16, 1964 (see 12H42-52).

5. It would be many years later, after the House Select Committee on Assassinations conducted its investigation during which it more thoroughly examined the Dallas Police radio recordings, that Decker's actual message that day would become available in full. And it would also be made clear at that point that the copy of the "edited transcript . . . from the Dallas police radio log for November 22, 1963," as printed for public inspection in volume 31 of the twenty-six volumes, was amended for more than just purposes of length. In this more recent version of the log, Curry's response about putting men onto the underpass remains unchanged from what the Commission published in 1964. But Decker's words, according to this later transcript, vary dramatically from what was shown in the Commission's transcript: "Have my office move all available men out of my office *into the railroad yard* [author's emphasis] to try to determine what happened in there and hold everything secure until Homicide and other investigators should get there" (see, for instance, Groden, 52).

6. 19H452-543.

7. I wrote Weisberg about my interview when I returned home. "Decker lied to you, as might have been expected," he responded on August 12. "All of his files are not in the 26. None of the pictures, which interested me most."

8. From handwritten notes made during a personal interview with Jarnagin, August 1, 1968.

9. I searched for Miss Mauldin in Dallas but could not find her.

10. See CE 2821 (as shown in 26H254-57).

11. 5H232.

12. Ibid., 239.

13. Ibid., 232.

14. Ibid., 234.

15. Ibid., 232.

16. From handwritten notes made during a telephone interview with Jones, August 1, 1968.

17. From handwritten notes made during a telephone interview with Miller, August 1, 1968.

18. 19H481.

19. CD 5, 30.

20. 7H560.

21. Ibid., 564.

22. From handwritten notes made during a personal interview with Hudson, August 2, 1968.

23. *Liebeler:* Did the shots seem evenly spaced or were some of them closer together? *Hudson:* They seemed pretty well evenly spaced. *Liebeler:* Evenly spaced; is that it? *Hudson:* Yes, sir. (7H565.)

24. Stenographers keeping the official record for the Warren Commission would routinely use the notation "(off the record)" to indicate that such discussions took place. It is interesting that despite Hudson's claims to the contrary, not a single mention of an off-the-record conversation can be found in his testimony, as published in the twenty-six volumes.

25. From handwritten notes made during a personal interview with Holland, August 2, 1968.

26. Several questions came to mind at this point. For instance, what happened to the two men that railroad-tower operator Lee Bowers had observed standing behind the fence only moments before he heard the shots? During his testimony in April 1964, Bowers told the Commission all about those men and how he felt "something out of the ordinary" had occurred at that location when the shooting started (6H288). He also related to author Mark Lane in 1966 that his attention was drawn to that area when the shots rang out and he felt there had been "a flash of light or smoke or something" (see Lane, 32). Wouldn't the two men he noticed have seen a gunman fire a weapon from there? And after years of worldwide controversy over this matter, why have those two individuals still not come forward to offer their observations?

27. Years later I would stare intently at a black-and-white picture, taken about five minutes after the assassination, by *Dallas Times Herald* photographer William Allen. Taken from the same side of the street and just west of where Mary Moorman snapped her famous shot, the Allen photograph shows a group of spectators converged on the sidewalk and street in front of the steps leading up to the knoll. In the background is the corner of the picket fence. At the exact spot where I had stood that August day, an unidentified police officer is shown standing behind the fence, gazing down onto the street where the shooting had just occurred, apparently after having been directed there by witnesses.

28. Holland died in 1969, apparently of natural causes.

29. From a taped interview with Craig, August 4, 1968.

30. It indeed would have been very revealing, and would have lent credence to what Craig was saying, had Fritz used the general term "car," while Oswald replied with the more specific and incriminating "station wagon." But when Commission attorney David

Belin questioned him in Dallas on April 1, 1964, Craig did not quote Fritz as saying "car" when the police captain was addressing Oswald:

Belin: Then, what did Captain Fritz say and what did you say and what did the suspect say?
Craig: Captain Fritz then asked him about the—uh—he said, "What about this station wagon?" And the suspect interrupted him and said, "That station wagon belongs to Mrs. Paine"—I believe is what he said. "Don't try to tie her into this. She had nothing to do with it." (6H270)

31. Craig provided a more detailed description in his testimony:

Craig: Oh, he was a white male in his twenties, five nine, five eight, something like that; about 140 to 150; had kind of medium brown sandy hair—you know, it was like it'd been blown—you know, he'd been in the wind or something—it was all wild-looking; had on—uh—blue trousers—
Belin: What shade of blue? Dark blue, medium or light?
Craig: No; medium, probably; I'd say medium. And, a—uh—light tan shirt, as I remember it.
Belin: Anything else about him
Craig: No; nothing except that he looked like he was in an awful hurry. (6H266)

32. 7H404.
33. WR, 160.
34. Ibid., 161.

Chapter 12
1. DE 5323 (as shown in 19H492).
2. CD 5, 65.
3. Lane, 33.
4. Ibid.
5. From handwritten notes made during a telephone interview with Price, August 6, 1968.
6. From a taped interview with Wise, August 7, 1968. Wise would later become mayor of Dallas.
7. It was this observed demeanor—Ruby with tears in his eyes at the thought of the slain president, his widow, and the now-fatherless children—that caused Wise to be called as a witness for the defense during the March 1964 murder trial of Ruby. Ruby's defense hinged on his claim that he killed Oswald to keep Mrs. Kennedy and her children from having to return to Dallas had Oswald's case gone before a jury. See CE 2413 (as shown in 25H498-505).
8. See, for instance, Elmer Gertz, *Moment of Madness: The People vs. Jack Ruby* (Chicago: Follett, 1968), 110-11.
9. 15H491.
10. See Hall (C. Ray) Exhibit 3 (as shown in 20H47-62).
11. WR, 340-42. At one point during the press conference, somehow-knowledgeable Ruby corrected District Attorney Henry Wade by saying Oswald was really a member of a *pro*-Castro group instead of the anti-Castro organization Wade had erroneously mentioned to the media.
12. During that trial testimony, Harkness responded as follows:

[Assistant District Attorney] *Alexander:* I'll ask you if you saw Jack Ruby in that crowd that you moved back from the jail entrance?
Harkness: Yes sir.

Alexander: And did you see which direction he went after you moved him back?
Harkness: No, sir. The last I had seen of him was at Elm and Houston, on the jail side, on the east side of Houston.
Alexander: Now that was on Saturday afternoon, just before four o'clock?
Harkness: Yes sir. (See 25H403.)

13. 6H314.
14. Ibid. Harkness introduced two other areas of importance during his testimony, both of which virtually cried out for elaboration. The first occurred behind the Depository, where the officer had gone to search after the assassination:

Belin: Was anyone around in the back when you got there?
Harkness: There were some Secret Service agents there. I didn't get them identified. They told me they were Secret Service. (6H312)

These were not two men who quickly flashed a badge or identification card that Harkness, under the circumstances, could have mistaken as being Secret Service credentials; these men actually "told" the officer they were from that agency. But no Secret Service agents had been assigned to the grounds of Dealey Plaza. Who were these men? What were they wearing? What did they look like? What happened to them? Instead of asking these questions or ones similar, Belin wanted to move on to what Harkness did when he returned to the front of the Depository. This led Harkness to mentioning the second area of ignored significance, which concerned what happened when he entered the railroad yards and searched a train that had been leaving the area until the alert tower operator, Lee Bowers, stopped it:

Harkness: Well, we got a long freight that was in there, and we pulled some people off of there and took them to the station.
Belin: You mean some transients.
Harkness: Tramps and hoboes. . . .
Belin: Do you know whether or not anyone found any suspicious people of any kind or nature down there in the railroad yard?
Harkness: Yes, sir. We made some arrests, I put some people in. (6H312)

What were these people doing that made them "suspicious" enough for police to "put them in"? In what I was finding typical of Belin's approach, he wasn't concerned, even though he initiated the question. Rather, convinced by Harkness that the hoboes and tramps were weaponless when arrested, he moved on to an unrelated area.
15. Wise interview. Why wasn't Ruby present when the presidential limousine passed by that Friday afternoon? This was someone who, during that weekend and in front of many people, openly cried at the mere thought of the president's death. His regard for Kennedy and his wife was so deep-seated, he said, that he became enraged at the mention or sight of the accused assassin. He ultimately was willing to sacrifice his own life for the sake of revenge. And yet, only a few blocks away and conducting business that easily could have waited, Ruby chose not to spare a few minutes to stroll up and see his beloved First Family.
16. CD 5, 40. The Commission, already aware of the frequency with which the FBI, Secret Service, and even David Belin himself had clicked a stopwatch for the express purpose of resolving important timing issues, chose to ignore this one involving Miss Adams.
17. Mrs. Davis told the FBI, "I, along with others, started to move forward in the direction of the President's car, but after moving about fifteen feet I turned and returned inside the Depository Building" (22H642). Following the shots, Molina "moved from

my position on the steps in the direction of where the Presidential car was proceeding," he told the agency. "I remained outside for a few moments and then went back inside" (22H664).

18. See Sawyer Exhibit A (as shown in 21H392).

19. Staff Working Papers, Liebeler, Wesley J. The comment was made in Liebeler's "Memorandum re Galley Proofs of Chapter IV of the Report," under the subheading "Oswald's Actions in Building After Assassination," 12.

20. Ibid. Liebeler's revision was submitted too late for any changes to be made. The opening two sentences regarding Miss Adams were thus left to read as originally written on page 154 of the Warren Report.

Chapter 14

1. In hindsight, I see that this line must have greatly amused Salandria.

2. From handwritten notes made during a personal interview with Salandria, August 20, 1968.

3. Harold Weisberg, letter to author, September 30, 1968.

4. WR, 87-88.

5. CE 386 (as shown in 16H977).

6. CE 385 (as shown in 16H977).

7. CD 107, Part One, 2. The actual report regarding the hole locations reads as follows: "The hole in the back of the coat is positioned approximately $5^3/8$" below the top of the collar and $1^3/4$" to the right of the middle seam. The hole in the shirt back is located in the same relative area, being $5^3/4$" below the top of the collar and $1^1/8$" to the right of the middle." See CD 205, 153.

8. Ibid.

9. Ibid.

10. 5H62. According to the FBI's laboratory analysis, "Spectrographic examination of the fabric surrounding the holes in the back of the coat and shirt revealed minute traces of copper. No bullet metal was found in the fabric surrounding the hole in the front of the shirt" (CD 205, 153-54).

11. 5H61.

12. Office Files of Staff, J. Lee Rankin.

13. CD 107, Part One, 2.

14. Ibid., Part Three, Exhibits 59 and 60.

15. CE 393 and 394 (in 17H23-26) show the president's coat and shirt respectively but are not distinct and do not contain enlargements of the actual bullet holes or pinpoint the exact locations of those holes in the clothing as do the FBI photographs.

16. 2H365.

17. Ibid., 366. It is interesting to note that at this point in his testimony, Humes hints that the Commission's drawing of the president's neck wound may not be faithful to its actual position and that photographs taken during the autopsy "would be more accurate as to the precise location." Those autopsy pictures were never shown to him.

18. Ibid.

19. Ibid. See also 17H28.

20. 7H495.

21. Hudson Exhibit 1 (as shown in 20H183). A much better copy of the Willis photograph appeared later in Groden, 20.

22. CE 2112 (as shown in 24H542).

23. CE 1024 (as shown in 18H760).

24. WR, 111.

25. 2H143.

26. CD 7, DL 100-10461.

27. Ibid.

28. 2H93.

29. Ibid., 103.

30. CE 397 (as shown in 17H45). Marginal notes on the face sheet do indeed give measurements for this wound that are in agreement with the higher location shown in CE 386. I found Sylvia Meagher's words interesting: "It is hard to understand why those measurements were recorded in the margin—recorded only for this particular wound but not for other wounds, scars, or incisions, and written in heavier ink than the other notations found on the same diagram." See Sylvia Meagher, *Accessories After the Fact* (New York: Bobbs-Merrill, 1967), 140-41.

31. Norman Redlich, memorandum to J. Lee Rankin, April 27, 1964. Office Files of Staff, Norman Redlich.

32. Ibid.

33. Ibid.

34. Ibid.

35. Ibid.

36. Ibid.

37. WR, 97.

38. Ibid. See also CE 887 (as shown in 18H86).

39. Ibid.

40. Ibid.

41. CE 886 (as shown in 18H85). In the picture published in the Bantam Books edition of the Warren Report (October 1964, inside front cover), a dotted line runs between the two stand-ins, indicating the path a bullet would have taken based on the location of the chalk marks on both men. The line shows the bullet emerging from the president's chest rather than his throat.

42. WR, 97.

43. CE 903 (as shown in 18H96). See also Groden, 125. In the Groden example, you can clearly see that the trajectory rod is now above the chalk mark on the Kennedy stand-in's coat.

44. 6H20.

45. Certificate of Death, Pres. John Fitzgerald Kennedy, 1.

46. Ibid., 2.

47. Many years later, I would ask Weisberg why the damaging death certificate had not been destroyed in the first place. He told me it was a federal crime to tamper with evidence, especially of this magnitude, and he felt that the only alternative was to "hide" it somewhere within the existing massive volumes of documentation, where it would most likely not be discovered by an ordinary researcher.

48. In a memorandum "To File" dated March 18, 1977, then acting counsel and director of the House Select Committee on Assassinations Richard A. Sprague wrote that an attorney representing Burkley had contacted him to say his client "had never been interviewed and that he has information in the Kennedy assassination indicating that others besides Oswald must have participated." The attorney said that he was calling Sprague with Burkley's consent and that Burkley had agreed to talk with Sprague in Washington. Unfortunately, and as a result of continuing pressure from his superiors, Sprague resigned his position two weeks later. Two HSCA staff members finally interviewed Burkley in January 1978. Based on an affidavit signed by Burkley in November 1978, that interview was routine in nature and concerned only the general duties Burkley performed during that fateful weekend. No mention was made of the death certificate or the information he claimed to possess regarding a possible conspiracy. (See JFK Collection: HSCA RG233.) Burkley died of pneumonia on January 2, 1991, in Los Angeles. He was eighty-eight.

49. Weisberg traveled to the Archives the next day and found the death certificate exactly where I told him it was. He announced the discovery in his next book, *Post Mortem*, self-published in 1975. The delay from 1969 to 1975, Weisberg explained to

me, was caused by his lengthy attempts to get his manuscript commercially published and the fact he "did not want to cause any sensationalism" by publicly releasing the death certificate separate from his book. He further said he had no fear of someone else finding it, due to its nearly concealed location. President Kennedy's death certificate now has its own file at the National Archives (Group 272, Entry 52, Folder 15).

Chapter 15

1. CD 5, 70.
2. See Jesse Curry, *JFK Assassination File* (Dallas: American Poster and Printing, 1969), 72.
3. 22H635.
4. CD 5, 41.
5. WR, 134. See also CE 142 (as shown in 16H513).
6. See, for example, Studebaker Exhibits A-J (as shown in 21H643-49).
7. Ibid., 647.
8. 3H286.
9. See, for instance, the testimony of Dallas Police members Gerald Hill (7H65) and J. B. Hicks (7H289).
10. See also Craig's testimony in 6H268.
11. 7H103.
12. 7H98.
13. Ibid., 102.
14. 4H267.
15. WR, 135.
16. Ibid., 134. The Report also neglected to mention that Frazier, the closest observer of the bag, was quoted on more than one occasion describing it as being completely different from the one said to have been used by Oswald: in a November 29 internal FBI memo as "definitely a thin flimsy sack like one purchased in a dime store" (FBI #62-109060-1111) and in a December 1 FBI report as "a light brown thin crinkly paper bag of the type used by five and ten cent stores" (FBI #62-109060-1253). The FBI would note as well that when Frazier was shown the paper sack for identification purposes at Dallas Police headquarters on the night of the assassination, he described the bag Oswald carried as "a flimsy, thin consistency" and said the sack being displayed by police that night "had never been seen by him before." The FBI continued, "He also said that this sack was definitely not the one he had observed in possession of Oswald the morning of November 22, 1963" (FBI File No. 89-43-1390).
17. WR, 136.
18. 4H81.
19. Ibid. During his testimony, Agent Stombaugh also provided a comical and self-incriminating aside to the Commission's steadfast contention that Oswald pilfered paper from the Depository for the sole purpose of using it to fashion a rifle container:

Stombaugh: When I looked at the bag and examined it, it struck me as being a homemade bag such as I could make. Occasionally I will have a need for something like this at home. Therefore, I will take some brown paper and a strip of tape home with me. Then when I get home I will fold the tape—fold the paper rather—in the shape I need—and to seal it up I will tear strips of the sealing tape from the little piece I have. (4H75)

The Commission attorney questioning Stombaugh chose not to pursue the agent's confession.

20. 4H97.
21. Ibid.
22. Ibid., 98. Cadigan was queried along these lines as the result of a March 23, 1964,

internal memo to Eisenberg from Commission attorneys Ball and Belin, in which that team suggested that questions be asked regarding the lack of rifle markings on the inside of the bag: "Do the markings on the bag permit a conclusion that a rifle was carried in this bag?" Ball and Belin wrote. "The FBI report, Document 5, page 165, reads 'the inside surface of specimen Q-10 [the paper bag] did not disclose markings identifiable with the rifle.' Does the absence of such markings compel the conclusion that the rifle was never carried in that bag? If the rifle had been carried in that bag would the rifle probably have left markings on that bag?" (Joseph Ball and David Belin, memorandum to Melvin A. Eisenberg, 2.)

23. See CE 2974 (as shown in 26H455). The description came from J. Edgar Hoover.

24. WR, 135. See also 4H93.

25. CD 5, 129.

26. FBI teletype from Dallas to New Orleans, File No. 100-10461-4653, March 23, 1964. The Commission had made the request to the FBI on March 20.

27. CD 205.

28. Ibid.

29. Tim would write in a January 31, 1970, letter that his show with me "was the best program I've ever had." This was not bad, considering he also had as guests one night members of the local chapter of the John Birch Society and a soothsayer who could predict the future.

Chapter 16

1. Harold Weisberg, letter to author, March 10, 1970.

2. The opening chapter to Ford's *Portrait of the Assassin* (New York: Simon and Schuster, 1965) contained details of the rumor Oswald may have been a government agent, a bombshell that up to that point had remained behind closed doors during the Warren Commission's investigation.

3. David Belin, *November 22, 1963: You Are the Jury* (New York: Quadrangle/The New York Times Book Co., 1973).

4. Ibid., 269.

5. Ibid., 270.

6. 6H340-41.

7. 6H331.

8. Belin, 271.

9. Fifteen years later, Belin wrote *Final Disclosure: The Full Truth About the Assassination of President Kennedy* (New York: Charles Scribner's Sons, 1988). This time, Miss Adams, a staple in the author's other evaluations, would not be mentioned at all.

10. Belin, *November 22, 1963*, 271. In the book's foreword, Harrison E. Salisbury, no newcomer to overstatement himself, described what he termed "the Belin study" as being "meticulous, precise and all-embracing." Ibid., xiii.

11. "Goodnight America," ABC Television, March 6, 1975.

12. See Hosty's explanation of the incident in his autobiography, *Assignment: Oswald* (New York: Arcade, 1996), 60. Hosty said the note was merely an admonishment, telling him to come to Oswald directly with any questions regarding Oswald's return from Russia rather than continue to bother his wife at the Paine residence. Hosty considered the letter to be "no big deal" (Hosty, 29).

13. WR, 327. See also CE 18 (as shown in 16H64 and 5H112).

14. Fidel Castro *was* present in Dealey Plaza during the assassination, if one chooses to believe the photograph on the April 7, 1992, front page of a grocery-store tabloid called the *Sun*. A blowup of a man standing along Elm Street, moments after the shooting began, reveals an obviously elated Castro watching as his archenemy is hit by an assassin's bullet. The same picture was published in the twenty-six volumes (21H781), but the man identified by the *Sun* as Castro is not present. Had the Warren Commission secretly

cropped him out, fearing public reprisal if it were known he was there? My judgment was that one couldn't expect credibility from a paper that enticed readers of the same issue with other such leading stories as "Top Model Has 73-inch Bust And Earns $10G A Day" and "Face On Mars Is UFO Beacon."

15. HSCA open hearings, September 11, 1978. See also HSCA, vol. 2, 209-10.

16. Ibid. See also HSCA, vol. 2, 279.

17. Ibid. See also HSCA, vol. 2, 282. General Walker, an outspoken anti-communist and member of the John Birch Society, had been relieved of his military command by President Kennedy in 1962 for distributing right-wing literature to subordinates. On April 10, 1963, someone fired a shot at Walker as he sat in his home in suburban Dallas. Oswald was later linked to the crime.

18. HSCA open hearings, September 21, 1978. See also HSCA, vol. 3, 614 and 641.

19. Ibid. See also HSCA, vol. 3, 615.

20. Ibid., 617. He couldn't have gotten far. When Oswald was arrested, his pockets held only $13.87 in cash (CE 2003, 289, as shown in 24H345). This was odd for a man who supposedly had the foresight to plan his murderous deed in advance and left his wife $170 in cash before departing for work on the morning of the assassination. Author Albert H. Newman would come up with a better idea. In his book, *The Assassination of John F. Kennedy: The Reasons Why* (New York: Clarkson N. Potter, 1970), Newman would assign Oswald the classic quality of tenacity: that the escaping assassin didn't require much money since he was on his way to a bus ride that would take him to the home of General Walker, where he could complete the job he had so miserably failed at more than seven months earlier (47-49).

21. HSCA open hearings, September 22, 1978. See also HSCA, vol. 4, 9.

22. Ibid. See also HSCA, vol. 4, 12.

23. 5H120-29.

24. HSCA open hearings, September 22, 1978. See also HSCA, vol. 4, 121. McCone had remained similarly mute when he appeared with Helms in front of the Warren Commission (5H120-29).

25. Ibid. See also HSCA, vol. 4, 160.

26. HSCA open hearings, September 25, 1978. See also HSCA, vol. 4, 467.

27. On September 4, 1976, six months before his death, De Mohrenschildt handwrote a two-page letter to George Bush, who was then director of the CIA. Opening with "Dear George," he asked Bush to help "bring a solution into the hopeless situation I find myself in." He continued, "My wife and I find ourselves surrounded by some vigilantes; our phone bugged and we are being followed everywhere." Referring to his recently completed manuscript titled "I Am a Patsy! I Am a Patsy!" he went on to say he had "tried to write, stupidly and unsuccessfully about Lee H. Oswald and must have annoyed a lot of people—I do not know." And he asked Bush to "do something to remove this net around us." He promised, "This will be my last request for help and I will not annoy you any more." On CIA letterhead, Bush replied three weeks later with a "Dear George" letter of his own, saying the delay on his end was due to the time it took "to explore thoroughly the matters you raised." He unfortunately could not offer the help De Mohrenschildt sought. "However, my staff has been unable to find any indication of interest in your activities on the part of Federal authorities in recent years. The flurry of interest that attended your testimony before the Warren Commission has long since subsided. I can only speculate that you may have become 'newsworthy' again in view of the renewed interest in the Kennedy assassination and, thus, may be attracting the attention of people in the media." (CIA Document 104-10322-10242.)

28. According to a February 28, 1964, FBI document, De Mohrenschildt would enter into a relationship with Oswald only after being assured by that agency that Oswald was "completely harmless." How the FBI knew this was not mentioned. (See FBI File No. DL 105-632.)

29. HSCA open hearings, September 25, 1978. See also HSCA, vol. 4, 468.

30. HSCA open hearings, September 8, 1978. See also HSCA, vol. 1, 414-15.

31. Ibid. See also HSCA, vol. 1, 503-5.

32. Ibid. See also HSCA, vol. 1, 502.

33. Mack would humbly tell me years later that his calculations regarding when he felt gunfire had occurred on the tape were off by one minute from the timing ultimately established by the Committee. Therefore, he said, he could take credit only for being the first to introduce the theory that the assassination had been recorded.

34. See HSCA, vol. 5, 554.

35. HSCA open hearings, September 11, 1978. See also HSCA, vol. 2, 94.

36. HSCA open hearings, December 29, 1978. See also HSCA, vol. 5, 556.

37. The testimony of McLain indicated he was the officer riding the motorcycle with the faulty microphone. He said he was unaware of any problems with his police radio on that day and may not have known about it even if there had been, and he admitted his microphone had become stuck in the open position on several earlier occasions. HSCA, vol. 5, 618-41.

38. Ibid., 583. See also HSCA open hearings, December 29, 1978.

39. Ibid., 592.

40. Ibid.

41. Ibid. See also 593.

42. Ibid.

43. Ibid.

44. Ibid., 674. In its final report, the Committee would cite Barger as saying there was a small possibility that the recorded sound from the grassy knoll represented "random noise" or something other than that of a gunshot, thereby reducing the 95 percent figure to 76 percent. It would sum up the matter by saying, "The Committee found no evidence or indication of any other cause of noise as loud as a rifle shot coming from the grassy knoll at the time the impulse sequence was recorded on the dispatch tape, and therefore concluded that the cause was probably a gunshot fired at the motorcade." See HSCA Report, 75.

45. Ibid. See also HSCA, vol. 5, 684.

46. Ibid. See also 694.

47. HSCA Report, 97.

48. Commission on Physical Sciences, Mathematics, and Resources of the National Research Council, *Report of the Committee on Ballistics Acoustics* (Washington, D.C.: National Academy Press, 1982).

49. Ibid.

50. HSCA open hearings, September 21, 1978. See also HSCA, vol. 3, 624-25.

Chapter 18

1. While I visited with him one day, Harold Weisberg told me the following story. In 1991, he had heard Oliver Stone was shooting a movie praising Garrison, and so he sent the producer a letter about his own knowledge of the district attorney's investigation. It fell on deaf ears. Weisberg then obtained a copy of the movie's script, despite extraordinary security precautions to keep it secret. (I asked him how he had been able to pull off such a feat, since Stone had had each copy numbered and kept under lock and key. Usually free with his information, Weisberg would this time only smile and say, "I had a good contact.") What he read in those pages, he said, sickened him to the point where he decided to leak the contents of the script to a writer for the *Washington Post*. The result was the beginning of the media frenzy that surrounds the film even to this day.

2. *People*, December 30, 1991.

3. HSCA Report, 57.

4. Ibid. There would be no mention, however, of the lack of gun oil on the inside of the sack or the absence of creasing to the paper from it containing a heavy and angular object.

5. Ibid.
6. Ibid.
7. See CE 3131 (as shown in 26H809).
8. WR, 249.
9. Ibid.
10. Ibid., 566.
11. HSCA Report, 54.
12. Ibid., 54-56.
13. Ibid., 51.
14. Ibid.
15. Ibid., p. 57.
16. Ibid.
17. Ibid., 58.
18. Ibid.
19. Ibid.
20. Ibid.
21. Ibid.
22. 3H252.
23. Ibid., 240.
24. HSCA Report, 58.
25. 3H275. Mrs. Reid's two-minute figure was based on the results of a timed test performed, stopwatch in hand, by David Belin, who had conducted her questioning. It is yet another example of the lengths to which Belin went to resolve timing questions—except when it came to Victoria Adams.
26. HSCA Report, 58.
27. Ibid.
28. Ibid., 601.
29. HSCA, vol. 11, attachment E, 227.
30. Ibid., attachment H, 447.
31. HSCA 180-10095-10363.
32. HSCA Report, 59.
33. Ibid.
34. The Committee was aware of what Craig said he saw, though. Under the heading of "Conspiracy Witnesses in Dealey Plaza," details of Craig's story as well as from others who saw suspicious activities are presented. See HSCA, vol. 12, 17-18.
35. HSCA Report, 59.
36. Ibid., 601.
37. Ibid., 60.
38. When Oswald's personal effects were searched by Dallas Police after his arrest, authorities found a photograph showing the back of Walker's home. By the time that picture was released by the FBI, a hole had been cut into the photograph, removing the license plate of a car that had been parked in Walker's driveway (see CE 5, as shown in 16H7). Much of what was used to link Oswald to the Walker shooting ultimately came from the testimony of Marina Oswald.
39. HSCA Report, 60.
40. HSCA, vol. 7, 370.
41. HSCA Report, 60.
42. Ibid., 61.
43. Ibid.
44. Ibid., 86. Then there were those who would say it was impossible for Holland to have seen gunfire because "modern" weapons do not emit smoke. Who's to say that a gunman on the knoll was not using an older weapon like Oswald's, which did emit smoke from the muzzle, as the Committee's Firearms Panel proved (see HSCA, vol. 7,

373)? The Committee would continue, "A firearms expert engaged by the Committee explained that irrespective of the exact type of ammunition used, it would be possible for witnesses to have seen smoke if a gun had been fired from that arena. According to the expert, both 'smokeless' and smoke-producing ammunition may leave a trace of smoke that would be visible to the eye in sunlight. That is because even with smokeless ammunition, when the weapon was fired, nitrocellulose bases in the powder which are impregnated with nitroglycerin may give off smoke, albeit less smoke than black or smoke-producing ammunition. In addition, residue remaining in the weapon from previous firings, as well as cleaning solution which might have been used on the weapon, could cause even more smoke to be discharged in subsequent firings of the weapon." (See HSCA, vol. 12, 24-25.)

45. WR, 219.
46. HSCA Report, 157.
47. Ibid.
48. Ibid.
49. Ibid., 158.
50. HSCA, vol. 3, 461.
51. Ibid., vol. 9, 1120.
52. HSCA Report, 241.
53. Ibid., 242.
54. Ibid., 243-44.
55. Ibid., 244.
56. Ibid.
57. Ibid., 255.
58. The Committee wrote in its Report, "Virtually all former Warren Commission members and staff contacted by the Committee said they regarded the CIA-Mafia plots . . . to be the most important information withheld from the Commission. They all agreed that an awareness of the plots would have led to significant new areas of investigation and would have altered the general approach of the investigation." (Ibid., 258.)
59. Ibid., 238-39.
60. Ibid., 261.
61. The comment was made by administrative assistant Howard P. Willens in an August 8, 1964, memo to J. Lee Rankin regarding Willens' thoughts on improving the wording in chapter 4 of the soon-to-be-published Warren Report. That chapter was titled, "The Assassin" and listed evidence linking Oswald with the crime. Willens' complete statement read, "It could be set forth by the Commission in a frank statement that the Commission has no scientific evidence as opposed to eyewitness and circumstantial evidence that Oswald fired the rifle on November 22." See, for example, HSCA, vol. 11, 447. During his stint with the Commission, Willens also served as liaison with the Department of Justice. The value Rankin attached to "circumstantial evidence" was shown in a closed-door meeting with Commission members in January 1964, when Rankin said, while discussing the rumor that Oswald was a paid FBI informant, "Now that is just circumstantial evidence, and it don't prove anything about this, but it raises questions." (See transcript, Executive Session Meeting, January 22, 1964, 11.)

Chapter 19

1. Alfred Goldberg, memorandum to J. Lee Rankin, April 28, 1964, 1.
2. Ibid.
3. Ibid.
4. Ibid., 2.
5. Ibid., 3.
6. Transcript, Executive Session Meeting, December 16, 1963, 47.
7. Associated Press wire story as published in the *Syracuse Herald-American*, May

9, 1976. In *Oswald and the CIA* (New York: Carroll and Graf, 1995), 39, author John Newman details how the CIA had similar concerns about the FPCC, going so far as to think it "a Castro-financed effort to foment insurrection in America."

8. There is no evidence Oswald ever visited the Soviet Embassy in Washington. The statement in the memo saying he did so undoubtedly refers to an FBI interview of Oswald on August 16, 1962, in Ft. Worth, not long after his return from Russia. During that interview, Oswald said he had *written* a letter to the Soviet Embassy in Washington, but only to forward his wife's current address. See CE 2758 (as shown in 26H143-44).

9. Document No. 92-226, LBJ Presidential Library. The copy I obtained was from the files of Harold Weisberg.

10. J. Edgar Hoover, memorandum to Gordon Shanklin, November 22, 1963. FBI Document No. 62-109060-58.

11. Ibid., FBI Document No. 62-109060-59.

12. Ibid., FBI Document No. 62-109060-57.

13. FBI Document No. 105-569-94.

14. Cartha D. DeLoach, memorandum, November 25, 1963.

15. Ibid.

16. J. Edgar Hoover, memorandum, November 26, 1963. FBI Document No. 62-109060-61.

17. Ibid.

18. HSCA, vol. 3, 644.

19. Ibid.

20. Ibid.

21. Ibid., 643.

22. Nicholas deB. Katzenbach, memorandum to Bill Moyers, November 25, 1963. Department of Justice Record No. 129-11, 2.

23. Ibid., 1.

24. Ibid., 2.

25. J. Edgar Hoover, memorandum, November 26, 1963. FBI Document No. 62-109060-1490.

26. Transcript, Executive Session Meeting, December 16, 1963, 12.

27. Ibid., 33.

28. Ibid., 55.

29. W. D. Griffith, memorandum to Mr. Conrad, November 28, 1964. Document No. 62-109060-2405, 2.

30. FBI Document No. 62-109060-4235.

31. Memo on Discussions with Mr. Allan W. Dulles on the Oswald Case, April 13, 1964. CIA Document 657-831.

32. Ibid.

33. Ibid.

34. Ibid.

35. 5H121. This is in contrast to a redacted CIA memo written November 25, 1963 (but not released until 1992), which notes the CIA did in fact have "OI," operational intelligence interest, in Oswald. The unknown author wrote that he or she was being moved into a new assignment and thus, "I would have left the country shortly after Oswald's arrival [from Russia]. I do not know what action developed thereafter."

36. CIA Document 579-250.

37. Ibid.

38. Ibid.

39. CIA Document 695-302A, 2. The briefing material was well accepted. Helms, for instance, himself no stranger to such tactics, called it "a first-class job . . . not only as to format but also as to content" (see CIA Document 694-302).

40. CIA Document 695-302A, Summary Outline, 3.

41. CIA Document 871-388A.

42. Ibid.

43. Ibid.

44. CIA Document 1035-960.

45. Ibid., 2.

46. Ibid.

47. Ibid.

48. Weisberg had a habit of writing himself explanatory notes that he would include in his files. Often lengthy, these personal notations included details on how he acquired certain documents and occasionally listed his feelings after having first read and thought about the material. Regarding this incident, Weisberg wrote that there were two obvious answers: one, the "Hunt" letter was real, which introduced questions of its own, or two, it was a "deliberate hoax designed to be used." The latter was his choice. He also said he sent a written inquiry to the return address in Mexico that was on the envelope but had not received a reply.

49. Harold Weisberg, letter to Jim Lesar, February 12, 1977.

50. "It is impossible to determine positively whether the letter to Hunt is or is not in the handwriting of the same person as the other writings purporting to be Oswald's," those experts would say. See HSCA, volume 8, 246.

51. For a full discussion of this tomfoolery, see Christopher Andrew and Vasili Mitrokhin, *The Sword and the Shield: The Mitrokhin Archive and the Secret History of the KGB* (New York: Basic Books, 1999).

Chapter 20

1. Transcript, Executive Session Meeting, December 5, 1963, 1.

2. Ibid.

3. Ibid.

4. Ibid., 2-3. One member, Senator Russell, actually went so far as to say he hoped the Commission would not be put into the position of having to hear the testimony of any witnesses. Another member, Senator Cooper, agreed, suggesting that witnesses simply be referred to the FBI to present their testimony and have it evaluated (ibid., 41).

5. Transcript, Executive Session Meeting, December 16, 1963, 18.

6. Ibid., 43.

7. Transcript, Executive Session Meeting, January 21, 1964, 61.

8. Transcript, Executive Session Meeting, December 16, 1963, 25.

9. Transcript, Executive Session Meeting, January 21, 1964, 13.

10. Ibid., 16-17.

11. Transcript, Executive Session Meeting, January 22, 1964, 10.

12. Ibid., 1.

13. Ibid., 6.

14. Ibid.

15. Ibid., 11.

16. Ibid., 12-13.

17. Ibid., 12.

18. Ibid., 13. Some researchers erroneously make mention of there being only twelve Executive Session meetings instead of thirteen. The mistake quite possibly originates from the fact that this particular meeting was not recorded like the others, perhaps because it was unscheduled and had been quickly called to order. Plus, an official transcription was not made until ten years later, based on this note on the cover page of that document: "Prepared by a Department of Defense stenotypist with the proper security clearance from reporter's notes among the records of the Commission in the National Archives at the request of the General Services Administration in August 1974."

19. Transcript, Executive Session Meeting, January 27, 1964, 153.

20. Ibid., 162.
21. Ibid., 166.
22. Ibid., 171.
23. Ibid., 176.
24. See CE 2758 (as shown in 26H143-44).
25. Transcript, Executive Session Meeting, January 27, 1964, 176.
26. Ibid., 193.
27. Ibid., 177.
28. Ibid., 212.
29. Transcript, Executive Session Meeting, April 30, 1964, 5880.
30. Ibid., 5870.
31. Ibid., 5873.
32. Transcript, Executive Session Meeting, June 4, 1964, 6653.
33. See, for example, Office Files of Staff, Francis Adams and Arlen Specter, box 1, entry 44.
34. Transcript, Executive Session Meeting, June 4, 1964, 6656.
35. FBI Document No. 62-109060-4199EBF. On page 2 of this document, the FBI concluded "the copy of Oswald's diary in possession of 'Life' magazine originated from the Office of the Dallas County Attorney." The allegation that Ford was involved apparently originated from there as well.
36. HSCA, volume 11, 54.
37. Ibid., vol. 3, 576-77.
38. Ibid.
39. Cartha D. DeLoach, *Hoover's FBI: The Inside Story by Hoover's Trusted Lieutenant* (Washington, D.C.: Regnery, 1997), 149. Ford told the HSCA that he *did* meet with DeLoach, but those meetings were during the organizational stages of the Commission. Ford said he could find no written records indicating he had any meetings with DeLoach after December 19, 1963 (see HSCA, vol. 3, 577).
40. Robert Kennedy would say nothing during the interview, except for this sole question at the very end of the proceeding. It was printed only in the official and unedited transcript of Mrs. Kennedy's testimony (released in June 1988, p. 6817).

Rankin: Yes. You have told us what you remember about the entire period as far as you can recall, have you?
Mrs. Kennedy: Yes.
Mr. Robert Kennedy: Can we go off the record just a minute?

The request by Kennedy to go off the record was not shown in the printed version of Mrs. Kennedy's interview in the twenty-six volumes. The discussion in private may have concerned the condition of Mrs. Kennedy, since immediately after returning to the record, Warren ended the session.

41. Arlen Specter, memorandum to J. Lee Rankin, March 31, 1964.
42. 5H178-81.
43. Ibid., 180.
44. Unedited transcript of Mrs. Kennedy's testimony, 6815.
45. WR, 50.
46. Ibid., 54.
47. Howard P. Willens memorandum to J. Lee Rankin, December 19, 1963, 1.
48. 5H180.
49. Unedited transcript of Mrs. Kennedy's testimony, 6815.
50. A complete set of the twenty-six volumes, providing one can even be found, is currently valued at over two thousand dollars.
51. Transcript, Executive Session Meeting, September 18, 1964, 7654.

52. Ibid., 7655.

53. Ibid., 7657.

54. Leon Jaworski, *Confession and Avoidance: A Memoir* (Garden City, NY: Anchor Press, 1979), 106.

55. Ebersole described that moment to the HSCA: "I believe by ten or ten thirty approximately a communication had been established with Dallas and it was learned that there had been a wound of exit in the lower neck that had been surgically repaired. I don't know if this was premortem or postmortem but at that point the confusion as far as we were concerned stopped." (See testimony of John H. Ebersole, M.D., March 11, 1978, HSCA Record Number 180-10075-10063, 4-5.)

56. Ebersole is further supported by the fact that tissue samples were taken during the autopsy from the president's throat wound, an unusual procedure if doctors believed it to have been caused only by a tracheotomy.

57. Gil Delaney, *Lancaster Intelligencer Journal*, March 8, 1978.

58. Testimony of John H. Ebersole, M.D., March 11, 1978, HSCA Record Number 180-10075-10063, 3. During a recorded interview in 1992, Ebersole said he "saw a big wound" on the back of Kennedy's head. He would also describe the bullet hole in Kennedy's back as being at the level of "T4" (thoracic vertebra number four), a position even lower down the back than where Admiral Burkley placed it, at T3, in the president's official death certificate. See James H. Fetzer, ed., *Murder in Dealey Plaza* (Chicago: Catfeet Press, 2000), 434.

59. Signed affidavit of Francis X. O'Neill, HSCA Document No. 013073, November 8, 1978, 3.

60. Ibid.

61. Ibid. "The autopsy room had a phone and a coffee pot," O'Neill had written on p. 4.

62. HSCA Document No. 180-10089-10178, 2.

63. Ibid., 3.

64. Ibid.

65. Ibid., 4.

66. Ibid., 8.

67. *Journal of the American Medical Association* (May 27, 1992): 2794-2803. The other member of the autopsy team, Pierre Finck, was living in Switzerland and declined an invitation to be interviewed. Included in the article is a picture of Humes and Boswell with *JAMA* editor George Lundberg. The caption ironically reads that the trio "finally got together on a *grassy knoll* in Florida to discuss the 1963 autopsy of President John F. Kennedy [author's emphasis]." See p. 2799.

68. Ibid., 2794.

69. Ibid., 2799.

70. Ibid., 2800.

71. 2H374-75.

72. See, for example, transcript, Executive Session Meeting, December 16, 1963, 23. At that meeting, Warren made the comment, "I would think a man who was a trial lawyer and who had that experience in the biggest police department in this country should be an asset to this Commission."

73. Office Files of Staff, Francis Adams and Arlen Specter, box 1, entry 44. The application was signed on January 10, 1964.

74. HSCA, volume 11, attachment G, 388.

75. Staff Working Papers, Adams, Francis W. H. His objectives were listed in a 106-page memo to Rankin dated February 18, 1964, and titled, "Phase I—The Assassination: President Kennedy's Agenda and Activities From Planning the Dallas Trip Through Autopsy."

76. Edward J. Epstein, *Inquest: The Warren Commission and the Establishment of Truth* (New York: Viking, 1966), 79. When I wrote Epstein about this matter, he responded

that Adams had told him "Rankin did not correctly represent what his [Adams'] work would be" (Edward J. Epstein, e-mail to author, June 9, 2001). Epstein did not reply when I sought clarification on that comment and also denied me access to his transcript of the Adams interview. When I asked on September 13, 2001, if his interview with Adams would be posted on Epstein's Web page or anywhere else, he answered, "They will eventually be listed there. They are not available elsewhere." To date, it has not appeared.

77. From handwritten notes made during a telephone interview with Adams, June 6, 1999.

78. Arlen Specter briefly discussed his association with team member Adams in his autobiography, *Passion for Truth: From Finding JFK's Single Bullet to Questioning Anita Hill to Impeaching Clinton* (New York: William Morrow, 2000). He described his relationship with Adams as "difficult" and said Adams thought the Commission's work was "too microscopic" and should instead be a more "incisive, piercing investigation" (48-49). Specter portrayed him as a man too busy with his New York law firm to pay much attention to the Commission's work. "By mid-March Adams seemed to feel removed from the commission's activities," Specter wrote. "He came less frequently and was even less engaged than before. He seemed troubled by his situation but unable to change it" (51). Specter went on to say that Adams "was not popular at the commission" (50). I wondered why Adams was disliked so much, especially when Commission members spoke so highly of him when he was hired. On two separate occasions, I sought clarification on that issue by attempting to speak with Specter at his Washington, D.C. office. Both times I left detailed messages regarding my request with his subordinates. I never received a response.

79. In his *November 22, 1963* (15), Belin reminisced about Adams, even though he couldn't get his name straight. "One of the best-kept secrets inside the Commission," Belin offered, "was that Francis W. K. [*sic*] Adams, one of the two lawyers assigned to Area I, performed virtually no work. He should have been asked to resign when it first became apparent that he was not going to undertake his responsibilities, but because of some mistaken fear that this might in some way embarrass the Commission, Mr. Adams was kept on in name only and the entire burden in Area I fell upon Arlen Specter."

Chapter 21

1. The Commission gratefully acknowledged the able assistance that had been provided to it by both of these individuals, thanking "in particular Harold Barefoot Sanders, Jr., U.S. attorney for the northern district of Texas, and his conscientious assistant, Martha Joe Stroud." See WR, 481.

2. Based on a review of Miss Adams' testimony in the twenty-six volumes, the corrections were never made. Curious also was the fact that a copy of Miss Stroud's letter was not in Rankin's correspondence or working files, nor could I find it in any "Victoria Adams" files.

3. Martha Joe Stroud, letter to J. Lee Rankin, June 2, 1964.

4. Ibid. The parenthetical notation of "(Miss Garner)" is as shown in the original.

5. WR, 154.

6. Ibid.

7. From handwritten notes made during a personal interview with Weisberg, May 2, 1999.

8. The comment was made in court papers filed during the case of *Harold Weisberg v. United States Department of Justice* (Civil Action 75-226), his lawsuit to acquire the results of spectrographic analysis tests conducted by the FBI for the Warren Commission. "In the motion to strike," those papers say, "plaintiff [Weisberg] also alleges the existence of certain documents which he claims have not been provided by the FBI. In a sense, plaintiff could make such claims ad infinitum since he is perhaps more familiar with

events surrounding the investigation of President Kennedy's assassination than anyone now employed by the FBI." See p. 3.

Chapter 22

1. Harold Weisberg, letter to Robert Groden, September 10, 1993.

2. From handwritten notes made during a personal interview with Groden, October 3, 1999.

3. On his personal Web page, Groden includes this unusual message: "$5000 Reward. For information leading to the return of all of the unique JFK assassination photo slide transparencies, photographic materials and other items which were stolen from Robert Groden's home on September 9, 1999, and the arrest and conviction of the perpetrators of the thefts. The identities of the culprits are known."

4. When I returned home, I wrote Groden a letter, reminding him who I was and specifically asking for information about purchasing a video he had for sale. I received no reply.

Chapter 23

1. Gary Mack, letter to author, June 30, 1999.

2. Joseph Cody, letter to author, July 13, 1999.

3. Ibid.

4. From the taped interview with Cody, October 4, 1999.

5. City of Dallas Archives, JFK Collection, box 15, folder 3.

6. 7H268.

7. Joseph Ball, memorandum to Alfred Goldberg, June 26, 1964.

8. *Dallas Morning News,* December 5, 1992.

9. From handwritten notes made during a telephone interview with Leavelle, October 7, 1999.

10. From handwritten notes made during a telephone interview with Day, October 6, 1999.

11. See, for example, CE 718 (as shown in 17H501).

12. From handwritten notes made during a telephone interview with Walther, October 6, 1999.

13. In *Case Closed* (New York: Random House, 1993), a celebrated book that defends the Warren Commission, author Gerald Posner discusses Mrs. Walther in a single paragraph on page 231. It is important to examine how Posner shaded her words from her FBI statement in an attempt to discredit this witness. First, Posner writes, "She claimed one man had his arms extended and was holding a machine gun outside the window, for all to see." The reader can judge Posner's accuracy from what the FBI quoted Mrs. Walther as saying (CE 2086, as shown in 24H522): "This man had the window open and was standing up leaning out this window with both his hands extended outside the window ledge. In his hands, this man was holding a rifle with the barrel pointed downward, and the man was looking south on Houston Street. The man was wearing a white shirt and had blond or light brown hair. She recalled at the time that she had not noticed the man there a few moments previously when she looked toward the building and thought that apparently there were guards everywhere. The rifle had a short barrel and seemed large around the stock or end of the rifle. Her impression was that the gun was a machine gun. She noticed nothing like a telescopic sight on the rifle or a leather strap or sling on the rifle. She said she knows nothing about rifles or guns of any type, but thought that the rifle was different from any she had ever seen."

Posner also writes, "Walther also said a second man, with another gun, stood directly behind the first one." That is *not* what Mrs. Walter stated, and it displays a lack of care on Posner's part in his reading of the FBI report. Immediately following what she said about the man in the window, Mrs. Walther was quoted by the FBI as saying, "This man was standing in about the middle of the window. In the same window, to the left of this man, she could see a portion of another man standing by the side of this man with a rifle." It is clear that "this man with a rifle" was in reference to the individual Mrs. Walther had already described and in no way was intended to mean that the second man also held a gun. That is apparent moments later in her statement, when she is quoted as saying, "Almost immediately after noticing this man with the rifle and the other man standing beside him, someone in the crowd said 'Here they come,' and she looked to her left."

Posner then cites the fact that Mrs. Walther had a companion with her: "A friend, Pearl Springer, was with her and did not notice any gunmen." The implication was that because Mrs. Springer did not see any "gunmen," the erroneous use of the plural "men" notwithstanding, then Mrs. Walther must have been wrong. But Posner does not share with his readers why Mrs. Springer saw no one in the window, a reason that is clear in that woman's FBI statement (CE 2087, as shown in 24H523): "They [Mrs. Walther and Mrs. Springer] stood there for about fifteen minutes waiting for the parade. During that time, she [Mrs. Springer] looked around at the crowd but never looked up above the ground floor of the Texas School Book Depository building located diagonally across the street from where she was standing." Posner also undermines Mrs. Walther's testimony when he tells readers she never told Mrs. Springer about what she had seen. Since the source of the shots was unknown at this point and she believed "there were guards everywhere," her silence does not necessarily induce suspicion, unless one wants it to do just that.

14. A sign on this display reads, "Investigators disturbed the arrangement of book cartons and other evidence in searching the corner window area. Official photographs taken on Friday and Monday at the scene were all reconstructions of the arrangement, and showed different configurations of cartons."

15. Portions of Mrs. Dorman's film became part of an updated video produced and sold by the Sixth Floor Museum titled, *JFK: The Dallas Tapes* (1998).

16. From a taped interview with Mack, October 7, 1999.

17. Lovelady died on January 14, 1979, after suffering a heart attack. He was forty-one years old.

18. Figure IV-67 (as shown in HSCA, vol. 6, 288).

Chapter 26

1. The *real* Victoria Elizabeth Adams, e-mail to author, February 3, 2002.

Chapter 27

1. Quoted material and details regarding the story of Ms. Adams are compiled from numerous e-mails and telephone conversations that began in February 2002.

2. At the time, Ms. Adams was five feet, three and three-quarters inches tall.

3. There is nothing on record indicating such a fire occurred. If it had, it is a sure bet the story would have been picked up, since the media basically had been monitoring every move of the Dallas Police.

Chapter 29

1. Curiously, Officer Marrion Baker also saw a black man in the same general area. During a December 2004 telephone interview, the now-retired Baker told me when he and building manager Roy Truly reached the rear of the Depository on their way to the stairs, he noticed an "older, large black man sitting toward the back stairs, near the elevators there." Baker said the man was the only person he saw in that area. When he asked Truly about him, Truly replied that the man was an employee and was "slightly retarded." Baker went on to say that when he arrived on the second floor, he saw a man later identified as Oswald through a window in the vestibule door. The door was definitely closed when he spotted Oswald, Baker recalled. Oswald said nothing during the entire encounter with the

police officer, which took about thirty seconds, Baker said, and he appeared "very calm." I asked Baker if he heard any other sounds at the time, such as general office noise or perhaps commotion as someone ran down the stairs behind him. He said he heard nothing, although he admitted he was preoccupied with Oswald during that time.

Chapter 30
1. From handwritten notes made during a telephone interview with Butler, February 13, 2002.

2. Quoted material and details regarding the story of Mrs. Butler are compiled from numerous e-mails to the author from February 14 to 19, 2002.

3. Still nagged by this the following year, I would send another e-mail to Mrs. Butler, asking whether she had seen Shelley or Lovelady at *any* time on November 22, 1963. "I don't recall seeing them in person," she answered on January 26, 2003, "just in photographs later, in which they were identified as being among the group standing on the front steps watching the parade."

Chapter 31
1. The quote is from "I Did It My Way," a 1,200-word summation of her life that she struggled to compose during her final weeks.

Chapter 32
1. CE 1381 (as shown in 22H648).

2. From handwritten notes made during a telephone interview with Garner, June 27, 2011.

3. 3H182.

4. WR, 154.

Epilogue
1. *Washington Post*, February 23, 2002. On March 4, 2002, the *New York Times* wrote, "Unlike many other critics of the investigation, Mr. Weisberg cannot accurately be called [a] conspiracy theorist, because he did not speculate about who might have been involved in the assassination."

2. *People* (November 24, 2003): 15.

3. The show, "The Kennedy Assassination: Beyond Conspiracy," aired November 20, 2003.

4. The implication of Oswald's absence from the roll call, which was held shortly before 2 P.M. on the day of the assassination, was that he had fled the scene of the crime. It was in fact the basis on which Dallas Police labeled him a prime suspect. By the mid-1990s, though, many authors were reporting on and showing a document uncovered in the Dallas Police Archives that contained a partial list of employees of the Depository. Among those on that list were the names of four employees who were described as being still outside the building at 2:55 P.M. or later and therefore also not present for any roll call.

5. While it *is* true that Oswald once achieved "sharpshooter" status during his stint in the U.S. Marines, that designation occurred in 1956 after weeks of "extensive" weapons training and a subsequent score of 212 on the rifle range, two points above the minimum needed to be classified a sharpshooter. At that time, he was evaluated as being a "fairly good shot." But what Jennings failed to mention, even though it was clearly stated in the Warren Report, was the fact that when Oswald was tested again in 1959, he scored 191, just one point above the minimum necessary to be ranked a "marksman." That was the lowest level on the Marines' marksman-sharpshooter-expert classification scale. Oswald, at that point, was evaluated as being a "rather poor shot." See WR, 191.

6. Bugliosi, *Reclaiming History*, 832. In a related endnote, the author writes, "Conspiracy theorists see Victoria Adams's testimony as evidence Oswald couldn't have

used the stairs to get to the second floor (otherwise Adams would have seen or heard him), and therefore couldn't have been Kennedy's assassin." Bugliosi, without any further analysis or factual foundation, believes Miss Adams came down the stairs later than she thought. And also like the Warren Commission, he discredits Miss Adams because she said she saw Shelley and Lovelady on the first floor. But he goes a step farther and cites the testimony of Eddie Piper, a Depository employee who told the Commission he was standing on the first floor moments after the shooting and did not see Miss Adams come down the stairs before Officer Marrion Baker and Roy Truly ran up them (7H389). Bugliosi, who is quick to dismiss other researchers for their dependence on unreliable and dubious witnesses, does not tell his readers that even the Warren Report called Piper a "confused" witness who "had no exact memory of the events of that afternoon" (WR, 153).

7. Theodore H. White, in *The Making of the President 1964* (New York: Signet, 1966), 48, writes that on the return flight to Washington aboard Air Force One, "the party learned that there was no conspiracy; learned of the identity of Oswald and his arrest." This occurred only a few hours after Kennedy had been shot.

Vincent Salandria related the story that Pierre Salinger, Kennedy's press secretary, received the same message while he was on a Cabinet-level plane returning to Washington from Hawaii. Salinger personally instructed the National Archives to release copies of the cockpit transmission tapes to Salandria in order to confirm the incident. Those copies, however, were reported to be missing from the Archives. Salandria then requested the information from the White House Communication Agency and was told the radio tapes were made for official use only and could not be released. That incident is "conclusive evidence of high-level U.S. government guilt," Salandria would say. "The first announcement of Oswald as the lone assassin, before there was any evidence against him, and while there was overwhelmingly convincing evidence of conspiracy, had come from the White House Situation Room. . . . This announcement had been made while back in Dallas, District Attorney Henry Wade was stating that 'preliminary reports indicated more than one person was involved in the shooting'" (from a transcript of the speech Salandria delivered to the Coalition on Political Assassination conference in Dallas, Texas, November 21, 1998, 14). Wade's comment was published in the *Dallas Morning News* on November 23, 1963.

8. I was able to obtain several handwriting samples of Victoria Adams from her son. Although I don't claim to be an expert, those samples do appear to be a match with the signature and correctional notations made on this later version of her testimony.

9. For example, three corrections apparently in Miss Adams' handwriting on page 75 of the latest version of her testimony do not appear on the same page that was reviewed by the HSCA. See HSCA 180-10095-10363 versus version two of Miss Adams' testimony.

10. Four of the twenty-three typewritten pages of the transcript of Miss Adams' testimony contain references to Shelley and Lovelady. Three of those four pages have no notations made by Miss Adams. The fourth page shows a one-word correction near the middle of that page, with the reference to Shelley and Lovelady appearing near the bottom. Interesting as well is that on one of those four pages, immediately after he first mentions the names "Mr. Shelley and Mr. Lovelady," David Belin refers to those two as "Truly and Lovelady." His error remained uncorrected.

11. Amy DeLong, archivist, National Archives and Records Administration, e-mail to author, September 20, 2012. Still not satisfied, I filed a Freedom of Information Act request with the Archives on November 1, 2012, seeking a list of the contents of Entry 39. When I received a reply a month later, I was told that the stenographic tapes in those sixteen boxes are arranged chronologically by the date the transcripts were taken (from January 21 through September 15, 1964) and not by the name of the person being deposed. Strangely, all of the stenographic tapes made on April 7, 1964—the date Miss Adams was questioned by David Belin—are missing from the collection. Gone as well are those of Billy Lovelady and William Shelley, who also were deposed on that date.

12. Even the discovery of something as minor as the clipboard raises suspicions. Despite the Dallas Police and other investigative agencies scouring the sixth floor for evidence in the aftermath of the assassination, the clipboard Oswald used was not found until some ten days later. That's surprising, since Frankie Kaiser, the employee credited with first spotting it, testified, "It was just laying there in the plain open." (See 6H343.)

Index

331